Albert Welles

The Pedigree and History of the Washington Family

Albert Welles

The Pedigree and History of the Washington Family

ISBN/EAN: 9783743400405

Manufactured in Europe, USA, Canada, Australia, Japa

Cover: Foto ©ninafisch / pixelio.de

Manufactured and distributed by brebook publishing software (www.brebook.com)

Albert Welles

The Pedigree and History of the Washington Family

THE

PEDIGREE AND HISTORY

OF THE

WASHINGTON FAMILY:

DERIVED FROM

ODIN, THE FOUNDER OF SCANDINAVIA, B. C. 70,

INVOLVING A PERIOD OF

EIGHTEEN CENTURIES, AND INCLUDING

FIFTY-FIVE GENERATIONS,

DOWN TO

GENERAL GEORGE WASHINGTON,

FIRST PRESIDENT OF THE UNITED STATES.

BY

ALBERT WELLES,

President of the American College for Genealogical Registry and Heraldry.

NEW-YORK :
SOCIETY LIBRARY.

1879.

PREFACE.

M Y position as President of the "American College for Genealogical Registry and Heraldry" enables me to obtain *correct* pedigrees and history of Foreign Families, and as the *English* history of the WASHINGTON Family, by several authors, has been *confessedly suppositious*, it is deemed important that a correct and authentic volume should be written that would become the standard for reference on the subject.

My correspondent in London, from whom I have obtained the material for the WASHINGTON Pedigree in *England*, is a lineal descendant of the progenitor in England, and has been engaged over thirty years in gathering evidence. He thus writes: "If I had not taken upon myself the great labor of examining those inestimable Records, the 'Common Pleas Rolls,' the truth of that great man's lineage would not have been revealed. They are of immense value, and I hope you will make them known to your countrymen by the *publication* of the WASHINGTON History. The pedigree I now send I can establish by *legal evidence.*"

The *uncertainty* hitherto existing in regard to the English progenitors of the WASHINGTON Family, which has led to the numberless and fruitless controversies among the Genealogists, will be entirely removed and cleared up by this volume. Beginning with ODIN, the Founder of Scandinavia, B. C. 70, the history is followed down through the

ROYAL LINE OF DENMARK in the thirty-two generations to
"THORFIN THE DANE," nat. circa A. D. 1000, whose ancestors were of Schleswig, Denmark. He settled in Yorkshire, England, prior to the Norman Conquest. The
descent is traced in Denmark and England, from father to
son, down through the centuries, including branches in
different shires, to JOHN WASHINGTON, the great-grandfather of General GEORGE WASHINGTON, in twenty generations from THORFIN; with interesting personal matter
regarding nearly 500 members of the Family and their
alliances in England and America.

The FAMILY OF WASHINGTON derives its *name* from the
Village of *Wassington*, juxta Ravensworth (now called
Wharleton), in the Parish of Kirkby-Ravensworth, in the
North Riding of Yorkshire. Originally Evervicscire—the
Eboricure of the Romans, or Evereux,—afterwards Ebor,
at the time of the Conquest, and lastly Yorkshire.

The people of this part of the country were *all* of *Scandinavian* descent, and spoke the same language with the
Normans themselves, which was the language of the
Ancient *Angles*. The *Saxons* never settled here, and were
of a *different race*. The City of York having been long
before that time especially a *Danish* City, and the Chief
City in all England.

With respect to the *Anglo*-Saxons, there were no *Saxons*
in *these* parts, which was settled by the *Angles*, who spoke
the same language as is spoken this day in these parts of
Yorkshire; and all those *Saxon* inscriptions, about which
so many wonders are made, is simply plain *Yorkshire*. The
Angles were a branch of the *Danes*, who lived in Schleswig
(a seaport town of Denmark), and came over to England,
men, women, children, beasts, &c., and left that country
desolate for 300 years, as is confirmed by the *Saxon* chronicles.

The 174 manors given to Earl Alan by the Conqueror,
were only so many shadows. There were only about six

manors really attached to the Earldom of Richmondshire; of all the others he was merely nominally the Chief Lord ; and each was held by an owner whose ancestors held for many generations before the Conquest.

There was never in Richmondshire above *six* families descended from *Norman* Ancestors; and they acquired their lands by marrying heiresses.

The growing importance and value of such a work as this, is illustrated by the *increasing interest* in everything pertaining to General WASHINGTON, and it is, in fact, the only genealogy and Family History of *national* importance in *this* country.

The Bible, is a History of the earliest races of Mankind ; and a Record of the Jewish Lineage—Religion, the Science of Immortality—Genealogy cognate with both, inasmuch as it is a study embracing the present life, combined with departed generations, giving results of vast import in the future, and may therefore be considered next only in importance to Religion and Bible History.

The Songs with which the Northern Bards regaled the Heroes at their "Feasts of Shells" were but versified chronicles of each Ancestral line, symphonied by their stirring deeds.

Through the oak fire's uncertain flame, the Chieftain saw descend the shadowy forms of his Fathers ; they came from the HALLS OF ODIN, as the harper swept the strings, and deployed before their descendant, *rejoicing in the sound of their praise.* No parchment told his Lineage to the Warrior of those days, but the Heroic Names were branded each night upon his swelling heart by the burning numbers of the Bards.

Thus did the Northman chronicle his Ancestry in those unlettered times. Afterward, when the oak fire was extinguished, the shell thrown by, and the night came no more with songs; when we reach the age of Records we find this love of Lineage availing itself of the new method of com-

memoration. This strong Ancestral spirit of the Northman
may traced, partly to the profound sentiment of perpetuity
which formed the principal and noblest element of his
character, and partly to the nature of the property to which
he was linked by immemorial customs of the race.

The Family History, or Record, of the Sovereigns of the
World before Christ, furnish almost the *only* Histories of
the Countries over which they reigned, as Egypt, Chaldea,
Babylonia, Greece, &c. The *Chinese* annals, the most
ancient known, were written with the most perfect exact-
ness, and preserved with the greatest care ; composed
originally by order of the Emperors—each of whom on his
accession to the throne, *commanded* the acts of his predecessors to be *written* by some learned philosopher—so that the
whole form one uniform continued series of the *History* of
the *Ancient Chinese Empire*, from the beginning of the monarchy (Fo Hi B. C. 2538), for some thousands of years.
And *thus* was the *history* of *China obtained* and *preserved* more
correctly, and *for a longer period* than that of *any other nation
in the world.* Had not the Hebrew race cherished this love
of Kindred and Lineage we should not have any Bible
to-day, and to this feeling we owe our knowledge of the
History of the most ancient Kingdoms of the World and
most of our Modern History. The *English Registers* have,
for *upwards* of a *thousand* years, been the *protection* and
authority of *many* families ; and the *means* of *preserving* large
property interests.   A. W

We are indebted to Mr. HENRY J. JOHNSON for the use of
several of the beautiful steel-plate illustrations from his
publication, entitled " The Life and Times of Washington."
Also to Messrs. G. P. PUTNAM'S SONS for similar favors ;
and to JOHN C. BUTTRE, Esq., Steel-plate engraver. Also
to JAMES PHILLIPPE, Esq., of London, for the *English*
Pedigree.

DERIVATION

OF

"THORFIN, THE DANE,"

EARL OF THE ORKNEY ISLES,

FOUNDER OF THE WASHINGTON FAMILY IN ENGLAND,

CIRCA A. D. 1030–35,

FROM

ODIN,

FIRST KING OF SCANDINAVIA, B. C. 70.

Page v. ODIN, the son of Fridulf, supreme ruler of the Scythians, in Asaland, or Asaheim, Turkestan, between the Euxine and Caspian Seas, in Asia. He reigned at Asgard, whence he removed in the year B. C. 70, and became the first King of Scandinavia. He died in the year B. C. 50, and was succeeded by his sons, who reigned in different parts of Scandinavia. His son

Page vii. SKIOLD became King of Zealand and Jutland, B. C. 50, and died B. C. 40. His son was:

Page viii. FRIDLEIF, who became the first King of Denmark, B. C. 40. He died B. C. 23. His son was:

Page viii. FRODE FREDIGOD, who became King of Denmark, B. C. 23. He died A. D. 35. His son was:

Page viii. FRODE II., who became King of Denmark, A. D. 59. He died A. D. 87. His son was:

Page viii. VERMUND, THE SAGE, who became King of Denmark, A. D. 87, and died A. D. 140. His son was:

Page viii. OLAF, THE MILD, who became King of Denmark, A. D. 140. Obit A. D. 190. His

Page viii. DAUGHTER, became Queen of Denmark,—and
    "   "   DAN MYKILLATI, her husband, became King of

7

Denmark, A. D. 190. He died A. D. 270. His son was:

Page ix. FRODE III., who became King of Denmark, A. D. 270. He died A. D. 310. His son was:

Page ix. HALFDAN, who became King of Denmark, A. D. 310. Obit A. D. 324. His son was:

Page ix. FRIDLEIF III., who became King of Denmark, A. D. 324. He died A. D. 348 His son was:

Page ix. FRODE IV., who became King of Denmark, A. D. 348. He died A. D. 407. His son was:

Page ix. HALFDAN II., who became King of Denmark, A. D. 456. Obit A. D. 457. His son was:

Page ix. ROE, who became King of Denmark, A. D. 460. He died A. D. 494. His son was:

Page x. FRODE VI., who became King of Denmark, A. D. 494. He died A. D. 510. His son was:

Page x. FRODE VII., who became King of Denmark, A. D. 522. He died A. D. 548. His son was:

Page x. HALFDAN III., who became King of Denmark, A. D. 548. He died A. D. 580. His son was:

Page xi. IVAR VIDFADME, who became King of Denmark, A. D. 588. Obit A. D. 647. His daughter,

Page xi. AUDA DIUPHRAUDZA, Queen of Holmgard, married RERICK, King of Holmgard. Her son was:

Page xi. HARALD HILDETAND, who became King of Denmark, A. D. 647. Obit A. D. 735. His son was:

Page xv. THROUD, King of Frondheim, who married A. D. 750, a daughter of SIGURD HRING. His son was:

Page xv. EISTEN, King of Frondheim, born about A. D. 755. Married A. D. 780. His son was:

Page xv. HALFDAN, King of Frondheim, born about A. D. 785. Married A. D. 810. His son was:

Page xv. EISTEN GLUMRU, King of Thrandia, born about A. D. 815, became King of Thrandia, A. D. 840. His

Page xv. Daughter married, A. D. 850, IVAR, Earl of Upland. Their son was:

8

Page xv. EISTEN GLUMRU. He was living A. D. 870. His son was :

Page xv. ROGVALD, who was Earl of Moere, A. D. 885. His son was :

Page xx. EINAR, Earl of the Orkney Isles. His son was :

Page xx. TORFIDUR, who was Earl of the Orkney Isles, A. D. 942. His son was :

Page xx. LODVER, who was Earl of the Orkney Isles. His son was :

Page xx. SIGURD, who was Earl of the Orkney Isles. His son was :

Page xxii. "THORFIN, THE DANE," Earl of the Orkney Isles, also called TORKILL, of Richmondshire, England, Baron, and Lord of Tanfield, Founder of the Washington Family of England.

DERIVATION

OF

GEORGE WASHINGTON,

FIRST PRESIDENT OF THE UNITED STATES,

FROM

"THORFIN, THE DANE."

Page 1. "THORFIN, THE DANE," Earl of the Orkney Isles, also called Torkill, of Richmondshire, England, Baron and Lord of Tanfield, Founder of the Washington Family in England, was born about A. D. 1010, and settled in Yorkshire, England, about 1030–35. Obit about A. D. 1080. His son was:

Page 4. BARDOLF FIL THORFIN, born about A. D. 1035. Obit about A. D. 1120. His son was:

Page 5. AKARIS FIL BARDOLF, born about A. D. 1080. Obit A. D. 1161. His son was:

Page 11. BONDO FIL AKARIS, born about A. D. 1122. Obit about A. D. 1200. His son was:

Page 14. WALTER FIL BONDO DE WASHINGTON, born about A. D. 1160. Obit about A. D. 1245. His son was:

Page 17. ROBERT DE WASHINGTON, born about A. D. 1195. Obit about A. D. 1260. His son was:

Page 25. ROBERT DE WASHINGTON, born about A. D. 1230. Obit about A. D. 1300. His son was:

Page 31. ROBERT WASHINGTON, born about A. D. 1265. Obit about A. D. 1325. His son was:

Page 36. JOHN WASHINGTON, born about A. D. 1305. He died before A. D. 1386. His son was:

Page 38. JOHN WASHINGTON, born about A. D. 1330. He died about A. D. 1405. His son was:

Page 41. JOHN WASHINGTON, born about A. D. 1365. He died about A. D. 1425. His son was:

Page 43. ROBERT WASHINGTON, born about A. D. 1400. He died about A. D. 1479. His son was:

Page 44. JOHN WASHINGTON, born about A. D. 1430. He died 4 May, A. D. 1501. His son was:

Page 47. ROBERT WASHINGTON, born A. D. 1467. He died 20 September, A. D. 1517. His son was:

Page 51. THOMAS WASHINGTON, born A. D. 1493. He died about A. D. 1560. His son was:

Page 65. LAURENCE WASHINGTON, born about A. D. 1515. He was living A. D. 1543. His son was:

Page 77. LAURENCE WASHINGTON, born about A. D. 1540. He was living A. D. 1588. His son was:

Page 86. LAURENCE WASHINGTON, born A. D. 1569. He was living A. D. 1629. His son was:

Page 96. LEONARD WASHINGTON, born about A. D. 1595. He died A. D. 1657. His son was:

Page 105. COLONEL JOHN WASHINGTON, born A. D. 1627. He died in January, A. D. 1677. His son was:

Page 111. LAURENCE WASHINGTON, born about A. D. 1661. He died A. D. 1697. His son was:

Page 114. AUGUSTINE WASHINGTON, born A. D. 1694. He died 12 April, A. D. 1743. His son was:

Page 126. GENERAL GEORGE WASHINGTON, first President of the United States, born February 22, A. D. 1732, and died 14 December, A. D. 1799.

INTRODUCTION.

All the Ancient Records of England are written in abbreviated Latin, and in writing varying in character from Hebrew, or Arabic to Greek, so that very few can read or understand them properly.

An attempt was made some years ago to publish some of these Records, but the parties employed to transcribe them could not read the originals correctly and left out much of the most important information.

With respect to the "Domesday Book," it is simply a schedule of the lands belonging to the King's Geld, and does not include any of the independent freeholders of the period, and is therefore not of that importance, ignorantly attributed to it. William the Conqueror, although he confiscated some of the great fiefs of the Anglo-Saxon nobles, yet he did not touch the lands belonging to any of the tenants holding feudally under them. It embraces the whole of Yorkshire, with which is included part of Lancashire and Westmoreland.

YORKSHIRE.

The County of York gave William the Conqueror more trouble than any other of the shires. The eminent General Herreward le Wake, who resisted the Norman invasion more successfully than even Harold, was a native of what was then the North Riding. The Eboricans, after the country was subdued, allied themselves with the Angles, and were in constant revolt. The original Anglo-Saxon families disgusted with Norman severities, retired into Scotland, and it is from the "Ragged Roll" that the investigator can find trace of these families, after their removal. In view of this, there is good ground for the statement made by several writers, that there was actually no Survey made in the County of York at the period of the

Conquest. The " Ragged Roll," copied by Nesbit, was returned to Scotland by Edward III.

The Saxons settled in the middle and southern portions of England, and were of a different race, the city of York having been long before that time especially a Danish city, and the chief city in all England.

The uncertainty hitherto existing in regard to the early progenitors of the Washington Family in England, which has led to the numberless and endless controversies among the English and American genealogists, will be entirely removed and cleared up by this History, which is based upon and, compiled mainly from the " Common Pleas Rolls " of England.

These Rolls run over 2,000 skins of parchment for every year, and are closely written on both sides in abbreviated Latin. They contain everything relating to law, both civil and criminal, in all parts of England, with the Coronors' Rolls, &c. They form an extensive and valuable historical depository, and have been the means of clearing up and correcting a vast amount of the early history of the country at the time of, and subsequent to the Norman Conquest.

This Washington Family History therefore being *authentic*, must become important and valuable in England and America. The above Rolls having been inaccessible because inscrutable, have never been used by other Genealogists who have attempted to compile a " Washington Pedigree," and their disputes and controversies have been bitter and fruitless. General Washington's ancestors for many generations before they emigrated to America were agriculturists, and the reason that the names of the two brothers, Laurence and John, who came in 1659, do not appear in the *published* lists, was because they were *not* " *subsidy men*," but farmers of good estate, and this accounts also for the fact that the Genealogists were unable to trace the pedigree of the Washington Family in England, as it could not be found in any of the Public Records, except the " Common Pleas Rolls," all of which may be plainly seen in *this* History of the Family.

Washington Irving states that the progenitor of the Washington Family in England, from whom was derived George Washington, first President of the United States, was William de Hertburn, of Durham, 1183 who exchanged his village of Hertburn for the manor and village of Wessyng on, in Durham, and changed his *name* with the estate to de Wessyngton, and cites the " Bolden Book " to prove him the ancestor of the Washington Fam-

.ly, which the said book fails to do, but only recites that de Hertburn made the exchange. As Irving does not give account of the descendants of above William, he fails to prove *him* the *ancestor* of the American Washingtons.

He mentions next a William de Wessyngton who was at the battle of Lewes in 1264, *inferentially* son or grandson of said William de Hertburn. which he was not, as *he* was son of Walter fil Bondo de Wessington of Ravensworth, *Yorkshire*. He next mentions Sir Stephen de Wessyngton, of Durham, 1334, but does not state *who he* was. And next in 1350 a *William de Wessyngton, manifestly also descended from above William de Hertburn— as being lord of the manor of Wessyngton in Durham, and died 1367, whose son William succeeded to the estate, and as *he* left *no male heir*, the *name* and line *died* out, being merged into the Tempest (not Temple) family by marriage of his daughter with Sir William Tempest, of Studley in Yorkshire, who gave up the manor, and it passed to the family of Blackstone. Thus it is seen by Irving's own showing that William de Hertburn *could not* have been the ancestor of the American Washingtons.

He next refers to a John de Wessyngton, Prior of the Benedictine Convent in Durham, 1415. He does not state *who he was*, but that he died in 1446. Having abandoned the *de Hertburn* founders, he next takes up for ancestor the Hon Laurence Washington, Mayor of Northampton, and states that he was son of John Washington, of Warton, Co. Lancaster. The above Laurence was son of John Washington, of Tuwhitfield, Co. Lancaster, who was derived from Robert de Washington, of Milleburn, Westmoreland, but General Washington was *not* derived from said Laurence. He next states that "John and *Andrew* Washington were great grandsons of above Laurence, and emigrated to Virginia in 1657." The two brothers Laurence and John, who emigrated in 1659, were sons of Leonard Washington, of Warton, Co. Lancaster, who died at Warton in 1657. His father and grandfather were named Laurence, born and died at Warton, Co. Lancaster.

Irving winds up the English pedigree thus: "We have entered with some minuteness into this genealogical detail, tracing the family step by step through the pages of historical documents, for upwards of six centuries."

---

* Above William, who died in 1367 was descended from William de Washington. son of Walter fil Bondo, of Wessington, juxta Ravensworth, Yorkshire. As there were several *villages* in different parts of England named Wessyngton, either might have served for ancestors.

Those who will read the first chapter of his book may see the length of the steps, and the genealogical detail.

I have taken Irving as a type of the class. Many others have made similiar derivations. If any of these gentlemen had *traced the lineage* of the Washington Family *from* William de Hertburn, down through the generations from father to son, they might have named *him* as the progenitor in England, but as they have all failed in this, it is simply absurd to have adopted him. Furthermore the family was founded in England nearly two centuries prior to the time of said William de Hertburn.

WASHINGTON.

Of all the noble families of England, that of Washington is the most ancient and one of the most illustrious. Tracing back through the Royal line of Denmark to that great hero King Odin, the Founder of Scandinavia B. C. 70, whose life and character were so great and glorious that his people deified himself and family, and thus established a Scandinavian mythology of equal magnitude and grandeur with that of ancient Greece and Egypt, and of such minuteness in detail as to have confused some historians who were unable to separate the real from the mythological history.

The remarkable resemblance of character between Odin and his descendant Washington, separated by a period of eighteen centuries, is so great as to excite the profound and devout astonishment of the genealogical student—one the Founder of the most eminent race of Kings and Conquerors, and the other of the Grand Republic of America.

SCANDINAVIA.

There is a nation, even now extant, possessing a history as brave as that of the Romans, as poetic as that of the Greeks—a nation that has controlled the world's history in many things and at many times, and whose achievements in war and in letters, are worthy the most heroic age of Rome and the most finished period of Greece ; a nation whose philosophy outran their age and anticipated results that have been slowly occurring ever since. This reference can be true of but one people, the Norsemen, the dwellers in Scandinavia, who lived as heroes, lords and conquerors ; who, sailing out of the ice and desolation in which they were born and nurtured, conquered England, Scotland and Ireland, ravaged Brittany and

Normandy, discovered and colonized Iceland and Greenland, and crossed
the Atlantic in their crazy barks and discovered this very continent long
before Columbus; anchored in Vineland Sound, and left a monument behind
them ; and wheresoever they went they were lords and rulers.

And then their religion—what a wild, massive, manly mythology !
With nothing of the soft sentimentalities of more southern people, but continent of much that revelation has assured us to be true in doctrine—presenting ever the necessity of right and doing right—of manliness, honesty and
responsibility ; rewards and punishments.

All the ancient traditions of the North agree in describing the first inhabitants of Scandinavia as men of colossal stature and incredible strength.
These giants (or trolls as they were called by the Eddas) were alleged to
have been a remnant of the Canaanitish Anakim (descendants of Anek, derived from Canaan, the son of Ham, the son of Noah), whom Caleb and
Joshua, by Divine command, drove out of Palestine, and who ultimately
settled in *Scandia* after fighting many battles with the Scythian emigrants
from Asia.

1. ODIN.

The most important epoch in the historical antiquities of the North, and
the most memorable from the extraordinary revolutions it accomplished, is
the arrival of Odin, the Mars as well as the Mohammed of Scandinavia, the
founder of those religious and political institutions which universally prevailed there until the introduction of Christianity.*

The account of the historical Odin, as narrated by Snorre in the Yng-
lina Saga, states that he came from Asaland or Asaheim, a district east-
ward of the river Tanais, the capital of which was called Asgard, and the
people Asen or Aesir.

By his superior military talents Odin had endeared himself to his
Asiatic subjects. He was successful in every combat, whence his warriors
believed that victory hung on his arm. When he sent forth his soldiers to
any expedition he laid his hands upon them and blessed them ; they then

---

* It was in the reign of Emund Biorn, King of Sweden — 820 to 859 — that the
light of the gospel first dawned in the north, although it did not become the established
religion until the accession of Olaf Skotkanung, A.D. 1001, who, with his whole family, was
baptized in 1001. The surname of Skotkanung or Tribute King, was given to Olaf on account of a yearly tax he paid to the Pope to carry on the war against the Infidels. Olaf
was baptized by Sigefroy, an English monk whom King Ethelred of England had sent to
Sweden.

believed themselves invincible. The invasion of the Romans at length compelled him to flee towards the North, "where he knew that a place of refuge was reserved for him and his people."

Leaving his two brothers to rule at Asgard, he proceeded with his pontiffs and a vast concourse of followers (evidently the Sviar or Suiones of Tacitus) through Gardarike, or Russia, to Saxland, subduing all the nations as he passed, and bestowing their dominions as kingdoms upon his sons. Having disposed of these countries he next crossed the Baltic, and chose the agreeable island of Fionia for his residence, where he is said to have built the city of Odense. The whole of Denmark submitted with little re- sistance. .Passing into Sweden, where a prince named Gylfe then reigned, he fixed his abode near the Lake Logur (the Maelar Sea), in the modern province of Stockholm, and erected a splendid temple at Sigtuna for cele- brating the rites of the new faith. The surrounding territory, which formed the cradle of his empire, was called the Lesser Svithiod, or Sweden, in con- trast to the Larger Svithiod or Scythia, from whence they had emigrated, and Mannheim, the "Home of Man," to distinguish it from Asgard or God- heim, the abode of the Asen or celestial deities. In Upsula and the neigh- boring districts places were assigned for the residence of the pontiffs.

" The migration of this renowned adventurer with a band of followers from the banks of the Tanais is generally placed about the middle of the first century before Christ. Among the fugitive princes of Scythia who were expelled from their country in the Mithridatic war by the superior genius and resources of Pompey, tradition has placed the name of Odin, the ruler of a potent tribe in Turkestan, between the Euxine and Caspian seas."

" His true name. according to tradition, was Sigge, son of Fridulph, but he assumed that of Odin, the Supreme Deity of the Scythians, of whose religion he was chief priest. After achieving so many glorious conquests Odin retired to Sweden, where he ended his days B.C. about 50."

After the death of Odin his authority, both regal and pontifical, was transmitted to his sons and chiefs, whom he had placed on the neighboring thrones. Heimdall was made ruler of Scania. Skiold established himself with a colony of Goths at Ledra in Zealand, which he erected into a mon- archy; and from him descended the Skioldungs, a race of Kings which long swayed the sceptre of Denmark. Yngve, another son, reigned in Sweden; and from him sprang the Ynglings, a name by which the ancient Sovereigns of that country are distinguished in history. Balder was appointed viceroy over the Angles, in the southern part of the Cimbric Chersonese, or ancient Holstein, and hence the Anglo-Saxon princes all traced their origin to that venerable progenitor. Horsa und Hengist, the two Saxon chiefs that conquered England in the fifth century, reckoned Odin (or Woden in their dialect) as their ancestor; and even in Lower Germany the greater part of the reigning families calculated their descent from the same stock.*

The following are the five sons of Odin, who, after his death, about B. C. 30, divided Scandinavia into equal parts, viz :—

2 HEIMDAL, reigned in Skania.

2 NIORD or YNGVE, reigned in Sweden. Died B. C. 20.

2 SEMING or SUABONE, reigned in Norway.

Tradition placed Seming, a son of Odin, on the throne of Norway, and from him descended a race of Pontiff Kings, of whom nothing but their names are recorded.

2 BALDER, Viceroy of the Angles at Schloswig Holstein, in the southern part of the Cimbria Chersonese.

2 SKIOLD, reigned at Ledra, in Zealand, and at Jutland. He became the head of an illustrious race of Kings called Skioldunger, who reigned at Leire (Ledra), in Zealand, twenty miles from Copenhagen. He died B. C. 40. The island of Zealand was ceded by Gylfe to Gefyon, who had married Skiold, one of the sons of Odin.

The small States forming the Kingdom of Denmark continued three or four centuries under the sway of various petty princes, the chief of whom were the Skioldungs, that branch of the family of Odin which established the seat of their authority at Ledra in Zealand. Skiold, the founder of this dynasty, reigned about forty years before the Christian era. Tradition has ascribed to Skiold the usual qualities of the heroic age, great bodily strength and the most indomitable courage. Among his other military

---

* In the district of Loftahammars, close to the Swedish town of Vestervik, a most interesting collection of ancient Russian coins, to the number of 610, in good condition, have been discovered at a little distance below the surface of the earth. The large number of these rare coins shows the extent of the commercial relations which existed some thousand years ago between Sweden and the interior of the present empire of Russia, where Swedish colonies were established all along the great rivers, down to the Black Sea. It is now also an established fact that when Scandinavia became Christian most of the pilgrims to the Holy Land proceeded thence through Russia, where the original commercial Swedish colonies for several centuries retained their native tongue.—*New York Paper*, *Nov.* 30, 1876.

exploits he is said to have conquered the Saxons and subjected them to the payment of an annual tribute.   The son and successor of Skiold was:

3 FRIDLEIF THE FIRST, who was called the First King of Denmark of the Skioldungers, or descendants of Skiold, the son of Odin.   He succeeded to Skiold B. C. 40, and died B. C. 23.   His sons were:

    4 Frode Fredigod.

    4 Fridlief.

    4 Havar.

4 " FRODE FREDIGOD (Pacific) was King of Denmark at the time of Christ." He succeeded King Fridleif in year B. C. 23 and died A. D. 35.

Frode I. enjoyed the reputation of unrivalled prowess as a warrior, having carried his victorious arms into Sweden, Germany, Hungary, England and Ireland.   So strict was the administration of justice in his own dominions, that, if we may credit the Northern legends, bags of gold might have been safely exposed on the highways.   It is alleged that he compiled a civil and military code, which Saxo Grammaticus states to have been extant in his time.   He was succeeded by his brother Fridleif.   His son was:

    5 Frode, born at Ledra about A. D. I.

4 FRIDLEIF THE SECOND became King of Denmark in A. D. 35, and died A. D. 47.   He was succeeded by his brother

4 HAVAR, who became King of Denmark A. D. 47, and died A. D. 59. He was succeeded by his nephew

5 FRODE THE SECOND, son of Frode Fredigod above, who became King of Denmark A. D. 59, and died A. D. 87.   His successor was his son

6 VERMUND THE SAGE, who became King of Denmark A. D. 87, and died A. D. 140.   His successor was his son

7 OLAF THE MILD, who became King of Denmark and Zealand A. D 140, and died A. D. 190.   His daughter married Dan Mykillati, who was his successor.

8 DAN MYKILLATI (the Splendid), became King of Denmark in A. D. 190. He died A. D. 270, after having reigned eighty years, with the greatest justice and reputation.   Almost all historians agree that he was the founder of the kingdom of Denmark.

The first that united the Danish provinces (except Jutland, which formed a separate monarchy) under one government was Dan Mykillati (the Magnanimous), King of Scania, a descendant of Heimdal, and married to a

daughter of Olaf the Mild, Sovereign of Zealand and Denmark, and sixth in
descent from Skiold. He reduced the whole country, with the smaller
islands, to subjection, and is alleged to have given his name to the new
kingdom of which he was the founder. The union of his sister with Dyggve
of Sweden, is reckoned the earliest matrimonial alliance that was formed
between the two Crowns. The son and successor of Dan Mykillati was:

9 FRODE THE THIRD, who became King of Denmark A. D. 270, and died
A. D. 310. The son and successor of Frode the Third was:

10 HALFDAN THE FIRST, who became King of Denmark A. D. 310, and
died A. D. 324. He subdued Sweden, defeated Aun in many battles
and having driven him from the throne, he fixed his residence in Upsala, where he died A. D. 324. The son and successor of Halfdan was:

11 FRIDLEIF THE THIRD, who became King of Denmark A. D. 324, and
died A. D. 348. His son and successor was:

12 FRODE THE FOURTH, who became King of Denmark A. D. 348, and
died A. D. 407. The three sons of Frode the Fourth were:

13 INGILD, who succeeded to his father as King of Denmark A. D. 407,
and died A. D. 436. Another

12 HALFDAN THE SECOND, who succeeded to his brother Ingild as King
of Denmark A. D. 456, and died A. D. 457; and

13 FRODE THE FIFTH, who succeeded to his brother Halfdan A. D. 457,
and died A. D. 460. He was succeeded by Roe and Helge.
The dominions of Halfdan II. (above) were inherited by his sons,

14 ROE and } who reigned from 460 to 494. They agreed to divide the
14 HELGE, } sovereignty between them. The former is said to have built
the city of Roskilde, but he exchanged his patrimony in the North
for the Danish possessions in Northumberland, Eng., where he fixed
his residence and conquered several provinces from the Anglo Saxons.
His brother Helge invaded the Swedish territory, defeated King Adils
plundered the palace at Upsala and carried off the Queen, a Saxon
princess named Yrsa. The lady from being his prisoner became his
wife, and the mother of the celebrated hero (15) Rolf Krake, one of
the brightest ornaments of the throne. His stature was gigantic and
his strength extraordinary. Having perished ignobly by the treachery
of a nobleman on whom he had bestowed his daughter in marriage, the
crown became the prize of contending factions until the kingdom was

again united under the sceptre of Ivar Vidfadme, who transmitted it to his grandson, Harald Hildetand.

In the middle of the seventh century the brothers Rerik and Helge reigned jointly in Leire (Lethra) Zealand, and Ivar Vidfadme, King of Denmark, made himself ruler over a great part of the North, To obtain Sjelland (Zealand) he gave his daughter Audur in marriage to Rerik, although she preferred Helge. Afterward he kindled variance between the brothers so that Rerik in a fit of jealousy killed his brother Helge. Whereafter Ivar succeeded in conquering Rerik and acquired Zealand. He lost his life on an expedition to Russia (Garderige) A. D. 647. About this time Hamlet (son of Horvendill, hereditary prince of Jutland) was killed in a battle as he was endeavoring by force to succeed to the Crown of Denmark, to which he was entitled, as having married Gerutha, daughter of Rerik.

Harald Hildetand, a son of Rerik (and Audur), at the death of Ivar brought under subjection all the countries his grandfather Ivar had ruled, and became a mighty and sovereign King, but in 735, after a peaceful reign, his nephew Sigurd Hring, Viceroy in Sweden, raised an insurrection against him. The battle was fought at Bravallahede, Sweden, and Harald was killed.

15 **FRODE THE SIXTH,** son of Roe above, succeeded to Roe and Helge, and became King of Denmark A. D. 494. He died A. D. 510. His successor was his cousin, Rolf Krake, son of Helge above.

15 ROLF KRAKE became King of Denmark A. D. 510. He was of immense size ; his enormous stature and strength were so extraordinary that he was surnamed Krake. He kept 12 giants at his court. He was killed by his own sister, Skulda (married to Hjartvar, Rolf's Viceroy in Skane), in A. D. 522. He died childless.

The successor of Rolf Krake was Frode VII., son of his cousin Frode

16 **FRODE THE SEVENTH,** or OLAF THE SHARP EYED, became King of Denmark A. D. 522, and died A. D. 548. His two sons were :

17 Halfdan III., or Snaile, King of Denmark.

17 Rorik Slyngeband, also King of Denmark.

17 Ingiald Illrada, King of Sweden.

The successor of Frode VII. was his son

17 **HALFDAN THE THIRD,** or SNAILE I., became King of Denmark A. D. 548, and died A. D. 580. He was succeeded by his brother

17 RORIK SLYNGEBAND, who became King of Denmark A. D. 580, and died A. D. 588. He was succeeded by his nephew

18 IVAR VIDFADME, son of Halfdan III., who became King of Denmark A. D. 588, and of Sweden A. D. 630, and died A. D. 647.

Historians rank him among the most distinguished warriors of antiquity. He raised Denmark to an unprecedented height of power. He conquered all Sweden (allt Sviaveldi) and united it with all Denmark (allt Danaveldi) and a great part of Saxland, the whole of Estland and a fifth part of England. From him henceforth descend the supreme Kings of the Danes and the Swedes. The throne and extensive dominions of Ivar were inherited by his grandson, Harald Hildetand; from him they descended to Sigurd Ring and Ragnar Lodbrok, all of whom swayed the Danish sceptre in the eighth century. Ivar married Gothilda, by whom he had a daughter·

19 AUDA DIUPHAUDZA, who became the wife of

19 RERIK, or ROBERT, King of Holmgard, whose son was:

20 HARALD HILDETAND, or HILLDITUR (Golden Tooth), who succeeded to Ivar Vidfadme as King of Denmark A. D. 647, and died A. D. 735, when he was succeeded by his nephew, Sigurd Ring.

Harald Hildetand, grandson of Ivar Vidfadme, raised Denmark to an illustrious height of grandeur. Not content with chastising the neighboring States, he made frequent incursions into Germany, took the Vandals under his protection, reduced several nations on the Rhine, invaded the coasts of France and overran part of Britain, which, according to Saxo, had withdrawn its allegiance from the Danish Kings since the death of Frode III., A. D. 310. His fleets are described as covering the Sound, and like those of Xerxes bridging over the Northern Hellespont from shore to shore; but his life and reign terminated at the fatal battle of Bravala, fought on the coast of Scania in 735, against his nephew, Sigurd Ring, in consequence of his attempt to expel him from the throne. The son of Harald Hildetand was (21) Throud.

21 SIGURD HRING, (son of the King Randver, who married Hildetand's sister Asa), became King of Sweden and Denmark A. D. 735.

The Danish throne fell to the possession of Sigurd in 735, who, like other Danish Kings of his time, embarked in sea-roving expeditions to keep alive the military enthusiasm of his people. He recovered the English province of Northumberland, conquered by Ivar Vidfadme, which had as-

serted its independence, and at his death, A. D. 750, he left the crown to
his son, the famous Ragnar Lodbrok. He married Queen Alfhilda. His
children were:

      22 Ragnar Lodbrok, or Lodbrok the Elder (Hairy Breeches), and a

      22 Daughter, who was married A. D. 750, to Fronde or Throud, or
          Hoerk, King of Frondheim, son of Harald Hildetand above.

22 RAGNAR LODBROK, son of Sigurd Hring, became King of Denmark
    A. D. 750.

    This monarch while ruling his dominions in peace, his jealousy was
excited by rumors of the daring achievements of his sons in various regions
of Europe, and in A. D. 794 he determined to undertake an expedition that
should rival their fame. Two vessels were built of immense size, such as
had never before been seen in the North. "The arrow," the signal of war,
was sent through all his kingdom to summon his champions to arms. With
this apparently inadequate force he set sail, contrary to the advice of his
Queen, Aslanga, who presented him with a magical garment to ward off
danger. After suffering from storms and shipwreck he landed on the coast
of Northumberland, Eng. Ella, the Saxon King of that country, collected
his forces to repel the invader. A battle ensued, wherein the valiant Dane,
clothed in his enchanted robe and wielding the huge spear with which he
had slain the guardian serpent of the Princess Thora, four times pierced the
enemy's ranks, dealing death on every side, whilst his own person was in-
vulnerable. But the contest was unequal, his warriors fell one by one around
him until he was at last taken prisoner, stripped of his miraculous vest and
thrown alive, by order of Ella, into a dungeon full of serpents, in the midst
of which he expired with a laugh of defiance, chanting the famous death-
song called the Lodbrokar-quida, or Biarka-mal, which he is alleged to
have composed in that horrible prison. "The surname of Lodbrok or
Hairy Breeches he acquired from the rough garment, daubed with sand
and pitch, that he wore when he slew the serpent and gained the hand of
Thora, his first Queen."—*Torfaeus Hist. Nor. tom, I. lib. X. c. 29.*

    "Ragnar Lodbrok was remarkable for his exploits and enterprises of
hazard. Perpetually roving in defiance and war, partly on the southern and
eastern coasts of the Baltic, partly in Flanders, Scotland, Ireland and England, and being lord and ruler wherever he went, he was at last captured
by King Ella, of Northumberland, who threw him bound into a dungeon

of vipers. His four sons, avenging his death, divided the widespread realms which Ivar Vidfadme, Harald Hildetand and Sigurd Ring had gathered together."

The first wife of Ragnar Lodbrok was Thora, who bore no children. His second was Asloga, daughter of Sigurd and Byrnhilda. She was the mother of :

> 23 Biorn Jarnaside, who became King of Sweden A. D. 794
>
> 23 Gudrod, or Godefred Hvidsaerk, who became King of Jutland and Wendon, and died A. D. 810.
>
> 23 Ivar Beentoris, who became King of Northumberland.
>
> 23 Siguard Snogoje, who became King of Denmark.

After the death of Ragnar Lodbrok, A. D. 794, his son

23 SIGURD SNOGOJE (Snake Eye) inherited the Danish Crown, but was slain in battle with the Franks A. D. 803, after extending his sway over all Jutland, Scania, Holland and part of Norway. His son was :

> 24 Horda Knut or Harde-Canute, born about A. D. 790.

The historian Meursius speaks in high terms of Sigurd Snake Eye : "God enabled him to complete a reign as pregnant with real felicity as any which the annals of Denmark can show."

At the death of Sigurd Snogoje, A. D. 803, he was succeeded by his son :

24 HORDA KNUT, or HARDE CANUTE, who being young at the time of his father's death, was left to the guardianship of his uncle Gudrod, Regent of the Kingdom.

During the Prince's minority Jutland threw off its allegiance and the sovereignty was fiercely contested between the sons of Gudrod and Harald Klak, a petty King of Schloswig, and father of Rurik, who had taken violent possession of Frisia. He was repeatedly driven from his dominions and his flight became remarkable as the means of shedding the first rays of Christianity over the Pagan darkness of the North. The achievement of this desirable object was reserved for Louis le Debonnaire, son of Charlemagne, whose Court at Ingleheim on the Rhine, was visited (A. D. 826) by the exiled Prince of Jutland, accompanied with his Queen, his sons and numerous retinue, in a fleet of a hundred galleys. Here the solicitations of the Emperor and his prelates induced Harald to renounce the errors of Paganism. His wife and children and many of his followers were baptized. Harde-Canute died A. D. 850. His son was :

25 Gorm, surnamed "The Old."

Ragnar Lodbrok bestowed the Swedish Crown as a distinct possession on one of his sons, Biorn Jarnasida (Ironside), in whose grandson's reign (Biorn II.) it is generally admitted that the light of the gospel first dawned in the North, although it did not become the established religion until the accession of Olaf Skotkanung, who was baptized with his whole family in the year 1001, and exerted himself with great enthusiasm to propagate the true faith. His father Erik is said to have carried his zeal for Christianity so far as to cause the magnificent heathen temple at Upsala, with its idols. and images, to be destroyed, and the ancient sacrifices to be interdicted under the severest corporeal inflictions, but this imprudent mandate cost. him his life, as he was murdered in a tumult of the people enraged at the demolition of their Pagan worship.

OLAF.—He made a temporary conquest of Norway, and having annexed Gothland inalienably to his own dominions, he assumed the title of King of Sweden, his predecessors being merely styled Sovereigns of Upsala. His son Edmund Jacob contributed so much to the progress of Divine truth among his subjects as to obtain the designation of " Most Christian Majesty." A severe law which procured him the name of Kolbrenner (the coal-burner) enacted that if any man injured his neighbor, his effects to the same value, should be consumed with fire. His successor became involved in a dispute with the Danes about adjusting the frontiers of the two kingdoms, and fell at the head of an army which he had levied for recovering the ceded province of Scania. Indignant at the surrender of that valuable district, the Swedes raised Steukill to the throne, who founded a new dynasty to the exclusion of the race of Lodbrok. The Goths, who likewise claimed the right of election, chose Hakon the Red as their King ; but the rival monarchs came to an amicable arrangement by stipulating that the latter should enjoy the regal dignity for life, on condition that, at his demise, Gothland should revert inseparably to Sweden.

25 GORM, the son of Horda Knut, surnamed the Old from the length of his reign, fifty-eight years. He became King of Denmark A. D. 883, and died A. D. 941.

Profiting by the absence of many of the jarls and chiefs in distant predatory expeditions, he subdued Jutland. Other conquests followed until he succeeded in uniting into one State the territories which now con-

stitute the Danish monarchy, including the Swedish provinces of Scania
and Holland. He had espoused the beautiful Thyra Dannebod (ornament
of Denmark), daughter of Harald Klak, who had been baptized when a
child in France, and through her influence he was induced to tolerate the
preaching of the missionaries, although he still continued to worship the
idols of his ancestors. His sons were : Canute and Harald.

The son of Harald Hildetand (No. 20) above was :

21 **THROUD** or **FRONDE**, King of Frondheim, who married a daughter of
Sigurd Ring, A. D. 750, and was father of

22 **EISTEN**, King of Frondheim, who married A. D. 780, and was father of

23 **HALFDAN**, King of Frondheim, married A. D. 810, and was father of

24 **EISTEN GLUMRU**, King of Frondheim or Thrandia, A. D. 840. His

25 **DAUGHTER**, was married to

25 IVAR, Jarl or Earl of Upland, A. D. 850. He was son of Halfdan the
Aged, born about A. D. 800, whose father was Sveide the Viking, who
was living from A. D. 760 to 780. The son of Ivar was :

26 **EISTEN GLUMRU** or **VORS**. He was living A. D. 870. He was father of

27 Huldrich, ancestor of Raoul de Toeny.

27 Sigurd, the first Jarl or Earl of the Orkney Isles, and of

27 **ROGVALD**,* Jarl or Earl of Moere, A. D. 885. By his first wife, Rogvald
had four sons, viz.: 28 Hallidur. 28 Ivar. 28 Hrollagur, or Drugo
Turstain. 28 Einar, Jarl or Earl of the Orkneys.

By his second wife, Hilder, daughter of Rolf Nefio, he had :

28 Thorer, Jarl or Earl of Moere, and

28 Rollo, First Duke of Normandy, A. D. 912.

Rogvald was killed by Harald Harefoot's sons, and Harald granted
Rogvald's brother, Huldrich, the fief of Normandy, and Rollo conquered
it from the original Dukes of Neustria.

28 HROLLAGUR or DROGO, A. D. 896 third son of Rogvald, Jarl or Earl of
Moere. In the division of Normandy in fiefs, among his followers
in 912, Rollo, the conqueror and first ruler in Normandy, allotted the
northern district of La Manche to his half brother Drogo, who took the

---

* The line of Rogvald from Sulim *Histoire Critique du Danemarc ;* and Snorro,
Historia Regnum Septentrionalium. TURSTAIN, from M. le Compte de Toustain-Riche
bourg. *Hist. Généal de la Maison de Toustain-Frontebosq.* BERTRAND from Ordericus
Vitalis ; the Cartulary of the Abbey of St. Trinité at Caen ; and Leguin Histoire Militaire
des Bocains.

surname of Turstain.   The Bertrand family were derived from Drogo. Drogo married Ermina. His son was:

29 HROLF, or ROBERT TURSTAIN. He was living in 920.

This Robert Turstain was the potent baron " Vir nobilis et præpotens Torstingus " that in A. D. 960 gave certain lands to the Abbey of St. Wandrille (or Fontanelle), which Duke Richard I. sanctioned and confirmed By Gerlotte, his wife, daughter of Theobald, Count of Blois and Chartres, Robert Turstain was the father of three distinguished sons:

> 30 Anslech, Baron of Briquebec,
>
> 30 Onfroi, or Aunsfred, surnamed the Dane in memory of his northern origin, the sire of Turstain-Goz, and ancestor of Hugh Lupus, Earl of Chester, and
>
> 30 William, ancestor of the Lords of Bec Crespin, all of whose signatures appear on a charter A. D. 990, to the Abbey of Mount St. Michel.

80 ANSLECH TURSTAIN, the first son of Robert Turstain, was Baron of Briquebec in 943, and his grandson William, Baron of Briquebec, was the first to take the name of Bertrand, from whom descended the Russell family of England, Dukes of Bedford.

In the rebellion of Rioulf of St. Savour against Duke William Longsword, in A. D. 933, Anslech, Baron of Briquebec, is mentioned by Wace as one of the three barons who alone remained faithful to the Duke, by rendering him military service at the siege of Rouen ; and on the assassination of that Prince he was appointed by the barons of Normandy and Bretagne one of the three guardians to his son, the young Duke Robert, at a crisis which required a rare union of courage, firmness and discretion, and fulfilled his trust during that long and troublous minority with infinite reputation to himself and advantage to his country.   It was in the time of Anslech that the Castle of Briquebec was first erected, now one of the most beautiful and picturesque ruins in La Manche.

Anslech lived to witness the accession of Duke Richard II. At his death he left two sons :

> 31 Turstain, Baron of Briquebec and Lord of Bastenbourg.
>
> 31 Richard, or Turstain Haralduc or Halduc ; and a daughter
>
> 31 Ertemburga, who was married in A. D. 950, to Torf de Harcourt, son of Bernard the Dane, and who became the ancestress of the Harcourt family in England.

31 TURSTAIN DE BASTENBOURG, Baron of Briquebec, first son of Anslech Turstain, (No. 30 above), was born in La Manche, Normandy. He left at his death two sons and a daughter, viz. :

> 32 William Bertrand, Baron of Briquebec.
>
> 32 Hugh Cum Barba, (so denominated from wearing his beard un-shorn, which was not the regular habit of the Normans), and
>
> 32 Gisela. During the Government of Duke Richard II. she en-gaged the affections of Geroye, Lord of Montreuil and Echauffour, and became the mother of seven sons and four daughters, whence issued, says Ordenius, a race of hardy knights who were the terror of the barbarians in Apulia, Syria and Thrace.

32 WILLIAM BERTRAND, Baron of Briquebec, first son of Turstain de Bastenbourg, and first to take the name of Bertrand, was born at Bri-quebec, in La Manche, Normandy.

His name occurs on a charter in 1023, of Duke Richard II., confirm-ing to the Abbey of Mount St. Michel, all the deeds and privileges granted by his predecessors, and especially those of the Duchess Gunnora, his mother, wife of Duke Richard I. In this document he is styled "William the son of Turstain, and his name is followed by that of "Hugh, his brother," and their kinsman "Richard" (the Viscount d'Avranches), as witnesses. William Bertrand had issue three sons :

> 33 Robert, surnamed Le Tort, who succeeded to the barony of Briquebec. Wife Susanna.
>
> 33 Hugh de Rozel, born about 1020, was invested with the Castle of Rozel about 1045. Had possessions in the isles of Guernsey and Jersey.
>
> 33 William, the third son, and a daughter
>
> 33 Emma, who married Rabel Count de Montchenseye.

32 HUGH TURSTAIN, the Bearded, brother of William Bertrand, about 1030 obtained, by marriage of Lady Barbe de Montfort, the town and territory of Montfort, in Upper Normandy.

30 ONFROI or AUNSFRED, Viscount d'Exmes, second son of Robert Tur-stain, (No. 29 above) was born at Briquebec, in La Manche, Normandy.

In 1016 Richard II., Duke of Normandy, gave the county of Exmes to Aunsfred, the Dane, brother of Anslech, Baron of Briquebec. His son was :

31 TURSTAIN GOZ, Viscount d'Exmes and Argentan, who was born at Exmes, in Normandy. He married Judith de Monteroliers.

Turstain Goz, succeeded to Exmes, in which he was confirmed by the Barons during William's minority, who also made him Viscount of Argentan and Governor of the Castle of Falaise. His son was:

> 32 Richard Goz, Viscount d'Avranches. He married Emmeline de Montagne. He witnessed Duke Richard II. charter to Mount St. Michel, A. D. 1,001   His son was:

88 HuGH Lupus. He was Earl of Chester, and with Hugh de Montgomerie, Earl of Shrewsbury, united his forces in resisting the inroads of the Welsh into England.

The daughter of Anslech Turstain (No. 30 above) was :

81 ÉRTEMBURGA, who was married A. D. 950, to

81 TORF or TORFIN, Seigneur de Torraille, surnamed Le Riche, who was born at Schloswig, in Denmark, about A. D. 920. He wandered to the country of Greenland.

"In 1,007 a rich Greenlander, Torfin, determined to emigrate to Vinland, (now New England.) His followers numbered 60, and he was accompanied by his wife Gudrida, the widow of a previous explorer. Five other women were on board, and the ships were freighted with all kinds of domestic animals, tools and provisions for a permanent colony. Gudrida had been the first female to see the new world, having accompanied her former husband during the previous year. The expedition of Thorfin prospered. The natives came in great numbers and trafficked in furs and produce. Gudrida bore a son, Snorro, the first birth of European parentage in America, who is said to have been an ancestor of the sculptor Thorwaldsen. The family remained three years in the colony, but ultimately returned, and Thorfin settled and died in Iceland. The widow made a pilgrimage to Rome in her bereavement, and died in a cloister founded by her son in Iceland. Other chiefs went to Vinland, but their history throws no further light upon the colony. They, however; discovered land extending far away to the south-west and inhabited by natives of different caste, of darker color and more vigorous frame. The colony perished at last, destroyed probably like that of Greenland. Traces of it were found by Jesuit missionaries among the Indians Gaspé at the mouth of the St. Lawrence, a tribe which revered the symbol of the cross before the arrival of the missionaries. Physical constitution and peculiarities of manners and customs are also cited in confirmation of European descent. Father Charlevoix adds that 'many marks distinguishing them from other American Indians go far to make me believe that they are a colony of Europeans degenerated into savages through destitution.' "

His father was :

30 BERNARD THE DANE, Prince in Denmark, Governor and Regent in Normandy under ROLLO, with whom he received baptism at Rouen A. D. 912. The son of Torf (No. 31 above) was :

82 TOURODE, Sire de Pont Audemer, whose wife, Weva Duceline de Crèpon, was sister of the Duchess Gonnor,* wife of Richard I. (Sans Peur), Duke of Normandy, and thus was the great grandmother of WILLIAM THE CONQUEROR.

Weva Duceline was niece of Tourode. She was sister of Osberne de Crèpon, High Steward of Normandy, who married Avelina, and was the father of Walter Giffard, Earl of Buckingham, Eng., and daughter of Herfault, the brother of Tourode, and they were grandsons of " Bernard the Dane." Osberne was assassinated at Vandreuil when sleeping in the chamber of Duke William, who was then a child. Crèpon was an estate near Bayeux, Normandy.

Of the six children of Tourode the eldest was :

33 ONFROY or HUMPHROI DE VELUTIS, Count of Pont Audemer. Estates of Pont Audemer went to the Bardulf family of St. Mary's of Hoo, Kent, Eng. He married Aublice Dame de la Hare Auberèe about 1027. His son was :

84 ROGER DE BEAUMONT, who died Nov. 29, 1094. By his wife Adeline, Countess of Millent, he was father of :

85 ROBERT, EARL OF MILLENT, in the Vexin, afterward, in 1103, Earl of Leicester ; and of

85 HENRY, EARL OF WARWICK, in 1068, who married Margueritte, daughter of Rotrou, Count of Perche.

The youngest child of Tourode was :

33 JOSSELINE, who married Hugh de Montgomerie, Count of Montgomerie and Earl of Shrewsbury. Their children were : Roger, Robert, William, and Gilbert Montgomerie.

Another son of Torf (No. 31 above) was :

---

* Gunnora was the mother Richard II, Duke of Normandy, who by his wife Judith was father of Robert, Duke of Normandy, who by his wife Arlotta was the father of WILLIAM THE CONQUEROR.

82 TURCHETIL, Sire de Turchetil, from whom were descended the family of Harcourt in England.

28 EINAR, EARL OF THE ORKNEYS, 4th son of Rogvald, (No. 27 above), Earl of Moere, had three sons, viz. :

29 Torfidur.

29 Erlind, and

29 Arnkell.   These last two sons were both slain A. D. 942.

29 TORFIDUR, first son of Einar, (No: 28 above), became Earl of the Ork- neys A. D. 942, married Grelota, daughter of Dungad, Earl of Caith- ness, whose wife Groa was daughter of Turstain Rauda.   The sons of Torfidar were:

30 Arnfidur.

30 Havard.

30 Lodver, Earl of the Orkney Isles.

30 Liotur.

30 Skulo.

80 LODVER, third son of Torfidur, (No. 29 above).   He succeeded to his father as Earl of the Orkney Isles, and was succeeded by his son

81 SIGURD, as Earl of the Orkney Isles.   He married Thora, daughter of Malcolm, King of Scotland.   His sons were :

32 Sumarlis.

32 Bruso, whose son was Jarl Rogvald.

32 Einar, and

32 Thorfin, who was the father of Bardolf and Bodin of England.

28 THORER, Jarl or Earl of Moere, was fifth son of Rogvald, Earl of Moere, (No. 27 above).

He married Alofa Arbot, daughter of Harald, first King of Norway, A. D. 885, (son of Halfdan the Swart), whose wife Alfhilda was daughter of Hringo, son of Dagus, King of Upper Hringa.

The daughter of Thorer was :

29 Bergliotta, who became the wife of

29 Sigurd, Earl of of Hlatha, whose son

30 Earl Haquin became King of Norway, A. D. 921, and reigned un- til A. D. 996.   By his first wife he was father of

31 King Eric, who married Guda of Denmark, and was father of

32 King Haquin, whose wife was Thyra.

By his second wife Thora, daughter of Skage Skofteson, Earl Haquin above had children :

    31 Swein, whose wife was Holmfrida of Sweden.

    21 Hemingur.

    31 Erling.

    31 Bergliota, who married Einar Thamba-Scelfur, and had son, Earl Eindred, and

    31 Ragnhilda, who married Skopte Shakeson.

28 ROLLO, sixth son of Rogvald, (No. 27 above).

Rollo devastated Holland and appeared upon the Seine while Gottfried ravaged the valleys of the Meuse and Scheldt. They burned and sacked Cologne, Bonn, Treves, Metz and other cities, stabling their horses at Aix-la-Chapelle, in the Cathedral Church of Charlemagne. *A furore Normann-orum libera nos Domine*, came to be part of the Catholic litany. Hastings, at the head of a band of Northmen, sacked Bordeaux, Lisbon and Seville ; defeated the Moorish conquerors of Spain at Cordova ; crossed the Straits into Morocco ; repassed them ; overran Tuscany ; returned to France, where other chieftains had had various success against Charles the Bald, and embraced Christianity. (See Hastings.) His name, the most dreaded of all the Vikings, was adopted by many successors. With safe winter quarters in Spain, they extended their ravages to Naples, Sicily and the coasts of the Greek Empire. Anarchy, meanwhile, prevailing in France, in the autumn of 885 they laid siege to Paris. After a year the siege was converted into a blockade, but at last King Charles the Fat, bought off the Northmen with 700 pounds of silver and a free passage to the Upper Seine and Burgundy. The most redoubtable of the Northmen afterward was Hrolf, better known as ROLLO, chieftain, of Norwegian parentage, first Duke of Normandy, and direct ancestor, in the sixth generation, of WILLIAM THE CONQUEROR. In the words of Snorro Sturleson : "He was so mighty of stature that there was no horse of strength and size to bear him. He was therefore always on foot, and was called the Marcher." He ravaged Friesland and the countries watered by the Schieldt, and took Rouen, St. Lo Bayeux and Evreux. From Charles the Simple he accepted the hand of a daughter, together with a tract of Neustrian territory north of the Seine, from Andalye to the sea (modern Normandy), in exchange for Christian baptism and an oath of fealty (912). Thus was arrested the Scandinavian flood which had devastated France for more than a century. Rollo distributed among his followers the lands of Neustria, to be held of him as Duke of Normandy. Thus were laid the foundations of the feudal system which William (7th Duke) transplanted into England (1066-87). Few external traces of the Scandinavians are to be found in modern Normandy. Yet for a time the Scandinavian gods divided with the Saviour the religious reverence of the people of that country. Monasteries and cathedrals were built, however, with what extent and magnificence their splendid remains attest. The Normans adopted the language of the vanquished province, but greatly modified it. It was the *langue d'oni* (the *langue d'oc* being south of the Loire), which became under Norman inspiration the peculiar medium of romantic poetry.

32 THORFIN, THE DANE, or Torkill of Richmondshire Baron, Lord of Tanfield, founder of the WASHINGTON FAMILY in England, fourth son of Sigurd, (No. 31 above), Earl of the Orkney Isles, was born about A. D. 1000. He was Jarl or Earl of the Island of Orkney, that was held as a feif, under the Kings of Denmark.

These Earls were Sigurd, son of Eisten Glumru; Einar, son of Rogvald, Jarl or Earl of Moere; Torfidur, son of above Einar; Lodver, son of Torfidur; Sigurd, son of Lodver; and Einar and Thorfin, sons of Sigurd.

They were called LORDS OF THE ISLES. The present Duke of Argyle is descended from them. They were the ancient Marmours, one of the Marmours was represented in the Maring Charters with Thorfin.

ARMS: NORMANDY, *gules* two leopards or lions passant gardant. *or*, a bend compony *or* and *azure*. BLOIS *azure*, a bend *argent* coticed potencé contrepotencé, *or*. HARCOURT, lozengy *or* and *gules*. BERTRAND, *or*, a lion rampant *vert*, langued and raguled, *gules*, and crowned, *argent*. MONTFORT, bendy *or* and *azure*. MONTCHENSEYE, *or*, 3 escutcheons, 2 and 1, barry of *vaire* and *gules*. DU ROZEL, *argent*, a lion rampant *gules*. a chief *sable*. WAR-CRY of NORMANDY, " *Diex aie!* " Of TURSTAIN, " *Tons teines de sang!* " Of MONTCHENSEYE, " Montchenseye."

------ •◆ -- ------

The line of descent may be traced through the full face Caps.

AMERICA DISCOVERED

BY RELATIVES OF

THORFIN,

THE

PROGENITOR OF THE WASHINGTON FAMILY

IN ENGLAND.

———•———

THAT Columbus did not discover America, everybody who believes in the traditions of the Indians, that go to show an Asiatic descent of the gentle savage, is compelled to own.   But who discovered these descendants of the East, after their wanderings, is a question that promises to prove far more agitating than the vital one of what constitutes the "American drama."   Assuming that the original inhabitants of the American continent forced their way from the East through the icy regions of the North, and by way of Behring's Straits (as all scientific men assume, they being agreed that man sprung up in the East and found his way to the West), the question now is, who discovered their progeny on this continent?   Until a very few years ago the people of the temperate and torrid zones were quite agreed that one Christopher Columbus, a Genoese voyager, was that person.   These people took no heed of the Phœnician, Greek, Welsh, and Irish claims, and as they knew little and cared less for the Scandinavian literature, did not apprehend the cropping up of another and more formidable claimant than had yet appeared, from the icy North.   It will be seen, therefore, that from such a diversity of demands, nearly all of which seem genuine, it will be rather difficult to select the justest, and settle the matter in an agreeable manner to all concerned. In the first place, it is maintained that the Greek philosopher Pythias traversed the Atlantic Ocean 340 B. C., and discovered the different length of days in different climates. It is also well known that the Phœnicians colonized the Canary Isles, and, it is said, these bold sailors pushed their way to the West and found this continent ages ago. The Welsh declare that one of their ancestors, named Madoc, settled here in 1322, one hundred and seventy years before Columbus landed. Ninety-one years before this, a Norseman was driven on the coast, and found people who appeared to him to speak Irish, although he did not understand that language. The Norsemen themselves, whose claims we are about to examine, insist that America was accidentally discovered in the year 986 by Bjarne Herjulfson, who did not land, although he came near the land three times, first, where the present Nantucket stands, second, at Nova Scotia, and the third time at Newfoundland. When Bjarne went home to Norway two or three years later, and recounted his strange adventures, he was censured by his chief for not landing and exploring the strange land. Still, what he had done was sufficient to arouse Leif Erikson, son of the Jarl, and he determined to find what kind of regions these were that were so much talked about. He bought Bjarne's ship, selected a crew, and found the land just as had been described. They landed at Newfoundland and Nova Scotia, then sailed South, and entered the bay now known as Mount Hope Bay. Here they resolved to spend the winter, and built a large house. There was a captive German in the party named Tryker, who had become a great favorite with Leif Erikson. One day he was missing, and great was Leif's sorrow, for he feared some disaster had befallen his friend; but the German was descried toward evening coming home in a most excited state, singing and shouting, and bearing in his hands bunches of grapes. On his arrival, he continued shouting and singing in German, which greatly increased the wonder of his auditors, who did not understand that language. At length he explained to them that he found grapes growing even as they grew in Germany, upon which information Leif promptly christened the place Vinland. This was that part of the country now known as Massachusetts, the year was 1000, and the Sagas insist that Leif Erikson was the first pale-faced man who planted his feet on this continent. These Sagas of the Norsemen, the contents

of which are now becoming gradually known to reading men, promise to
revolutionize many of the old theories the world has held to.   In the
spring Leif returned to Greenland, and there found his brother Thorwald,
who declared, after listening to his story, that the land had not been half
explored.   So he started out in 1002 and remained in Vinland three years.
At the end of that time he was killed by a Skrælling (Indian), and buried
there.   He was the first Christian and first white man that died and was
buried in America, and it is now declared that the skeleton in armor
found in Fall River, Mass., in 1831, and made famous in Longfellow's
poem, was no other than the bold explorer, Thorwald Erikson, who was
killed by Indians A. D. 1005.   When the Norsemen had buried their
chief they at once returned to Greenland.   The same year, the Sagas tell
us, Thorstein, youngest brother to Leif and Thorwald, fitted out a vessel,
manned it with twenty-five men, selected for their strength and stature,
and accompanied by his wife Gudrid, a most remarkable woman, set out
for the new land ; but they met with tempestuous weather, and during all
the summer were tossed about on the deep, and driven they knew not
where.   At length they made Lysefjord, on the coast of Greenland.   Here
Thorstein and several of his men died, and Gudrid returned home.
The next year Gudrid married Thorfinn Karlsefne, a wealthy and influen-
tial person, who, through her persuasions, was induced to fit out an expedition for Vinland.   This party consisted of one hundred and fifty-one
men and seven women, and, unlike prior excursions, started fully
equipped, and resolved on colonization.   It was provided with cattle and
sheep, and arrived safely.   Here the party remained for three years, until
hostilities with the Skrællings compelled them to give up the colony.
The Sagas give full accounts of Thorfinn's enterprises in Vinland, about
the traffic with the Skrællings ; and about the development of the colony.

They also record the interesting fact, that a son was born to Thorfinn
and Gudrid, a year after the colony was settled, who was named Snorre
Thorfinnson.   He was born in the present State of Massachusetts, in the
year 1008, and was the first man of European blood of whose birth in
America we have any record.   From him the famous sculptor Albert
Thorwaldsen is lineally descended, beside a long train of learned and
distinguished men, who have flourished during the last eight centuries
in Iceland and Denmark.   The author of " America not discovered by

Columbus" calls attention to the Dighton Writing Rock Inscription in the Taunton River (which has been translated, "Thorfinn, with one hundred and fifty-one Norse sea-faring men took possession of this land "), and says, that this inscription removes all doubt of the presence of Thorfinn and the Norsemen in the Taunton River in the beginning of the eleventh century. The Sagas give elaborate accounts of other expeditions that took place in 1011 and in 1121, when Bishop Erik Upsi went as a missionary to Vinland. There were other expeditions that went as far south as Florida. The last expedition made by them was in the year 1347, the year the Black Plague started in Europe. This Plague spread over Europe, and at length reached Vinland, and cut off communication between the two countries. It reduced the population of Norway from 2,000,000 to 300,000, and left no surplus for expeditions. Thus the New World remained until Columbus visited it in 1492. It is believed that Columbus knew of these voyages of the Norsemen. Fifteen years before he sailed for America, he was in Iceland, and undoubtedly was made familiar with the Norsemen's expedition, and the reason why he should know of them, was the visit of Gudrid to Rome,* after the death of her husband. Rome at that time took great interest in geographical discoveries, and took pains to collect all charts and reports that were brought in. The Romans might have heard of Vinland before, but Gudrid brought them personal evidence. That Vinland was known to the Vatican, is proved by the fact that Pope Paschal II., in the year 1112, sent Erik Upsi, as Bishop, to Iceland, Greenland, and Vinland. Recent developments also prove that Columbus had the opportunity to see the map of Vinland in the Vatican, and it would appear, indeed, strange that with his nautical knowledge, he would not, in the age of discovery and literary activity in which he lived, have heard as much as he did. Beside all this, there is another fact which goes to show that Columbus knew of this continent. Adam, of Bremen, a canon and historian of high authority, visited and described the North of Europe, and Iceland and Greenland. Having given an account of these countries, he says, "beside these there is another region which has been visited by many, lying in that ocean (the Atlantic), which is called Vinland, where vines grow spontaneously, and where corn springs up without being sown. This we know, not by fabulous conjecture, but from positive statements of the Danes." This book

*See page xviii.

was printed in 1073, and, as it was read by all educated men, must have been read in time by Columbus. He says himself that he based his conviction that there was land in the West on the authority of learned writers. Another evidence that he was certain of finding land, after he had "sailed seven hundred leagues," was his promise given to his mutinous crew when they insisted upon turning back, that if land did not appear in three days he would do as they desired. The land appeared, and here is a subject quite as interesting as the question, "Who wrote Shakespeare?" It can be decided by anybody who will read up in Scandinavian litera-ture.

It is certain that the Iceland rovers who settled in Greenland explored the coast of New England down to Rhode Island. In their intercourse with the Skrællinger (Esquimaux) these Danes learned that "farther southward, beyond Chesapeake Bay, there dwelt white men, who clothed themselves in long white garments, carried before them poles to which cloths were attached, and called with a loud voice." In the Sagas, the history of Thorfinn Karlsefne, and the famous chronicle, the Landnama-bok, this country is styled the "Land of the White Men" (Hvitramanna-land). The Landnama Book says : "To the south of inhabited Greenland are wild and desert tracts and ice-covered mountains ; then comes the land of the Skrællings (Esquimaux), beyond this Markland (Nova Scotia), and then Vinland the Good (Massachusetts and southwards). Next to this, and somewhat behind it, lies Albania, that is to say, Hvitramanna-land, *whither vessels formerly sailed from Ireland.* It was there that several Irishmen and Icelanders recognized Ari, the son of Mar and Katla of Reykjanes, whom they had not for a long time had any tidings of, and whom the natives of the country had made their chief." The Landnama-bok also states that Ari Marsson was driven by a tempest to Hvitraman-naland, and detained and baptized there. The Northmen are reputed to have received their account of Hvitramannaland, which was also called Irland it Mikla (Ireland the great) from Limerick traders, vessels from that port having sailed thither before the Icelandic discovery of Vinland. (Compare Rafu, *Antiquit. Amer.*, 203, 206, 211, 446, 451 ; and Wilhelmi, *Ueber Island*, &c., &c., s. 75, 81.) This Ari Marsson, referred to above, was of the race of Ulf the Squint-eyed, a heathen family of great influence in Iceland. It is the opinion of some, indeed, that the earliest settlements of Iceland were made from Irland it Mikla, the first chronicles and Sagas speaking of "west men who had come across the sea."

In Sir Richard Grenville's voyage to Roanoke he found natives, who, as he claimed, saluted him in the purest Erse or Gaelic, calling out to him *hao, hui, iach*. Owen Chapelain, who in 1669 was captured by the Tuscaroras, saved himself when they were about to scalp him by addressing them in Gaelic. They did not understand his words, but were familiar with the sounds of his language. Gallatin says that the language of these Tuscaroras is a branch of the Iroquois dialect. But this singular tribe of Indians, all of whom are white, and many of them blue-eyed, could scarcely be akin to the dark Iroquois. Catlin is strongly inclined to think them a mixed race, and believes them to be the descendants of the Welsh prince Madoc, son of Owen Gwinneth, who voyaged westward in 1170. Humboldt is quite inclined to think with Catlin. He says in a note to *Cosmos :* "Although no connection of language has yet been proved, I by no means wish to deny that the Basques and the people of Celtic origin inhabiting Ireland and Wales, who were early engaged in fisheries on the most remote coasts, may have been the constant rivals of the Scandinavians in the northern parts of the Atlantic, and even that the Irish preceded the Scandinavians in the Faroe Islands and in Iceland. It is much to be desired that in our days, when a sound and severe spirit of criticism, devoid of a character of contempt, prevails, the old investigations of Powell and Richard Hackluyt (*Voyages and Navigations,* vol. iii., p. 4) might be resumed in England and Ireland."

This Thorfinn Karlsefne was Torf or Torfinn, Seigneur de Torraille, surnamed "Le Riche," (see page xviii.,) born about A. D. 920, whose father was "Bernard the Dane," Governor and Regent in Normandy, (see page xix.) under Rollo, *with whom* he received baptism at Rouen, A. D. 912. The first wife of Thorfinn Karlsefne was Ertemburga, (married A. D. 950,) daughter of Anslich Turstin, Baron of Briquebec, son of Hrolf or Robert Turstin, Baron, whose father was Hrollagur, or Drogo, the son of Rogvald, Jarl or Earl Moere, A. D. 885, and he was the father of another son, Einar, Jarl or Earl of the Orkneys, whose son, Torfidur, Earl of the Orkneys, A. D. 942, was father of Lodvar, Earl of the Orkneys, whose son, Sigurd, also Earl of the Orkneys, was the father of THORFIN, ancestor of the Washington Family in England.

TABLE SHOWING THE DERIVATION OF THORFIN, ANCESTOR OF WASHINGTON, AND THORFINN KARLSEFNE,

WHO CAME TO AMERICA A. D. 1007.

HILDER, second wife. Daughter of Rolf Neho.

ROGVALD, Jarl or Earl of Moere, A. D. 885. = First wife.

THORER, Jarl or Earl of Moere.

ROLLO, First Duke of Normandy, A. D. 912.

ANSLECK TURSTAIN, Baron of Briquebec, A. D. 943.

TURSTAIN DE BASTENBOURG, Baron of Briquebec.

RICHARD, or Turstain Haralduc.

ONFROI, or "Aunsfred, the Dane," TURSTAN GOZ

WILLIAM, Ancestor of the Lords of Bec Crespin.

ERTEMBERGA, 950 — TORF DE HARCOURT, 1007 — Son of Bernard the Dane, or Torfin, Seigneur de Touraille, or Thorfinn.

GUDRIDA, Widow of Thorstain.

TURSTAIN DE BASTENBOURG

WILLIAM BERTRAND, Baron of Briquebec.

HUGH CUM BARBA.

GISELA

JOURODE, = WEVA, Sire de Pont Duccline Andemer, de Crepon.

KARLSEFNE, or THORFINN KARLSEFNE,

SNORRE THORFINNSEN, Nat. 1008, in Vinland.

HALLIDUR IVAR HROLLAGUR,

GERLOTTE, daughter of THEOBALD, Count of Blois and Chartres.

HROLF, or ROBERT TURSTAIN, Baron.

ERMINA = TURSTAIN, Jarl or Earl of Moere.

DROGO

EINAR, Jarl or Earl of the Orkneys.

ARNFIDUR HAVARD EARL LODVER LIATUR SKULO

TORFIDUR ERLIND ARNKELL

SUMARLIS BRUSO EINAR THORFIN, Nat. 1000.

EARL SIGURD = THORA, daughter of Malcolm, King of Scotland.

BARDOLF BODIN

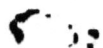

DERIVATION

OF THE

AMERICAN WASHINGTONS,

FROM

THORFIN THE DANE,

EARL OF THE ORKNEY ISLES.

———•◦•———

It has been annunciated by authors and others that the great-grand-father of George Washington was John Washington of Bridge's Creek, Westmoreland Co., Va., who emigrated to America about 1657, and that the great-grandfather of said John was Lawrence Washington, sometime Mayor of Northampton, and the first lay proprietor of the Manor of Sulgrave, in Northamptonshire, which was granted to him in 1538.

Also that Lawrence, brother of John above, had studied at Oxford, and John had resided on an estate at South Cave, in Yorkshire, a circumstance that gave rise to the erroneous tradition that the family sprang from that region.

The above, partly suppositious, has been copied over and over again by writers, and being without dates, seems to defy contradiction. The lack of dates has occasioned all the inferences, which are errors. The following is the correct pedigree or line of descent from father to son, from

32.—1 "THORFIN THE DANE," thirty-second generation from ODIN, who had two sons :

2 BODIN, born at Ravenswath, York, about A. D. 1040.

2 BARDOLF, born at Ravenswath, York, about A. D. 1045.

" In Molsonby and Diddaston bailiwick of the Geld, 11 carucates and 10 ploughs. There TORFIN had one manor ; now BODIN has there 1 carucate and 15 villans, and 3 borders, with 7 ploughs. There is a church there.

The whole was 1 league in length, and 1 in breadth, temp. Edward the Confessor."—(1041–1066.)

The above is from the Domesday Book, and is a translation of that portion respecting the North Riding in Yorkshire, including the district of Wharleton, alias Washington.—1070–1080.

2 BARDOLF, a Monk, and Lord of Ravenswath, second son of TORFIN, was born in the parish of Kirkby Ravenswath, about A. D. 1045.

"Bardolf possessed Ravenswath, with divers other fair Lordships in Richmondshire, in the time of WILLIAM THE CONQUEROR, but desiring in his age to end his days in the devout service of God, forsook the world, and with his brother BODIN, took upon him the habit of a monk of the Abbey of St. Marie's, at York ; whereunto, at the special instance of BODIN, he gave the churches of Patrick-Brompton and Ravenswath in pure alms. To this BARDOLF succeeded his son and heir AKARIS."

"The Manor of Egginton, Derbyshire, was held at Domesday Survey by Azelin, under Geffrey de Alselyn.

"BARDOLF married the heiress of Hanselyn (or Alselyn) of this Baronial Family, and she carried this manor to BARDOLF."

His sons were :

3 AKARIS, born at Ravenswath, Yorkshire, about A. D. 1080.

3 HENRY, born at Ravenswath, Yorkshire, about A. D. 1090.

3 AKARIS, or AKARY FIL BARDOLF, Lord of Ravenswath, first son of BARDOLF, was born at Ravenswath about A. D. 1080.

"AKARIS was the pious founder of Jourvaulx, a famous Abbey of the Cisterian order in this northern track." "In 5 Stephen (1,139), AKARIS founded also an Abbey at Tors, in Wensley-dale in Com. Ebor, then called the 'Abbey of Charity.' He departed this life 7 Henry II (1,161). He gave three carucates of land in Warton, and one carucate and a half at Tors to the Abbey, where he was buried, leaving nine sons." Of whom were:

4 HERVEY FITZ AKARIS, born at Kirkby, Rav., about A. D. 1120.

4 BONDO FIL AKARIS, " " " " 1122.

4 ROBERT FIL AKERY DE ASHTON, " " " 1125.

4 HERASCULFUS FIL AKERY, " " " 1130.

4 BONDO FIL AKARIS, Lord of Wessyngton, juxta Ravenswath, Richmondshire Co., York, a younger son of AKARIS, was born at Ravenswath about 1122. The manor came to him from his father temp. Henry II. (1154).

He was called indifferently BONDO DE WASSYNGTON or WASHINGTON, and BONDO DE RAVENSWATH.   These two places join each other (as per map in main body of this work).   His sons were :

  5 WILLIAM FIL BONDO,   born at Wassyngton about A. D. 1150.
  5 CONAN DE WASHINGTON,   " " " 1155.
  5 WALTER FIL BONDO,   " " " 1160.
  5 RALPH FIL BONDO DE RAVENSWATH, " " 1165.
  5 ROBERT DE WASHINGTON,   " " 1170.

5 WALTER FIL BONDO DE WASHINGTON, of Wassyngton, Co. York, son of BONDO FIL AKARIS, was born there about A. D. 1160.

He was Lord of Milleburne in Westmoreland in right of his wife Agnes temp. King John (1199–1215).   He acquired large estates in the counties of Northumberland and Westmoreland in right of his wife Agnes, Lady Milleburne, daughter and heiress of Ivo de Welleburne, or Milleburne, and resided at Milleburne.   He had issue by wife Agnes :

  6 ROBERT DE WASHINGTON, born at Milleburne about A. D. 1195.
  6 WILLIAM DE WASHINGTON, " " " 1200.

His second wife Juliana, who survived him, claimed dower in the estates, and was living 30, Henry III. (1245).   She claimed dower in the lands of her husband in Northumberland and Westmoreland, and amongst others against her step-son ROBERT DE WASHINGTON, the third part of the Manor of Milleburne (or Welleburn), Co. Westmoreland, 30 Henry III. (1245).

6 ROBERT DE WASHINGTON, of Milleburne, Westmoreland Co., first son of WALTER FIL BONDO DE WASHINGTON, was born there about A. D. 1195.

" ROBERT DE WASHINGTON, Lord of Milleburne, Co. Westmoreland, in right of his mother, 3 Henry III. (1218), against whom Juliana, second wife of his father WALTER DE WASHINGTON, claimed the third part of the Manor of Milleburne as her dower, 30 Henry III." (1245).   He was seized of divers lands in Strickland Ketell, Co. Westmoreland, by the gift of Walter de Strickland, chevalier, and Elizabeth his wife, in free marriage with Johanna their daughter.   His wife's mother Elizabeth was daughter and heiress of Sir Ralph Deincourt, Knt.   He had issue, son :

  7 ROBERT DE WASHINGTON, born at Milleburne about A. D. 1230.

7 ROBERT DE WASHINGTON, of Milleburne, Co. Westmoreland, first son of ROBERT DE WASHINGTON, was born there about A. D. 1230.

" He was son and heir, was seized of a capital messuage and divers
lands in Kerneford, Co. Lancaster, in right of his wife, where he resided 29
Edward I. (1302). He married Amercia, daughter and heiress of Hugh de
Kerneford and Lady Kerneford, Co. Lancaster." Had two sons :

  8 JOHN DE WASHINGTON, born at Milleburne about A. D. 1260.

  8 ROBERT WASHINGTON,   "   "   " 1265.

8 ROBERT WASHINGTON, Lord of Welleburne, Co. Westmoreland, or
Milleburne, Co. Westmoreland, second son of ROBERT DE WASHING-
TON, was born there about A. D. 1265, and removed to Kerneford,
Co. Lancaster, where he settled.

He was second son of ROBERT DE WASHINGTON, upon whom his father
and mother settled in fee tail the lands of Kerneford, Co. Lancaster. He
took part with Thomas, Earl of Lancaster, and was pardoned by King Edward II. in the 12th year of his reign (1319).

He married Agnes, daughter and heiress of Adam Derling.

Had four sons :

  9 ROBERT WASHINGTON, born at Kerneford, about A. D. 1300.

  9 JOHN WASHINGTON,   "   "   " 1305.

  9 THOMAS WASHINGTON, "   "   " 1310.

  9 WILLIAM WASHINGTON, "   "   " 1315.

9 JOHN WASHINGTON, of Kerneford, Co. Lancaster, second son of
ROBERT WASHINGTON, was born there about A. D. 1305. He settled
at Warton, Co. Lancaster.

He married 26 Edward II. (1333), Alianora, daughter and heiress of
John de Warton, of Warton, in Lonesdale, Co. Lancaster, and died before
10 Richard II. (1386) when his widow was living at Warton. She was
executrix of the will of William de Lancaster. He had two sons :

  10 JOHN WASHINGTON, born at Warton, A. D. 1334.

  10 EDMUND WASHINGTON,   "   " 1340.

10 JOHN WASHINGTON, of Lonesdale, Co. Lancaster, first son of JOHN
WASHINGTON of Kerneford, was born there A. D. 1334. He was living
at Lonesdale 26 Edward III. (1352), and 10 Richard II. (1386), and
4 Henry IV. (1402). By wife Johanna he had son :

  11 JOHN WASHINGTON, born at Warton, about A. D. 1365.

11 JOHN WASHINGTON, of Warton, Lancaster, first son of JOHN WASH-
INGTON, of Lonesdale, was born there about A. D. 1365. He was of

Warton and was living there 4 Henry IV. (1402). He was commonly called "JOHN FIL JOHN WASHINGTON." His sons were :

 12 ROBERT WASHINGTON, born at Warton, about 1400.

 12 WILLIAM WASHINGTON,   "   " 1405.

12 ROBERT WASHINGTON, of Warton, Co. Lancaster, first son of JOHN WASHINGTON, of Warton, was born there about A. D. 1400. He was living there temp. Henry V. and Henry VI., and died 16 Edward IV. (1479). His sons were :

 13 JOHN WASHINGTON, born at Warton, about A. D. 1430.

 13 RICHARD WASHINGTON,   "   "   " 1435.

 13 ROBERT WASHINGTON,   "   "   " 1440.

13 JOHN WASHINGTON, of Warton, Co Lancaster, first son of ROBERT WASHINGTON, of Warton, was born there about A. D. 1430. He succeeded to the Warton Estates, and died 4 May, 17 Henry VII. (1501). He was succeeded by his eldest son :

 14 ROBERT WASHINGTON, born at Warton, A. D. 1467.

14 ROBERT WASHINGTON, of Warton, Co. Lancaster, first son of JOHN WASHINGTON, of Warton, was born there A. D. 1467. He was 34 years of age at the death of his father, 17 Henry VII. (1504). He was Sergeant-at-Arms to King Henry VII., and to King Henry VIII. (circa 1500 to 1510). He died Sept. 20, 9 Henry VIII. (1517). He disinherited his eldest son and heir THOMAS, son of his first wife.

 15 THOMAS WASHINGTON, born at Warton, A. D. 1493.

His second wife was Amy, sister to Sir Richard Whytell, Knt. Her will dated 2 June, 1525. She died 20 June, 19 Henry VIII. (1527). Her husband at his death in 1517, gave to her and her issue, all his inheritance.

He married his second wife about 1505. Issue:

 15 RICHARD WASHINGTON, born at Warton, A. D 1506.

 15 HENRY WASHINGTON,   "   "   " 1508.

 15 ROBERT WASHINGTON,   "   "   " 1510.

 15 LAUNCELOT WASHINGTON, "   "   " 1512.

 15 MARY WASHINGTON,   " (died) "   " 1515.

 15 MARY WASHINGTON,   "   "   " 1517.

 15 ANNE WASHINGTON,   "   "   " 1520.

15 THOMAS WASHINGTON, of Warton, Co. Lancaster, first son of ROBERT WASHINGTON, of Warton, was born there A. D. 1493. He was son and heir, and was aged 24 at his father's death, 9 Henry VIII. (1517).

He was disinherited by his father, and filed his bill in Chancery for the recovery of the Estates, but did not recover them. His sons were:

16 LAURENCE WASHINGTON, born at Warton, about A. D. 1515.
16 LEONARD WASHINGLON,   "   "   "   " 1520.

16 LAURENCE WASHINGTON, of Warton, Co. Lancaster, first son of THOMAS WASHINGTON, of Warton, was born there about 1515. He was living there 35 Henry VIII. (1543). His sons were:

17 LAURENCE WASHINGTON, born at Warton about A. D 1540.
17 LEONARD WASHINGTON,   "   "   " 1545.
17 ROBERT WASHINGTON,   "   "   " 1550.

17 LAURENCE WASHINGTON, of Warton, first son of LAURENCE WASHINGTON, of Warton, was born there about A. D. 1540. He was living there 30 Elizabeth (1588). Had only son:

18 LAURENCE, born at Warton, A. D. 1569.

18 LAURENCE WASHINGTON, of Warton, Co. Lancaster, first son of LAURENCE WASHINGTON, of Warton, was born there A. D. 1569. He was of Warton 1 James I. (1603), 1st and 4th Charles I. (1625–28). His children were:

19 LEONARD WASHINGTON, born at Warton, about A. D. 1595.
19 LAURENCE WASHINGTON,   "   "   1597.
19 THOMAS WASHINGTON,   "   "   1600.

19 LEONARD WASHINGTON, first son of LAURENCE WASHINGTON, of Warton, was born there about A. D. 1595. He was recusant A. D. 1640, obit A. D. 1657. His wife was named Anne, and she was also recusant A. D. 1640. His children were:

20 ROBERT WASHINGTON, born and bapt. at Warton, A. D. 1616.
20 JANE WASHINGTON,   "   "   "   " 1619.
20 FRANCIS WASHINGTON,   "   "   "   " 1622.
20 LAURENCE WASHINGTON,   "   "   "   " 1625.
20 JOHN WASHINGTON,   "   "   "   " 1627.

These two youngest sons emigrated to Virginia, A. D. 1659.

20 COL. JOHN WASHINGTON, of Warton, Co. Lancaster and Bridges' Creek, Va., the fifth child of LEONARD WASHINGTON of Warton, Eng., was born at Warton, A. D. 1627, and emigrated to America with his brother LAURENCE, A. D. 1659, two years after their father's death. He died early in Jan. 1677, will proved Jan. 10, 1677.

He was married near Pope's Creek, Va,, in Westmoreland County, about A. D. 1660, to Anne Pope, who was his second wife. Their children were:

    21 **LAURENCE WASHINGTON**, born at Bridge's Creek, about A. D. 1661.

    21 JOHN WASHINGTON, born at Bridge's Creek, about A. D. 1664.

    21 ELIZABETH WASHINGTON,   "   "   " 1665.

    21 ANNE WASHINGTON,   "   "   " 1667.

From Col. JOHN WASHINGTON, the great-grandfather of Gen'l GEORGE WASHINGTON I have carried this lineage back to the progenitor in England, to demonstrate that William de Hertburn (1183) *was not the Ancestor of the* AMERICAN WASHINGTONS, and also to show the errors of all the usually received pedigrees.

The line of descent may be traced through the full face Caps.

COAT ARMORIAL OF THE WASHINGTON FAMILY.

The following, from " BURKE'S ARMORY," will show the Coat Armorial as granted to branches of the Washington Family in several shires of England :

YORKSHIRE.

Arms—Vert, (green), a lion rampant, argent, (silver), within a bordure gobonated or (gold) and azure. (blue).

Crest—Out of a Ducal coronet, or, (gold), an eagle, wings addorsed, sable. (black).

Motto—*Eritus acta probat.*

LANCASHIRE, LEICESTERSHIRE, NORTHAMPTON-SHIRE, BUCKINGHAMSHIRE, WAR-WICKSHIRE, AND KENT.

Arms—Argent, (silver), two bars gules, (red), in chief three mullets (stars) of the second, gules. (red).

Crest—A raven with wings addorsed, sable, (black), issuing out of a Ducal coronet, or. (gold).

LANCASHIRE.

Arms—Barry of four, argent (silver) and gules. (red). On a chief of the second, gules, (red), three mullets (stars) of the first. (argent).

Crest—On a Ducal coronet or, (gold), a martlet sable.

Arms—Argent, (silver), on a fesse gules, (red), three mullets (stars) of the first. (silver).

Arms—Gules, (red), on a fesse argent, (silver). three mullets (stars) pierced of the field. (gules).

Arms—Gules, (red), two bars argent, (silver), in chief three mullets of the second. (silver).

The second variety above described was the Coat Armour used by General Washington, but the YORKSHIRE Escutcheon was the *original* Arms of the *Family*.

WASHINGTON.

T HE Family of Washington was founded in England
by

I THORFIN THE DANE,

whose ancestors came from Schleswig, in Denmark, and
settled in ancient Ebor or Yorkshire, prior to the Norman
conquest.

The name of "Washington" was derived from a village
juxta Ravenswarth, called originally, "Wessyngton."

The *name* is of Saxon origin, and it existed in England
prior to the Norman conquest. The village "Wassyngton" is mentioned in a Saxon charter, as granted by King
Edgar in 973, to Thornby Abbey.—*Collectanea Typographica*, vol. 4, p. 55. This village is now called "Wharlton,"
and is in the parish of Kirkby Ravensworth, in the North
Riding of Yorkshire.

This Torfin was a great man, of Danish-Scandinavian
descent, as were all of the great men of these parts.

FROM THE DOMESDAY SURVEY, 1070–1080.

"In Benningham, Torfin had a hall and 2 carucates of
land of the Geld, and 2 ploughs, held by Enisan of the

Earl. The whole 2 leagues in length, and 1 in breadth; and underwood, 1 league in length, and a half in breadth."

" In Laton, Torfin had 3 carucates of the Geld, with sack and soke, and there were 3 ploughs, held by Bodin his son, of the Earl. In the time of King Edward the Confessor, it was 1 league in length, and 1 in breadth."

" In Stannigges, Torfin had 3 carucates of land, with sack and soke, and 3 ploughs, now Enisan holds of the Earl in demesne, 1 carucate and 3 villains, with 2 ploughs. In the time of King Edward, the whole was half a league in length, and a half in breadth."

" In Ravenswarth of the Geld are 12 carucates of land and 8 ploughs. There Torfin had one manor. Now Bodin holds there, half a carucate, and 16 villains, and 4 borders, with 8 ploughs. There is a church there, and a priest, and 4 acres of meadow. The whole was 1 league in length, and a half broad. temp. Edward the Confessor."

The above is from " Domesday Book," and is a translation of that portion respecting the North Riding in Yorkshire, including the district of Wharleton alias Washington, about 1070 to 1080.

Two sons of Torfin were:

2 BODIN, born in Ravensworth, Yorkshire, about 1040.
2 **BARDOLF,** "   "   "   "   1045.

" In Malsonby and Diddaston bailiwick of the Geld, 11 carucates and 10 ploughs. There Torfin had one manor. Now Bodin has there 1 carucate, and 15 villains, and 3 borders, with 7 ploughs. There is a church there. The whole was 1 league in length and 1 in breadth, in time of Edward the Confessor."—1040–1066.

The manor of *Wharton* or *Washington*, or any of the adjoining manors are not mentioned, *because* there was no land there belonging to the King's Geld.

RAVENSWATH CASTLE.

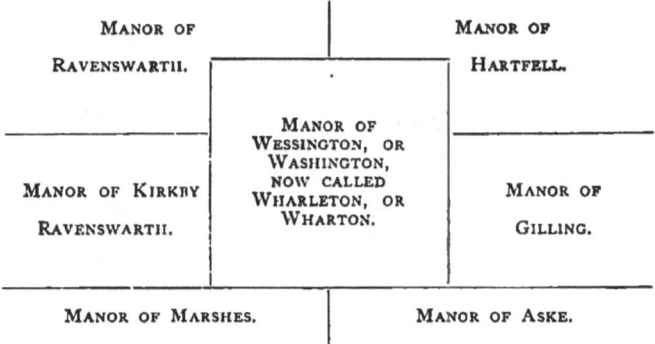

MANOR OF RAVENSWARTH.		MANOR OF HARTFELL.
MANOR OF KIRKBY RAVENSWARTH.	MANOR OF WESSINGTON, OR WASHINGTON, NOW CALLED WHARLETON, OR WHARTON.	MANOR OF GILLING.
MANOR OF MARSHES.		MANOR OF ASKE.

Bodin and Bardolf have been mentioned as the sons of Eudo de Bayeux, Earl of Britanny, and therefore derived from the ancestor of the Earls of Richmond, England. This error arose from the supposition, that William the Conqueror confiscated *all* of the lands of the *Englishmen*, and gave them to his followers. This is not true, as he confiscated only the lands of a few rebels, which he divided into Baronies, and gave them to his leaders. Being too vast for occupation by single persons, they were sub-let to Knights and Vassals, and oftentimes to the previous tenants.

The Saxon Earl, Edwin of Mercia, after he had revolted "over and over again," when he died without issue, the Conqueror was much grieved at the loss of so great a lord, and it was only *because* the Earl Edwin died without issue, that William the Conqueror gave his lands to Alan, first Earl of Richmond, who was second cousin to William I.

The 174 manors *given* to Earl Alan by the Conqueror— one of which was the manor of Ravensworth, held by Torfin and his son Bodin,—were only so many shadows in the hands of the Earl. There were only about 6 manors really attached to the Earldom of Richmond. Of all the others, he was merely nominally chief lord, and *each was held by an owner whose ancestors held for many generations before the Conquest.* There was never in Richmondshire, above six families descended from *Norman* ancestors, and these acquired their lands by marrying heiresses.

2 BODIN, "the Monk of Richmondshire," was born at Ravensworth, Yorkshire, Eng., about 1040. He was son of "TORFIN THE DANE." Bodin had issue, a son :

   3 ALET fil BODIN, born in Richmondshire about year 1070.

Bodin, Lord of Ravensworth, at the time of the compilation of the survey of the lands belonging to the King's Geld, called "Domesday Book," held Ravensworth, Yorkshire, of Alan Rufus, first Earl of Richmond, who held of the king. This Bodin gave all his estate to his brother Bardolf, and retired to the monastery of York, where he assumed the religious habit.

2 BARDOLF, " Lord and Monk of Ravensworth," was born about 1045. He was second son of TORFIN THE DANE. Bardolf possessed Ravensworth with divers other fair lordships in Richmondshire, in the time of King William the Conqueror, but, desiring in his age, to end his days in the devout service of God, forsook the world, and, with his brother Bodin, took upon him the habit of a monk of the Abbey of St. Marie's at York. Whereunto, at the especial instance of *Bodin*, he gave the churches of Patrick-Brompton and Ravensworth, in pure Almes. To this Bardolf succeeded his son and heir :

   3 AKARIS, Lord of Ravensworth, born at Ravensworth, about year 1080. He had another son :

   3 HENRY, Lord of Ravensworth, born at Ravensworth, about year 1090.

" The manor of Eggington, Derbyshire, was held at Doomsday Survey, by Azelm, under Geffrey de Alselyn, or Aseline. Bardolf married the heiress of Hanselyn, of this baronial family, and she carried the manor to the Bardolfs."—*Valor Ecclesciasticus.*

3 ALET fil BODIN, son of Bodin, son of TORFIN THE D̶A̶N̶E̶, was born in Richmondshire, England, about 1070.

Alet, son of Bodin, held 3 carucates of land at Bradwell in Essex.—*Testa de Neville*, p. 268. He had issue :

    4 WALTER BARDOLF, born in Richmondshire, about 1130, and WILLIAM DE BRADWELL. about 1135.

Walter Bardolf, son of Alet, dropped out of the Pedigree by Dugdale, was born about 1130. He is referred to in the *Abbre Plact*, 88th page. At the assize Hugo, his son, claimed Manton Priory, that had been given to the priors. He is styled as of the county of York.

3 HENRY fil BARDOLF, second son of Bardolf, second son of "Torfin the D̶a̶n̶e̶," was born at Ravensworth, county York, about 1090.

3 AKARIS or AKAR, or AKARY, called also Akary fil Bardolf, or Fitz Bardolph, Lord of Ravensworth, born about 1080, first son of Bardolf, Lord and Monk of Ravensworth, in Richmondshire, second son of "Torfin the D̶a̶n̶e̶."

"And Bardolf, whose son Akar was the pious founder of 'Jourvaulx,' a famous Abbey of the Cisterian order in the Northern Tract."

"To this Bardolf succeeded Akaris, his son and heir, who in 5 Stephen, 1139, founded an Abbey at Fors, in Wenslay-dale in Com. Ebor, then called the 'Abbey of Charity.' He departed this life in Ann. 1161, 7 Henry II." *Dugdale's Baronage*, vol. 1, p. 403. He gave 3 carucates of land in Wharton, and 1 carucate and a half in Fors, to the abbey, where he was buried, leaving nine sons, of whom only five are mentioned :

    4 HERVEY FITZ AKARIS, born at Kirkby Ravensworth, about 1120.

    4 WALTER fil AKARIS, born at Kirkby Ravensworth, about 1122.

4 ROBERT fil AKERY DE ASHTON, **born at Kirkby Ra-**
vensworth, about 1125.

4 HERESCULFUS fil AKERY, **born at Kirkby Ravens-**
worth, about 1127.

4 BONDO FITZ AKARIS, born at Kirkby Ravensworth,
about 1130.

"Akaris was one of the great Vassals of Stephen, Earl of
Richmond, and, as such, appears upon the great Pipe Rolls
in 1st Henry 2 (1154). He was the father of Hervey fil
Akary, who was Lord of Ravensworth, and ancestor of the
Lords Fitz Hugh of that place, and of Bondo, Lord of Oual-
sington, juxta Ravensworth, which was given to him by
his father, temp. King Stephen."

HISTORY OF JOREVAULX ABBEY.

"In the time of King Stephen (1134 to 1154) Akeris son of Bardolph,
and Nephew of Boden, (says Dugdale, in the Monasticon), was Lord of
many possessions in Yorkshire. Having given to Peter de Quinciano
one Carucate and a half of Land in Waunleysdale at Fors, called Dela-
grange, and three Carucates in Warton, where the said Peter and his
Companions began to found an Abbey, and to erect simple edifices for
their habitations, in A. D. 1145. This was afterward made subject to
the Abbey of Byland, from which—A. D. 1150, an Abbot and twelve
Monks were sent, who, A. D. 1166, on account of the poorness of the land
and bad air were removed with consent of Hervius (or Hervey) son of
Akaris, their original founder, to a pleasant valley upon the river Eure in
East Witton, given to them by Conan, Duke of Brittany and Earl of Richmond, taking the bones of their founder, Akeris, and his wife, along with
them. Their first Abbot John De Kingston, then began to build a church
(dedicated to St. Mary) and called it Jourvaix."—*Dugdale's Monasticon,*
vol. 5, p. 569.

CHARTER.

CHARTER OF LAND ON RIVER EURE, AT EAST WITTON, YORKSHIRE.

"Conan, Duke of Brittany and Count of Richmond, his Steward, his
Constable, his Chamberlain and Bailiffs, and all others, French and English; All take notice that I have given, and that this paper confirms the
donation of land to Roger de Ask, which was made to certain Barons of
mine, to the Church of St. Andrew's of Marring, and the fees of two vil-

lains, neai the termination of the Barony, and me and my heirs do grant and give and confirm in Wood, in field, in pasture, in moor or water, in crop or in seed, and all other places in and belonging to the Barony. I prohibit the Churchmen or Laymen, and all others from disturbing or molesting the grantees, nor any other man shall receive it for debt. And I command all the Barons of mine and all others in love and duty to see this maintained. If any do injury, I command all ministers to see that full redress be made. Witnessed by Henry fil Acheris, Alan the Constable, Walter fil Acheris, Nigello the Chamberlain, Henry son of Henry, Conan de Ask, Thomas his brother, Radulpho the Chamberlain, and many others. Given at Richmond." Seal of white wax, (dependent by a silk string), a Knight on horseback.

This was Conan the 4th, Duke of Richmond, called le Petit, grantor of Jourvaux Abbey, whose founders were sons of Bardolf and Bodin.

This is the territory granted to the Monks on River Eure at East Witton, where they removed in 1166 from Wandleysdale, the original site of Journaulx Abbey. St. Mary's and St. Andrew's were the same as Jourvaulx Abbey, with only change of locality.

4 HERVEY fil AKARY, first son of Akaris, first of Bardolf, second of Torfin the Dane, was born about 1120 at Ravensworth. He was Lord of Ravensworth, in the time of Henry II. (1154–1189). Ancestor of the family of the Lords Fitz Hugh of Ravensworth. Died 28 Henry II. (1182).

"Which Hervey, being a noble and good knight, and highly esteemed in his country, gave his assent that Conan, then Earl of Britanny and Richmond, should translate the 'Abbey of Charity,' into the Fields of East Witton, and to place it upon the verge of the river Jore, whereupon thenceforth it took the name of Jorevaulx ; and caused the bones of Akaris, his Father, to be brought thither and there entombed ; himself and his heirs being reputed the Founders of that Monastery. After which, viz. in Ann. 1182 (28 Henry II.), he departed this life, leaving issue three sons : Henry, Hugh and William."—*Dugdale's Baronage*, vol. 1, p. 403.

5 HENRY DE RAVENSWORTH, born in Yorkshire, circa 1160.

5 HUGH DE RAVENSWORTH, born in Yorkshire, circa 1165.

5 WILLIAM DE RAVENSWORTH, born in Yorkshire, circa 1170. Sons of Hervey fil Akery.

LITERAL COPIES FROM DUGDALE'S MONASTICON.

Charters of St. Andrew's Priory, in the Parish of Meering, North Riding, County Ebor (York). Kirkby Ravensworth (or Kirkly on the Hill); Patrick-Brompton, Aiskew Garritson, and Little Fleming, *olim* Lemingford.

These charters are properly ecclesiastical surveys, and the advent of the parties named, antedates the confirmation of them in the reign of Edward III. 1327–77. The persons must be anterior to this date, who are referred to as the donors or grantors of the charities earlier.

CHARTER I.

Hervi fili Acharil omibz sce eccle sal. Sciatis me dedisse t presenti carta confirmasse do t eccle Sce Marie t Sce Andre t monialibz in Marring do servientibus, nonn garb d bladi Dominioz meoz quiscug ea colat, hoz vidilicet et d Rauenswart d Brutn d Aichescon t d Gurrestñn t una crofter in Lemingford qd fuit Robti Snarri t sibi t hoibz suis in pfata elemasina, manentibus comunia pascura peceribz suis in pura t perpetua elemasina liba t qeta ab omni serviti q sutudine t exactione. Hic testif Haresculfus fil Acharie Cuñano fil Elie, Robert fil Rob, d Sacles. Bondo d Wassigetu.

TRANSLATION.

I, Hervey, son of Akery to all the sons of the church greeting. Know that I have given, and the present Charter of mine confirms the gift, to the church of St. Mary's and St. Andrews, the fees in Marring, and two villains, and nine shocks of grain, and everything else, there gathered and other possessions, that is to say: in the Lordship of Ravensworth, in that of Lord Britto de Aichescon, and in Lord Garretsuns, also one croft in Lemingford, that belonged to Robert Snarri, himself and heirs, in the said village remaining, with the common sheep-pasture, to have and to hold in pure and perpetual gift, free and in quiet, without any service or tax, *lying and held by Lord Ravensworth, Lord Brutu or Brittville of* Aichescon, and Lord Guerreston, and one croft in Lemingford (or Flemingford), that belonged to Robert Snarris, remaining in said village, common, and pasture, to have and to hold by said grantees, without service or exaction whatsoever.

Witnessed by Herescui fil Acharie (Heresculfus de Clesby), Conan son of Helie, Robert son of Robert Lacelles, and Bondo Washington.— *Collectanea Typographica et Genealogica,* vol. 5, page 221.

CHARTER II.

Hervius fili Acarisii oibz eccle filiis sal. Sciatis me dedisse t concessisse t psenti Carta confirmasse quadraginta to IIIIor acras, tre in Ravensward t sexdecem acras si mora d Kirkeby t comune pastura i eadem Mora do t scimonialibz do servientibus in Marring cu uxore mea t ancessoz t successoriz meoriz. Et ut has tras habeant de me t heredibus meis in pura t ppetua elemosina liba t qeta ab oi servitio ab oi exactione et auxilio in ppetuo.

Witnesses : Roberto Camerario Guarnerio, Henrico fil Hervei, Roger de Ask, t Conano de Ask, Bertra Haget, Bondo d Whasingetu.

Note.—These grants were outside of the territory of Meering Priory, and these donations were made to the church, by the lords of the surrounding villages, who were the grandsons of the original founders, under the same name of Akeris and Hervie.

TRANSLATION.

"Hervius, son of Akery, To all the sons of the church sends greeting. Know that I have given and granted, and the present charter confirms 40 acres and 1 quarter in Ravensworth, and 16 acres of meadow in Kirkby, common pasturage in said meadow, given in fee tail with 2 servants in Marring, which my wife and daughter, and ancestors of mine held. And the same territory, to be held of me and my heirs, in pure and perpetual gift, to hold free and unmolested, of all exaction perpetually.

"Witnesses : Robert (Camorario, or) the Chamberlain, Warner, son of Wymer, Henry fil Hervey, Roger de Ask, and Conan de Ask, Bertrand Haget, and Bondo de Whashington.—*Collectanea Typographica et Genealogica,* vol. 5, 221.

4 WALTER fil AKARIS, second son of Akaris, was born at Ravensworth, Yorkshire, about A. D. 1122.

4 ROBERT fil AKERY de Ashton, third son of Akaris, born at Kirkby, Ravensworth, York, about 1125, settled at Ashton, and took the name of Robert de Ashton, after of Shropshire.

ASTON vel WASHINGTON, the ancestor of the Aston family, was seated in Shropshire, and was called Aston Aer, known also by the name of Wheaton-Aston. The grant of the underwritten charter, took place, from the date of the York records, near Kirkby Ravensworth, 1164. This is quoted in the early deeds, relating to Shropshire.

CHARTER OF ROBERT DE ASHTON.

"Sciant as q sciunt t quit fut i t q d in die dedicationes cimiterii de Estona ego Robt fil Acherii dedi deo & capelle de eade villa de Eston una vigata tre Sexaginta contiente and tota decima de Domino meo ei de nille."

TRANSLATION.

"Know ye who are and who were or may be, in this day of the dedication of the cemetery of Eston, that I, Robert, son of Achery, gave to God and the chaplain, 1 virgate of land containing 60 acres, and the whole of my tythings in the lordship of mine, in said village."

Eston in York, near Dalton-Travers, is the locality whence the grantor emanated. He is mentioned in connection with the grants to Achery, of 11 bovates of land in Eston to Robert Ulram, juxta Bridlington. Witnessed by Roger fil Richard de Hedon, Willo de Eston, Huestachio Karlyle, Robert, Constable de Flemingburg, Henry fil Ranulf.

Hedon refers to the town in Holderness. Bridlington is also in Holderness.

4 HERESCULFUS fil AKERY, son of Akeris, was born at Kirkby Ravensworth, York, about 1130. His name appears as witness on a charter of Agnes, Prioress of Marrick Abbey, in 1165. He settled at Clesby, and was called Heresculfus de Clesby.

In the reign of Stephen, 1134–1154, the territory of the County of York, Durham, Northumberland, and land adjoining, was all annexed to the Earldom of Bourlogne, and to that of Brittany. The date of these charters belongs to that period.

CHARTER OF AGNES, PRIORESS OF MARRICK.

Endenture fait p entre Agnes, Prioress de Marrick, t Sa covent dune pt et Ricardus Akersmith, de Hertipole, dantre pt temoigne qu le dit Prioress t sa conent ont grantez t ferme lessez a dit Richard une gardeyn a Hertipool, jardis en le tenet. Walter Backster al fyne de XII. anns rendent annualment 11 South. Don a Marryk le ventissime for de May, lan du Reign du Henry quint puys le Conquest premier.

TRANSLATION.

"Indenture made between Agnes, Prioress de Marrick, and her convent on one part, and Richard Ackersmith (Ackeryth), of Hertipool (Durham), of the other part. In testimony of which, the said Prioress and her convent have conveyed a quit claim to the said Richard, a garden at Hertipool, leased anciently by Walter Backster, to the extent of 12 ells, paying annually 11 shillings. Done at Marring, the 20th of May, the year of the Reign of Henry, one hundred years from the first conquest."

Witnesses : Heresculfus fil Achery ; Conan, son of Helia, Robert, son of Robert de Lasscelles ; BOND DE WASSIGETU. [Seal gone.]

This would bring the period to a precise agreement with the advent of Agnes, a few months after the death of Stephen, 1165.

4 **BONDO** fil AKARIS, a younger son of Akaris, was born at Ravensworth about 1122. Lord of Wessyngton, juxta Ravensworth, Richmondshire Co., York, which manor was given to him by his father in the time of King Henry II. (1154 to 1189). He is called sometimes Bondo de Washington, and sometimes Bondo de Ravensworth. These two places join each other. His sons were :

    5 WILLIAM fil BONDO, born at Wassington about 1150.

    5 CONAN DE WASHINGTON, born at Wassington about 1155.

    5 WALTER fil BONDO, born at Washington about 1160.

    5 RALPH fil BONDO DE RAVENSWORTH, born at Washington about 1165.

    5 ROBERT DE WASHINGTON, born at Washington about 1170.

LATIN TEXT OF CHARTER OF BONDO.

Omibz sce eccle filiis Bondo de Wassingetun Sat. Sciatas me dedisse t psenti carta confirmasse do t scimonialib sci Andree d Marring q'cessu dui mei Hervio filii Acarissi t concessu heredu meoz dimidia carrucata tre i *Wassingetu* t unn toftu cu qu tofta ad pdicta tra ptinent. Et hauc dinnida carrucata tre do t concedo eis in pura t ppetua elemosina libam t q'eta ab oi Servitio t ab oi q'suetudine t exactione in basco i plano i prato i aqra t pascius in viss t Semitis t oib locis eid ville p tinentibz. His testib. Hervie fil Acarissi t Heneric fil ei, Robt et Lasscelles t Gerard fil ei, Rogeri d Ask, Will fil Bondo, t plures alii. Qur sine sigillo, fui cu hauc donative face bauc cata Sigillo dui mei Hervei Sigillavi.

TRANSLATION.

CHARTA OF BONDO DE WYSSINGTON.

WASHTON YORK.

To all of the Sons of the Church, greeting.

Know that I, Bondo de Wassington, have given, and the present charta confirms the gift, the fees of Marring, which the Lord Hervey son of Acery gave my heirs. One half a carrucate of land in Wyssington, and one toft belonging to the aforesaid territory. And this half a carrucate of land is given in pure and perpetual charity, free of all service and of any tax whatsoever, in plain, or meadow, or pasture, and in crop or in seed, or water, in any place belonging to said village.

Witnesses: Hervey, son of Ackery, Henry, his son, Robert de Lascelles, Gerard, his son, Roger de Ask, William, son of Bond, and others.

In a historical sense nothing could be more interesting. This is the *first* instance where the name of Wassington is mentioned in early annals.

4 WALTER BARDOLF, younger son of Alet fil Bodin, son of Bodin, son of Torfin the Dane, was born in Richmondshire about 1130. He is referred to in the abbreviated Plact., page 88. He had issue:

5 HUGO fil WALTER, born in Richmondshire about 1160.

5 HENRY fil HERVEY DE RAVENSWORTH, first son of Hervey fil Akary, see page 7, first son of Akaris, first of Bardolf, second of Torfin the Dane, was born at Ravensworth, Yorkshire, about 1160.

"Which Henry took to wife Alice, the daughter of Randolf Fitz-Walter (ancestor to the Barons of Greistoke), with
whom he had the lordship of Mikelton, and service of Guy
de Bovencourt, for certain lands there and in Northumberland; as also the services of Lonton and Thirngarth, with
the forest of Loun and free chase, and departed this life
in An. 1201 (3 John), leaving issue." He was the ancestor
of the Fitz-Hugh family of England.

CHARTA.

Henry fil Hervius de Wyssington of Hinton, 1201, of Richmondshire,
1 caracute of land, in Scorton, that Walter fil Acherie, and Arkilgarde,
gave, confirmed by Conan, Duke of Brittany, to Hervic, the aforesaid,
and Henry and Lord Warine le Scargil, land that belonged to Nigel Caus-
eriro, part of his estate at Middleton.—*Nigelus de Wass.*

5 HUGH DE RAVENSWORTH, second child of HENRY fil
AKARY, was born at Ravensworth about 1155.

5 WILLIAM DE RAVENSWORTH, third child of HENRY fil
AKARY, born at Ravensworth about 1170.

5 WILLIAM fil BONDO, first son of Bondo fil Akaris, first
of Akaris, first of Bardolf, second of Torfin the Dane,
was born at Wassington about 1150. He was "Lord of
Wassington."

"He divided his lands amongst his sons in the time of
King John" (1199–1216). He was the ancestor of the fam-
ily of Washington, of Wassington, juxta Ravensworth,
North Riding of Yorkshire. His sons were:

    6 HENRY fil WILLIAM, born at Wassington about 1175.

    6 PETER DE WASHINGTON, born at Wassington about
    1178.

    6 SIMON DE WASHINGTON, born at Wassington about ·
    1180.

    6 EUDO fil WILLIAM, born at Wassington about 1182.

6 WILLIAM DE WASHINGTON, born at Wassington about 1185.

6 GILBERT DE WASHINGTON, born at Wassington about 1190.

5 CONAN DE WASHINGTON, second son of BONDO fil AKARIS (see page 11), was born at Wassington about 1155.

" Conan accused certain parties of robbery, but died before their trial, 6 Richard I. (1194), whereupon they were acquitted." No issue.

5 **WALTER** fil **BONDO DE WASHINGTON,** third son of Bondo fil Akaris, was born at Wassington about 1160.

" Walter was Lord of Milburn in Westmoreland, in right of his wife Agnes, in the time of King John " (1199-1216). " Walter de Washington acquired large estates in the counties of Northumberland and Westmoreland, in right of his wife Agnes, Lady of Milburn, daughter and heiress of Ivo de Welleburne, county Westmoreland, and resided at Welleburne, in Westmoreland."

He had issue by wife Agnes :

6 ROBERT DE WASHINGTON, born at Welleburne about 1195.

6 WILLIAM DE WASHINGTON, born at Welleburne about 1200.

" His second wife Julianna, who survived him, claimed dower in his estates, and was living, 30 Henry III. (1245). She claimed dower in the lands of her husband, in Northumberland and Westmoreland, and amongst others, she claimed, against Robert de Washington, the third part of the manor of Milleburne (or Welleburne), county Westmoreland, 20 Henry III." (1245).

5 RALPH fil BONDO DE RAVENSWARTH, fourth son of BONDO fil AKARIS, was born at Wassington about 1165.

" In 13 Henry III. (1228), Ralph de Ravenswarth was fined for default." He died without issue.

5 ROBERT DE WASHINGTON, fifth son of Bondo fil Akaris, was born at Wassington about 1170.

"From Robert de Washington descended a younger branch of the family of Washington juxta Ravensworth."

"He was defendant, with Brian fil Alan, at the suit of Eudo de Stanwigges, who claimed common of pasture at Stanwigges, against them, 3 Henry III." (1218). Robert de Washington had issue :

      6 ALAN DE WASHINGTON, born at Wassington about 1195.

      6 GALFRIDUS DE WASHINGTON, born at Wassington about 1200.

      6 NICHOLAS DE WASHINGTON, born at Wassington about 1205.

5 HUGO fil WALTER, son of WALTER BARDOLF, son of Alet, son of Bodin, son of Torfin the Dane, was born in county Richmond about 1160.

"At the assize he claimed Meanton Priory that had been given to the priors. He is styled as of the county of York."

He is also described as of Suffolk temp. John, 1199–1215. He had issue :

      6 THOMAS fil HUGO, born in Suffolk, about 1200.

6 THOMAS fil HUGO, son of Hugo fil Walter, son of Walter Bardolf, son of Alet, son of Bodin, son of Torfin the Dane, was born in Suffolk county, about 1200.
He is mentioned as of Suffolk, 3 Edward I. (1276).

6 RANDOLF DE RAVENSWORTH, first son of Hervey, first of Hervey, first of Akaris, first of Bardolf, second of Torfin the Dane, was born at Ravensworth, Yorkshire, about 1190. He died 1262, 49 Henry III., and was buried in the Abbey of Jourvaulx. Married Alice, daughter and heir of Adam de Staveley, Lord of Staveley, Dent and Sadbergh. He had issue :

7 HENRY DE RAVENSWORTH, born at Ravensworth, about 1220.

7 ADAM DE RAVENSWORTH, born at Ravensworth, about 1225.

6 HENRY DE WASHINGTON, first son of William de Washington, first of Bondo, second of Akaris, first of Bardolf, second of Torfin the ~~Dane~~, was born at Wassington, about 1175.

"He was seized of one half the Manor of Washington juxta Ravensworth, except one carucate and two bovates of land, by the gift of his father, temp. King John" (1199–1216).

"Having with Stephen, the chaplain's son, beheaded two thieves between Marwood and Langdale, county York, they were arrested at York to answer the king for that act," 15 Henry III. (1230). He had issue :

7 RANULPH DE WASHINGTON, born at Wassington, about 1210.

7 HENRY DE WASHINGTON, born at Wassington, about 1215.

7 EUDO DE WASHINGTON, born at Wassington, about 1220.

6 PETER DE WASHINGTON, second son of William de Washington, born at Wassington, about 1178.

"He was seized of lands in Dalton Travers, Lancashire, 25 Henry III." (1240). He had issue :

7 JOHN DE WASHINGTON, born at Wassington, about 1215.

7 ROBERT DE WASHINGTON, born at Wassington, about 1220.

6 SIMON DE WASHINGTON, third son of William de Washington, was born at Wassington, about 1180.

"He had lands in Washington by gift of his father, 10 John " (1208).

6 Eudo de Washington, fourth son of William de Washington, was born at Wassington, York, about 1182.

"He had one half of the Manor of Washington by gift of his father. He died before 35 Henry III." (1249). His wife was Alice, sister to Hugh fil Ranulph, Lord of Ravensworth. He had issue :

  7 Alicia de Washington, born at Wassington, York, about 1220.
  7 Henry de Washington, born at Wassington, York, about 1222.
  7 Michael de Washington, born at Wassington, York, about 1225.
  7 John de Washington, born at Wassington, York, about 1230.
  7 William de Washington, born at Wassington, York, about 1232.
  7 Robert de Washington, born at Wassington, York, about 1235.

6 William de Washington, fifth son of William de Washington, was born at Wassington, about 1185.

"He was defendant in a plea of trespass, 3, 4 Henry III." (1249). He had issue :

  7 Thomas de Washington, born at Wassington, about 1230.

6 Gilbert de Washington, sixth son of William de Washington, was born at Wassington, about 1190.

"He was surety for his cousin John fil Eudo de Washington, 30 Henry III." (1245).

6 ROBERT DE WASHINGTON, first son of Walter fil Bondo de Washington. fourth of Bondo, second of Akaris, first of Bardolf, second of Torfin, was born at Wellebourne, in Westmoreland, Eng., about 1195.

"Robert de Washington, Lord of Milleburne, county

Westmoreland, in right of his mother, 3 Henry III. (1218), against whom Juliana (who was his step-mother), second wife of his father, Walter de Washington, claimed the third part of the Manor of Welleburne, as her dower, 30 Henry III." (1245).

"He was seized of divers lands in Strickland Ketell, county Westmoreland, by gift of Walter de Strickland, Chèvalier, and Elizabeth, his wife, in free marriage with Johanna, their daughter."

His wife's mother, Elizabeth, was daughter and heiress of Sir Ralph Deincourt, Knt. He had issue :

> 7 ROBERT DE WASHINGTON, born at Milleburne, about 1230.

6 WILLIAM DE WASHINGTON, called William de Wessington, second son of Walter fil Bondo de Washington, was born at Welleburne, or Milburne, Westmoreland, about 1200.

"He is said to have held the Manor of Wessyngton, alias Washington, county Durham, of the Bishop of Durham, 11 Henry III." (1226).

"In the 13th John (1212), he paid the king 40 marks to marry Alicia, the widow of John de Lexington, and was allowed 10 marks for 2 palfreys. He was at the battle of Lewes, in 1264." He had issue :

> 7 WILLIAM DE WASHINGTON, born at Wessyngton, Durham, about 1230.
>
> 7 THOMAS WASHINGTON, born at Wessyngton, Durham, about 1235.
>
> 7 JOHN WASHINGTON, born at Wessyngton, Durham, about 1240.
>
> 7 SIMON DE WASHINGTON, born at Wessyngton, Durham, about 1245.

"About 1260 occurred the wars of the Barons, during which the throne of Henry III. was shaken by the De Montforts. The chivalry of the Palatinate rallied under

the Royal standard. On the list of the loyal knights who
fought for their sovereign in the disastrous battle of Lewes
(1264), in which the king was taken prisoner, we find the
name of William de Washington."—*Hutchinson's Hist.
Durham*, vol. 1, p. 220.

6 ALAN DE WASHINGTON, first son of Robert de Washington, fifth of Bondo, second of Akaris, first of Bardolf, second of Torfin, was born at Wassington, about 1195.
"He was defendant in a plea of trespass, 5 Henry III."
(1220). He had issue :
> 7 ALAN DE WASHINGTON, born at Wassington, county
> York, about 1230.
> 7 ALICIA DE WASHINGTON, born at Wassington, county
> York, about 1235.
> 7 JOHANNA DE WASHINGTON, born at Wassington,
> county York, about 1240.

6 GALFRIDUS DE WASHINGTON, second son of Robert de
Washington, born at Wassington, about 1225.
He was living, 35 Henry III. (1250).

6 NICHOLAS DE WASHINGTON, third child of Robert de
Washington, was born at Wassington, about 1230.
He was living, 35 Henry III. (1250).

7 HENRY DE RAVENSWORTH, first son of Randolf, first of
Henry, first of Hervey fil Akary, first of Akaris, first of
Bardolf, second of Torfin the Dane, was born at Ravensworth, York, about 1220.
"Which Henry had also issue two sons, Randolf, who
died issueless, and Hugh, who succeeded his brother Randolf, in the inheritance, died at Berewyk, upon Teise, upon
the fourth ides of March, An. 1304 (32 Ed. I.), and was
buried at Rurnaldkirk. But Albreda, his wife, departing
this life at Harworth upon Teise, had sepulture at Jore-

vaulx, near to the grave of Henry Fitz-Randolf, her husband's father."

8 RANDOLF DE RAVENSWORTH, born at Ravensworth, about 1245. Died s. p.

8 HUGH DE RAVENSWORTH, born at Ravensworth, about 1250.

7 ADAM DE RAVENSWORTH, second son of Henry, was born at Ravensworth, York, about 1225.

7 RANULPH DE WASHINGTON, first son of Henry de Washington, first of William de Washington, first of Bondo, second of Akaris, first of Bardolf, second of Torfin the Dane, was born at Wassington, about 1200.

"He claimed half the Manor of Washington, against Robert fil Eudo de Washington, 35 Henry III." (1250).

"He claimed lands in Washington against Robert Warde and Alicia, his wife (daughter of Eudo de Washington, and sister of above Robert), in 52 Henry III." (1267).

"He claimed 100 acres of wood, in Washington, of which William fil Bondo de Washington, his grandfather, died seized, against Hugh fil Henry de Washington of Ravensworth, in 9 Edward I." (1282). He had issue :

8 HENRY DE WASHINGTON, born at Wassington, York, about 1235.

8 ALAN DE WASHINGTON, born at Wassington, York, about 1240.

8 ADAM DE WASHINGTON, born at Wassington, York, about 1245.

7 HENRY DE WASHINGTON, second son of Henry de Washington, was born at Wassington, about 1205.

"He was defendant in a plea of 'Morte Anteceperis,' at the suit of Henry fil Ranulph de Washington (his nephew), in 35 Henry III." (1250). He had issue :

8 ALEXANDER DE WASHINGTON, born at Wassington, about 1240.

8 JOHN DE WASHINGTON, born at Wassington, about 1245.

7 EUDO DE WASHINGTON, third son of Henry de Washington, was born at Wassington, about 1210.

"He was a juryman at the trial of a plea at York, between Hugh fil Henry de Ravensworth, and John de la Ware, touching common of pasture in Ravensworth, in 9 Edward III." (1282).

7 JOHN DE WASHINGTON, first son of Peter de Washington, second of William, first of Bondo, second of Akaris, first of Bardolf, second of Torfin the Dane, was born at Dalton Travers, Lancashire, about 1205.

"Robert de Travers claimed against him common of pasture, in Dalton Travers, Lancashire, in 30 Henry III." (1245). Had issue, only child:

8 MATILDA, born at Dalton Travers, Lancashire, about 1230.

8 MATILDA WASHINGTON, daughter, heiress, and only child of John de Washington, first of Peter, second of William, first of Bondo, second of Akaris, first of Bardolf, second of Torfin the Dane, was born at Dalton Travers, Lancashire, about 1230.

She married in 1252, James, son of and successor to Sir Robert Lawrence, of Ashton Hall, Lancashire, whose father, Sir Robert, accompanied the lion-hearted Richard to Palestine, and distinguished himself at the siege of Acre, in 1191, was made Knight Banneret, and obtained for his arms "Argent, a cross raguly gules." James Lawrence acquired by his marriage the Manor of Washington (changed from Dalton), Sedgwick, &c., in that county. His son and successor was:

John Lawrence, who levied a fine of Washington and Sedgwick, in 1283. He married Margaret, daughter of Walter Chesford, and was father of

John Lawrence, who presented to the church of Washington, in 1326, and died about 1360, leaving by Elizabeth, his wife, daughter of Holt of Stably, Lancashire, a son and heir :

Sir Robert Lawrence, Knt., who married Margaret Holden of Lancashire, and had four sons, viz. :

1 Sir Robert, his son and heir.

2 Thomas, whose son Arthur was ancestor of Sir John Lawrence, of Chelsea, who was created a Baronet in 1628. Now extinct.

3 William, born 1395, served in France, and afterward joining Lionel, Lord Welles, fought under the Lancastrian banner at St. Albans, in 1455, where he was slain, and buried in the Abbey Church.

4 Edward, born about 1400.

7 ROBERT DE WASHINGTON, second of Peter de Washington, born at Dalton Travers, about 1210.

" He was defendant in a plea of trespass in 7 Edward I." (1280).

7 ALICIA DE WASHINGTON, first child of Eudo de Washington, fourth of William, first of Bondo, second of Akaris, first of Bardolf, second of Torfin the Dane, was born at Wassington, York, about 1220.

" Her father gave her lands in Washington juxta Ravensworth."

She married Robert Ward, of Washington juxta Ravensworth. Children in his line :

7 HENRY fil EUDO DE WASHINGTON, second child of Eudo
de Washington, was born at Wassington, York, about
1222.

"He was defendant in a plea of land at the suit of his
brother John, 28 Henry III." (1243). His son was :

    8 Roger fil Henry de Washington, was born at Was-
    sington, York, about 1245. He was living, 50 Henry
    III. (1265). His son was :

        9 Henry fil Roger de Washington, born at Was-
        sington, York, about 1270. He was living,
        30 Edward I. (1303), 2 Edward II. (1309), 4 Ed-
        ward III. (1330). His son was :

            10 Roger fil Henry de Washington, born at
            Wassington, York, about 1300. He was de-
            fendant conjointly with Warren de Wash-
            ington in a plea touching lands in Neusam,
            7 Edward III. (1333), and in a plea of debt,
            30 Edward III. (1356).

7 MICHAEL fil EUDO DE WASHINGTON, third child of Eudo
de Washington, was born at Wassington, York, about
1235. He was living, 50 Henry III. (1265).

7 JOHN fil EUDO DE WASHINGTON, fourth child of Eudo de
Washington, was born at Wassington, York, about 1230.
He devised one bovat of land in Ravensworth, &c.,
against his brothers Henry and William, 28 Henry III.
(1243). His son was :

    8 Warren fil John de Washington, born at Was-
    sington, York, about 1255. He was attorney and
    chief steward to Henry fil Henry, Lord of Ravens-
    worth, 21 Edward I. (1294), and died 10 Edward II.
    (1317).

7 WILLIAM fil EUDO DE WASHINGTON, fifth child of Eudo
de Washington, was born at Wassington, York about

1232. He was defendant in a plea of land at the suit of his brother John, 28 Henry III. (1243). His children were :

8 John fil William de Washington, born at Wassington, York, about 1255. He was seized of lands at Washington, 8 Edward II. (1315). His son was :

  9 William de Washington, born at Wassington, York, about 1280. He claimed the arrears of an annual rent of eight marks against Robert le Constable of Hamburgh, county York, Knt., 19 Edward II. (1326). He died 1 Edward III. (1327). He married Elizabeth, daughter of Robert le Constable of Hamburgh, county York, Knt. She was living at the time of her husband's death, 1327.

8 ELENA, second child, was born at Wassington, York, about 1260. She married 19 Edward I. (1292). William fil William fil Abraham de Aldborough.

7 ROBERT DE WASHINGTON, sixth child of Eudo de Washington, was born at Wassington, York, about 1235.

" He was under age in 35 Henry III. (1250), and in the custody of his uncle Henry, his mother's brother, fil Ranulph de Ravensworth, when his cousin Ranulph fil Henry de Washington claimed against him and his mother Alicia, half the Manor of Washington juxta Ravensworth."

" He married Isolda, daughter of Robert Werry, of Dalton Travers." She was a widow 20 Edward I. (1293). He had issue :

8 ROBERT DE WASHINGTON, born at Wassington, about 1255.

8 STEPHEN DE WASHINGTON, born at Wassington, about 1257.

8 ISOLDA DE WASHINGTON, born at Wassington, about 1260.

7 THOMAS DE WASHINGTON, first son of William de Washington, fifth of William, first of Bondo, second of Akaris,
second of Torfin the Dane, was born at Wassington,
York, about 1230.

"He was seized of lands in Washington juxta Ravensworth, in 20 Edward I." (1293). He had issue :

    8 WALTER DE WASHINGTON, born at Wassington, York,
       about 1265.

    8 THOMAS DE WASHINGTON, born at Wassington, York,
       about 1270.

    8 JOHN DE WASHINGTON, born at Wassington, York,
       about 1275.

    8 WILLIAM DE WASHINGTON, born at Wassington, York,
       about 1280.

7 **ROBERT DE WASHINGTON,** Lord of Welleburne, county
Westmoreland, first son of Robert de Washington, first
of Walter, fourth of Bondo, second of Akaris, first of Bardolf, second of Torfin the Dane, was born at Milburne,
or Welleburne, county Westmoreland, circa 1230.

"Son and heir, was seized of a capital messuage and
divers lands in Kerneford, in county of Lancaster, in right
of his wife, where he resided, 29 Edward I." (1302).

"He married Amercia, daughter and heir of Hugh de
Kerneford, Lady Kerneford, county Lancaster," by whom
he had issue :

    8 JOHN DE WASHINGTON, born at Welleburne, about
       1260.

    8 ROBERT DE WASHINGTON, born at Welleburne, about
       1265.

7 WILLIAM DE WASHINGTON, first son of William de Washington, second of Walter, fourth of Bondo, second of
Akaris, first of Bardolf, second of Torfin the Dane, was
born at Wassington, county Durham, about 1230.

"William de Washington, or Wessyngton, of Washington, county Durham, to whom his father gave half the Manor of Halton Fletham, county Westmoreland, 6 Edward I." (1279), was living 29 Edward I. (1302). He was living 29 Edward I. (1302). He had issue :

    8 ROBERT DE WASHINGTON, born at Wessington, Durham, about 1260.

7 THOMAS WASHINGTON, of Usseworth, Durham, second son of William de Washington, born at Wessington, county Durham, about 1235.

"He was living at Usseworth, county Durham, 28 Edward I." (1301).

"He married Isabella, daughter and co-heir of James de Usseworth, county Durham." He had issue.

7 JOHN WASHINGTON, third son of William de Washington, was born at Wessington, county Durham, about 1240.

"To whom his father gave half the Manor of Helton Fletham, county Westmoreland. He was living 29 Edward I." (1302). He had issue :

    8 WALTER WASHINGTON, born at Wessington, Durham, about 1270.

    8 JOHANNA WASHINGTON, born at Wessington, Durham, about 1275.

7 SIMON DE WASHINGTON, fourth son of William de Washington, was born at Wessington, county Durham, about 1245.

"He was of Essewell, county Hertford, 19 Edward I." (1292).

7 ALAN DE WASHINGTON, first child of Alan de Washington, first of Robert, fifth of Bondo, second of Akaris, first of Bardolf, second of Torfin, was born at Wassington, county York, circa 1230.

"Clericus, died s. p."

7 ALICIA DE WASHINGTON, second child of Alan de Washington, was born at Wassington, county York, about 1235. "She died before 17 Edward I." (1290).
"She married Roger de Hertford of Washington. He was living 21 Edward I." (1294). Her daughter was:

    8 ALICIA, born about 1260, niece and co-heir to Alan de Washington, 17 Edward I. (1290). She married, 17 Edward I. (1290), Stephen de Hudderwell. Had issue, given in his line.

7 JOHANNA DE WASHINGTON, third child of Alan de Washington, was born at Wassington, York, about 1240.
She died before 17 Edward I. (1290). She married Roger de Scargill. Had issue:

    8 ROGER fil ROGER DE SCARGILL.

8 RANDOLF DE RAVENSWORTH, first child of Henry de Ravensworth, first of Randolf, first of Henry, first of Hervey, first of Akaris, first of Bardolf, second of Torfin the Dane, was born at Ravensworth, York, about 1245.
He was heir to the inheritance of the Ravensworth estates, and died without issue. He was succeeded by his brother Hugh.

8 HUGH DE RAVENSWORTH, second child of Henry, born at Ravensworth, about 1250, d. 1304.
He succeeded his brother Randolf in the inheritance, see above. He had issue:

    9 HENRY DE RAVENSWORTH, born at Ravensworth, about 1275.

8 HENRY DE WASHINGTON, first son of Ranulph de Washington, first of Henry, first of William, first of Bondo, second of Akaris, first of Bardolf, second of Torfin the Dane, was born at Wassington, York, about 1235.
He claimed lands in Washington against Thomas

Godgram and others, 17 Edward I. (1290), and 3 Edward II. (1310). He had issue :

> 9 RANULPH DE WASHINGTON, born at Wassington, York, about 1270.
>
> 9 HUGH DE WASHINGTON, born at Wassington, York, about 1275.

8 ALAN DE WASHINGTON, second son of Ranulph de Washington, born at Wassington, York, about 1240.

He was killed by a fall from his horse at Wassington, juxta Ravensworth, 7 Edward I. (1280).

8 ADAM DE WASHINGTON, third son of Ranulph de Washington, born at Wassington, York, about 1245.

He held lands in Lastington of John fil Henry de Ravensworth, 20 Edward I. (1293). He had issue :

> 9 JOANNA, daughter and heir, born at Lastington, about 1280. She married about 1300, Hugh de Lastington. He was seized of lands in Lastington, in right of his wife. Had issue.

8 ALEXANDER DE RAVENSWORTH, first son of Henry de Washington, second of Henry, first of William, first of Bondo, second of Akaris, first of Bardolf, second of Torfin the Dane, born at Wassington, York, about 1240.

He was surety for William de Hertford, 21 Edward I. (1294).

8 JOHN DE WASHINGTON, second son of Henry de Washington, born at Wassington, York, about 1245.

He was living, 21 Edward I. (1294).

8 ROGER DE WASHINGTON, son of Henry de Washington, second child of Eudo de Washingon, fourth of William, first of Bondo, second of Akaris, first of Bardolf, second of Torfin the Dane, was born at Wassington, York, about

1250. He was living, 50 Henry III. (1265). Had issue :
9 HENRY DE WASHINGTON, born at Wassington, York,
about 1280.

8 WARREN DE WASHINGTON, son of John de Washington,
fourth child of Eudo, fourth of William, first of Bondo,
second of Akaris, first of Bardolf, second of Torfin the
Dane, was born at Wassington, York, about 1260.
He was attorney and chief steward to Henry fil Henry,
Lord of Ravensworth, 21 Edward I. (1294), and died 10
Edward II. (1317). He had issue.

> 9 Alicia, born at Wassington, York, about 1290, eldest
> daughter and co-heir. Was living 18 Edward III.
> (1355). Married John de Laton, of West Laton,
> county York. He was living, 18 Edward III. (1355).
> Had issue.
>
> 9 Agnes, born at Wassington, York, about 1295, second
> daughter and co-heir. Was living in 18 Edward III.
> (1355). She married Thomas Roter, of Wessington.
> He was living in 18 Edward III. (1355). Had issue.
>
> 9 Matilda, born at Wassington, York, about 1297, third
> daughter and co-heir. Was living in 18 Edward III.
> (1355).
>
> 9 Elizabeth, born at Wassington, York, about 1300,
> fourth daughter and co-heir. Was living in 18
> Edward III. (1355).

8 JOHN DE WASHINGTON, first child of William, fifth of
Eudo, fourth of William, first of Bondo, first of Akaris,
first of Bardolf, second of Torfin the Dane, was born
at Wassington, York, about 1255.
He was seized of lands in Washington in 8 Edward II.
(1315). He had issue :

> 9 WILLIAM DE WASHINGTON, born at Wassington, York,
> about 1280.

8 ROBERT DE WASHINGTON, first child of Robert, sixth of Eudo, fourth of William, first of Bondo, second of Akaris, first of Bardolf, second of Torfin the Dane, was born at Wassington, York, about 1255.

He was surety for William de Hertford, 26 Edward I. (1298).

8 STEPHEN DE WASHINGTON, second child of Robert de Washington, was born at Wassington, York, about 1257.

He was seized of 1 messuage and 1 bovate of land with the appurtenances, in Washington, 20 Edward I. (1293). He married Elizabeth, daughter of John de Ulvington, of Washington juxta Ravensworth. He had issue:

    9 ADAM DE WASHINGTON, born at Wassington, York, about 1285.

8 ISOLDA DE WASHINGTON, third child of Robert de Washington, born at Wassington, York, about 1260. She was living in 7 Edward I. (1280).

She married William fil Alicia de Neusum, who was seized of lands in Dalton Travers, in right of his wife, by gift of her father, in 7 Edward I. (1280). Had issue.

8 WALTER DE WASHINGTON, first son of Thomas, first of William, fifth of William, first of Bondo, second of Akaris, first of Bardolf, second of Torfin the Dane, was born at Wassington, York, about 1265.

He was living 30 Edward (1302).

8 THOMAS DE WASHINGTON, second son of Thomas de Washington, was born at Wassington, York, about 1268.

He was living 23 Edward I. (1296).

8 JOHN DE WASHINGTON, third son of Thomas de Washington, was born at Wassington, York, about 1270.

He was living 23 Edward I. (1296).

8 WILLIAM DE WASHINGTON, fourth son of Thomas de Washington, was born at Wassington, York, about 1272. He was living 23 Edward I. (1296).

8 JOHN DE WASHINGTON, first son of Robert de Washington Lord Milleburne, first of Robert, first of Walter, fourth of Bondo, second of Akaris, first of Bardolf, second of Torfin the Dane, was born at Milburne or ·Welleburne, county Westmoreland, about 1260.

He was the son and heir of Robert, Lord Milburne, and ancestor of the Washington family of Welleburne, Hull-hede, Barton and Shappe, county Westmoreland ; the latter branch being the ancestors of the Washingtons of Ardwich le Street, county York. He was of Milburne, 30 Edward I. (1303), and 10 Edward II. (1317). He had issue :'

> 9 PETER DE WASHINGTON, born at Milburne, Westmoreland, about 1300.
>
> 9 JOHN DE WASHINGTON, born at Milburne, Westmoreland, about 1305.

8 **ROBERT WASHINGTON**, second son of Robert de Washington, was born at Welleburne, county Westmoreland, about 1265, and removed to Kerneford, county Lancaster.

He was second son, upon whom his father and mother settled in fee tail the lands of Kerneford, county Lancaster. He took part with Thomas, Earl of Lancaster, and was pardoned 12 Edward II. (1319).

He married Agnes, daughter and heir of Adam Derling, by whom he had issue :

> 9 ROBERT WASHINGTON, born at Kerneford, county Lancaster, about 1300.
>
> 9 JOHN WASHINGTON, born at Kerneford, county Lancaster, about 1305.
>
> 9 THOMAS WASHINGTON, born at Kerneford, county Lancaster, about 1310.

9 WILLIAM WASHINGTON, born at Kerneford, county Lancaster, about 1315.

8 ROBERT DE WASHINGTON, first son of William de Washington, first of William, second of Walter, fourth of Bondo, second of Akaris, first of Bardolf, second of Torfin the Dane, was born at Wessyngton, Durham, about 1260. He was living in 6 and 10 Edward II. (1313–1317), and 1 Edward III. (1327). He had issue :

9 SIR WILLIAM DE WASHINGTON, born at Wessyngton, Durham, about 1300.

8 WALTER WASHINGTON, first child of John, third of William, second of Walter, fourth of Bondo, second of Akaris, first of Bardolf, second of Torfin the Dane, was born at Wessyngton, Durham, about 1270, and removed to Helton Fletham, county Westmoreland, where he was living 1 Edward III. (1327).

His first wife was Alicia, who bore one child. His second wife, Elizabeth, was administratrix to his will.

Christina, his daughter and heir, married Sir Roger de Blakiston, of Blakiston, county Durham. Had issue, given in his line.

8 JOHANNA WASHINGTON, second child of John Washington, was born at Wessyngton, county Durham, about 1275.

She had the Manor of Benwell, in the county of Northumberland. She was married to Robert de Whitchester.

9 LORD HENRY DE RAVENSWORTH, first son of Hugh, second of Henry, first of Randolf, first of Akaris, first of Bardolf, second of Torfin the Dane, was born at Ravensworth, York, about 1275.

"To Hugh succeeded his son Henry, who being called Henry Fitz-Hugh, gave the first occasion for all his descendants to assume that sirname, and in 3 Edward II.

(1310), was in that expedition made into Scotland. So, likewise, in 4 Edward II. (1311), and in 8 Edward II. (1315.) In consideration of which services and great expenses therein, the King gave him the sum of four hundred marks, to be received at the hands of Eleanor, the widow of Henry Lord Percy, she being indebted to the Exchequer in the like sum. Moreover, in 9 Edward II. (1316) he was constituted Governor of Bernard Castle, in the Bishoprick of Durham, by reason of the Earl of Warwick's minority, it being of his inheritance, and in 10 and 11 Edward II. (1317 and 1318), having again been employed in the Scottish wars, was in 14 Edward II. (1321) first summoned to Parliament amongst the Barons of this Realm.

"In 20 Edward II. (1327) having a debt of five hundred marks due to him from Sir Henry Vavasor, Knight, he did by a special instrument under his seal, acquit the same Henry thereof, upon condition that Henry le Vavasor, son to the same Henry, should take to wife Annabil, his daughter. In 7 Edward III. (1333) he was again in the Scottish wars, so likewise in 8 and 9 Edward III. (1334-5).

"And having married Eve, the daughter of Sir John Bulmer, Knight, left issue by her, Henry, his son and heir, which Henry took to wife Joane, the daughter of Sir Richard Fourneys, Knight; sister and heir of William, with whom he had the Lordships of Carleton, Ringstone, Beghton and Bothomfall, and left issue by her two sons, viz.: Hugh and Henry, which Hugh having wedded Isabel, the daughter of Ralph Lord Nevill, died without issue."

9 RANULPH DE WASHINGTON, first son of Henry de Washington, first of Ranulph, first of Henry, first of William, first of Bondo, second of Akaris, first of Bardolf, second of Torfin the Dane, was born at Wassington, York, about 1270.

He was defendant in a plea of land, 16 Edward III. (1342). He had issue:

3

10 ALEXANDER DE WASHINGTON, born at Wassington, York, about 1300.

9 HUGH DE WASHINGTON, second of Henry de Washington, was born at Wassington, York, about 1275.

He was one of the defendants with Adam de Bowes and others, at the suit of Hugh de Ask, for forcibly seizing his cattle and goods at Richmond, 3 Edward III. (1329). Plaintiff in a plea of accounts against John de Huddeswell and John de Watts, 36 Edward III. (1357).

9 HENRY DE WASHINGTON, first son of Roger, first of Henry, second of Eudo, fourth of William, first of Bondo, second of Akaris, first of Bardolf, second of Torfin the Dane, was born at Wassington, York, about 1280.

He was named 30 Edward I. (1303), 2 Edward II. (1309), 4 Edward III. (1330). He had issue:

10 ROGER DE WASHINGTON, born at Wassington, York, about 1310.

9 WILLIAM DE WASHINGTON, first son of John de Washington, first of William, fifth of Eudo, fourth of William, first of Bondo, second of Akaris, first of Bardolf, second of Torfin the Dane, was born at Wassington, York, about 1285.

He claimed arrears of an annual rent of eight marks, against Sir Robert le Constable, of Hamburgh, county York, Knt., 19 Edward II. (1326). He died 1 Edward III. (1327). He married Elizabeth, daughter of Sir Robert le Constable, of Hamburgh, county York, Knt. She was living 1 Edward III. (1327). He had issue.

9 ADAM DE WASHINGTON, first son of Stephen, second of Robert, sixth of Eudo, fourth of William, first of Bondo, second of Akaris, first of Bardolf, second of Torfin the Dane, was born at Wassington, York, about 1285.

He claimed lands in Washington juxta Ravensworth, against Elizabeth, wife of John de Ulvington, 10 Edward III. (1336). He had issue.

9 PETER DE WASHINGTON, first son of John, first of Robert, first of Robert, first of Walter, fourth of Bondo, second of Akaris, first of Bardolf, second of Torfin the Dane, was born at Welleburne, county Westmoreland, about 1300.

He claimed his wife's dower in her first husband's lands, in Strickland, 23 Edward III. (1349). ·

He married Matilda, widow of William L'Engleys, of Strickland. He had issue :

> 10 JOHN DE WASHINGTON, born at Welleburne, county Westmoreland, about 1323.
>
> 10 ROGER DE WASHINGTON, born at Welleburne, county Westmoreland, about 1325.

9 JOHN WASHINGTON, second son of Peter de Washington, was born at Welleburne, county Westmoreland, about 1305, and removed to Barton, county Westmoreland.

He was defendant in a plea of trespass, 36 Edward III. (1362).

9 ROBERT WASHINGTON, first child of Robert, second of Robert, first of Robert, first of Walter, fourth of Bondo, second of Akaris, first of Bardolf, second of Torfin the Dane, was born at Kerneford, county Lancaster, about 1300.

He was the eldest son, and ancestor of the Washingtons of Kerneford. He was living 47 Edward III. (1373). By wife Margaret he had issue :

> 10 ROBERT WASHINGTON, born at Kerneford, county Lancaster, about 1325.
>
> . 10 JOHN WASHINGTON, born at Kerneford, county Lancaster, about 1330.

9 JOHN WASHINGTON, second child of Robert Washington, was born at Kerneford, county Lancaster, about 1305.

He settled at Warton, county Lancaster. He married Alianna, daughter and heir of John de Warton, of Warton, in Lonesdale, county Lancaster, about year 1329, and died before 10 Richard II. (1386), when his widow was living at Warton. She was executrix of the will of William de Lancaster. He had issue :

> 10 JOHN WASHINGTON, born at Warton, Lancaster, about 1330.
>
> 10 EDMUND WASHINGTON, born at Warton, Lancaster, about 1340.

9 THOMAS WASHINGTON, third child of Robert Washington, born at Kerneford, Lancaster, about 1310.

He settled at Bolton, county Lancaster, was there 27 Edward III. (1353). He had issue :

> 10 THOMAS WASHINGTON, born at Bolton, county Lancaster, about 1340.

9 WILLIAM WASHINGTON, fourth child of Robert Washington, was born at Kerneford, county Lancaster, about 1315.

He was living 26 Edward III. (1352). He had issue :

> 10 WILLIAM WASHINGTON, born at Kerneford, county Lancaster, about 1340.

9 SIR WILLIAM DE WASHINGTON, Chevalier, first child of Robert de Washington, first of William, first of William, second of Walter, fourth of Bondo, second of Akaris, first of Bardolf, second of Torfin the Dane ; was born at Wessyngton, county Durham, Eng., about 1300.

He was Lord of Washington, county Durham, 1 Edward III. (1327), was living 47 Edward III. (1373). He had issue :

10 WILLIAM WASHINGTON, born at Wessington, Durham, about 1330.

10 ROGER WASHINGTON, born at Wessington, Durham, about 1335.

10 ALEXANDER DE WASHINGTON, first child of Ranulph, first of Henry, first of Ranulph, first of Henry, first of William, first of Bondo, second of Akaris, first of Bardolf, second of Torfin the Dane; was born at Wassington, York, about 1300.

He was defendant in a plea of trespass, at the suit of John Alayn, for depasturing cattle at Washington, and injuring his corn and meadow to the value of 10 marks, 3 Richard II. (1379). He had issue:

  11 ROBERT DE WASHINGTON, born at Wassington, York, about 1340.

  11 WILLIAM DE WASHINGTON, born at Wassington, York, about 1345.

10 ROGER DE WASHINGTON, Clericus, first of Henry, first of Roger, first of Henry, second of Eudo, fourth of William, first of Bondo, second of Akaris, first of Bardolf, second of Torfin the Dane; was born at Wassington, York, about 1310.

He was defendant conjointly with Warren de Washington, in a plea touching lands in Neusum, 7 Edward III. (1317), and in a plea of debt, 30 Edward III. (1356).

10 JOHN DE WASHINGTON, first child of Peter, first of John, first of Robert, first of Robert, first of Walter, fourth of Bondo, second of Akaris, first of Bardolf, second of Torfin the Dane; was born at Welleburne, county Westmoreland, about 1323.

He was living there, 40 Edward III. (1366), and 21 Richard II. (1397). He married Alicia, 40 Edward III. (1366). He had issue:

11 ROBERT WASHINGTON, born at Milburne, Westmoreland, about 1350.

10 ROGER DE WASHINGTON, second child of Peter, born at Welleburne, county Westmoreland, about 1325.

He settled at Strickland Ketell, county Westmoreland, was living there, 16 and 17 Richard II. (1392–3). He had issue :

   11 NICHOLAS WASHINGTON, born at Strickland Ketell, about 1348.

   11 RICHARD WASHINGTON, born at Strickland Ketell, about 1350.

   11 JOHN WASHINGTON, born at Strickland Ketell, about 1352.

10 ROBERT WASHINGTON, first child of Robert, first of Robert, second of Robert, first of Robert, first of Walter, fourth of Bondo, second of Akaris, first of Bardolf, second of Torfin the Dane, was born at Kerneford, county Lancaster, about 1325.

He was living there, 13 Richard II. (1389).

10 JOHN WASHINGTON, second child of Robert, was born at Kerneford, county Lancaster, about 1330.

He removed and settled at Catton, Lincolnshire, where he was living 40 Edward III. (1366).

10 JOHN WASHINGTON, first of John, second of Robert, second of Robert, first of Robert, first of Walter, fourth of Bondo, second of Akaris, first of Bardolf, second of Torfin the Dane ; was born at Warton, in Lonesdale, county Lancaster, about 1330.

He was living there, 26 Edward III. (1352), and 10 Richard II. (1386), and 4 Henry IV. (1402). By wife Johanna, he had issue :

   11 JOHN WASHINGTON, born at Warton, county Lancaster, about 1365.

10 EDMUND WASHINGTON, second of John, was born at Warton, county Lancaster, about 1340.

He was plaintiff in a plea of debt, 40 Edward III. (1366). He was then of Warton, Lancaster.

10 THOMAS WASHINGTON, first of Thomas, third of Robert, first of Robert, second of Robert, first of Robert, first of Walter, fourth of Bondo, second of Akaris, first of Bardolf, second of Torfin the Dane; was born at Bolton, county Lancaster, about 1340.

He was living there, 16 Richard II. (1392).

10 WILLIAM WASHINGTON, first of William, fourth of Robert, second of Robert, first of Robert, first of Walter, fourth of Bondo, second of Akaris, first of Bardolf, second of Torfin the Dane; was born at Kerneford, county Lancaster, about 1340.

He was living there, 26 Edward III. (1352), and 10 Richard II. (1386).

10 WILLIAM WASHINGTON, first child of Sir William de Washington, Chevalier, first of Robert, first of William, first of William, second of Walter, fourth of Bondo, second of Akaris, first of Bardolf, second of Torfin the Dane; was born at Wessyngton, county Durham, about 1330.

He held half the Manor of Helton Flatham, county Westmorcland. He had issue :

    11 WILLIAM WASHINGTON, born at Wessyngton, county Durham, about 1365.

"In 1350 William de Wessyngton, Lord of the Manor of Wessyngton, Durham, had license to settle it, and the village upon himself, his wife, and 'his own right heirs.' He died in 1367, and his son and heir William succeeded to the estate."

10 ROGER WASHINGTON, Bishop of Durham, second child

of Sir William, was born at Wessyngton, county Durham, about 1335. He had issue :

   11 WILLIAM WASHINGTON, born at Wessington, county Durham, about 1370.

11 ROBERT DE WASHINGTON, first child of Alexander, first of Ranulph, first of Henry, first of Ranulph, first of Henry, first of William, first of Bondo, second of Akaris, first of Bardolf, second of Torfin the Dane ; was born at Wassington, York, about 1340.

He was defendant in a plea at the suit of Richard Tekyll and Margaret, his wife, who claimed against him certain lands in Kerkan, Forrett, and Dalton Norreys, 2 Henry IV. (1400). He had issue.

11 WILLIAM DE WASHINGTON, clerk or clergyman, second child of Robert de Washingon, born at Wassington, York, about 1345.

He was defendant with his brother in a plea touching 2 messuages, 1 toft and 2 bovats of land in Kerkan, Forrett, and Dalton Norreys, 2 Henry IV. (1400).

11 ROBERT WASHINGTON, first child of John de Washington, first of Peter, first of John, first of Robert, first of Robert, first of Walter, fourth of Bondo, second of Akaris, first of Bardolf, second of Torfin the Dane ; was born at Milburne, county Westmoreland, about 1350.

He was living there, 12 Henry IV. (1412). He had issue :

   12 JOHN WASHINGTON, born at Milburne, about 1380.

11 NICHOLAS WASHINGTON, first son of Roger de Washington, second of Peter, first of John, first of Robert, first of Robert, first of Walter, fourth of Bondo, second of Akaris, first of Bardolf, second of Torfin the Dane ; was born at Strickland Ketell, county Westmoreland, about 1348. He was living there, 3 Henry IV. (1402).

11 RICHARD WASHINGTON, second of Roger, was born at Strickland Ketell, county Westmoreland, about 1350.

He was living there, 3 Henry IV. (1402).

11 JOHN WASHINGTON, third of Roger, was born at Strickland Ketell, county Westmoreland, about 1352.

He was defendant in a plea for debt, 49 Edward III. (1375).

11 JOHN WASHINGTON, first son of John, first of John, second of Robert, second of Robert, first of Robert, first of Walter, fourth of Bondo, second of Akaris, first of Bardolf, second of Torfin the Dane; was born at Warton, county Lancaster, about 1365.

He was of Warton, 4 Henry IV. (1402). He was commonly called "John fil John Washington." He had issue :

    12 ROBERT WASHINGTON, born at Warton, Lancaster, about 1400.

    12 WILLIAM WASHINGTON, born at Warton, Lancaster, about 1405.

11 SIR WILLIAM DE WASHINGTON, Knt., first child of William, first of Sir William, first of Robert, first of William, first of William, second of Walter, fourth of Bondo, second of Akaris, first of Bardolf, second of Torfin the Dane; was born at Wessyngton, county Durham, about 1365.

He married Margaret, daughter and heir of John de Morville. He had issue :

    12 ELEANOR, daughter and heir, born at Wessyngton, Durham, about 1390.

"He is mentioned as 'Sir William de Weschington.' His father died in 1367, when he succeeded to the Manor and estates of Wessyngton. He was one of the knights who sat in the privy council of the county during the espis-

copate of John Fordham."—*Hutchinson's Hist. Durham,*
vol. 2.

"For upwards of two hundred years the de Wessyngtons had sat in the councils of the Palitinate; had mingled
with horse and hound in the stately hunts of the Prelates,
and followed the banner of St. Cuthbert to the field, but
this Sir William was the last of the family that rendered
this feudal service. He was the last male of the line to
which the inheritance of the Manor, by the license granted
to his father, was confined. It passed away from the de
Wessyngtons, after his death, by the marriage of his only
daughter and heir, with Sir William Tempest, of Studley,
county York."

ELEANOR WASHINGTON, daughter, heiress and only child
of Sir William de Washington, of Wassington, Durham.
Died 1451.

She married, about 1420, Sir William Tempest of Studley,
son of Sir Richard Tempest of Studley (M. P. for county
of York, 2 Henry IV. 1400). Had issue two sons:

1 WILLIAM, of Studley, who died 1444, left two daughters, his co-heirs, viz.:

   1 ISABELLA, married to Richard Norton, of Norton Conyers, in Yorkshire, and

   2 DIONYSIA, married to William Mallorie, to whom
she conveyed the Manor of Studley, and from
this marriage the present (1833) Mrs. Lawrence
of Studley derives.

2 SIR ROWLAND, of Holmside, which he acquired by
gift of Sir Robert Umfraville, and in 18 Henry VI.
(1446), he also obtained lands from his brother.
He married Isabella, daughter and co-heir of Sir
William Elmdon, Knt. From this Sir Rowland Tempest descended the Tempests of Holmside, Stella,
Bracepath, Wyngard, &c., in the county of Durham,
and the Tempests in Kent.

11 WILLIAM WASHINGTON, first child of Roger Washington, Bishop of Durham, second of Sir William, Chevalier, first of Robert, first of William, first of William, second of Walter, first of Bondo, second of Akaris, first of Bardolf, second of Torfin the Dane ; was born at Wassyngton, county Durham, about 1370. He was son and heir.

12 JOHN WASHINGTON, first child of Robert, first of John, first of Peter, first of John, first of Robert, first of Robert, first of Walter, fourth of Bondo, second of Akaris, first of Bardolf, second of Torfin the Dane ; was born at Milburne, county Westmoreland, about 1380.

He was seized of the Manor of Hullhede, county Westmoreland, 11 Henry VI. (1439). He had issue :

    13 ROBERT WASHINGTON, born at Hullhede, Westmoreland, about 1420.

12 **ROBERT WASHINGTON,** first child of John, first of John, first of John, second of Robert, second of Robert, first of Robert, first of Walter, fourth of Bondo, second of Akaris, first of Bardolf, second of Torfin the Dane ; was born at Warton, Lancaster, about 1400.

Was living, temp. Henry V. and Henry VI. Died about 16 Edward IV. (1479). He had issue :

    13 JOHN WASHINGTON, born at Warton, Lancaster, about 1430.

    13 RICHARD WASHINGTON, born at Warton, Lancaster, about 1435.

    13 ROBERT WASHINGTON, born at Warton, Lancaster, about 1440.

12 REV. WILLIAM WASHINGTON, second of John Washington, was born at Warton, county Lancaster, about 1405.

He was living at Diegge, county Lancaster, 11 Henry VI. (1438). He was clergyman at Diegge.

13 ROBERT WASHINGTON, first child of John, first of Robert, first of John, first of Peter, first of John, first of Robert, first of Robert, first of Walter, fourth of Bondo, second of Akaris, first of Bardolf, second of Torfin the Dane; was born at Hullhede, county Westmoreland, about 1420.

He was seized of the Manor of Hullhede, county Westmoreland, where he resided, 40 Henry VI. (1468). He had issue:

> **14** THOMAS WASHINGTON, born at Hullhede, Westmoreland, about 1450.
>
> **14** JOHN WASHINGTON, born at Hullhede, Westmoreland, about 1455.
>
> **14** ROBERT WASHINGTON, born at Hullhede, Westmoreland, about 1460.

13 JOHN WASHINGTON, first son of Robert, first of John, first of John, first of John, second of Robert, second of Robert, first of Robert, first of Walter, fourth of Bondo, second of Akaris, first of Bardolf, second of Torfin the Dane; was born at Warton, county Lancaster, about 1430.

He succeeded to the Warton estates, and died 4 May, 17 Henry VII. (1501), and was succeeded by his eldest son Robert. He had issue:

> **14** ROBERT WASHINGTON, born at Warton, Lancaster, in 1467.

13 RICHARD WASHINGTON, second son of Robert, was born at Warton, county Lancaster, about 1435.

He was an officer of the Yeomen of the Guard to Henry VII., circa 1490.

13 ROBERT WASHINGTON, third son of Robert, was born at Warton, county Lancaster, about year 1440.

Removed and settled at Tewhitfield, county Lancaster.

He was the ancestor of the Washington family of North-amptonshire.

By first wife, Elizabeth, daughter of Ralph Westfield, of Westfield, county Lancaster, he had issue :

14 JOHN WASHINGTON, born at Tewhitfield, county Lancaster, about 1465.

14 THOMAS WASHINGTON, born at Tewhitfield, county Lancaster, about 1467.

13 ELEANOR WASHINGTON, born at Tewhitfield, county Lancaster, about 1470.

By second wife, Jane, daughter of Miles Whittington, of Barwick, county Lancaster, he had issue :

14 ROBERT WASHINGTON, born at Tewhitfield, county Lancaster, about 1475.

14 MILES WASHINGTON, born at Tewhitfield, county Lancaster, about 1477.

By third wife, Agnes, daughter of John Bateman, of Hersham, county Westmoreland, he had issue :

14 WILLIAM WASHINGTON, born at Tewhitfield, county Lancaster, about 1480.

14 ANTHONY WASHINGTON, born at Tewhitfield, county Lancaster, about 1482.

14 WALTER WASHINGTON, born at Tewhitfield, county Lancaster, about 1485.

14 ELIZABETH WASHINGTON, born at Tewhitfield, county Lancaster, about 1490.

14 THOMAS WASHINGTON, first son of Robert, first of John, first of Robert, first of John, first of Peter, first of John, first of Robert, first of Robert, first of Walter, fourth of Bondo, second of Akaris, first of Bardolf, second of Torfin the Dane ; was born at Hullhede, county Westmoreland, about 1450.

He died 10 Aug., 7 Henry VIII. (1515). Inquisition proved, 8 Henry VIII. (1516). By wife Anne he had issue :

15 KATHARINE, eldest daughter and co-heir, was aged

10 years, 7 Henry VIII. (1515). She married Miles
Beck. Issue given in his line.

15 ELIZABETH, second daughter and co-heir, was aged
8 years, 7 Henry VIII. (1515). She married William
Gilpin. Issue given in his line.

15 MARGARET, third daughter and co-heir, was aged
3 years, 7 Henry VIII. (1515). She married Thomas
Carus. Issue given in his line.

15 JOHANNA, fourth daughter and co-heir, was aged 2
years, 7 Henry VIII. (1515). She married Walter
Chambre. Issue given in his line.

14 JOHN WASHINGTON, second son of Robert, was born at
Hullhede, county Westmoreland, circa 1455.

His father gave him lands in Rosegill, county Westmoreland. He resided at Kendall, county Westmoreland. He
was defendant in a plea of trespass, 17 Henry VII. (1501).
By wife Elizabeth, he had issue :

15 RICHARD WASHINGTON, born at Kendall, Westmoreland, about 1490.

15 ELIZABETH WASHINGTON, born at Kendall, Westmoreland, about 1492.

15 JANE WASHINGTON, born at Kendall, Westmoreland,
about 1495.

15 THOMAS WASHINGTON, born at Kendall, Westmoreland, about 1497.

14 ROBERT WASHINGTON, third son of Robert, was born
at Hullhede, county Westmoreland, circa 1460.

He settled at Stanley, county Westmoreland, obit circa
8 Henry VIII. (1516). He had issue :

15 RICHARD WASHINGTON, born at Stanley, Westmoreland, circa 1490.

15 JOHN WASHINGTON, born at Stanley, Westmoreland,
circa 1495.

X 14 ROBERT WASHINGTON, first child of John, first of
Robert, first of John, first of John, first of John, second
of Robert, second of Robert, first of Robert, first of Walter, fourth of Bondo, second of Akaris, first of Bardolf,
second of Torfin the Dane; was born at Warton, county
Lancaster, in 1467. He was 34 years of age at the death
of his father, 17 Henry VII. (1501).

He was sergeant-at-arms to King Henry VII. and King
Henry VIII. (circa 1500 to 1510). He died 20 Sept., 9
Henry VIII. (1517). He disinherited his eldest son and
heir, Thomas, son of his first wife.

By his first wife Robert Washington had issue :

15 THOMAS WASHINGTON, born at Warton, Lancaster,
in 1493.

His second wife was Amy, sister to Sir Richard Whytell,
Knt. Her will dated 2 June, 1525, obit 20 June, 19 Henry
VIII. (1527). Her husband gave to her and her issue all
his inheritance. Issue by second wife :

15 RICHARD WASHINGTON, born at Warton, county Lancaster, in 1506.

15 HENRY WASHINGTON, born at Warton, county Lancaster, about 1508.

15 ROBERT WASHINGTON, born at Warton, county Lancaster, about 1510.

15 LAUNCELOT WASHINGTON, born at Warton, county
Lancaster, about 1512.

15 MARY WASHINGTON, born at Warton, county Lancaster, about 1515. Died infant.

15 MARY WASHINGTON, born at Warton, county Lancaster, about 1517.

13 ANNE WASHINGTON, born at Warton, county Lancaster, about 1520.

14 JOHN WASHINGTON, first child of Robert, third of Robert,
first of John, first of John, first of John, second of Robert, second of Robert, first of Robert, first of Walter,

fourth of Bondo, second of Akaris, first of Bardolf, second of Torfin the Dane ; was born at Terwhitfield, county Lancaster, circa 1470.

He married Margaret, daughter of Robert Kitson, of Warton, county Lancaster (sister of Sir Thomas Kitson, Alderman of London), by whom he had issue :

> 15 LAURENCE WASHINGTON, born at Terwhitfield, county Lancaster, about 1500.
>
> 15 NICHOLAS WASHINGTON, born at Terwhitfield, county Lancaster, about 1502.
>
> 15 LEONARD WASHINGTON, born at Terwhitfield, county Lancaster, about 1505.
>
> 15 PETER WASHINGTON, born at Terwhitfield, county Lancaster, about 1507.
>
> 15 THOMAS WASHINGTON, born at Terwhitfield, county Lancaster, about 1510.
>
> 15 JANE WASHINGTON, born at Terwhitfield, county Lancaster, about 1515.

14 THOMAS WASHINGTON, second child of Robert, was born at Terwhitfield, county Lancaster, circa 1467.   Had issue two sons.

14 ELEANOR WASHINGTON, third child of Robert, was born at Terwhitfield, county Lancaster, circa 1470.

She married James Mason, of Warton, county Lancaster. Issue given in his line.

14 ROBERT WASHINGTON, fourth child of Robert, was born at Terwhitfield, county Lancaster, circa 1475.   Had issue :

> 15 THOMAS WASHINGTON, born at Terwhitfield, county Lancaster, about 1500.

14 MILES WASHINGTON, fifth child of Robert, was born at Terwhitfield, county Lancaster, circa 1477.

14 WILLIAM WASHINGTON, sixth child of Robert, was born at Terwhitfield, Lancaster, about 1480.

14 ANTHONY WASHINGTON, seventh child of Robert, was born at Terwhitfield, Lancaster, about 1482.

14 WALTER WASHINGTON, eighth child of Robert, was born at Terwhitfield, Lancaster, about 1485.

14 ELIZABETH WASHINGTON, ninth child of Robert, was born at Terwhitfield, Lancaster, about 1490.

15 RICHARD WASHINGTON, first of John, second of Robert, first of John, first of Robert, first of John, first of Peter, first of John, first of Robert, first of Robert, first of Walter, fourth of Bondo, second of Akaris, first of Bardolf, second of Torfin the Dane ; was born at Kendall, county Westmoreland, about 1490.

He was seized of the tythes of Rosegill, &c. He levied a fine on the Manor of Docker, county Westmoreland, 30 Henry VIII. (1538).

He married Philippa, and had issue :

16 ROBERT WASHINGTON, born at Kendall, Westmoreland, about 1525.

16 ANNE WASHINGTON, born at Kendall, Westmoreland, about 1528.

16 MARGARET WASHINGTON, born at Kendall, Westmoreland, about 1530.

16 JOHN WASHINGTON, born at Kendall, Westmoreland, about 1532.

16 SOPHIA WASHINGTON, born at Kendall, Westmoreland, about 1535.

16 THOMAS WASHINGTON, born at Kendall, Westmoreland, about 1538.

16 HENRY WASHINGTON, born at Kendall, Westmoreland, about 1504.

4

16 Francis Washington, born at Kendall, Westmoreland, about 1545.

15 Elizabeth Washington, second child of John Washington, was born at Kendall, county Westmoreland, about
1492.

15 Jane Washington, third child of John Washington,
was born at Kendall, county Westmoreland. about 1495.

15 Rev. Thomas Washington, fourth child of John Washington, Rector of Germanstown, county Derby, was born
at Kendall, county Westmoreland, about 1497.

He removed to Germanstown, county Derby. where he
was Rector. He died intestate.

His wife, Joanna, had administration to her husband's
goods, 23 Elizabeth (1580), was residing at Porloch, county
Somerset, a widow, 26 Elizabeth (1583).

15 Richard Washington, first son of Robert, third of
Robert, first of John, first of Robert, first of John, first
of Peter, first of John, first of Robert, first of Robert,
first of Walter, fourth of Bondo, second of Akaris, first
of Bardolf, second of Torfin the Dane ; was born at Stanley, county Westmoreland, about 1490. Removed to
Shappe, county Westmoreland.

He was seized of the Rectory of Shappe and lands, &c.,
in Slegill, Shaftfield, Strickland, &c., county Westmoreland. Will dated 26 June, 1553, obit 2 Jan. 1554, 3 Philip
and Mary. By wife, Anne Lund, he had issue :

16 James Washington, born at Stanley, Westmoreland, about 1520.

16 Ranulph Washington, born at Stanley, Westmoreland, about 1525.

15 John Washington, second son of Robert, was born

at Stanley, county Westmoreland, about 1495. He removed and settled at Delicar, county Westmoreland.
He had issue :

    16 THOMAS WASHINGTON, born at Delicar, Westmore-
      land, about 1520.

15 THOMAS WASHINGTON, first child of Robert, first of
John, first of Robert, first of John, first of John, first of
John, second of Robert, second of Robert, first of Rob-
ert, first of Walter, fourth of Bondo, second of Akaris,
first of Bardolf, second of Torfin the Dane ; was born at
Warton, county Lancaster, in 1493.

    He was son and heir. Was aged 24 years at his father's
death, 9 Henry VIII. (1517). He was disinherited by his
father, and filed his bill in chancery for the recovery of the
estates, but did not succeed therein. He had issue :

    16 LAURENCE WASHINGTON, born at Warton, county
      Lancaster, about 1515.

    16 LEONARD WASHINGTON, born at Warton, county
      Lancaster, about 1520.

15 SIR RICHARD WASHINGTON, Knt., second child of Robert, was born at Warton, county Lancaster, in year 1506.

    He was aged 21, 19 Henry VIII. (1527). He was
knighted, 29 Henry VIII. (1537).

15 HENRY WASHINGTON, third child of Robert, was born
at Warton, county Lancaster, about 1508.

15 ROBERT WASHINGTON, fourth child of Robert, was born
at Warton, county Lancaster, about 1510.

15 LAUNCELOT WASHINGTON, fifth child of Robert, was
born at Warton, county Lancaster, about 1512.

15 MARY WASHINGTON, sixth child of Robert, was born at
Warton, county Lancaster, about 1515. Died infant.

15 MARY WASHINGTON, seventh child of Robert, was born at Warton, county Lancaster, about 1517.

15 ANNE WASHINGTON, eighth child of Robert, was born at Warton, county Lancaster, about 1520.

15 HON. LAURENCE WASHINGTON, first child of John, first of Robert, third of Robert, first of John, first of John, first of John, second of Robert, second of Robert, first of Robert, first of Walter, fourth of Bondo, second of Akaris, first of Bardolf, second of Torfin the Dane; was born at Terwhitfield, county Lancaster, about 1500.

He removed and settled at Grey's Inn, county Middlesex, was Mayor of Northampton, 1532 and 1545. Had a grant of the Manor of Sulgrave, Northamptonshire, by purchase from the crown, 30 Henry VIII. (1538). He died, 19 July, 26 Elizabeth (1584).

He married, first, Elizabeth, widow of William Gough, of Northampton, who died 2 Oct., 1564.

He married, second, Ann or Aimee, daughter of Robert Pargiter, of Glentworth. He had issue :

 16 ROBERT WASHINGTON, born at Grey's Inn, Middlesex, in 1544.

 16 WILLIAM WASHINGTON, born at Grey's Inn, Middlesex, about 1548.

 16 JOHN WASHINGTON, born at Grey's Inn, Middlesex, about 1550.

 16 FRANCES WASHINGTON, born at Grey's Inn, Middlesex, about 1555.

 16 ANN WASHINGTON, born at Grey's Inn, Middlesex, about 1560.

 16 MARY WASHINGTON, born at Grey's Inn, Middlesex, about 1565.

 16 MARGARET WASHINGTON, born at Grey's Inn, Middlesex, about 1567.

 16 ELIZABETH WASHINGTON, born at Grey's Inn, Middlesex, about 1570.

16 MARGARET WASHINGTON, born at Grey's Inn, Mid-. dlesex, about 1573.

16 BARBARA WASHINGTON, born at Grey's Inn, Middlesex, about 1576.

16 SIR LAURENCE WASHINGTON, born at Grey's Inn, 19 May, 1579.

His numerous daughters formed alliances in the Midlands, and elsewhere, both patrician and plebeian.

"When Henry VIII. made an end of the English Monasteries, 1528–9, he gave all the lands in Sulgrave and Woodford, and certain lands in Stotesbury and Cotton, near Northampton, lately belonging to the priory of St. Andrew's in that town, and all lands in Sulgrave, lately belonging to the dissolved priories of Canons Ashby and Catesby, to Laurence Washington, of Northampton, gentleman.

"Like many other persons who profited by the burly Tudor's *coup,* Laurence was a lawyer, being of Grey's Inn, London, and son of John Washington, of Whitfield, or Warton, Lancaster. He was also Mayor of Northampton in 1532 and 1545. He died possessed of these lands, 19 July, 26 Elizabeth (1584). His son and heir, Robert, jointly with his eldest son, Laurence, sold the property, 43 Elizabeth (1600), to his nephew, Laurence Makepeace, of the Inner Temple, London."

THE OLD HOME OF THE WASHINGTONS,

At Sulgrave, Northamptonshire, England, built by Hon. Laurence Washington, Mayor of Northampton. Visitation of 1846.

"It was in a quiet, rural neighborhood, where the farmhouses were quaint and antiquated. A part only of the manor-house remained, and was inhabited by a farmer. The Washington crest, in colored glass, was to be seen in a window of what was now the buttery. Another relic of the ancient manor of the Washingtons was a rookery in a venerable grove hard by. The rooks, those staunch adherents to old family abodes, still hovered and cawed about their hereditary nests. In the pavement of the parish church we were shown a stone slab bearing effigies on plates of brass, of Laurence Washington, gentleman, and Aimee, his wife, and their four sons and seven daughters. The inscription in black letter was dated 1564.

"The house stands at the eastern extremity of the village —indeed just outside of it ; in its own grounds, and is approached on the west by a pretty green croft, separated from the almost encircling road by a hedge. Crossing by one of the paths one catches, through a gap on the right, a charming glimpse of Sulgrave church, gray with the rains, frost and sunshine of 300 years. A little to the left, not far from the building, are three fine elms, planted triangularly as regards one another, which at the time of my visit kept up a continual mournful rustling in the west wind, as if bewailing the loss of their six fellows cut down seven years ago ; and also of the inhabiting rooks, which then incontinently forsook their old abode. That was the end of Washington Irving's "grove" and "rookery," and as the farmer occupying the house tells me that one of the remaining trees is decayed, I suppose that before long not one of them will be left standing. They used to shear sheep under them, which, with the rooks wheeling and cawing above and the old house behind, must have made a pretty picture.

"From this side one first sees a dead gable-end, with two narrow, stopped-up windows, and a partly stone, partly tiled roof ; of which former material the whole mansion is composed, though curiously defaced by plaster. This, having dropped off here and there, gives the edifice an equally dilapidated and venerable appearance. The ivy, which profusely mantles the northern side of the house, has climbed up the left side of the gable-end and ridge of

THE OLD HOME OF THE WASHINGTONS AT SULGRAVE, ENGLAND.

WASHINGTON COAT-OF-ARMS.

SULGRAVE CHURCH, NORTHAMPTONSHIRE.

the roof, and seems to intend an ascent up the two rather ornamental chimneys' surmounting the gable. To the left is the high wall of a kitchen garden, with a fragrant elder tree peeping over its coping, and standing in a shallow ditch or trench, boasting a luxuriant growth of nettles. A tall-ish young fir at the further end of the garden wall, near a gate affording access to the road, finishes the prospect in this direction.

"To the right of the gable-end is a low stone wall with a larch gate, fencing a small court, partly paved, partly in grass. This court was occupied by a brood of young ducks, resting together in very white and loving proxim-ity, and only now and then giving themselves the trouble to quack. In respect to behavior they were much wiser than a fussy hen with her family of scared-looking chick-ens, which comported themselves after the fashion of their kind, as if the whole solar system had no other purpose than their molestation. From this court-yard one enters the house by a handsomish old stone doorway. Above, two little attic windows project from the tiled roof. To the right of the court-yard are various modern buildings, proper to a farm-house, sheds, out-houses, and odoriferous pig-sties. All the foregoing is visible at one *coup d'œil* from the close behind the rustling elms.

"The southern aspect of the old mansion is accurately de-lineated, which may spare me some description. Only one-third of the original edifice is here remaining. Once it extended eastwards over the garden—some 30 or 40 feet —to a declivity, where there was more recently a wall six feet high. The joining of the gable-end is plainly per-ceptible on the wall. The projection at right angles with the main building was formerly the porch, but the fine old Tudor doorway of brown-stone, with its square-headed mouldings and depressed arch, has been converted into a dairy window by bricking up the lower portion. In the spandrels (or triangular spaces to the right and left of the arch) are two shields containing the Washington coat-of-arms, as shown in my sketch. Three centuries have somewhat worn off their original sharpness, but they are still clear-cut and unmistakable.

"What a fortune had that shield of a private English gentleman—to become the most notable blazon of all the world ! Strange to think that this little obscure stone coat-of-arms in a secluded Northamptonshire village should be the original of so much—should still be extant ! As strange to think of the contrast between the torpid and monotonous rustic life surrounding it for so many generations with the rush and roar of existence in our great republic !

"There can be no question that the three stars and three stripes furnished the idea for the American flag, albeit the details of the transaction are involved in obscurity. Tradition attributes the suggestion to that great inventor, Benjamin Franklin (whose ancestors, by the way, also came from Northamptonshire). Tupper is probably right in his Centennial drama when he makes Franklin say :

> " ——I proposed it to the Congress.
> It was their leader's old crusading blazon,
> Washington's coat, his own heraldic shield.
> And on the spur, when we must choose a flag
> Symboling independent unity,
> We and not he—all was unknown to him—
> Took up his coat-of-arms and multiplied
> And magnified it every way to this,
> Our glorious national banner.

"He adds, also, some allusions to the identical old mansion which I am now describing :

> " ——The Washingtons, of Wessyngton,
> In County Durham, and of Sulgrave manor,
> County Northampton, bore upon their shield
> Three stars atop, three stripes below the fess,
> Gules—that is red—on white, and for the crest

> An eagle's head upspringing to the light.
> *The architraves at Sulgrave testify,*
> As sundry painted windows in the hall
> At Wessyngton, this was their family coat.
> And at Mount Vernon I myself have noted
> An old cast-iron, scutcheoned chimney-back
> Charged with that heraldry.

"Mr. Tupper tells us that he himself made the Mount Vernon discovery, in 1851, and 'long after verified the matter at Herald's College;' and the crest and coat-of-arms appear upon the cover of his unpublished but privately printed drama. The motto is : *Exitus acta probat* (Issue proveth acts). Baker, who gives his authority for the genealogy as 'from visitations and title-deeds : the American line from monumental inscriptions,' states the Washington arms as follows :

"*Argent*, two bars *gules*, in chief three mullets of the second. Crest, a raven with wings endorsed proper, issuing out of a ducal coronet *or*.

"And these are yet to be seen in Fawsley and Brington churches, Northamptonshire, differenced by a crescent. Dugdale also quotes these as the arms of Washington in the windows of Radway and of Leekington churches, Warwickshire ; and thus Mr. Evelyn Philip Shirley gives them in 'Stemmata Shirleiana.' In so large and scattering a family as the Washingtons, it is easy to imagine how some variations might occur in the crest or coat-of-arms—especially when we remember the queer, conventional drawing of the old heralds. A mullet is the rowel of a spur (used as the filial distinction of a third son), hence the difference between it and a star would not be perceptible. And the crest on Mr. Tupper's book is more like a raven's head than an eagle's—certainly a less appropriate national emblem than the king of birds. It is asserted that Franklin objected to the latter symbol, and indeed to all heraldic beasts and birds, conventionally used as types of sovereignty, saying they were invariably creatures of prey and therefore unworthy of representing modern civilization. In lieu of an eagle, he characteristically proposed a turkey, as a valuable domestic fowl, particularly suitable to an exclusively agricultural country, as America then was. But the utilitarianism of the project had too comic an aspect for adoption, and old-fashioned ideas prevailed.

"Let us return to the ancient manor house at Sulgrave. Over the blocked-up doorway, and midway between it and the window above, is what appears to have been another coat-of-arms, also in stone, but so plastered that only the shape of the shield is discernible. It is more than twice the size of those in the spandrels. And above the common upper window there is yet another coat-of-arms, similarly disfigured. It is circular and surmounted by a sheaf or coronet with feathers, having also mutilated 'supporters,' probably a griffin and a lion. Each of these animals holds a flag. If these be indeed the Washington supporters the latter fact is a curious coincidence. Like the motto, it might be regarded as prophetic.

"The lower window in the main building to the right of the porch is that alluded to by Irving as having once contained the Washington arms in stained glass. It is mentioned also by Baker as 'the arms and alliances of the family ornamenting the kitchen window.' The fate of this memorial was peculiar. Colonel Henry Hely-Hutchinson, the late lord of the manor, an old Waterloo soldier, had the panes removed for their better preservation, when they were either stolen from or accidentally broken in his desk. So the very means taken for insuring their safety precipitated their destruction or disappearance. 'What,' asked a writer in the *Quarterly Review* of 1857, alluding to the circumstance in an article on 'The History and Antiquities of Northamptonshire,' 'would the Americans, who, having at first expunged "Heraldry" from their cyclo-

pædias, are now the chief clients of the Heralds' College,
give to recover those purloined or broken quarries ?'

"There is nothing remarkable in the appearance of the
eastern and northern sides of the house, which are almost
entirely covered with ivy, even to the obscuring of the
windows. The south-east gable has three common, mutilated chimneys, but some others, further on, seem ancient.

"During the time of their ancestors' ownership of the
Sulgrave lands, they unquestionably lived there, and in all
probability the Laurence who first acquired them built the
old manor house. Let me relate what is known, in addition, of the English Washingtons. They seem to have
been a good old family, numerous, and, as an American
would say, pretty scattering, for one reads of them as in
Lancashire, Yorkshire, Leicestershire, Durham, Warwickshire, Wiltshire, and Sussex, as well as Northamptonshire.
They were country gentlemen, soldiers, lawyers, scholars,
and the like. One—a Thomas Washington, of Compton,
Sussex—fought as a captain in Flanders in the reign of
Elizabeth. Another, brother to the Robert who sold the
Sulgrave manor, appears to have attained knighthood, for
he figures as Sir Laurence Washington, of Garsdon, Wiltshire, and was buried there on the 21st of May, 1643, aged
sixty-four. Laurence, the second, who abetted his father in
the sale, was born at Brington, where his grandfather and
namesake, the mayor and lawyer, seems to have settled.
This branch of the family subsequently became allied to the
important one of the Spencers, but hardly prospered until
Sir William Washington, of Packington, Leicestershire
(according to Baker—Washington Irving says Kent), got
married to Anne, half sister to George Villiers, Duke of
Buckingham, the imperious favorite of Charles the First.
Perhaps William was knighted after and in consequence of
this connection ; anyway it benefited the family. The
younger Washingtons are said to have been courtiers before, in the reign of James the First.

"Colonel Henry Washington distinguished himself in 1646, when elevated to the command of Worcester, the governor having been captured by the enemy. It was a time of confusion and dismay. The King had fled from Oxford in disguise, and gone to the Parliamentary camp at Newark. The royal cause was desperate. In this crisis Sir Henry received a letter from Fairfax, who, with his victorious army, was at Haddington, demanding the surrender of Worcester. ·The following was Colonel Washington's reply :

" SIR :—It is acknowledged by your books, and by report of your own quarter, that the King is in some of your armies. That granted, it may be easy for you to procure His Majesty's commands for the disposal of this garrison. Till then I shall make good the trust reposed in me. As for conditions, if I shall be necessitated, I shall make the best I can. The worst I know and fear not ; if I had, the profession of a soldier had not been begun nor so long continued by your Excellency's humble servant,
HENRY WASHINGTON.

" In a few days Colonel Whalley invested the city with 5,000 troops. Sir Henry despatched messenger after messenger to the King to know his pleasure. None of them returned. A female emissary was equally unavailing. Week after week elapsed until nearly three months expired. Provisions began to fail, the city was in confusion, the troops grew insubordinate, yet Sir Henry persisted in the defence. General Fairfax, with 1,500 horses and foot, was daily expected. Still Sir Henry 'awaited His Majesty's commands.' At length news arrived that the King had issued an order for the surrender of all towns, castles, and ports. A printed copy of the order was shown to Sir Henry, and on the faith of that document he capitulated (19th July, 1646) on honorable terms, won by his fortitude and preseverance. Those who believe in hereditary virtues may see foreshadowed in the conduct of this Washington of Worcester, the magnanimous constancy of purpose, the disposition to 'hope against hope,' which bore our Washington triumphantly through the darkest days of our Revolution." He was son of Sir William Washington, of Packyngton (page 87).

15 NICHOLAS WASHINGTON, second child of John, was born at Terwhitfield, county Lancaster, about 1502.
He was of Warton, county Lancaster, 37 Henry VIII. (1545).

15 LEONARD WASHINGTON, third child of John, was born at Terwhitfield, county Lancaster, about 1505.

15 PETER WASHINGTON, fourth child of John, was born at Terwhitfield, county Lancaster, about 1507.

15 THOMAS WASHINGTON, born at Terwhitfield, county Lancaster, about 1510.

15 JANE WASHINGTON, born at Terwhitfield, county Lancaster, about 1515.

15 THOMAS WASHINGTON, first of Robert, fourth of Robert, third of Robert, first of John, first of John, first of John, second of Robert, second of Robert, first of Robert, first of Walter, first of Bondo, second of Akaris, first of Bardolf, second of Torfin the Dane; was born at Terwhitfield, county Lancaster, about 1500.
He removed and settled at Compton, county Sussex; was a captain in Flanders.
He had issue by wife, who was daughter of a Deering, viz.:
>   **16** RICHARD WASHINGTON, born at Compton, about 1525. Died s. p.
>   **16** LUCY WASHINGTON, born at Compton, about 1527. Married Mr. Thezelwright, of Cambridge. Had issue.
>   **16** ANN WASHINGTON, born at Compton, about 1530. Married Robert Bateman. Had issue.
>   **16** KATHARINE WASHINGTON, born at Compton, about 1532. Married Melchior Reynolds. Had issue.

16 ROBERT WASHINGTON, first child of Richard, first of
John, second of Robert, first of John. first of Robert,
first of John, first of Peter, first of John, first of Robert,
first of Robert, first of Walter, fourth of Bondo, second
of Akaris, first of Bardolf, second of Torfin the Dane ;
was born at Kendall, county Westmoreland, about 1525.
He lived at Docker, county Westmoreland, also at Kendall. He was seized of the tythes of Rosegill and Waste-
land. Will dated 14 Nov., 1583. Inquisition post morten,
20 April, 27 Elizabeth (1584). He had issue :

    17 RANDALL WASHINGTON, born at Docker, county
    Westmoreland, in 1568.

    17 RICHARD WASHINGTON, born at Docker, county
    Westmoreland, about 1570.

    17 JAMES WASHINGTON, born at Docker, county West-
    moreland, about 1572.

16 ANN WASHINGTON, second child of Richard, was born
at Kendall, county Westmoreland, about 1527.

16 MARGARET WASHINGTON, third child of Richard, was
born at Kendall, county Westmoreland, about 1530.

16 JOHN WASHINGTON, fourth child of Richard, was born
at Kendall, county Westmoreland, about 1532.
Obit 1598. He had issue :

    17 FRANCIS WASHINGTON, born at Kendall, Westmore-
    land, about 1555.

    17 JOHN WASHINGTON, born at Kendall, Westmore-
    land, about 1560.

16 SOPHIA WASHINGTON, fifth child of Richard, was born
at Kendall, county Westmoreland, about 1535.

16 THOMAS WASHINGTON, sixth child of Richard, was born
at Kendall, county Westmoreland, about 1538.

He died 1587. He married Ellen (obit 1599). He had issue :

 17 ALAN WASHINGTON, born at Kendall, county Westmoreland, about 1565.

 17 THOMAS WASHINGTON, born at Kendall, county Westmoreland, about 1568.

 17 JAMES WASHINGTON, born at Kendall, county Westmoreland, about 1570.

16 HENRY WASHINGTON, seventh child of Richard, was born at Kendall, county Westmoreland, about 1540.

He removed and lived at Sedburgh, county Westmoreland. By wife, Elizabeth, he had issue :

 17 SIMON WASHINGTON, born at Kendall, county Westmoreland, about 1580.

 17 JOHN WASHINGTON, born at Kendall, county Westmoreland, about 1583.

 17 THOMAS WASHINGTON, born at Kendall, county Westmoreland, about 1585.

 17 MARGARET WASHINGTON, born at Kendall, county Westmoreland, about 1587.

 17 AGNES WASHINGTON, born at Kendall, county Westmoreland, about 1590.

16 FRANCIS WASHINGTON, eighth child of Richard, was born at Kendall, county Westmoreland, about 1545.

He removed to Gravigg, county Westmoreland.

16 JAMES WASHINGTON, first child of Richard, first of Robert, third of Robert, first of John, first of Robert, first of John, first of Peter, first of John, first of Robert, first of Robert, first of Walter, fourth of Bondo, second of Akaris, first of Bardolf, second of Torfin the Dane ; was born at Stanley, county Westmoreland, about 1520.

To whom his father gave half the rectory and tytlics of Shappe, county Westmoreland, in fee tail. He purchased the manors of Ardwick le Street, Hampall and Armsthorp, county York, temp. Elizabeth. He was plaintiff in a plea, conjointly with his brother Ranulph, touching lands in Blasterfield, county Westmoreland, and Penrith, county Cumberland, 6 and 8 Elizabeth (1564–6). Will dated, 15 August, and he died 29 August. Inquest, p. 19 October, 22 Elizabeth (1580). He was buried at Ardwick le Street.

He married Margaret, daughter of John Anlaby, of Etton, county York. She lived at Ardwick le Street, and died there, 1579, aged 35, and was buried at Ardwick. He had issue :

    17 MARTIN WASHINGTON, born at Ardwick le Street, county York, 17 Aug., 1565.

    17 RICHARD WASHINGTON, born at Ardwick le Street, county York, 25 Nov., 1566.

    17 PHILIP WASHINGTON, born at Ardwick le Street, county York, about 1568.

    17 FRANCIS WASHINGTON, born at Ardwick le Street, county York, about 1570.

    17 BARTHOLOMEW WASHINGTON, born at Ardwick le Street, county York, about 1572.

    17 LUCY WASHINGTON, born at Ardwick le Street, county York, about 1574.

    17 MARY WASHINGTON, born at Ardwick le Street, county York, about 1576.

    17 CATHARINE WASHINGTON, born at Ardwick le Street, county York, about 1578.

    17 JANE WASHINGTON, born at Ardwick le Street, county York, about 1580.

16 RANULPH WASHINGTON, second of Richard, was born at Stanley, county Westmoreland, about 1525.

He removed and lived at Bibleker, county Westmoreland. He was living 1 James I. (1603).

He was plaintiff, conjointly with his brother James, in a

plea touching lands in Blasterfield, county Westmoreland, and Penrith, county Cumberland, 6 and 8 Elizabeth (1564–6). By wife Eleanor, he had issue :

17 RANULPH WASHINGTON, born at Billeker, county ·Westmoreland, about 1560.

16 THOMAS WASHINGTON, first child of John, second of Robert, third of ·Robert, first. of John, first of Robert, first of John, first of Peter, first of John, first of Robert, first of Robert, first of Walter, fourth of Bondo, second of Akaris, first of Bardolf, second of Torfin the Dane ; was born at Delicar, county Westmoreland, about 1520. He had issue.

16 LAURENCE WASHINGTON, first child of Thomas, first of Robert, first of John, first of Robert, first of John, first of John, first of John, second of Robert, second of Robert, first of Robert, first of Walter, first of Bondo, second of Akaris, first of Bardolf, second of Torfin the Dane ; was born at Warton, county Lancaster, about 1515.

He was living 35 Henry VIII. (1543). He had issue :

17 LAURENCE WASHINGTON, born at Warton, county Lancaster, about 1540.

17 LEONARD WASHINGTON, born at Warton, county Lancaster, about 1545.

17 ROBERT WASHINGTON, born at Warton, county Lancaster, about 1550.

16 LEONARD WASHINGTON, second child of Thomas, was born at Warton, county Lancaster, about 1520.

He was living 37 Henry VIII. (1545). He had issue :

17 ROBERT WASHINGTON, born at Warton, county Lancaster, about 1550.

16 ROBERT WASHINGTON, first child of Hon. Laurence, first of John, first of Robert, third of Robert, first of John,

5

first of John, first of John, second of Robert, second of
Robert, first of Robert, first of Walter, fourth of Bondo,
second of Akaris, first of Bardolf, second of Torfin the
Dane ; was born at Grey's Inn, county Middlesex, in
1544.

He removed and lived at Sulgrave, Northamptonshire.
He was aged 40 at his father's death, 26 Elizabeth (1584).
He died at Althorp, 10 Mar., 162♦

He had license to alienate or sell his lands, 36 Elizabeth
(1593), and sold the Manor of Sulgrave to his nephew,
Laurence Makepeace, 43 Elizabeth (1600), of the Inner
Temple, London.

He married Elizabeth, daughter of Walter Light, of Redway, county Warwick, his first wife, by whom he had issue :

    17 LAURENCE WASHINGTON, born at Sulgrave, county
       Northampton, about 1565.

    17 ROBERT WASHINGTON, born at Sulgrave, county
       Northampton, about 1567.

    17 WALTER WASHINGTON, born at Sulgrave, county
       Northampton, about 1570, died infant.

    17 WALTER WASHINGTON, born at Sulgrave, county
       Northampton, about 1575.

Married second, Ann, daughter of Mr. Fisher, of Hanslape, county Bucks. She died 1602. Had issue :

    17 ROBERT WASHINGTON, born at Sulgrave, Northam-
       tonshire, about 1595.

    17 MARGARET WASHINGTON, born at Sulgrave, North-
       amptonshire, about 1597.

    17 ALBANY WASHINGTON, born at Sulgrave, Northamp-
       tonshire, in 1599.

    17 GUY WASHINGTON, born at Sulgrave, Northamp-
       tonshire, in 1602.

"The Washingtons were a gentle family, although
greatly reduced in circumstances, having been compelled
to part with the estate of Sulgrave, upon which they retired
to Brington. The Lord Spencer of that day befriended

them, and as they had frequently been his guests at Wormleighton, on their settlement at Brington they were wel-
comed at Althorp."

16 WILLIAM WASHINGTON, second child of Hon. Laurence,
was born at Grey's Inn, county Middlesex, about 1546.
Had issue three sons.

16 JOHN WASHINGTON, third child of Hon. Laurence, was
born at Grey's Inn, county Middlesex, about 1548. Had
issue four sons.

16 FRANCES WASHINGTON, fourth child of Hon. Laurence,
was born at Grey's Inn, county Middlesex, about 1550.
Married John Thompson, of Sulgrave.

16 ANN WASHINGTON, fifth child of Hon. Laurence, was
born at Grey's Inn, county Middlesex, about 1552. Married Edmund Fisher, of Hanslape.

16 MARY WASHINGTON, sixth child of Hon. Laurence, was
born at Grey's Inn, county Middlesex, about 1555. Married Abel Makepeace, of Chipping Warden. Had son :
   17 LAURENCE, to whom his uncle Robert sold the
   Manor of Sulgrave, 43 Elizabeth (1600). He was of
   the Inner Temple, London.

16 MARGARET WASHINGTON, seventh child of Hon. Laurence, was born at Grey's Inn, county Middlesex, about
1557, died infant.

16 ELIZABETH WASHINGTON, eighth child of Hon. Laurence, was born at Grey's Inn, county Middlesex, about
1560.

16 MARGARET WASHINGTON, ninth child of Hon. Laurence.
was born at Grey's Inn, county Middlesex, about 1563.
Married Gerard Hawtyer.

16 BARBARA WASHINGTON, tenth child of Hon. Laurence, was born at Grey's Inn, county Middlesex, about 1576.

16 SIR LAURENCE WASHINGTON, Knt., eleventh child of Hon. Laurence, was born at Grey's Inn, county Middlesex, 19 May, 1579.

He was of Garsdon, Wiltshire, was Register in Chancery, 46 Elizabeth (1603). Obit 1643, aged 64 years.

Married Anne, who died 1645, aged 75 years. He had issue :

> **17** LAURENCE WASHINGTON, JR., born at Garsdon, Wiltshire, about 1605.
>
> **17** MARTHA WASHINGTON, born at Garsdon, Wiltshire, about 1607.
>
> **17** MARY WASHINGTON, born at Garsdon, Wiltshire, about 1610.

SIR LAURENCE WASHINGTON, OF GARSDON.

"Garsdon, a parish in England, in the county of Wiltshire, has the honor of containing in its venerable church a monument erected to the memory of Sir Laurence Washington. The village of Garsdon is about two miles from Malmesbury, and the church is a quaint Gothic structure, situated in the bosom of a rich country and surrounded with ancient trees.

"The monument was once a superb specimen of rich and curious workmanship. It is to be seen in the chancel on the left side of the altar, and is finely carved out of the stone of that part of the country. It is surrounded with the family Coat-of-Arms, which forms a handsome Emblazonment of Heraldry, and although erected more than two hundred years ago, they are still burnished with gilding, and the following interesting inscription appears :

To y^e
Memory of
Sir Laurence Washington, Nite,
Lately Chief Register
Of ye Chancerye,
Of Renown, Piety and Charitye.
An Exemplyarye, and Loving Husband, a Tender
Father, a Bountefulle· Master, a Constante
Reliever of ye Poore : and to Thoas of His Parish
A Perpetual Benefactor.
Whom it Pleased
God to Take into His Peace
From ye Furye of ye Inzuing. Warrs.
Born May XIX.
He was Heare Interred
May XXIV, An. Dni. 1643
Æ, 64,
Heare also Lyete
Dame Anne
is Wife, who Deceased
January XIIth, and who
Was Beryed XIVth,
Anno Dni. 1645.

' Hic Patrios cineres, eruruit filius urna,
Conderre qui Tumulo, nunc jacet itle prius.'

'The pyous Son His Parents here interred,
Who hath his share in time, for them prepared.'

" The ancient English homestead of the Washington
family, at Garsdon, is handsome, very old-fashioned, and·
built of stone, with immense solidity and strength. The
timber about it is chiefly oak, and in several of the rooms,
particularly the old hall or banqueting room, there are
rich remains of gilding, carved work in cornices, ceilings
and panels, polished floors and wainscoting, also shields
containing the same Coat-of-Arms as in the mural Monument in the church, carved over the lofty antique mantel-
pieces. Beneath the house are extensive cellars, which,
with the banqueting room, seem to indicate the genuine
hospitality and princely style of living peculiar to a " fine
old English gentleman, all of the olden time," and, indeed,
according to the traditions and chronicles of that region of
country, such was the general character of the heads of the

Washington family.   The walls of the house are *five* feet thick, and the entire residence is surrounded by beautiful gardens and orchards."

17 LAURENCE WASHINGTON, first child of Sir Laurence, of Garsdon, eleventh of Hon. Laurence, of Grey's Inn, first of John, first of Robert, third of Robert, first of John, first of John, first of John, second of Robert, second of Robert, first of Robert, first of Walter, fourth of Bondo, second of Akaris, first of Bardolf, second of Torfin the Dane ; was born at Garsdon, Wiltshire, about 1605.

He was Register in Chancery, 2 Charles I. (1626).   Died in 1662.

Married Elizabeth, daughter of William Guise, of Elmore, county Gloucester.   Issue :

    18 ELIZABETH WASHINGTON, daughter and heiress, and only child, born at Garsdon, about 1630, died 1693.

She married Sir Robert Shirley, Knt., first Earl of Ferrers, at Garsdon, about 1650.   He died 1717.   Had ten sons and seven daughters, of whom only five survived infancy, viz.:

    1 ROBERT, who predeceased his father, died 1699, leaving one son and a daughter, viz.:

        ROBERT, Viscount Tamworth, who also died *vitâ patris,* 1714, unmarried.

        ELIZABETH, who married James, fifth Earl of Northumberland, and succeeded, as heiress of her brother, to the Baronies of Chartley, Bouchier and Lovaine.

    2 WASHINGTON, who succeeded his father, in 1717, as second Earl of Ferrers, but died s. p., when the honors devolved upon his brother.

    3 HENRY, third Earl, at whose decease, unmarried, the title passed to his nephew.

4 LAURENCE, who married Anne, fourth child of Sir Walter Clarges, Bart., and had six sons and four daughters, of whom the three eldest sons :

    1 LAURENCE, born anno 1720, fourth Earl of Ferrers, died s. p.

    2 WASHINGTON, fifth Earl of Ferrers, died s. p.

    3 ROBERT, sixth Earl of Ferrers, had issue :

        1 ROBERT, seventh Earl of Ferrers, and

        2 WASHINGTON, present Earl.

Robert married, second wife, Anne, daughter of Sir Humphrey Ferrers, Knt., of Tamworth Castle, and heir of her grandfather, John de Ferrers.

On the 14th Jan. 1661–2, Laurence Washington, of Garsdon, county Wiltshire, made his will, in which he left an annuity of £40 per annum to his cousin John, son of Sir John Washington, of Thrapston, county Northampton, Knt.

His widow, Elizabeth, married Sir William Pargetar, Knt.

17 MARTHA WASHINGTON, second child of Sir Laurence, was born at Garsdon, Wiltshire, about 1607.

Married Sir John Tyrrell, Knt., of Springfield, county Essex.

17 MARY WASHINGTON, third child of Sir Laurence, was born at Garsdon, Wiltshire, about 1610.

Married a Horspole, of Maidstone, county Kent.

17 RANDALL WASHINGTON, first son of Robert, first of Richard, first of John, second of Robert, first of John, first of Robert, first of John, first of Peter, first of John, first of Robert, first of Robert, first of Walter, fourth of Bondo, second of Akaris, first of Bardolf, second of Torfin the

Dane; was born at Docker, county Westmoreland, in 1568.

He was aged 16 years and 6 months, at his father's death, 1584. He was living and was recusant, in 1640. First wife, Mabilla, obit 1623. Issue:

> 18 JOHN WASHINGTON, born at Docker, county Westmoreland, about 1595.
>
> 18 STEPHEN WASHINGTON, born at Docker, county Westmoreland, about 1600.
>
> 18 MARY WASHINGTON, born at Docker, county Westmoreland, in 1611.

Second wife, Maria, obit 1640.

17 RICHARD WASHINGTON, second son of Robert, was born at Docker, county Westmoreland, about 1570.

His father bequeathed to him and his brother James, the tithes of Rosegill, &c., for their lifetime.

17 JAMES WASHINGTON, third son of Robert, was born at Docker, county Westmoreland, about 1572.

His father bequeathed to him and his brother Richard, the tithes of Rosegill, &c., for their lifetime.

17 FRANCIS WASHINGTON, first child of John, fourth of Richard, first of John, second of Robert, first of John, first of Robert, first of John, first of Peter, first of John, first of Robert, first of Robert, first of Walter, fourth of Bondo, second of Akaris, first of Bardolf, second of Torfin the Dane; was born at Kendall, county Westmoreland, about 1555.

By wife Agnes, he had issue:

> 18 JOHN WASHINGTON, born at Kendall, county Westmoreland, about 1580.
>
> 18 RICHARD WASHINGTON, born at Kendall, county Westmoreland, about 1585.

18 MARGARET WASHINGTON, born at Kendall, county Westmoreland, about 1590. Married Henry Newby.

17 JOHN WASHINGTON, second child of John, was born at Kendall, county Westmoreland, about 1560.

He died there in 1685. By wife Margaret, he had issue :
18 THOMAS WASHINGTON, born at Kendall, county Westmoreland, about 1583.

18 AGNES WASHINGTON, born at Kendall, county Westmoreland, about 1585.

17 ALAN WASHINGTON, first child of Thomas, sixth of Richard, first of John, second of Robert, first of John, first of Robert, first of John, first of Peter, first of John, first of Robert, first of Robert, first of Walter, fourth of Bondo, second of Akaris, first of Bardolf, second of Torfin the Dane; was born at Kendall, county Westmoreland, about 1565.

17 THOMAS WASHINGTON, second child of Thomas, was born at Kendall, county Westmoreland, about 1568.

He settled at Grarigg, county Westmoreland. Died 1619. He had issue by his wife Ann (who was living in 1619), viz. :
18 RANDALL WASHINGTON, born at Grarigg, county Westmoreland, about 1595.

18 RICHARD WASHINGTON, born at Grarigg, county Westmoreland, about 1597.

18 MARGARET WASHINGTON, born at Grarigg, county Westmoreland, about 1600.

18 AGNES WASHINGTON, born at Grarigg, county Westmoreland, about 1605.

17 JAMES WASHINGTON, third child of Thomas, was born at Kendall, county Westmoreland, about 1570.

He settled at Grarigg, county Westmoreland. He died, 1619. By wife Anne, he had issue :

18 HENRY WASHINGTON, born at Grarigg, county Westmoreland, about 1600.

17 SIMON WASHINGTON, first child of Henry, seventh of Richard, first of John, second of Robert, first of John, first of Robert, first of John, first of Peter, first of John, first of Robert, first of Robert, first of Walter, fourth of Bondo, second of Akaris, first of Bardolf, second of Torfin the Dane; was born at Kendall, county Westmoreland, about 1580.

He settled at Sedburgh, Yorkshire. Married at Kendall, 1618, Anna Atkinson. Had issue:

18 HENRY WASHINGTON, born at Sedburgh, Yorkshire, about 1620.

17 JOHN WASHINGTON, second child of Henry, was born at Kendall, county Westmoreland, about 1582.

17 THOMAS WASHINGTON, third child of Henry, was born at Kendall, county Westmoreland, about 1585.

17 MARGARET WASHINGTON, fourth child of Henry, was born at Kendall, county Westmoreland, about 1587.

17 AGNES WASHINGTON, fifth child of Henry, was born at Kendall, county Westmoreland, about 1590.

17 MARTIN WASHINGTON, first child of James, first of Richard, first of Robert, third of Robert, first of John, first of Robert, first of John, first of Peter, first of John, first of Robert, first of Robert, first of Walter, fourth of Bondo, second of Akaris, first of Bardolf, second of Torfin the Dane; was born at Ardwick le Street, county York, 17 Aug., 1565.

"He was son and heir, aged 15 years and 12 days at his father's death, 29 Aug., 22 Elizabeth (1580)." He died 3 Aug., 23 Elizabeth (1581).

17 RICHARD WASHINGTON, second child of James, was born at Ardwick le Street, York, 25 Nov., 1566.

Heir to his brother Martin, at the time of whose death he was aged 14 years, 8 months and 8 days. To whom his father gave the Manor of Hampall, county York. He suffered a recovery of his land, 30 Elizabeth (1588). Had license to alienate the Manor of Armethorpe, 40 Elizabeth (1598). He purchased the site of the priory of Hampall, 41 Elizabeth (1599). He was treasurer of the lame soldiers, 22 James I. (1624), and died 20 April, 10 Charles I. (1634).

He married Marie, daughter of Thomas Wombwell, of Wombwell, county York. Had issue :

> **18** D'ARCY WASHINGTON, born at Ardwick le Street, county York, in 1594. .
>
> **18** PHILIP WASHINGTON, born at Ardwick le Street, county York, about 1596.
>
> **18** GREGORY WASHINGTON, born at Ardwick le Street, county York, about 1598.
>
> **18** WILLIAM WASHINGTON, born at Ardwick le Street, county York, about 1600.
>
> **18** THOMAS WASHINGTON, born at Ardwick le Street, county York, about 1602.
>
> **18** RICHARD WASHINGTON, born at Ardwick le Street, county York, about 1605.
>
> **18** FRANCIS WASHINGTON, born at Ardwick le Street, county York, about 1607.
>
> **18** ELIZABETH WASHINGTON, born at Ardwick le Street, county York, about 1610. ˙
>
> **18** MARY WASHINGTON, born at Ardwick le Street, county York, about 1612.

17 PHILIP WASHINGTON, third child of James, was born at Ardwick le Street, county York, about 1568.

His father gave him an annuity for life, of £6 13s. 4d.

17 FRANCIS WASHINGTON, fourth child of James, was born at Ardwick le Street, county York, about 1570.

His father gave him an annuity for life, of £6 13s. 4d.

17 REV. BARTHOLOMEW WASHINGTON, fifth child of James, was born at Ardwick le Street, county York, about 1572.

His father gave him an annuity for life, of £6 13s. 4d. He was executor to his father's will. He was Rector of Burgh Walys, now Wallis, county York. He died 1622.

His wife, Isabella, was executrix to his will, in 1622. He had issue :

> **18** MARMADUKE WASHINGTON, born at Ardwick le Street, county York, about 1595.
>
> **18** GREGORY WASHINGTON, born at Ardwick le Street, county York, about 1597.
>
> **18** BARTHOLOMEW WASHINGTON, born at Ardwick le Street, county York, about 1600.
>
> **18** ANNE WASHINGTON, born at Ardwick le Street, county York, about 1602.
>
> **18** MARGARET WASHINGTON, born at Ardwick le Street, county York, about 1605.

17 LUCY WASHINGTON, sixth child of James, was born at Ardwick le Street, county York, about 1575.

17 MARY WASHINGTON, seventh child of James, was born at Ardwick le Street, county York, about 1577.

17 CATHARINE WASHINGTON, eighth child of James, was born at Ardwick le Street, county York, about 1580.

17 JANE WASHINGTON, ninth child of James, was born at Ardwick le Street, county York, about 1582.

17 RANULPH WASHINGTON, first child of Ranulph, second of Richard, first of Robert, third of Robert, first of John, first of Robert, first of John, first of Peter, first of John, first of Robert, first of Robert, first of Walter, fourth of Bondo, second of Akaris, first of Bardolf, second of Torfin the Dane; was born at Billeker, county Westmoreland, about 1560.

He settled at Threapland, county Westmoreland. Sold his lands, 27 James I. (1629). He had issue :

 18 RICHARD WASHINGTON, born at Threapland, county Westmoreland, about 1600.

17 **LAURENCE WASHINGTON,** first son of Laurence, first of Thomas, first of Robert, first of John, first of Robert, first of John, first of John, first of John, second of Robert, second of Robert, first of Robert, first of Walter, fourth of Bondo, second of Akaris, first of Bardolf, second of Torfin the ~~Dane~~; was born at Warton, county Lancaster, about 1540.

He was living 30 Elizabeth (1588). He had issue :

 18 LAURENCE WASHINGTON, born at Warton, county Lancaster, A. D. 1569.

17 LEONARD WASHINGTON, second child of Laurence, was born at Warton, county Lancaster, about 1545.

He married Elizabeth Crofts. She died in year 1588. He had issue :

 18 JOHN WASHINGTON, born at Warton, county Lancaster, about 1580.

17 ROBERT WASHINGTON, third child of Laurence, was born at Warton, county Lancaster, about 1550.

He was living in 1588. He had issue :

 18 ROBERT WASHINGTON, born at Warton, county Lancaster, about 1580.

17 ROBERT WASHINGTON, first son of Leonard, second of Thomas, first of Robert, first of John, first of Robert, first of John, first of John, first of John, second of Rob-

ert, second of Robert, first of Robert, first of Walter, fourth of Bondo, second of Akaris, first of Bardolf, second of Torfin the Dane ; was born at Warton, county Lancaster, about 1550.

Will dated 1588, bequeathed his lands to his son, and the heirs begotten of his body. Default to Robert, the son of Robert, who was the son of Laurence Washington. He had only son :

18 LEONARD WASHINGTON, born at Warton, county Lancaster, about 1575.

17 LAURENCE WASHINGTON, first child of Robert, first of Hon. Laurence, first of John, first of Robert, third of Robert, first of John, first of John, first of John, second of Robert, second of Robert, first of Robert, first of Walter, fourth of Bondo, second of Akaris, first of Bardolf, second of Torfin the Dane ; was born at Sulgrave, county Northampton, about 1565.

He died at Brington, Northampton, 13 Dec., 1616. He married, 3 Aug., 1588, Margaret, daughter of William Butler, of Tighes, county Sussex. His children were :

18 SIR WILLIAM WASHINGTON, baptized at Sulgrave, county Northampton, about 1589.

18 SIR JOHN WASHINGTON, baptized at Sulgrave, Northamptonshire, about 1591.

18 ROBERT WASHINGTON, baptized at Sulgrave, Northamptonshire, about 1593.

18 LUCY WASHINGTON, baptized at Brington, Northamptonshire, about 1595.

18 LAURENCE WASHINGTON, baptized at Sulgrave, Northamptonshire, about 1597.

18 RICHARD WASHINGTON, baptized at Sulgrave, Northamptonshire, about 1600.

18 AMY WASHINGTON, baptized at Sulgrave, Northampton, about 1602.

18 THOMAS WASHINGTON, baptized at Sulgrave, North-amptonshire, about 1605.

18 GREGORY WASHINGTON, baptized at Brington, North-amptonshire, 16 Jan., 1607. Died, and was buried, 17 Jan., 1607.

18 GEORGE WASHINGTON, baptized at Wormleighton, county Warwick, 3 Aug., 1608.

18 JOAN WASHINGTON, baptized at Brington, North-amptonshire, about 1610.

18 ELIZABETH WASHINGTON, baptized at Brington, Northamptonshire, about 1612.

18 BARBARA WASHINGTON, baptized at Brighton, Sussex, about 1615.

At his death he held a Manor of Lord Spencer, named Wicke, in Northamptonshire.

"There is a monument erected to the memory of Laurence Washington, in the chancel of the Brington church, in Northamptonshire, a slab displaying the family arms with those of his wife ; and an inscription in Latin and English. From the first we learn that he had eight sons and nine daughters."

17 ROBERT WASHINGTON, second child of Robert, was born at Sulgrave, county Northampton, about 1567.

He settled at Brighton, county Sussex, and died 1612. He married Elizabeth, daughter of John Cheshall, of Moore Hall, Essex.

"Married Elizabeth, who survived her husband. She left, by her will, dated 17 Mar., 1722–3, among other legacies, to her nephews and nieces, £100 to her nephew, Sir William Washington."

17 WALTER WASHINGTON, third child of Robert, was born at Sulgrave, county Northampton, about 1570. Died infant.

17 WALTER WASHINGTON, fourth child of Robert, was born at Sulgrave, county Northampton, about 1575.

He settled at Redway, county Warwick. He married Katharine Murdon, of Radcliff, county Warwick.

17 ROBERT WASHINGTON, fifth child of Robert, was born at Sulgrave, county Northampton, about 1595.

17 MARGARET WASHINGTON, sixth child of Robert, was born at Sulgrave, county Northampton, about 1597.
She married John Gardiner, of London. Children given in his line.

17 ALBANY WASHINGTON, seventh child of Robert, was born at Sulgrave, county Northampton, in year 1599.
"He was aged 19 years in 1618."

17 GUY WASHINGTON, eighth child of Robert, was born at Sulgrave, county Northampton, about 1602.

18 JOHN WASHINGTON, first child of Randall, first of Robert, first of Richard, first of John, second of Robert, first of John, second of Robert, first of John, first of Peter, first of John, first of Robert, first of Robert, first of Walter, fourth of Bondo, second of Akaris, first of Bardolf, second of Torfin the Dane; was born at Docker, county Westmoreland, about 1595.
He was recusant in 1640. His wife, Jane, was also recusant in 1640. He had issue:
    19 WILLIAM WASHINGTON, born at Docker, county Westmoreland, about 1620. Obit 1624.

18 STEPHEN WASHINGTON, second child of Randall, was born at Docker, county Westmoreland, acout 1600.
He settled at Kendall, county Westmoreland. He purchased lands in Sedburgh and Hewgill, 2 Charles I. (1626). He had issue:
    19 RICHARD WASHINGTON, of Kendall, who was living 20 Charles II. (1668).

18 MARY WASHINGTON, fifth child of Randall, was born at Docker, county Westmoreland, about 1611.

18 JOHN WASHINGTON, first child of Francis, first of John, fourth of Richard, first of John, second of Robert, first of John, first of Robert, first of John, first of Peter, first of John, first of Robert, first of Robert, first of Walter, fourth of Bondo, second of Akaris, first of Bardolf, second of Torfin the Dane; was born at Kendall, county Westmoreland, about 1580.

18 RICHARD WASHINGTON, second child of Francis, was born at Kendall, county Westmoreland, about 1585.

18 MARGARET WASHINGTON, third child of Francis, was born at Kendall, county Westmoreland, about 1590. Married Henry Newby.

18 THOMAS WASHINGTON, first child of John, second of John, fourth of Richard, first of John, second of Robert, first of John, second of Robert, first of John, first of Peter, first of John, first of Robert, first of Robert, first of Walter, fourth of Bondo, second of Akaris, first of Bardolf, second of Torfin the Dane; was born at Kendall, county Westmoreland, about 1583. He died 1617.

He married, in 1606, Elizabeth Moore. She died 1616. He had issue :

    19 MARGARET WASHINGTON, born at Kendall, county Westmoreland, in 1607.

    19 THOMAS WASHINGTON, born at Kendall, county Westmoreland, in 1609.

    19 JOHN WASHINGTON, born at Kendall, county Westmoreland, in 1612.

    19 ISABELLA WASHINGTON, born at Kendall, county Westmoreland, in 1616.

    19 ELIZABETH WASHINGTON, born at Kendall, county

6

Westmoreland, about 1620. Married, 1641, to Richard Jordan.

18 AGNES WASHINGTON, second child of John, was born at Kendall, county Westmoreland, about 1585.

18 RANDALL WASHINGTON, first child of Thomas, second of Thomas, sixth of Richard, first of John, second of Robert, first of John, first of Robert, first of John, first of Peter, first of John, first of Robert, first of Walter, fourth of Bondo, second of Akaris, first of Bardolf, second of Torfin the Dane ; was born at Grarigg, county Westmoreland, about 1595.
He was recusant, 3 Charles I. (1627), and died in 1627.

18 RICHARD WASHINGTON, second child of Thomas, was born at Grarigg, county Westmoreland, about 1597.

18 MARGARET WASHINGTON, third child of Thomas, was born at Grarigg, county Westmoreland, about 1601.

18 AGNES WASHINGTON, fourth child of Thomas, was born at Grarigg, county Westmoreland, about 1605.

18 HENRY WASHINGTON, first child of James, third of Thomas, sixth of Richard, first of John, second of Robert, first of John, second of Robert, first of John, first of Peter, first of John, first of Robert, first of Robert, first of Walter, fourth of Bondo, second of Akaris, first of Bardolf, second of Torfin the Dane ; was born at Grarigg, county Westmoreland, about 1600.
He settled at Kinkley, Lonesdale. By wife Anne Binks, of Sudburgh, he had issue :

19 SIMON WASHINGTON, born at Kinkley, Lonesdale, in 1629.

19 MATILDA WASHINGTON, born at Kinkley, Lonesdale, in 1634.

19 DOROTHY WASHINGTON, born at Kinkley, Lonesdale, about 1636.

18 HENRY WASHINGTON, first child of Simon, first of Henry, seventh of Richard, first of John, second of Robert, first of John, second of Robert, first of John, first of Peter, first of John, first of Robert, first of Robert, first of Walter, fourth of Bondo, second of Akaris, first of Bardolf, second of Torfin the Dane; was born at Sedburgh, county York, about 1620.

He was of Kinkley, in Lonesdale, in 20 Charles II. (1680). By wife Dorothy, he had issue :

19 SIMON WASHINGTON, of Kinkley, in Lonesdale. He was living in 1700.

18 D'ARCY WASHINGTON, first child of Richard, second of James, first of Richard, first of Robert, third of Robert, first of John, first of Robert, first of John, first of Peter, first of John, first of Robert, first of Robert, first of Walter, fourth of Bondo, second of Akaris, first of Bardolf, second of Torfin the Dane · was born at Ardwick le Street, county York, in 1594.

"He was 40 years of age at his father's death, 10 Charles I. (1634)." He was seized of the Manor of Hamphall. He sold lands at Ardwick le Street, 31 Charles II. (1691).

He married, 9 James I. (1611), Anne, daughter of Mathew Wentworth, of Bretton. He had issue :

19 JAMES WASHINGTON, born at Ardwick le Street, county York, about 1612.

19 D'ARCY WASHINGTON, born at Ardwick le Street, county York, about 1615.

19 MATHEW WASHINGTON, born at Ardwick le Street, county York, about 1617.

19 ANNE WASHINGTON, was born at Ardwick le Street, county York, about 1620.

19 GRACE WASHINGTON, born at Ardwick le Street, county York, about 1622.

19 MARY WASHINGTON, born at Ardwick le Street, county York, about 1625.

19 SARAH WASHINGTON, born at Ardwick le Street, county York, about 1630.

19 ELIZABETH WASHINGTON, born at Ardwick le Street, county York, about 1632.

19 ROBERT WASHINGTON, born at Ardwick le Street, county York, about 1635.

18 PHILIP WASHINGTON, second child of Richard, was born at Ardwick le Street, county York, about 1596.
He was of the university of Oxford, and died, 1635.

18 GREGORY WASHINGTON, third child of Richard, was born at Ardwick le Street, county York, about 1598.

18 WILLIAM WASHINGTON, fourth child of Richard, was born at Ardwick le Street, county York, about 1600.

18 THOMAS WASHINGTON, fifth child of Richard, was born at Ardwick le Street, county York, about 1602.

18 RICHARD WASHINGTON, sixth child of Richard, was born at Ardwick le Street, county York, about 1605.
He was of the University College of Oxford, and Provost of Trinity College, of Dublin, in 1640.

18 FRANCES WASHINGTON, seventh child of Richard, was born at Ardwick le Street, county York, about 1607.
She married Roger Kelvert, of London, merchant. Children given in his line.

18 Elizabeth Washington, eighth child of Richard, was born at Ardwick le Street, county York, about 1610.

18 Mary Washington, ninth child of Richard, was born at Ardwick le Street, county York, about 1612.

18 Marmaduke Washington, first child of Rev. Bartholomew, fifth of James, first of Richard, first of Robert, third of Robert, first of John, first of Robert, first of John, first of Peter, first of John, first of Robert, first of Robert, first of Walter, fourth of Bondo, second of Akaris, first of Bardolf, second of Torfin the Dane ; was born at Ardwick le Street, county York, about 1595.

18 Gregory Washington, second child of Rev. Bartholomew, was born at Ardwick le Street, county York, about 1597.

18 Bartholomew Washington, third child of Rev. Bartholomew, was born at Ardwick le Street, county York, about 1600.
He was of Lincolnshire.

18 Anne Washington, fourth child of Rev. Bartholomew, was born at Ardwick le Street, county York, about 1602.

18 Margaret Washington, fifth child of Rev. Bartholomew, was born at Ardwick le Street, county York, about 1605.

18 Richard Washington, first child of Ranulph, first of Ranulph, second of Richard, first of Robert, third of Robert, first of John, first of Robert, first of John, first of Peter, first of John, first of Robert, first of Robert, first of Walter, fourth of Bondo, second of Akaris, first

of Bardolf, second of Torfin the ~~Dane~~; was born at Threapland, county Westmoreland, about 1600.

Son and heir, joined his father in the sale of his estates, 22 James I. (1624).

18 **LAURENCE WASHINGTON**, first son of Laurence, first of Laurence, first of Thomas, first of Robert, first of John, first of Robert, first of John, first of John, first of John, second of Robert, second of Robert, first of Robert, first of Walter, fourth of Bondo, second of Akaris, first of Bardolf, second of Torfin the ~~Dane~~; was born at Warton, county Lancaster, in year 1569.

He was of Warton, 1 James (1603), 1 and 4 Charles I. (1625–1629). He had three sons, viz. :

19 Leonard Washington, born at Warton, county Lancaster, about 1595.

19 Laurence Washington, born at Warton, county Lancaster, about 1597.

19 Thomas Washington, born at Warton, county Lancaster, about 1600.

18 John Washington, first son of Leonard, second of Laurence, first of Thomas, first of Robert, first of John, first of Robert, first of John, first of John, first of John, second of Robert, second of Robert, first of Robert, first of Walter, fourth of Bondo, second of Akaris, first of Bardolf, second of Torfin the Dane; was born at Warton, county Lancaster, about 1580. He had issue :

19 Alicia Washington, baptized at Warton, county Lancaster, A. D. 1616.

19 James Washington, baptized at Warton, county Lancaster, A. D. 1619.

18 Robert Washington, first child of Robert, third of Laurence, first of Thomas, first of Robert, first of John,

first of Robert, first of John, first of John, first of John,
second of Robert, second of Robert, first of Robert, first
of Walter, fourth of Bondo, second of Akaris, first of
Bardolf, second of Torfin the Dane ; was born at Warton, county Lancaster, about 1580.
He was living in 1588.

18 LEONARD WASHINGTON, only child of Robert, first of
Leonard, second of Thomas, first of Robert, first of John,
first of Robert, first of John, first of John, first of John,
second of Robert, second of Robert, first of Robert,
first of Walter, fourth of Bondo, second of Akaris, first
of Bardolf, second of Torfin the Dane ; was born at
Warton, county Lancaster, about 1575.
He was of Yeland, in Warton, county Lancaster... He
had issue :
    19 JOHN WASHINGTON, born at Yeland, Warton, county
    Lancaster, about 1597.

18 SIR WILLIAM WASHINGTON, Knight, of Pakyngton,
county Leicester, first child of Laurence, first of Robert,
first of Hon. Laurence, first of John, first of Robert,
third of Robert, first of John, first of John, first of John,
second of Robert, second of Robert, first of Robert,
first of Walter, fourth of Bondo, second of Akaris, first
of Bardolf, second of Torfin the Dane ; was born at Sulgrave, county Northumberland, about 1589. Obit 1643.
He was buried at St. Martin in the Field, at London, 22
June, 1643.
He married Agnes or Anne, half sister of Geo. Villars,
Duke of Buckingham. She was buried at Chelsea, 25
May, 1643. He had issue :
    19 HENRY WASHINGTON, born at Sulgrave, county
    Northumberland, in 1615.
    19 GEORGE WASHINGTON, born at Sulgrave, county
    Northumberland, about 1617.

19 CHRISTOPHER WASHINGTON, born at Sulgrave, county Northumberland, about 1620.

19 ELIZABETH WASHINGTON, born at Sulgrave, county Northumberland, about 1622.

19 SUSANNA WASHINGTON, born at Sulgrave, county Northumberland, about 1625.

19 CATHARINE WASHINGTON, born at Sulgrave, county Northumberland, about 1627.

"Sir William Washington owned the Manor of Lack-hampstead, county Bucks, at time of death."

His aunt Elizabeth, widow of his uncle Robert, by her will, dated 17 Mar., 1723, bequeathed £100 to her nephew, Sir William Washington.

He was knighted at Theobalds, 17 Jan., 1622. After the marriage of his half sister, the Duke of Buckingham appears to have taken the whole family under his protection, and advanced their fortunes in various ways until the time of his death.

Sir William Washington was of Packington, county Lancaster, in 1618.

In his will, 6 June, 1643, he gives his residence as at Thistleworth (Isleworth), county Middlesex, and directs his Manor of Wicke, and Wicke farm, shall be sold. This Manor was in the parish of Isleworth, and had been purchased, in 1638, by Sir William Washington, from the co-heirs of Sir Michael Stanhope, but he was compelled to mortgage it, in 1640, to Sir Edward Spencer and Sir Richard Wynne, and it was in possession of the latter at his death, in 1649.

18 SIR JOHN WASHINGTON, Knight, of Thrapston, county Northampton, second child of Laurence, was born at Sulgrave, Northamptonshire, about 1591. Obit 1663. He married, by license, at St. Leonard's, Shoreditch, 14 June, 1621, Mary, daughter of Philip Curtis. She died 1 Jan.,

1625. Her mother's will, dated 6 Dec., 1622, bequeathed
£50 to her daughter's son Mordaunt as a legacy. Issue :
  19 MORDAUNT WASHINGTON, born at Thrapston, county
  Northampton, in 1622.
  19 JOHN WASHINGTON, born at Thrapston, county
  Northampton, about 1624.
  19 PHILIP WASHINGTON, born at Thrapston, county
  Northampton, about 1626.

He married second wife, widow Dorothy Kirkbey. No
child by second wife.

He was knighted at Newmarket, 21 Feb., 1623.

Mary, wife of Sir John Washington, died, Jan. 1, 1625,
and was buried in the church of Islip, Northamptonshire, where her monument still exist, bears the following
inscription : "Here lieth yᵉ body of Dame Mary, wife unto
Sir John Washington, Knight, daughter of Phillipe Curtis,
gent, who had issue by hur sayd husbande, three sonns, Mordaunt, John, and Phillipe. Deceased the 1 Janu. 1624-5."

Among the Royalist Composition Papers at the Public
Revenue office, in the case of the Earl of Northampton,
there is an affidavit of a tenant who had paid £218 to
Thomas Farrer, for the use of the said Earl and Sir John
Washington. Farrer responds that what sums of money
he had received out of the estate of James, Earl of Northampton, had been so received, " as Agent, and on behalf of
Sir John Washington, by virtue of an extent, which the said
Sir John had on said estate in the county of Bedford,".
whereupon it was ordered on the 23 Feb., 1653-4, "that a
letter be written to Sir John Washington, to pay in the
money or show cause."

Sir John Washington died before Oct. 6, 1678, on which
day his widow Dorothy made her will, and described her-
self as "Relict of Sir John Washington, Knight, deceased."
She directed to be buried in the chancel of the church of
Fordham, in Cambridgeshire, near her grandchild Mrs.
Penelope Audley. She had no issue by second husband.

18 ROBERT WASHINGTON, third child of Laurence, was born at Sulgrave, Northamptonshire, about 1593.

18 LUCY WASHINGTON, fourth child of Laurence, was born at Sulgrave, Northamptonshire, about 1595.

18 REV. LAURENCE WASHINGTON, fifth child of Laurence, was born at Sulgrave, Northamptonshire, about 1597. He was a student at Oxford, in 1622. Parson of the church at Purlingham, county Essex, in 1633. He was of Brasenose College, and matriculated, 2 Nov., 1621. Record, " Laurent Washington, Northamp. Gen. fil. an nat. 19,"—*i. e.*, Laurence Washington, of Northamptonshire, whose father's rank was that of a gentleman, and whose own age was 19 at his last birthday.

The will of his aunt Elizabeth, widow of his uncle Robert, dated 17 Mar., 1623, leaves him her husband's seal ring, and states that he was then of Oxford.

He took his B. A. degree in 1623, and became Fellow of Brasenose, in 1624. He served as lector, the principal educational office in the college, from 1627 to 1632 inclusive.

26 Aug., 1631, he became one of the proctors of the University ; 14 Mar., 1632–3, he was presented to the then very valuable living of Purleigh, in Essex, and resigned his fellowship. He continued at Purleigh until 1643, when he was " ejected by sequestration for his loyalty in the late rebellion of 1642."

He continued in his profession of clergyman after the Restoration.

18 RICHARD WASHINGTON, sixth child of Laurence, was born at Sulgrave, Northamptonshire, about 1600.

He was apprenticed, 7 July, 1614, under the auspices of the Clothworker's Company, to Richard Brent, of London.

18 AMY WASHINGTON, seventh child of Laurence, was born at Sulgrave, county Northampton, about 1602.

She married at Brington, Philip Curtis, of Brington, Northampton, 3 Aug., 1620. Daughter :

    19 KATHARINE CURTIS, born at Sulgrave, county Northampton, about 1622.

The will of Philip Curtis was nuncupative, and made 19 May, 1636, in presence of Sir John Washington, Knight, and another. He bequeathed £1,000 to his daughter Katharine, when of age or married, and to his nephews John and Philip Washington, each £50, when of age. His nephew Mordaunt, he commended to the kindness of his wife, to whom he bequeathed the residue of his .estate, and appointed as guardians of his daughter, the clergyman of the parish, and "Sir John Washington, of Thrapston, in the county of Northampton, Knight." The will was proved on 30 May, 1636, by his relict Amy Curtis, and on the ensuing 30 June, she made her own will. After directing to be buried in the Chancel of Islip, near her husband, she proceeds substantially as follows :

"Whereas, there was given to my nephew Mordaunt Washington, the eldest son of Sir John Washington, Knight, by the last will and testament of his grandmother Curtis, deceased, the sum of £50. .I now give to said Mordaunt £250 more, to be employed for his benefit till he becomes of age or married.

"Whereas, my husband, lately deceased, gave to John Washington, second son of Sir John Washington, Knight, £50. I now give to said John, my nephew, £50 more, to be employed to his use till he be of age, &c.

"Whereas, my husband, lately deceased, gave by his last will, to my nephew Philip Washington, third son of Sir John Washington, Knight, £50. I now give him £50 more, &c.

"Whereas, my husband, Philip Curtis, by his last will, gave me and my heirs forever, all his lands, houses, &c. I now give the same to my only daughter, Katharine Curtis, and her heirs forever, as well as the residue of all my es-

tate, and appoint 'my dear and loving mother, Margaret
Washington, and my loving brother, Sir John Washington,
Knight,' to be her guardians."

One of the witnesses was her brother, William Washington.   Administration granted to Sir John Washington,
Knight, 19 Nov., 1636.

18 THOMAS WASHINGTON, eighth child of Laurence, was
    born at Sulgrave, county Northumberland, A. D. 1605.

He died in Spain.   He was attached to the Suite of
Prince Charles, on the occasion of his memorable matrimonial expedition to Spain.   He died at Madrid, in 1623,
aged 18 (*Howell's Letters*).

18 GREGORY WASHINGTON, ninth child of Laurence, was
    baptized at Brington, Northamptonshire, 16 Jan., 1607.
    Died 17 Jan., 1607.

18 GEORGE WASHINGTON, tenth child of Laurence, was
    baptized at Wormleighton, Warwickshire, 3 Aug., 1608.
    He went as a soldier to Bergen ap Zoon, in 1631.

18 JOAN WASHINGTON, eleventh child of Laurence, was
    born at Brington, Northamptonshire, about 1610.
    She married Francis Pill, of Midford.

18 ELIZABETH WASHINGTON, twelfth child of Laurence,
    was born at Brington, county Northampton, about 1612.
    She married Francis Mauce, or Mewce, or Mews, of
Holdenby.

18 BARBARA WASHINGTON, thirteenth child of Laurence,
    was born at Brington, county Northampton, about
    1615.
    She married Simon Butler, of Appleton, or Appletree,

Northamptonshire. She thus became the ancestress of Alban Butler, author of the " Lives of the Saints."

19 RICHARD WASHINGTON, first child of Stephen, second of Randall, first of Robert, first of Richard, first of John, second of Robert, first of John, second of Robert, first of John, first of Peter, first of John, first of Robert, first of Robert, first of Walter, fourth of Bondo, second of Akaris, first of Bardolf, second of Torfin the Dane ; was born at Kendall, county Westmoreland, about 1625.. He was living, 20 Charles II. (1668).

19 MARGARET WASHINGTON, first child of Thomas, first of John, second of John, fourth of Richard, first of John, second of Robert, first of John, second of Robert, first of John, first of Peter, first of John, first of Robert, first of Robert, first of Walter, fourth of Bondo, second of Akaris, first of Bardolf, second of Torfin the Dane ; was born at Kendall, county Westmoreland, in 1607.

19 THOMAS WASHINGTON, second child of Thomas,.was born at Kendall, county Westmoreland, in 1609.

19 JOHN WASHINGTON, third child of Thomas, was born at Kendall, county Westmoreland, in 1612.

19 ISABELLA WASHINGTON, fourth child of Thomas, was born at Kendall, county Westmoreland, in 1616.

19 ELIZABETH WASHINGTON, fifth child of Thomas, was born at Kendall, county Westmoreland, in 1618. Married, 1641, Richard Jordan.

19 SIMON WASHINGTON, first child of Henry, first of James, third of Thomas, sixth of Richard, first of John, second of Robert, first of John, second of Robert, first of John, first of Peter, first of John, first of Robert, first of Robert, first of Walter, fourth of Bondo, second of Akaris, first of Bardolf, second of Torfin the ~~Dane~~ ; was born at Kinkley, Lonsdale, Eng., in 1629.

He was of Cockermuth, county Cumberland. He was living, 20 Charles II. (1668).

19 MATILDA WASHINGTON, second child of Henry, was born at Kinkley, Lonsdale, Eng., in 1634. Died, 1636.

19 DOROTHY WASHINGTON, third child of Henry, was born at Kinkley, Lonsdale, Eng., 1636. Died 1643.

19 SIMON WASHINGTON, first child of Henry, first of Simon, first of Henry, seventh of Richard, first of John, second of Robert, first of John, second of Robert, first of John, first of Peter, first of John, first of Robert, first of Robert, first of Walter, fourth of Bondo, second of Akaris, first of Bardolf, second of Torfin the ~~Dane~~ ; was born at Kinkley, Lonsdale, Eng., about 1645.

He was living in 1700.

19 JAMES WASHINGTON, first child of D'Arcy, first of Richard, second of James, first of Richard, first of Robert, third of Robert, first of John, first of Robert, first of John, first of Peter, first of John, first of Robert, first of Robert, first of Walter, fourth of Bondo, second of Akaris, first of Bardolf, second of Torfin the ~~Dane~~ ; was born at Ardwick le Street, county York, about 1612.

He was Lieutenant Colonel in the army of King Charles I., and slain at the siege of Pontifract. He married Elizabeth, daughter of William Copley, of Sportborough, county York. He had issue :

    20 RICHARD WASHINGTON, born at Ardwick le Street, county York, in year 1639.

    20 FOLJAMBE WASHINGTON, born at Ardwick le Street, county York, about 1641.

20 GODFREY WASHINGTON, born at Ardwick le Street, county York, about 1643.

20 DOROTHY WASHINGTON, born at Ardwick le Street, county York, about 1645.

20 MARY WASHINGTON, born at Ardwick le Street, county York, about 1646.

20 FRANCIS WASHINGTON, born at Ardwick le Street, county York, about 1648.

His widow married second husband, Stephen Eyre.

19 D'ARCY WASHINGTON, second child of D'Arcy, was born at Ardwick le Street, county York, about 1615.

19 MATHEW WASHINGTON, third child of D'Arcy, was born at Ardwick le Street, county York, about 1617.

19 ANNE WASHINGTON, fourth child of D'Arcy, was born at Ardwick le Street, county York, about 1620.
Married George Gill, of Notton, county Derby.

19 GRACE WASHINGTON, fifth child of D'Arcy, was born at Ardwick le Street, county York, about 1622.
Married Thomas Stanhope, of Hamphall, county ——.

19 MARY WASHINGTON, sixth child of D'Arcy, was born at Ardwick le Street, county York, about 1625.
Married John Robinson, of Pickburne.

19 SARAH WASHINGTON, seventh child of D'Arcy, was born· at Ardwick le Street, county York, about 1630.
Married Godfrey, son of Godfrey Copley, of Shelbrook, county York.

19 ELIZABETH WASHINGTON, eighth child of D'Arcy, was born at Ardwick le Street, county York, about 1632.

19 ROBERT WASHINGTON, ninth child of D'Arcy, was born
   at Ardwick le Street, county York, about 1635. He settled
   at Leeds, county York. He had issue :
 20 JOSEPH WASHINGTON, born at Leeds, county York,
  about 1660.

19 **LEONARD WASHINGTON**, first child of Laurence, first
   of Laurence, first of Laurence, first of Thomas, first of
   Robert, first of John, first of Robert, first of John, first of
   John, first of John, second of Robert, second of Robert,
   first of Robert, first of Walter, fourth of Bondo, second
   of Akaris, first of Bardolf, second of Torfin the Dane ;
   was born at Warton, county Lancaster, about 1595.
 He was recusant 1640. Obit 1657. He married Anne.
She was recusant 1640. He had issue :
 20 ROBERT WASHINGTON, baptized at Warton, county
  Lancaster, A. D. 1616.
 20 JANE WASHINGTON, baptized at Warton, county
  Lancaster, A. D. 1619.
 20 FRANCIS WASHINGTON, baptized at Warton, county
  Lancaster, A. D. 1622.
 20 LAURENCE WASHINGTON, baptized at Warton, county
  Lancaster, A. D. 1625.
 20 JOHN WASHINGTON, baptized at Warton, county
  Lancaster, A. D. 1627 (Laurence and John emigrated
  to America, A. D. 1659).

19 LAURENCE WASHINGTON, second child of Laurence, was
   born at Warton, county Lancaster, about 1597. He was
   recusant 1640. He had issue :
 20 ELEANOR WASHINGTON, baptized at Warton, county
  Lancaster, 1638.
 20 LEONARD WASHINGTON, baptized at Warton, county
  Lancaster, 1645.

19 THOMAS WASHINGTON, third child of Laurence, was born
   at Warton, county Lancaster, about 1600. Obit 1658.

19 ALICIA WASHINGTON, first child of John, first of Leonard, second of Laurence, first of Thomas, first of Robert, first of John, first of Robert, first of John, first of John, first of John, second of Robert, second of Robert, first of Robert, first of Walter, fourth of Bondo, second of Akaris, first of Bardolf, second of Torfin the ~~Dane~~; was baptized at Warton, county Lancaster, in 1616.

19 JAMES WASHINGTON, second child of John, was baptized at Warton, county Lancaster, in 1619.

19 JOHN WASHINGTON, first child of Leonard, first of Robert, first of Leonard, second of Thomas, first of Robert, first of John, first of Robert, first of John, first of John, first of John, second of Robert, second of Robert, first of Robert, first of Walter, fourth of Bondo, second of Akaris, first of Bardolf, second of Torfin the Dane; was born at Yeland, in Warton, county Lancaster, about 1597. He had issue:

    20 CHRISTOPHER WASHINGTON, baptized at Yeland, in Warton, county Lancaster, in 1619.

19 HENRY WASHINGTON, first child of Sir William Washington, Knight, of Pakyngton, county Leicester, first of Laurence, first of Robert, first of Hon. Laurence, first of John, first of Robert, third of Robert, first of John, first of John, first of John, second of Robert, second of Robert, first of Robert, first of Walter, fourth of Bondo, second of Akaris, first of Bardolf, second of Torfin the Dane; was born at Sulgrave, county Northampton, in 1615.
"He was aged 3 years, in 1618. He levied a fine on the Manor of North Cave, county York, in 1694." He had issue:

    20 RICHARD WASHINGTON, born at North Cave, county York, about 1640.

7

19 GEORGE WASHINGTON, second child of Sir William Washington, Knight, was born at North Cave, county York, about 1617.

19 CHRISTOPHER WASHINGTON, third child of Sir William Washington, Knight, was born at North Cave, county York, about 1620.

19 ELIZABETH WASHINGTON, fourth child of Sir William Washington, Knight, was born at North Cave, county York, about 1622.
Married George Legg, Lord Dartmouth.

19 SUSAN WASHINGTON, fifth child of Sir William Washington, Knight, was born at North Cave, county York, about 1625.
Married Reginald Graham.

19 CATHARINE WASHINGTON, sixth child of Sir William Washington, Knight, was born at North Cave, county York, about 1627.

19 MORDAUNT WASHINGTON, first child of Sir John Washington, Knight, of Thrapston, county Northampton, seventh of Laurence, first of Robert, first of Hon. Laurence, first of John, first of Robert, third of Robert, first of John, first of John, first of John, second of Robert, second of Robert, first of Robert, first of Walter, fourth of Bondo, second of Akaris, first of Bardolf, second of Torfin the Dane; was born at Thrapston, county Northampton, A. D. 1622.
He settled at Althorpe, in 1640.

19 JOHN WASHINGTON, second child of Sir John Washington, Knight, of Thrapston, was born at Thrapston, county Northampton, about 1624.
Was living, 1640.

19 PHILIP WASHINGTON, third child of Sir John Washington, Knight, of Thrapston, was born at Thrapston, county Northampton, about 1626.

Was living, 1640.

20 RICHARD WASHINGTON, first child of James, first of D'Arcy, first of Richard, second of James, first of Richard, first of Robert, third of Robert, first of John, first of Robert, first of John, first of Peter, first of John, first of Robert, first of Robert, first of Walter, fourth of Bondo, second of Akaris, first of Bardolf, second of Torfin the Dane ; was born at Ardwick le Street, county York, in year 1639.

He was captain of the trained band at the age of 38. In 1666 he levied a fine on the Manor of Ardwick. He died in 1678, aged 39.

He married Elizabeth ap Rees, of Washingly, county Huntingdon. Had issue :

> 21 RICHARD WASHINGTON, baptized at Ardwick le Street, county York, in 1673.
>
> 21 JAMES WASHINGTON, born at Ardwick le Street, county York, about 1675.
>
> 21 ROBERT WASHINGTON, born at Ardwick le Street, county York, about 1677.
>
> 21 ELIZABETH WASHINGTON, born at Ardwick le Street, county York, about 1680.
>
> 21 MARY WASHINGTON, born at Ardwick le Street, county York, about 1682.

20 FOLJAMBE WASHINGTON, second child of James, was born at Ardwick le Street, county York, about 1641. Died s. p., in 1678.

He was buried at Barnesley, county York, 1678.

20 GODFREY WASHINGTON, third child of James, was born at Ardwick le Street, county York, about 1643. Died unmarried, in 1709.

20 DOROTHY WASHINGTON, fourth child of James, was born at Ardwick le Street, county York, about 1645.

She married Henry Dore, of Tolmyth, county York.

20 MARY WASHINGTON, fifth child of James, was born at · Ardwick le Street, county York, about 1646.

Married Robert Eyre, of Holmsfield, county York.

20 REV. FRANCIS WASHINGTON, sixth child of James, was born at Ardwick le Street, county York, about 1648.

He was Rector of Sprotsborough, county York. He married, in 1669, Elizabeth Bower, of Sprotsborough, county York. Had issue :

    21 GEORGE WASHINGTON, born at Sprotsborough, county York, about 1670.

    21 ELIZABETH WASHINGTON, born at Sprotsborough, county York, about 1672.

    21 ANNE WASHINGTON, born at Sprotsborough, county York, about 1675.

    21 FRANCES WASHINGTON, born at Sprotsborough, county York, about 1677.

    21 GRACE WASHINGTON, born at Sprotsborough, county York, about 1680. Died infant.

20 JOSEPH WASHINGTON, first child of Robert, ninth of D'Arcy, first of Richard, second of James, first of Richard, first of Robert, third of Robert, first of John, first of Robert, first of John, first of Peter, first of John, first of Robert, first of Robert, first of Walter, fourth of Bondo, second of Akaris, first of Bardolf, second of Torfin the Dane ; was born at Leeds, county York, about 1660.

He was of the Inner Temple, London, a favorite of Sir John Somers, the Lord Keeper. He was buried in the Temple Church, London, 1 Mar., 1693.

20 ROBERT WASHINGTON, first child of Leonard, first of
Laurence, first of Laurence, first of Laurence, first of
Thomas, first of Robert, first of John, first of Robert,
first of John, first of John, first of John, second of Robert, second of Robert, first of Robert, first of Walter,
fourth of Bondo, second of Akaris, first of Bardolf, second of Torfin the Dane; was baptized at Warton, county
Lancaster, in 1616. Obit 1623.

20 JANE WASHINGTON, second child of Leonard, baptized
at Warton, county Lancaster, in 1619.

20 FRANCIS WASHINGTON, third child of Leonard, baptized
at Warton, county Lancaster, in 1622.

20 LAURENCE WASHINGTON, fourth child of Leonard, was
baptized at Warton, county Lancaster, in 1625.
Emigrated to America in 1659. He settled in Virginia.

The two brothers, Laurence and John, purchased land
for their plantations, in Westmoreland county, between the
Potomac and Rappahannock rivers, and located at or near
Bridge's Creek. He died on his estate, in Rappahannock
county, early in Jan., 1677. His will, dated 27 Sept., 1675.
Proved, 6 Jan., 1677. His wife, Jane, his second wife,
daughter of Captain Fleming, was appointed executrix of
his will. He had issue, named:

    21 MARY WASHINGTON, born at Warton, England,
    about 1648.

    21 JOHN WASHINGTON, born at Bridge's Creek, Vir-
    ginia, about 1660.

    21 ANN WASHINGTON, born at Bridge's Creek, Vir-
    ginia, about 1662.

He first settled with his brother John near the Potomac,
and afterward removed into Rappahannock county, where
he died. In Tappahannock, the county seat of Essex, in
the records of the old county of Rappahannock, is recorded

the will of Laurence Washington, and in the Court House
of Westmoreland is recorded the will of his brother John.
Both of the wills were made in the same year, that of Laurence, 27 Sept., 1675, and of John, 26 Feb., 1675. The latter, proved 10 Jan., 1677, the former, 6 Jan., same year,—an
interval of only four days,—so that it is probable that they
died about the same time, or within a few days of each
other.

THE WILL OF LAURENCE WASHINGTON.

" In the name of God, Amen.

"I, Laurence Washington, of the county of Rapp*ac*,
being sick and weak in body, but of sound and perfect
memory, do make and ordain this, my last will and testament, hereby *revoking, annulling,* and making void all
former wills and *Codicells,* heretofore by me made, either
by word or writing, and this only to be taken for my last
will and testament. Impr*s*. I give and bequeath my *Soule*
into the hands of Almighty God, hoping and trusting
through the mercy of Jesus Christ, my one *Savior* and re-
deemer, to receive full pardon and forgiveness of all my
sinns, and my body to the earth, to be buried in comely
and decent manner, by my Executrix hereafter named, and
for my worldly goods I thus *dispose* them. Item, I give and
bequeath unto my loving daughter, Mary Washington, my
whole estate in England, both *reall* and *personall,* to her
and the heirs of her body, lawfully begotten, forever, to be
delivered into her possession *immediately* after my decease,
by my Executrix hereafter named. I give and bequeath
unto my aforesaid daughter, Mary Washington, my smallest stone ring and one silver cup, now in my possession,
to her and her heirs, forever, to be delivered to her *imme-
dia'e'y* after my decease. I give and bequeath unto my
loving son, John Washington, all my bookes, to him and
his heirs, forever, to be delivered to him when he shall
come to the age of Twenty-one *yeares.* I give and bequeath

unto my son, John, and daughter, Ann Washington, all
the rest of my plate, but what is before *exprest* to be
equally divided between them, and delivered into their
possession when they come of age. Item, my will is,
that all my debts which of right and justice I owe to any
man be justly and truly paid, as *allso* my funerall expenses,
after which my will is, that all my whole estate, both *reall.*
and *personall*, be equally divided between my loving wife,
Jane Washington, and the two children God hath given
me by her Vizt John and Ann Washington. I give and
bequeath it all to them, and the *heires* of their bodies, lawfully begotten, forever, my *sonn's* part to be delivered to
him when he comes of age, and my daughter's part when
she comes of age or day of marriage, which shall first
happen. Item, my will is, that that land which became
due to me in right of my wife, lying on the South Side of
the river, formerly belonging to Capt. Alexander Flemm-
ing, and commonly known by the name of West Falco, be
sold by my Executrix hereafter named, for the payment of
my debts, immediately after my decease. Item, my will
is, that the land I have formerly *entred* with Capt. Wm.
Mosely, be forthwith after my decease, surveyed and *pat-
tented* by my Execx hereafter named, and if it shall amount
to the quantity of one thousand acres, then I b.ve and bequeath unto Alexander Barrow, two hundred acres of the
sd land, to him and his heires, forever, the remainder I give
and bequeath unto my loving wife aforesd and two children, to them and their heires, forever, to be equally *divided*
between them. Item, my will is, that if it shall please
God to take my daughter Mary out of the world before
she comes of age, or have heirs lawfully begotten of her
body, then I give and bequeath my land in England, which
by my will I have given to her, unto my son, John Washington and his heirs, and the *personall* estate which I have
given to her, I give and bequeath the same unto my daughter, Ann Washington and her heires, forever. Item, I do

hereby make and ordain my loving wife, Jane Washington, Executrix of this my last will and testament, to see it performed, and I do hereby make and appoint my dear and *loveing* Brother Coll John Washington, and my *loving* friend Thomas Hawkins (in case of the death or neglect of my executrix), to be the overseers and guardians of my Children *untill* they come of age to the truth whereof I have hereunto *Sett* my hand and *Seale*, this 27th of September, 1675.

"LAURENCE WASHINGTON. [*Seale.*]

"Signed Sealed and declared to be his last will and testament, in the presence of us.

"CORNELIUS WOOD.
"Signed.
"JOHN B. BARROW,
"HENRY SANDY, Junr.

"A codicil of the last will and testament of Laurence Washington, annexed to his will, and made Septembr 27th, 1675.

"Item, my will is, that my part of the land I now live upon, which became due to me by marriage of my wife, I leave it *wholy* and solely to her disposable after my decease, as witness my hand, the day and year above written.

LAURENCE WASHINGTON. [*Seale.*]

"Signed, Sealed and declared to be a Codicil of my last will and tastament, in the *presence* of us.

"CORNELIUS WOOD,
"HENRY SANDY, Junr.

"The above named Henry Sandy, Junr., aged 70 *yeares*, or thereabts, sworn and examined, saith, that he did see the above named Laurence Washington, Sign, *Seale* and publish the above mentioned, to be his last will and testament, and that he was in perfect sence and memory at the Signing, Sealing and publishing thereof, to the best of your deponent's Judgment.

" HENRY SANDY.

      .

"Juratus est Henricus Sandy, in Cur Com Rappk^{ac}. Sexto die. Jany, An^o 1677. Jr Saca end p^r and probat.
" Sc st
" EDM^D CRASK, Cl Cy.

    " A Copy Teste
" JAMES RAY MICON, Clerk,
" Essex County Court,
" State of Virginia."

20 COL. JOHN WASHINGTON, fifth child of Leonard, was baptized at Warton, county Lancaster, Eng., in 1627. Emigrated to America in 1659, and settled in Virginia, on Bridge's Creek, near the confluence of the Potomac.

" John Washington, ancestor of the first President of the United States, arrived in America in 1659, a passenger in a ship owned by Edward Prescott, of which one John Greene was captain.· During the voyage, Elizabeth Richardson, who may have been only an enthusiastic Quakeress, was suspected of witchcraft, and hung by the crew. John Washington, incensed by the transaction, upon landing preferred charges against the owner of the vessel, and Fendall, governor of Maryland, took bonds for his appearance to answer at the next Provincial Court, held at St. Mary's.

" On Sept. 30, 1659, Washington, who lived in Westmoreland county, Virginia, on the opposite side of the Potomac river, wrote to Fendall :

" Hon'ble Sir. Yo'rs of this 29th instant, this day I received. I am sorry y^t my extraordinary occasions will not permit mee to bee att·yᵉ next Provincial Court, to be held in Maryland yᵉ fourth of this next month. Because then, God willing, I intend to gett my young Sonne baptized. All yᵉ Company and Gossips being already invited. Besides in this short time witnesses cannot be gott to come over. But if Mr. Prescott bee bound to answer att yᵉ next Provincial Court after this, I shall doe what lyeth in my power to gett them over.

"Sr I shall desire you for to acquaynt mee whether Mr. Prescott be bound over to yᵉ next court, and when yᵉ court is, that I may have some time for to provide evidence, and soe I rest.

"Your ffriend and servant,

"30 September, 1659.   JOHN WASHINGTON."

He died early in January, 1677, within a few days of his brother Laurence. "He was interred in a vault which had been erected at Bridge's Creek." His will, dated 26 Feb., 1675, at Bridge's Creek, Westmoreland county, Virginia, was proved 10 Jan., 1677, and recorded in the Court House of Westmoreland. He was colonel of the Virginian forces, co-operating with those of Maryland, against the Seneca Indians, who were ravaging the settlements along the Potomac.

John Washington was church-warden of old "White Chapel," Lancaster county, Virginia, in 1661. The two brothers, Laurence and John, purchased lands for their plantations in Westmoreland county, between the Potomac and Rappahannock rivers. They located at Bridge's Creek.

John Washington was married first in England, and brought his wife and two children with him in 1659. They all died soon after arrival, and in his will he requests to be buried "on his plantation by the side of his wife and two children."

He was married near Pope's Creek, in Westmoreland

county, about 1660, to his second wife Anne Pope, whose
father resided at Pope's Creek.   Had issue :

    21 LAURENCE WASHINGTON, born at Bridge's Creek,
      Virginia, about 1661.

    21 JOHN WASHINGTON, born at Bridge's Creek, Vir-
      ginia, about 1663.

    21 ELIZABETH WASHINGTON, born at Bridge's Creek,
      Virginia, about 1665.

    21 ANNE WASHINGTON, born at Bridge's Creek, Vir-
      ginia, about 1667.

Colonel John Washington became an extensive planter,
Magistrate, and member of the House of Burgesses.   In
honor of his public services and private virtues, the parish
in which he resided was called after him, and still bears the
name of Washington.   He lies buried in a vault on Bridge's
Creek, which for generations was the family sepulchre.

WILL OF JOHN WASHINGTON.

"In the name of God, Amen.   I, John Washington, of
Washington Parish, in the county of Westmoreland, in
Virginia, gentleman, being of good and perfect memory,
thanks be unto Almighty God for it ; and calling to remembrance the uncertain state of this transitory life, that
all flesh must yield unto death, do make, constitute, and
ordain this my last will and testament, and none other.
And first, being heartily sorry from the bottom of my
heart, for my sins past, most humbly desiring forgiveness
of the same from the Almighty God, my Saviour and Re-
deemer, in whom and by the merits of Jesus Christ I trust
and believe assuredly to be saved, and to have full remis-
sion and forgiveness of all my sins, and that my soul with
my body at the general resurrection shall rise again with
joy."

Again he repeats the same sentiment, hoping "through
the merits of Jesus Christ's death and passion to possess
and inherit the kingdom of heaven, prepared for his elect

and chosen." He directs his body to be buried on the plantation upon which he lived, by the side of his wife and two children. He then proceeds to distribute his property, which he says it has pleased God to give him "far above his deserts." After dividing a number of landed estates between his second and surviving wife and his children—John, Laurence and Anne—and also his property in England, he directs that a funeral sermon be preached and no other funeral kept, and that a tablet with the Ten Commandments be sent for to England and given to the church. He also directs four thousand weight of tobacco to be given to the minister. He leaves one thousand pounds to his brother-in-law, Thomas Pope, and one thousand pounds and four thousand weight of tobacco to his sister, who had come or was coming over to this country. He makes his wife and brother, Laurence, his executors. From the above it would be seen that, great as were his military talents, being Commander-in-Chief in the Northern Neck, high as he stood in the Government, so that the parish was called after him, and large as was his property in England and America, he was also a sincerely pious man, and in his will emphatically testifies to those great Gospel principles which are so prominent in the church of his fathers.

20 ELEANOR WASHINGTON, first child of Leonard, second of Laurence, first of Laurence, first of Laurence, first of Thomas, first of Robert, first of John, first of Robert, first of John, first of John, first of John, second of Robert, second of Robert, first of Robert, first of Walter, fourth of Bondo, second of Akaris, first of Bardolf, second of Torfin the Dane ; was baptized at Warton, county Lancaster, in 1638.

20 LEONARD WASHINGTON, second child of Leonard, was

born at Warton, county Lancaster, and baptized at Warton, county Lancaster, in 1645.   Obit 1698.

20 CHRISTOPHER WASHINGTON, first child of John, first of Leonard, first of Robert, first of Leonard, second of Thomas, first of Robert, first of John, first of Robert, first of John, first of John, first of John, second of Robert, second of Robert, first of Robert, first of Walter, fourth of Bondo, second of Akaris, first of Bardolf, second of Torfin the Dane ; was baptized at Yeland, in Warton, county Lancaster, in 1619.

20 RICHARD WASHINGTON, first child of Henry, first of Sir William, first of Laurence, first of Robert, first of Hon. Laurence, first of John, first of Robert, third of Robert, first of John, first of John, first of John, second of Robert, second of Robert, first of Robert, first of Walter, fourth of Bondo, second of Akaris, first of Bardolf, second of Torfin the Dane ; was born at North Cave, county York, about 1640.
He sold the Manor of North Cave, in 1720.

21 RICHARD WASHINGTON, first child of Richard, first of James, first of D'Arcy, first of Richard, second of James, first of Richard, first of Robert, third of Robert, first of John, first of Robert, first of John, first of Peter, first of John, first of Robert, first of Robert, first of Walter, fourth of Bondo, second of Akaris, first of Bardolf, second of Torfin the Dane ; was baptized at Ardwick le Street, county York, in 1673.
He was buried in 1703.   He had issue :

    22 JAMES WASHINGTON, born at Ardwick le Street, county York, about 1700.

    22 GEORGE WASHINGTON, born at Ardwick le Street, county York, about 1703.

22 JOHN WASHINGTON, born at Ardwick le Street, county York, about 1705.

22 JUDITH WASHINGTON, born at Ardwick le Street, county York, about 1707.

22 ELIZABETH WASHINGTON, born at Ardwick le Street, county York, about 1710.

22 MARY WASHINGTON, born at Ardwick le Street, county York, about 1712.

21 JAMES WASHINGTON, Coroner, second child of Richard, was born at Ardwick le Street, county York, about 1675.

21 ROBERT WASHINGTON, third child of Richard, was born at Ardwick le Street, county York, about 1677.

21 ELIZABETH WASHINGTON, fourth child of Richard, was born at Ardwick le Street, county York, about 1680. Married Peter Hudson.

21 MARY WASHINGTON, fifth child of Richard, was born at Ardwick le Street, county York, about 1682. Married Dr. John Neale, second husband.

21 GEORGE WASHINGTON, first child of Rev. Francis, sixth of James, first of D'Arcy, first of Richard, second of James, first of Richard, first of Robert, third of Robert, first of John, first of Robert, first of John, first of Peter, first of John, first of Robert, first of Robert, first of Walter, fourth of Bondo, second of Akaris, first of Bardolf, second of Torfin the Dane ; was born at Sprotsborough, county York, about 1670.

21 ELIZABETH WASHINGTON, second child of Rev. Francis, was born at Sprotsborough, county York, about 1672.

ANNE WASHINGTON, third child of Rev. Francis, was born at Sprotsborough, county York, about 1675.

21 FRANCES WASHINGTON, fourth child of Rev. Francis, was born at Sprotsborough, county York, about 1677.

21 GRACE WASHINGTON, fifth child of Rev. Francis, was born at Sprotsborough, county York, about 1680.

21 MARY WASHINGTON, first child of Laurence by first wife, fourth of Leonard, first of Laurence, first of Laurence, first of Laurence, first of Thomas, first of Robert, first of John, first of Robert, first of John, first of Robert, first of John, first of John, first of John, second of Robert, second of Robert, first of Robert, first of Walter, fourth of Bondo, second of Akaris, first of Bardolf, second of Torfin the Dane ; was born at Warton, Eng., about 1648.

Remained there at her father's emigration to America, in 1659. Named in his will.

21 JOHN WASHINGTON, first child by second wife, Jane, of Laurence, of Warton, Eng , and Bridge's Creek, Virginia, was born at Bridge's Creek, Virginia, about 1660.

21 ANNE WASHINGTON, second child of Laurence, was born at Bridge's Creek, Virginia, about 1662.

"She married Major Francis Wright. He was interred in a vault on the banks of Bridge's Creek."

21 LAURENCE WASHINGTON, first child of Col. John, by second wife, fifth of Leonard, first of Laurence, first of Laurence, first of Laurence, first of Thomas, first of Robert, first of John, first of Robert, first of John, first of John, first of John, second of Robert, second of Robert, first of Robert, first of Walter, fourth of Bondo, second of Akaris, first of Bardolf, second of Torfin the Dane ; was born at Bridge's Creek, Westmoreland county, Virginia, about 1661.

He resided, and died there in 1697. He was married in Gloucester county, Virginia, about 1690, to Mildred, daughter of Col. Augustine Warner, of Gloucester county, Virginia. Issue :

 22 JOHN WASHINGTON, born at Bridge's Creek, Westmoreland county, Virginia, about 1692.

 22 AUGUSTINE WASHINGTON, born at Bridge's Creek, Westmoreland county, Virginia, in 1694.

 22 MILDRED WASHINGTON, born at Bridge's Creek, Westmoreland county, about 1696.

"Laurence Washington was interred in the family vault, at Bridge's Creek." His widow was married to George Gale.

21 JOHN WASHINGTON, second child of Col. John, was born at Bridge's Creek, Westmoreland county, Virginia, about 1663.

21 ELIZABETH WASHINGTON, third child of Col. John, was born at Bridge's Creek, Westmoreland county, about 1665.

She married Thomas Lanier, son of Lewis Lanier, of Bordeaux, France, about 1687. Had issue :

 22 RICHARD LANIER, born at Bridge's Creek, Westmoreland county, Virginia, about 1688.

 22 THOMAS LANIER, born at Bridge's Creek, Westmoreland county, Virginia, about 1690.

 22 JAMES LANIER, born at Bridge's Creek, Westmoreland county, Virginia, about 1692.

 22 ELIZABETH LANIER, born at Bridge's Creek, Westmoreland county, Virginia, about 1695.

 22 SAMSON LANIER, born at Bridge's Creek, Westmoreland county, Virginia, about 1700.

21 ANNE WASHINGTON, fourth child of Col. John, was born

at Bridge's Creek, Westmoreland county, Virginia, about 1667.

22 JAMES WASHINGTON, first child of Richard, first of Richard, first of James, first of D'Arcy, first of Richard, second of James, first of Richard, first of Robert, third of Robert, first of John, first of Robert, first of John, first of Peter, first of John, first of Robert, first of Robert, first of Walter, fourth of Bondo, second of Akaris, first of Bardolf, second of Torfin the Dane ; was born at Ardwick le Street, county York, about 1700.

22 GEORGE WASHINGTON, Coroner, second child of Richard, was born at Ardwick le Street, county York, about 1703.

22 JOHN WASHINGTON, third child of Richard, was born at Ardwick le Street, county York, about 1705.

22 JUDITH WASHINGTON, fourth child of Richard, was born at Ardwick le Street, county York, about 1707.

22 ELIZABETH WASHINGTON, fifth child of Richard, was born at Ardwick le Street, county York, about 1710. Married William Hutchinson, merchant, of Yorkshire. Children given in his line.

22 MARY WASHINGTON, sixth child of Richard, was born at Ardwick le Street, county York, about 1712. Married John Smith, of Skelton Grange, county York.

22 JOHN WASHINGTON, first child of Laurence, first of Col. John, fifth of Leonard, first of Laurence, first of Laurence, first of Laurence, first of Thomas, first of Robert, first of John, first of Robert, first of John, first of John,

8

first of John, second of Robert, second of Robert, first of Robert, first of Walter, fourth of Bondo, second of Akaris, first of Bardolf, second of Torfin the Dane; was born at Bridge's Creek, Westmoreland county, Virginia, about 1692.

He settled and died in Gloucester county, Virginia. He married Catharine Whiting, of Gloucester county, Virginia. He was buried in Gloucester county. He had issue :

23 WARNER WASHINGTON, born at Bridge's Creek, Virginia, about 1715.

23 HENRY WASHINGTON, born at Bridge's Creek, Virginia, about 1718.

23 MILDRED WASHINGTON, born at Bridge's Creek, Virginia, about 1720. Married.

23 ELIZABETH WASHINGTON, born at Bridge's Creek, Virginia, about 1722. Died unmarried.

23 CATHARINE WASHINGTON, born at Bridge's Creek, Virginia, about 1724. Married Fielding Lewis.

23 LAURENCE WASHINGTON, born at Bridge's Creek, Virginia, about 1726.

23 AUGUSTINE WASHINGTON, born at Bridge's Creek, Virginia, about 1728.

23 FRANCES WASHINGTON, born at Bridge's Creek, Virginia, about 1730.

22 AUGUSTINE WASHINGTON, second child of Laurence, was born at Bridge's Creek, Virginia, A. D. 1694.

He removed in 1722 to an estate in Stafford county, nearly opposite Fredericksburgh on the Rappahannock, where he died, 12 April, 1743, aged 49. He owned several fine estates on the Potomac and Rappahannock rivers. He was married, 20 April, 1715, to Jane, daughter of Caleb Butler, of Westmoreland county, by whom he had 4 children. She died 24 Nov., 1728. He had issue :

23 BUTLER WASHINGTON, born at Bridge's Creek, Virginia, A. D. 1716. Died young.

23 LAURENCE WASHINGTON, born at Bridge's Creek, Virginia, A. D. 1718.

23 AUGUSTINE WASHINGTON, born at Bridge's Creek, Virginia, A. D. 1720.

23 JANE WASHINGTON, born at Bridge's Creek, Virginia, A. D. 1722.   Died Jan. 17, 1735.

His wife died in Stafford county, Virginia, 24 Nov., 1728, and was interred in the Family Vault at Bridge's Creek, Virginia, near the remains of Colonel John Washington, the emigrant.

He was married, second, in Lancaster county, Virginia, 6 Mar., 1731, to Mary, daughter of Colonel William Ball, of Lancaster county, Virginia. (She died 25 Aug., 1789, aged 82.)   By whom he had six children :

23 GEORGE WASHINGTON, born at Wakefield, Westmoreland county, Virginia, 11 O. S. 22 N. S. Feb., 1732.

23 BETTY WASHINGTON, born at Wakefield, Westmoreland county, Virginia, 20 June, 1733.

23 SAMUEL WASHINGTON, born at Wakefield, Westmoreland county, Virginia, 16 Nov., 1734.

23 JOHN AUGUSTINE WASHINGTON, born at Wakefield, Westmoreland county, Virginia, 13 Jan., 1736.

23 CHARLES WASHINGTON, born at Wakefield, Westmoreland county, Virginia, 2 May, 1738.

23 MILDRED WASHINGTON, born at Wakefield, Westmoreland county, Virginia, 21 June, 1739.   Died 23 Oct., 1740.

"AUGUSTINE WASHINGTON and Mary Ball was Married the Sixth of March, 17$\frac{30}{31}$

GEORGE WASHINGTON son to Augustine & Mary his wife was Born ye 11th Day of February 173½ about 10 in the Morning & was Baptiz'd the 5th of April following Mrs Beverly Whiting & Capt Christopher Brooks Godfathers and Mrs Mildred Gregory Godmother.

BETTY WASHINGTON was Born the 20th of June 1733 about 6 in ye Mornin   Departed this life the 31st of March 1797 at 4 Oclock

SAMUEL WASHINGTON was Born ye 16 of Nov. 1734 about 3 in ye Mornin

JANE WASHINGTON Daughter of Augustine and Jane Washington Departed this Life Jany 17th 1735⁴

JOHN AUGUSTINE WASHINGTON was Born ye 13th of Jany. about 2 in ye Morn 1736⁵   •

CHARLES WASHINGTON was Borne ye 2 day of May about 3 in ye Morne 1738

MILDRED WASHINGTON was Born ye 21st of June 1739 about 9 at Night.

MILDRED WASHINGTON Departed this Life Octr ye 23d 1740 being thursday about 12 a Clock at Noon Aged 1 Year & 4 Months

AUGUSTINE WASHINGTON Departed this Life ye 12th Day of April 1743 Aged 49 Years"

The above is copied from the Family Bible of Augustine Washington.

Augustine Washington purchased the estate known as Mount Vernon, and at his death it became the property of his eldest son Laurence. He left large possessions distributed by will among his children. To Laurence the estate on the banks of the Potomac, with other real property, and several shares in iron works. To Augustine, the second son by the first marriage, the old homestead and estate at Bridge's Creek, Westmoreland county.

The children by the second marriage were well provided for, and George, when he came of age, was to have the house and lands on the Rappahannock.

22 MILDRED WASHINGTON, third child of Laurence, was born at Bridge's Creek, Virginia, about 1696.

"Her first husband was named Gregory, by whom she had three daughters :

 23 FRANCES, born at Bridge's Creek, Virginia, about 1716.

 23 MILDRED, born at Bridge's Creek, Virginia, about 1718.

 23 ELIZABETH, born at Bridge's Creek, Virginia, about 1720.

"Who married three brothers, Col. Francis Thornton, Col. John Thornton, and Reuben Thornton, all of Spottsylvania county, Virginia. She had for her second husband, Col. Henry Willis, of Fredericksburgh, and by him the present

 23 COL. LEWIS WILLIS, of Fredericksburgh."—*Washington's Letter*, 2 May, 1792.

. **22** RICHARD LANIER, first child of Thomas Lanier, the son of Lewis Lanier, of Bordeaux, France, and of Elizabeth Washington Lanier, third child of Col. John Washington, of Bridge's Creek, Virginia, was born at Bridge's Creek, Virginia, about 1688.

22 THOMAS LANIER, second child of Thomas Lanier, was born at Bridge's Creek, Virginia, about 1690.

22 JAMES LANIER, third child of Thomas Lanier, was born at Bridge's Creek, Virginia, about 1692.

22 ELIZABETH LANIER, fourth child of Thomas Lanier, was born at Bridge's Creek, Virginia, about 1695.

22 SAMSON LANIER, fifth child of Thomas Lanier, was born at Bridge's Creek, Virginia, about 1700. Had issue :

 23 LEWIS, born at Bridge's Creek, Virginia, about 1726.

 23 BUCKNER, "   "   ".   " 1728.

23 BURRILL, born at Bridge's Creek, Virginia, about 1732.
23 WINNIFRED,   "   "   "   " 1735.
23 NANCY,   "   "   "   " 1737.
23 REBECCA, .   "   "   "   " 1740.

·23 LEWIS LANIER, above, married Miss Ball, sister of General Washington's mother. Had son :

24 JAMES LANIER, Planter, born in Southampton county, Virginia, February 2, 1750. He removed to Nashville, Tennessee, in 1789, and to Bourbon county, Kentucky, in 1791. Thence to Pendleton, Kentucky, where he died April 27, 1806. He was married about 1774, to Sarah Chalmers (born October 30, 1755), of Scotland. (She was nearly related to the celebrated Dr. Chalmers.) Had issue :

25 ALEXANDER CHALMERS LANIER, born in Southampton county, Virginia, 31 Jan., 1779.

25 JAMES WALTERS LANIER, born about 1781. He was a surgeon in the United States army, in 1812. He died without issue.

25 A daughter and a son, died s. p.

25 ALEXANDER CHALMERS LANIER (above), was Court Clerk of the County Courts of Southampton county. He removed to Bourbon county, Kentucky, A. D. 1800, and to Eaton, Preble county, Ohio, A. D. 1807. He died in Lancaster, Garrard county, Kentucky, 25 Mar., 1820. He was married in Southampton county, Virginia, April 30, 1797, to Drusilla Cleaves Doughty (who was born Mar. 27, 1778, and died at Madison, Indiana, Feb. 8, 1838). His only child was :

26 JAMES FRANKLIN DOUGHTY LANIER, born at Washington, in Beaufort county,

North Carolina, Nov. 22, 1800. He
was taken to Eaton, Preble county,
Ohio, in 1807, to Madison, Indiana, in
1817. Removed to New York in 1849,
where he now (1878) resides, at No. 16
West Tenth Street.

He was married, first, at Madison,
Indiana, Dec. 8, 1819, to Elizabeth,
daughter of John Gardner, of Lexington, Kentucky. (She died April 15,
1846.) He was married, secondly, at
Madison, Indiana, 20 Jan., 1848, to Mary,
daughter of John McClure, of Carlisle,
Pennsylvania. Issue by first wife :

27 ALEXANDER CHALMERS LANIER,
   born at Madison, Indiana, on Fri-
   day, Oct. 6, 1820. Resides there
   (1878), not married.

27 ELIZABETH FRANCES LANIER, born
   at Madison, Indiana, on Tuesday, Feb. 26, 1822. Removed to
   Washington, D. C., in 1869, now
   (1878) there. She was married at
   Madison, Indiana, Mar. 11, 1841, by
   Rev. James Johnston, to Gen. William McKee Dunn, Judge Advo-
   cate, and General in the United
   States army, son of Williamson
   (and Mirian) Dunn, of Jefferson
   county, Indiana. She has issue :

   28 WILLIAM McKEE DUNN, born
      at Madison, Indiana, Aug. 20,
      1843. Now (1876) Major in the
      United States army, stationed
      at Fort Leavenworth, Kansas.

He was on General Grant's staff, before the battle of Vicksburg, Mississippi. He was married about 1844, to Mary, daughter of Hon. Lott Morrell (Secretary in 1876 of United States Treasury, at Washington), of Augusta, Maine. Has two children.

28 FRANCES ELIZABETH DUNN, born at Madison, Indiana, Dec. 6, 1847. Now (1876) at Washington, D. C. She was married about 1870, to David R. McKee, head of the Associated Press at Washington. Has two children.

28 LANIER DUNN, born at Madison, Indiana, Aug. 2, 1851. Now (1876) on the Wheeler Expedition Survey at the West. Not married.

28 MARY DUNN, born at Madison, Indiana, Sept. 22, 1853. At home. Not married.

28 GEORGE MARSHALL DUNN, born at Madison, Indiana, Mar. 20, 1856. Now (1876) on the Survey with his brother Lanier.

27 DRUSILLA ANN LANIER, born at Madison, Indiana, Dec. 21, 1824. Now (1876) there. She was married there, in 1844, to John Robert Cravens, of Madison, Indiana, and has ten children.

27 MARGARET D. LANIER, born at Madison, Indiana, on Saturday, Feb. 25, 1827.

27 JOHN JAMES LANIER, born at Madison, Indiana, on Thursday, July 23, 1829, and died there, 20 April, 1836.

27 MARY LANIER, born at Madison, Indiana, on Monday, Aug. 20, 1832. Removed to New York, and now (1876) resides at No. 15 West Ninth Street. She was married in New York, about 1858, to John Cameron Stone, of New York. Has two children :

　1 ELIZABETH GARDNER STONE, born Mar. 8, 1851.

　2 MARY LOUISA STONE, born April 21, 1860.

27 LOUISA MORRIS LANIER, born at Madison, Indiana, on Saturday, Jan. 31, 1835. Now (1876) resides in Madison, at the house of her sister, Mrs. Cravens. Not married.

27 CHARLES LANIER, born at Madison, Indiana, Jan. 19, 1837. Removed about 1849 to, and now (1878) resides in New York, No. 30 East Thirty-seventh Street. He was married in New York, by Rev. Gardiner Spring, Oct. 7, 1857, to Sarah E., daughter of Thomas Egleston, of New York. Has four children :

　1 JAMES FREDERICK DOUGHTY LANIER, born July 25, 1858.

2 Sarah Egleston Lanier, born
April 8, 1862.

3 Fannie Lanier, born Aug. 17,
1864.

4 Elizabeth Gardner Lanier,
born Oct. 29, 1870.

Issue of J. F. D. Lanier, by second wife :

27 Jane Lanier, born at Madison,
Indiana, in Jan., 1849, and died there
in 1857.

27 James Lanier, born at Madison,
Indiana, A. D. 1851, and died on
Staten Island, in 1856.

27 Katie McClure Lanier, born in
New York, 7 Jan. 1858. Resides
with her father, unmarried.

23 Warner Washington, first child of John, first of Laurence, first of Col. John, fifth of Leonard, first of Laurence, first of Laurence, first of Laurence, first of Thomas, first of Robert, first of John, first of Robert, first of John, first of John, first of John, second of Robert, second of Robert, first of Robert, first of Walter, fourth of Bondo, second of Akaris, first of Bardolf, second of Torfin the Dane ; was born at Bridge's Creek, Virginia, about 1715. He removed to Frederick county. Died in 1791. Married first, Elizabeth, daughter of Col. William Macon, of New Kent county, Virginia. Had one child :

24 Warner Washington, born in Gloucester county,
Virginia, 15 April, 1751.

Married secondly, at Fairfax, Virginia, about 1764, to Hannah, daughter of Hon. William Fairfax, of Fairfax, Clarke county, Virginia (then Frederick county). Children :

24 Mildred Washington, born at Fairfield, Virginia,
A. D. 1765.

24 HANNAH WASHINGTON, born at Fairfax, Virginia, April, 1767. Married P. B. Whiting, of Elmington, Gloucester county, Virginia.

24 CATHARINE WASHINGTON, born at Belvoir, Virginia, 7 April, 1769.

24 ELIZABETH WASHINGTON, born at Fairfield, Virginia, A. D. 1771.

24 LOUISA WASHINGTON, born at Fairfield, Virginia, about 1775.

24 FAIRFAX WASHINGTON, born at Fairfield, Virginia, about 1778.

24 WHITING WASHINGTON, born at Fairfield, Virginia, about 1780.

After his second marriage, Warner Washington removed to Frederick county, Virginia, where he died in 1791.

23 HENRY WASHINGTON, second child of John, was born at Bridge's Creek, Virginia, about 1718.

He married a daughter of Col. Thacker, of Middlesex county, Virginia, and had, beside two or three daughters, a son, viz.:

24 THACHER WASHINGTON, born at Bridge's Creek, Virginia, about 1740.

He married a daughter of Sir John Peyton, and had several children.

23 MILDRED WASHINGTON, third child of John, was born at Bridge's Creek, Virginia, about 1720.

Married twice; had no children.

23 ELIZABETH WASHINGTON, fourth child of John, was born at Bridge's Creek, Virginia, about 1722. Died unmarried.

23 CATHARINE WASHINGTON, fifth child of John, was born at Bridge's Creek, Virginia, about 1724.

She married Col. Fielding Lewis. Had a son and a daughter :

24 JOHN LEWIS, born at ——, about 1745.

24 FRANCES LEWIS, born at ——, about 1748, and died without issue.

(After the death of his wife Catharine, Col. Lewis married Betty Washington, second child of Augustine Washington by second wife.)

23 LAURENCE WASHINGTON, sixth child of John, was born at Bridge's Creek, Westmoreland county, Virginia, about 1726. Died s. p.

He bequeathed his estate to his cousin, General George Washington.

23 AUGUSTINE WASHINGTON, seventh child of John, was born at Bridge's Creek, Virginia, about 1728. He had issue :

24 WILLIAM WASHINGTON, born at Bridge's Creek, ·Virginia, about 1750.

23 FRANCIS WASHINGTON, eighth child of John, was born at Bridge's Creek, Virginia, about 1770.

23 MAJOR LAURENCE WASHINGTON, second child by first wife (Butler, first child, died young) of Augustine, second of Laurence, first of Colonel John, of Warton, Eng., and Bridge's Creek, Virginia; was born at Bridge's Creek, Virginia, in 1718.

In 1733 he was sent to England to complete his education. Returned in 1742. He served in the campaign in the West Indies 1740-2, with Admiral Vernon, and died at Mount Vernon, Virginia, 26 July, 1752, at the age of 34. He left a wife and infant daughter. He inherited an estate from his

father Augustine at his death, in April, 1743, in Fairfax county, lying eight miles below Alexandria, and sixteen from the
city of Washington. It was named by him, "Mount Vernon," in honor of Admiral Vernon, of the English navy,
with whom he had been intimate in the campaign of 1740–2.
At his death it descended to his next oldest brother George,
and it became his chosen home, and the place of his death
and burial.

"Major Laurence Washington died A. D., 1752, aged 34,
and was interred in a vault which he had caused to be
erected at Mount Vernon, in Fairfax county, Virginia,
where he settled after he returned from his Carthagena expedition."—*Washington Letter, May* 2, 1792.

"It was willed by General Washington to his nephew,
John Bushrod Washington, son of John Augustine, after
whose death it descended to his son, John Augustine Washington, who was, while aid to General Robert E. Lee with·
the rank of Colonel, killed near Cheat Mountain, in Sept.,
1861."

Major Laurence Washington was a member of the House
of Burgesses and Adjutant-General of the District, with
the rank of Major and a regular salary.

19 July, 1743, he married Anna, eldest daughter of Hon.
William Fairfax, of Belvoir, Fairfax county, Virginia. He
now gave up all thoughts of foreign service, and settled on
his estate, which he named Mount Vernon. Children of
Major Laurence Washington :

    24 JANE WASHINGTON, born at Mount Vernon, 27 Sept.,
        1744. Died in Jan., 1745.

    24 FAIRFAX WASHINGTON, born at Mount Vernon, 22
        Aug., 1747. Died Oct., 1747.

    24 MILDRED WASHINGTON, born at Mount Vernon, 28
      · Sept., 1748. Died 1749.

    24 SARAH WASHINGTON, born at Mount Vernon, 7 Nov.,
    ● 1750.

23 Augustine Washington, third child of Augustine, was born at Bridge's Creek, Virginia, about 1720.

He settled there at the old homestead. It was at his home that his half brother George resided, whilst attending the select school of Mr. Williams.

" He married, in 1743, Anne, daughter and co-heiress of Col. William Aylett, Esq., of Westmoreland county, by whom he had many children, all of whom died in their nonage and single, except Elizabeth, Anne and William." —*Letter of General Washington, May 2, 1792.* He had issue :

> **24** Elizabeth Washington, born at Wakefield, Bridge's Creek, Virginia, about 1750. Married Alexander Spotswood.
>
> **24** Jane Washington, born at Wakefield, Bridge's Creek, Virginia, about 1752. Married Col. John Thornton.
>
> **24** Anne Washington, born at Wakefield, Bridge's Creek, Virginia, about 1753. Married Burdet Ashton.
>
> **24** William Augustine Washington, born at Wakefield, Bridge's Creek, Virginia, Nov. 25, 1757.

" Augustine Washington lived at the ancient mansion, at Wakefield, and was buried in the family vault, at Bridge's Creek, Virginia."

23 Jane Washington, fourth child of Augustine, was born at Bridge's Creek. Died young.

23 GEORGE WASHINGTON, Planter, General and Commander-in-Chief of the American armies, and first President of the United States, was the first child by second wife, of Augustine Washington, of Bridge's Creek, Virginia, the second child of Laurence, of Bridge's Creek, Virginia, the first child of Col. John, of Warton, Lancaster, England, and Bridge's Creek, Virginia, the fifth child of Leonard, of Warton, county Lancaster, England, the

first child of Laurence, of Warton, the first child of
Laurence, of Warton, the first child of Laurence, of
Warton, the first child of Thomas, of Warton, the first
child of Robert, of Warton, the first child of John, of
Warton, the first child of Robert, of Warton, the first
child of John, of Warton, the first child of John, of Warton, the first child of John, of Warton, the second child
of Robert, of Warton, the second child of Robert, of
Kenneford, county Lancaster, the second child of Robert de Washington, Lord of Milburne, or Welleburne,
county Westmoreland, the first child of Robert de Washington, Lord of Milburne, or Welleburne, the first child
of Walter fil Bondo de Washington, called also Walter
de Washington, the fourth son of Bondo fil Akaris, or
Akary, the second son of Akary fil Bardolf, Lord of
Ravensworth, county York,—one of the great vassals
of Stephen, third Earl of Richmond,—the first child of
Bardolf, Lord of Ravensworth, in Richmondshire, the
second son of Torfin the Dane; who was the founder of
the Washington family in England, who was the fourth
son of Sigurd, Earl of the Orkney Isles, the son of Earl
Lodver, the third son of Torfidur, Earl of the Orkneys
A. D. 942, the first son of Earl Einar, the fourth son of
Earl Rogvald (These Earls were known as "THE LORDS
OF THE ISLES"). Rogvald was Jarl or Earl of Moere,
A. D. 885. He was the third son of Eisten Glumru (or
Vors), the son of Ivar, whose wife was daughter of
Eisten Glumru, King of Frondheim (or Thrandin), A. D.
840, the son of Halfdan, King of Frondheim, the son
of Eisten, King of Frondheim, the son of Throud (or
Frouds), King of Frondheim, the son of Harold Hilde-
tand (or Hildetur, King of Denmark, A. D. 647), the son
of Queen Auda Diuphaudza (wife of Rerik, King of
Holmgard), the daughter of Ivar Vidfadme, King of
Denmark, A. D. 588, the son of Halfdan III., King of
Denmark, A. D. 548, the first son of Frode VII., King of

Denmark, A. D. 522, the son of Frode VI., King of Denmark, A. D. 494, the son of Roe, King of Denmark, A. D. 460, the son of Halfdan II., King of Denmark, A. D. 456, died A. D. 457, the second son of Frode IV., King of Denmark, A. D. 348, the son of Friedlief III., King of Denmark, A. D. 324, the son of Halfdan I., King of Denmark, A. D. 310, the son of Frode III., King of Denmark, A. D. 270, the son of Dan Mykellati, King of Denmark, A. D. 190 (whose wife was daughter of Olaf, King of Denmark and Zealand, A. D. 140), the son of Vermund, King of Denmark, A. D. 87, the son of Frode II., King of Denmark, A. D. 59, son of Frode Fredigod, King of Denmark, B. C. 23 (and was King in Denmark in the time of Christ), the first son of Friedlief I., the first King of Denmark, B. C. 40 (of the Skioldingers, or descendants of Skiold, the son of Odin), the son of Skiold, who reigned at Ledra, Zealand, and at Jutland, about 40 years B. C., the fifth son of Odin, the founder of Scandinavia, B. C. 70 (see Introduction, page v.), from whom was descended, in 55 generations, GEORGE WASHINGTON, who was born at Wakefield, 11th O. S. and 22 N. S. Feb., 1732, near Bridge's Creek, Westmoreland county, Virginia, in the old Washington Homestead, on the estate where his great-grandfather, Col. John Washington, settled in 1659. He died at Mount Vernon, 14 Dec., 1799. His tomb is the Mecca of America. He was married at the White House, New Kent county, Virginia, a short distance from Williamsburgh, 6 Jan., 1759, to Martha (Widow of Col. Daniel Parke Custis (who died in 1757), of the White House, Virginia, at the time of her marriage), daughter of John Dandridge, of New Kent county, Virginia. The marriage was celebrated in the good old hospitable Virginia style, amid a joyous assemblage of relatives and friends. He adopted, when they were very young :

Eleanor Parke Custis, and
George Washington Parke Custis.

These were the children of John Parke Custis, the only child of Mrs. Martha Washington (*nee* Custis), by her first husband, Daniel Parke Custis, that lived to majority.

"Claymont, Del., Oct. 26, 1876.

"Harewood is the name of the estate on which the Washington family have resided for a long period. It was General Washington's country residence. The mansion is a fine old pretentious house of the old style. It is built of limestone, and has a costly finish in the interior. The property is owned by my sister, who has lived there many years.

"JOHN B. CLEMSON."

WASHINGTON'S BIRTHPLACE ON THE POTOMAC.

"This house commanded a beautiful view over many miles of the Potomac, and opposite shore of Maryland; it contained four rooms on the ground floor, and others in the attic. Such was the birthplace of our great and loved Washington. Not a vestige now remains of it; only a stone placed there by his wife's grandson, George Washington Parke Custis, marks the site of the "old low-pitched farm house," and an inscription denotes its being the birthplace of Washington, whose life and wonderful achievements as a soldier and statesman, are written as with a sunbeam upon the brilliant historic page which records the memorable struggle and liberation of the infant colonies from the tyranny of the mother country, and chronicles the stupendous growth of the vigorous young Republic during the first eight years of its existence."

A WASHINGTON ROMANCE.

A LETTER FROM GENERAL WASHINGTON ACKNOWLEDGING THE POWER
OF LOVE.

"In a collection of rare and valuable autograph letters we

9

find the accompanying letter written by General Washington at the age of twenty-six, and never before made public. The present owner purchased it in England some years ago for the sum of £15, where it was probably taken by members of the Fairfax family of Virginia. The letter is addressed to Sarah Fairfax, at Belvoir. This lady was a Miss Cary, to whom Washington at one time offered his hand, but was refused for his friend and comrade George William Fairfax. Irving asserts that it was a sister of Mrs. Fairfax, Miss Mary Cary, afterward Mrs. Edward Ambler. We have the authority of Mrs. Constance C. Harrison, a descendant of Lord Fairfax, who says, in a paper called 'A Little Centennial Lady,' published in *Scribner's Monthly* of July, 1876, that Sally Cary, Mrs. Fairfax, was the lady for whom Washington had a tenderness. Mrs. Harrison says :—

"'It is fair to say that papers which have never been given to the public set this question beyond a doubt. Mrs. George William Fairfax, the object of George Washington's early and passionate love, lived to an advanced age, in Bath, England, widowed, childless and utterly infirm. Upon her death, at the age of eighty-one, letters, (still in possession of the Fairfax family,) were found among her effects, showing that Washington. had never forgotten the influence of his youthful disappointment.'

"It is hardly probable that Washington means to express his love for Mrs. ~~Custis,~~ to whom he alludes here, for her husband was then living—in fact, did not die until twenty odd years after the date of this letter. For the matter of that, Mrs. Fairfax's husband did not die until 1787. The following letter is, without doubt, one of those letters which Mrs. Harrison declares will 'set this question beyond a doubt.' It will be found very interesting, as it shows Washington in quite a new light. Even as a lover

he has all the stateliness of the General and the Father of His Country :—

"'CAMP AT FORT CUMBERLAND, 12th September, 1758.
"'DEAR MADAM :—

"'Yesterday I was honored with your short but very agreeable favor of the first inst.—how joyfully I catch at the happy occasion of renewing a correspondence which I feared was disrelished on your part, I leave to time, that never failing expositor of all things—and to a monitor equally faithful in my own breast to testify. In silence I now express my joy. Silence, which in some cases—I wish the present—speaks more intelligently than the sweetest eloquence.

"'If you allow that any honor can be derived from my opposition to our present system of management, you destroy the merit of it entirely in me by attributing my anxiety to the animating prospect of possessing Mrs. Custis—when—I need not name it—guess yourself—Should not my own Honor and country's welfare be the excitement? 'Tis true, I profess myself a votary of Love—I acknowledge that a lady is in the case—and further I confess that this lady is known to you.—Yes, madam, as well as she is to one who is too sensible of her charms to deny the Power whose Influence he feels and must ever submit to. I feel the force of her amiable beauties in the recollection of a thousand tender passages that I could wish to obliterate, till I am bid to revive them,—but experience, alas! sadly reminds me how impossible this is,—and evinces an opinion which I have long entertained, that there is a Destiny, which has the sovereign control of our actions—not to be resisted by the strongest efforts of Human Nature.

"You have drawn me, dear madam, or rather I have drawn myself, into an honest confession of a simple Fact—misconstrue not my meaning—doubt it not, nor expose it—The world has no business to know the object of my

Love—declared in this manner to—you—when I want to conceal it.   One thing above all things in this world I wish to know, and only one person of your acquaintance can solve me that or guess my meaning—but adieu to this till happier times, if I ever shall see them.   The hours at present are melancholy dull, neither the rugged toils of war, nor the gentler conflict of A—— B——s is in my choice. I dare believe, you are as happy as you say.   I wish I was happy also.   Mirth, good humor, ease of mind and—what else?   Cannot fail to render you so and consummate your wishes.

"'If one agreeable lady could almost wish herself a fine gentleman for the sake of another; I apprehend, that many fine gentlemen will wish themselves finer e'er Mrs. Spotswood is possest.   She has already become a reigning toast in this camp; and many there are in it, who intend (fortune favoring) to make honorable scars speak the fullness of their merit, and be a messenger of their Love to Her.

"'I cannot easily forgive the unseasonable haste of my last express, if he deprived me thereby of a single word you intended to add,—the time of the present messenger is, as the last might have been, entirely at your disposal.   I can't expect to hear from my friends more than this once before the fate of the expedition will some how or other be determined.   I therefore beg to know when you set out for Hampton, and when you expect to return to Belvoir again —and I should be glad also to hear of your speedy departure as I shall thereby hope for your return before I get down; the disappointment of seeing your family would give me much concern.—From any thing I can yet see 'tis hardly possible to say when we shall finish, I don't think there is a probability of it till the middle of November. Your letter to Capt'n Gist I forwarded by a safe hand the moment it came to me.   His answer shall be carefully transmitted.

"'Col. Mercer, to whom I delivered your message and

General was always present. It was an occasion for emulous and aspiring belles to essay to win his attention. But he was never familiar; his countenance uniformly, even there, preserved its habitual gravity. A lady of his family said it was his habit, also, when without company, and that she only remembered him once to have made a hearty laugh in a narrative and incident in which she was a party. The truth was, his deportment was unavoidably grave; it was sobriety, stopping short of sadness. His presence inspired a veneration and a feeling of awe rarely experienced in the presence of any man. His mode of speaking was slow and deliberate, not as though he was in search of fine words, but that he might utter those only adapted to his purpose."

"George Washington, first President of the United States, was born at Bridge's Creek, Westmoreland county, Virginia, 22 Feb., 1732, and died at Mount Vernon, 14 Dec., 1799. Fourth son of Augustine. John, his ancestor, came to Virginia, A. D. 1659. He was educated by a private tutor, and became a surveyor, and was Adjutant-General, 1751. He was sent on a mission to the French commission on the Ohio, by Governor Dinwiddie, 31 Oct., 1753, returning 16 Jan., 1754, after much suffering. He was appointed Lieutenant-Colonel, Mar., 1754, and 28 May, captured a French detachment, near Great Meadows, killing its commander, Jumonville; surrendered his command at Fort Necessity to a superior French force, 4 July, 1754; volunteer aid to General Braddock, at the battle of Monongahela, 9 July, 1755; married, 6 Jan., 1759, to Martha, widow of John Parke Curtis, and daughter of John Dandridge; member of the House of Burgesses, 1760–75; delegate to the first Congress, Sept. 1774, and to the second, May, 1775, by which (15 June) he was chosen commander-in-chief of the American army, on the nomination of John Adams, and took command at Cambridge, Mass., 3 July.

He forced the British to evacuate Boston, 17 March, 1776 ; lost the battles of Brooklyn, 27 Aug., White Plains, 28 Oct., gained the victories of Trenton and Princeton, Dec. 26, and Jan. 3, was defeated at Brandywine, 11 Sept., 1777, and at Germantown, 4 Oct., 1777, fought an indecisive battle with Sir H. Clinton, 28 June, 1778, at Monmouth, and, in conjunction with the French army of Rochambeau, and the fleet of De Grasse, captured the army of Cornwallis, at Yorktown, 19 Oct., 1781, virtually ending the war. On 23 Dec., 1783, he resigned his command and retired to Mount Vernon. He was President of the Convention that formed the United States Constitution, 1787 ; inaugurated President of the United States at New York, 30 April, 1789, and returned to private life on the expiration of his second term, 4 March, 1797. In Sept., 1796, he published his Farewell Address. See *Life and Correspondence*, by Sparks, 12 vols. 8vo. Lives by Ramsay, Marshall, Bancroft, and Irving.

"Martha Washington, the widow of George Washington, died May 22, 1802, aged 70. She was the daughter of Mr. Dandridge, of the county of New Kent, in Virginia, and was born in May, 1732. Her first husband was Col. Daniel P. Custis, who lived on the Pamunkey river, a branch of York river. Of the children by this marriage, Martha died in womanhood at Mount Vernon, in 1770, and John Custis, in 1781, at the siege of Yorkton, aged 27, leaving several children. She married Washington in 1759. During the war she was accustomed to spend the winters at headquarters. The remains of husband and wife rest in the same vault. She was amiable and dignified, and adorned with the Christian virtues, and cheered with the Christian hope as she went down to the grave.

"Washington's close identification with the early history of our country, during his entire life, is without a parallel in the history of men or nations. Of all the great and good men our country has produced, he, whom the gallant Lee

aptly called " The Father of his Country," stands foremost
in the eyes of our own people and in the estimation of
mankind.   The whole world is filled with his glory, and
even after the moons of a century have come and gone, the
radiance of his glorious character shines with a lustre the
ages cannot dim.   Let all men study the life and character
of this truly wonderful man.   Let him ever be cited as a
model for all who aspire to fame, for their imitation in
every duty which adorns and dignifies distinguished men.

GENERAL WASHINGTON'S WILL.

" In the name of God, Amen.   I George Washington of
Mount Vernon a citizen of the United States and lately
President of the same, do make ordain and declare this
Instrument, which is written with my own hand and every
page thereof subscribed with my name, to be my last will
& testament, revoking all others.—

"*Imprimus* All my debts, of which there are but few,
and none of magnitude, are to be punctually and speedily
paid and the legacies hereinafter bequeathed, are to be discharged as soon as circumstances will permit, and in the
manner directed.

" Item—To my dearly beloved wife Martha Washington,
I give and bequeath the use, profit and benefit of my whole
Estate, real and personal, for the term of her natural life :
except such parts thereof as are specially disposed of hereafter : My improved lot in the Town of Alexandria, situated on Pitt and Cameron Streets, I give to her & her
heirs forever : as I also do my household and kitchen furniture of every sort and kind, with the liquors and groceries
which may be on hand at the time of my decease ; to be used
and disposed of as she may think proper.

" Item. Upon the decease of my wife, it is my will and desire, that all the slaves which I hold in my *own right*, shall
receive their freedom.—To emancipate them during her

life, would, tho' earnestly wished by me, be attended with
such insuperable difficulties, on account of their intermix-
ture by marriages with the dower negroes, as to excite the
most painful sensations, if not disagreeable consequences
from the latter, while both descriptions are in the occu-
pancy of the same proprietor : it not being in my power,
under the tenure by which the dower negroes are held, to
manumit them.—And whereas among those who will
receive freedom according to this devise, there may be
some, who from old age, or bodily infirmities : and others,
who on account of their infancy, that will be unable to
support themselves : it is my will and desire that all who
come under the first and second description, shall be com-
fortably clothed and fed by my heirs, while they live : and
that such of the latter description as have no parents living, or if living are unable, or unwilling to provide for
them, shall be bound by the Court, until they shall arrive
at the age of twenty-five years : and in cases where no
record can be produced, whereby their ages can be ascer-
tained, the Judgment of the Court, upon its own view
of the subject, shall be adequate & final. The negroes
thus bound, are (by their Masters or Mistresses), to be
taught to read and write, & to be brought up to some
useful occupation, agreeably to the Laws of the Commonwealth of Virginia, providing for the support of orphan
& other poor children. And I do hereby expressly forbid
the sale, or transportation out of the said Commonwealth
of any Slave I may die possessed of, under any pretence
whatsoever. And I do moreover most pointedly, and most
solemnly enjoin it upon my Executors hereafter named, or
the survivors of them, to see that *this* clause, respecting
slaves, and every part thereof, be religiously fulfilled at the
Epoch at which it is directed to take place : without evasion,
neglect or delay, after the crops which may then be on
the ground are harvested, particularly, as it respects the
aged & infirm : seeing that a regular & permanent fund be

established for their support so long as there are subjects requiring it : not trusting to the uncertain provision to be made by individuals.—And to my mulatto man, William (calling himself Wm : Lee.) I give immediate freedom, or if he should prefer it (on account of the accidents which have befallen him, and which have rendered him incapable of walking or of any active employment.) to remain in the situation he now is, it shall be optional in him to do so : In either case however, I allow him an annuity of thirty dollars during his natural life, which shall be independent of the victuals and clothes he has been accustomed to receive, if he chooses the last alternative : but in full with his freedom, if he prefers the first : & this I give him as a testimony of my sense of his attachment to me, and for his faithful services during the Revolutionary War.

"Item.   To the Trustees (Governors, or by whatsoever name they may be designated) of the Academy in the Town of Alexandria, I give and bequeath, in Trust, four thousand dollars, or in other words, twenty of the shares which I hold in the Bank of Alexandria, towards the support of a Free School, established at, and annexed to, the said Academy ; for the purpose of educating such orphan children, or the children of such other poor & indigent persons as are unable to accomplish it with their own means : and who in the Judgment of the Trustees of the said Seminary, are best entitled to the benefit of this donation.   The aforesaid twenty shares I give and bequeath in perpetuity : the dividends only of which are to be drawn for, and applied by the said Trustees, for the time being, for the uses above mentioned : the stock to remain entire and untouched : unless indications of a failure of the said Bank should be apparent, or discontinuance thereof should render a removal of this fund necessary : in either of these cases, the amount of the stock here devised, is to be vested in some other Bank or Public Institution, whereby the interest may with regularity & certainty be drawn and applied as above.—And to prevent misconception, my meaning is, and is hereby declared to be, that these twenty shares are in lieu of, and not in addition to, the one thousand pounds given by a missive letter some years ago : in consequence whereof an annuity of fifty pounds has since been paid toward the support of this Institution.

"Item : Whereas by a law of the Commonwealth of Virginia, enacted in the year 1785, the Legislature thereof was pleased (as an evidence of its approbation of the services I had rendered the public during the Revolution—& partly, I believe, in consideration of my having suggested the vast advantages which the community would derive from the extension of its Inland Navigation, under Legislative patronage,) to present me with one hundred shares of one hundred dollars each, in the incorporated company established for the purpose of extending the navigation of James River from tide water to the mountains : and also with fifty shares of one hundred pounds sterling each, in the corporation of another company, likewise established for the similar purpose of opening the navigation of the Potomac River from tide water to Fort' Cumberland : the acceptance of which, although the offer was highly honorable and grateful to my feelings, was refused, as inconsistent with a principle which I had adopted, and had never departed from—namely—not to receive pecuniary compensation for any services I could render my Country in its arduous struggle with Great Britain, for its Rights : and because I had evaded similar propositions from other States in the Union : adding to this refusal, however, an intimation that, if it should be the pleasure of the Legislature, to permit me to appropriate the said shares to *public uses*, I would receive them on those terms with due sensibility : and this, it having consented to, in flattering terms, as will appear by a subsequent Law and Sundry Resolutions, in the most ample and honorable man-

ner, I proceed after this recital, for the more correct understanding of the case, to declare that as it has always been
a source of serious regret with me, to see the youth of these
United States sent to foreign countries for the purpose of
education, often before their minds were formed, or they
had imbibed any adequate ideas of the happiness of 'their
own : contracting, too frequently, not only habits of dissipa-
tion and extravagance, but principles unfriendly to Repub-
lican Government & to the true and genuine liberties of
mankind : which, thereafter, are rarely overcome.—For
these reasons, it has been my ardent wish, to see a plan devised on a liberal scale which would have· a tendency
to spr^d systematic ides through all parts of this rising
Empire, thereby to do away local attachments, and State
prejudices, as far as the nature of things would, or indeed
ought to admit, from our National Councils. Looking
anxiously forward to the accomplishment of so desirable an
object as this is (in my estimation,) my mind has not been
able to contemplate any plan more likely to effect the
measure than the establishment of a University in a cen-
tral part of the United States to which the youths of fortune and talents from all parts thereof might be sent for
the completion of their Education, in all the branches of
polite literature in arts and sciences—in acquiring knowledge in the principles of politics & good government ;—
and (as a matter of infinite importance in my judgment)
by associating with each other, and forming friendships in
Juvenile years, be enabled to free themselves in a proper
degree from those local prejudices and habitual Jealousies
which have just been mentioned : and which, when carried
to excess, are never failing sources of disquietude to the
public mind, & pregnant of mischievous consequences to
this Country—Under these impressions, so fully dilated.

" Item. I give and bequeath in perpetuity, the fifty shares
which I hold in the Potomac Company (under the aforesaid Acts of the Legislature of Virginia.) towards the

endowment of a University to be established within the limits of the District of Columbia, under the auspices of the general Government, if that Government should incline to extend a fostering hand towards it—and until such Seminary is established, and the funds arising on these shares shall be required for its support, my further will & devise is that the profit accruing therefrom shall, whenever the dividends are made, be laid out in purchasing stock in the Bank of Columbia or some other Bank, at the discretion of my Executors : or by the Treasurer of the United States for the time being under the direction of Congress ; provided, that honourable body should patronize the measure, and the dividends proceeding from the purchase of such stock is to be vested in more stock, and so on, until a sum adequate to the accomplishment of the object is obtained, of which I have not the smallest doubt, before many years passes away : even if no aid or encouraged is given by Legislative authority, or from any other source.

"Item. The hundred shares which I held in the James River Company, I have given, and now confirm in perpetuity to, and for the use and benefit of Liberty Hall Academy, in the County of Rockbridge, in the Commonwealth of Virginia.

"Item. I release, exonerate and discharge the Estate of my deceased brother Samuel Washington, from the payment of the money which is due to me for the land I sold to Philip Pendleton (lying in the County of Berkeley,) who assigned the same to him, the said Samuel : who, by agreement was to pay me therefor : And whereas by some contract (the purport of which was never communicated to me.) between the said Samuel and his son, Thornton Washington, the latter became possessed of the aforesaid land, without any conveyance having passed from me, either to the said Pendleton, the said Samuel, or the said Thornton, and without any consideration having been made, by which neglect neither the legal nor equitable title has been

alienated : it rests therefore with me to declare my intentions concerning the premises : and these are to give and
bequeath the said land to whomsoever the said Thornton
Washington (who is also dead,) devised the same : or to his
heirs forever, if he died intestate : Exonerating the estate
of the said Thornton, equally with that of the said Samuel
from payment of the purchase-money: which, with interest,
agreeably to the original contract with the said Pendleton,
would amount to more than a thousand pounds. And
whereas, two other sons of my said deceased brother Samuel, namely, George Steptoe Washington & Laurence
Augustine Washington, were by the decease of those to
whose care they were committed, were brought under my
protection, and in conseqᵉ have occasioned advances on
my part for their education at College, and other schools,
for their board, clothing & other incidental expenses, to
the amount of near five thousand dollars, over and above
the sum furnished by their Estate, wᶜʰ sum may be incon-
venient for them, or their father's Estate to refund.—I do
for these reasons acquit them, and the said Estate from the
payment thereof.—My intention being, that all accounts
between them & me and their father's Estate and me, shall
stand balanced.

"Item. The balance due to me from the Estate of Bartholomew Dandridge, deceased, (my wife's brother,) and
which amounted on the first day of October, 1795, to four
hundred and twenty-five pounds (as will appear by an
account rendered by his deceased son John Dandridge,
who was the acting Exʳ of his father's Will,) I release
and acquit from the payment thereof.—And the negroes,
(then thirty-three in number,) formerly belonging to the
said Estate, who were taken in execution—sold and purchased in on my account in the year   and ever since
have remained in the possession, and to the use of Mary,
widow of the said Bartholomew Dandridge, with their increase, it is my will and desire, shall continue and be in her

possession, without paying hire, or making compensation for the same, for the time past or to come, during her natural life : at the expiration of which, I direct that all of them who are forty years old & upwards, shall receive their freedom : all under that age and above sixteen, shall serve seven years and no longer, and all under sixteen years shall serve until they are twenty-five years of age, & then be free: and to avoid disputes respecting the ages of any of these negroes, they are to be taken to the Court of the County in which they reside, and the Judgment thereof, in this relation, shall be final, and a record thereof made : which may be adduced as evidence at any time thereafter, if disputes should arise concerning the same : And I further direct that the heirs of the said Bartholomew Dandridge shall equally, share the benefits arising from the services of the said negroes according to the tenor of this devise, upon the decease of their mother.

"Item : If Charles Carter, who intermarried with my niece Betty Lewis, is not sufficiently secured in the title to the lots he had of me in the town of Fredericksburg, it is my will and desire that my Executors shall make such conveyances of them as the law may require to render it perfect.

"Item. To my nephew William Augustine Washington and his heirs (if he should conceive them objects worth prosecuting) and to his heirs, a lot in the town of Manchester, (opposite to Richmond.) No. 265, drawn on my sole account, and also the tenth of one or two, hundred acre lots, and two or three half acre lots in the city and vicinity of Richmond, drawn in partnership with nine others, all in the lottery of the deceased William Byrd are given—as is also a lot which I purchased of John Hood conveyed by William Willie and Samuel Gordon, Trustees, of the said John Hood, numbered 139 in the town of Edinburgh, in the County of Prince George, State of Virginia.

" Item. To my nephew Bushrod Washington, I give and
bequeath all the papers in my possession which relate to
my civil and military administration of the affairs of this
Country : I leave to him also such of my private papers
as are worth preserving : and at the decease of my wife, and
before if she is not inclined to detain them, I give and bequeath my Library of books, and pamphlets of every kind.

" Item : Having sold lands which I possessed in the state
of Pennsylvania, and part of a tract held in equal right
with George Clinton, late Governor of New York, in the
State of New York ; my share of land and Interest in the
Great Dismal Swamp, and a tract of land which I owned in
the County of Gloucester, withholding the legal titles
thereto, until the consideration money should be paid,—
and having moreover leased and conditionally sold (as
will appear by the tenor of the said leases,) all my lands
upon the Great Kanhawa,—and the tract of land upon Difficult Run in the County of Loudon, it being my will and
direction, that whensoever the Contracts are fully, and respectively complied with, according to the spirit, true intent,
and meaning thereof, on the part of the purchasers, their
heirs, or assigns, that then, and in that case, conveyances are
to be made, agreeably to the terms of the said Contracts &
the money arising therefrom, when paid, to be vested in
Bank Stock : the dividends whereof, as of that also wch is
already vested therein, to inure to my said wife during her
life, but the Stock itself is to remain and be subject to the
general distribution, hereafter directed.

" Item. To the Earl of Buchan, I recommit, " the box
made of the " Oak that sheltered the Great Sir William Wallace, after the battle of Falkirk," presented to me by his
Lordship, in terms too flattering for me to repeat,—with a
request " to pass it, on the event of my decease, to the man
in my Country, who should appear to merit it best, upon
the same conditions that have induced him to send it to
me." Whether easy, or not, to select *the man* who might

comport with his Lordship's opinion in this respect, is not for me to say : but conceiving that no disposition of this valuable curiosity can be more eligible than the re-commitment of it to his own cabinet, agreeably to the original design of the Goldsmith's Company of Edinburgh, who presented it to him, and at his request, consented that it should be transferred to me ; I do give and bequeath the same to his Lordship, and in case of his decease, to his heir, with my grateful thanks for the distinguished honor of presenting it to me : and more especially for the favourable sentiments with which he accompanied it.

"Item. To my brother Charles Washington I give and bequeath the gold-headed cane left me by Doct^r Franklin in his will—I add nothing to it because of the ample provision I have made for his issue. To the acquaintances and friends of my Juvenile years, Lawrence Washington & Robert Washington, of Chotanck. I give my other two gold-headed canes, having my arms engraved on them, and to each (as they will be useful where they live,) I leave one of the spy glasses which constituted part of my Equipage during the late war. To my compatriot in arms and old and intimate friend Doct^r Craik, I give my Bureau (or as the Cabinet Makers called it, Tambour Secretary,) and the circular chair, an appendage of my sturdy :—To Doctor David Stuart, I give my large shaving and dressing table, and my Telescope. To the Reverend, now Bryan, Lord Fairfax, I give a Bible in three large folio volumes, with notes, presented to me by the Right Reverend Thomas Wilson, Bishop of Sodor and Man. To General de la Fayette, I give a pair of finely wrought steel pistols, taken from the enemy in the Revolutionary war. To my sisters in law Hannah Washington and Mildred Washington ; to my friends Eleanor Stuart, Hannah Washington, of Fairfield, and Elizabeth Washington of Hayfield, I give each a mourning ring of the value of one hundred dollars. These bequests are

10

not made for the intrinsic value of them, but as mementors of my esteem and regard. To Tobias Lear, I give the use of the farm which he now holds, in virtue of a lease from me to him, and his deceased wife (for and during their natural lives,) free from Rent during his life : at the expiration of which, it is to be disposed as is hereinafter directed. —To Sally B. Haynie (a distant relation of mine,) I give and bequeath three hundred dollars.—To Sarah Green daughter of the deceased Thomas. Bishop, & to Ann Walker, daughter of Jn° Alton, also deceased, I give, each, one hundred dollars, in consideration of the attachment of their fathers to me, each of whom having lived nearly forty years in my family.   To each of my nephews, William Augustine Washington, George Lewis, George Steptoe Washington, Bushrod Washington, & Samuel Washington, I give one of the swords or cutteaux of which I may die possessed : and they are to *chuse* in the order they are named.   These swords are accompanied with an injunction not to unsheath them for the purpose of shedding blood, except it be for self defence, or in defence of their Country & its rights : and in the latter case, to keep them unsheathed, and prefer falling with them in their hands, to the relinquishment thereof.

" And now

" Having gone through these specific devises, with explanations for the more correct understanding of the meaning and design of them, I proceed to the distribution of the more important parts of my Estate, in manner following.

"First : To my nephew Bushrod Washington and his heirs (partly in consideration of an intimation to his deceased father, while we were Bachelors, & he had kindly undertaken to superintend my Estate during my military services in the former war between Great Britain and France, that if I should fall therein, Mount Vernon (then less extensive in domain than at present,) should become his property,) I give and bequeath all that part thereof which is comprehended within the following limits, · viz : Beginning at the ford of Dogue run, near my mill, and extending along the road, and bounded thereby, as it now goes, and ever has gone since my recollection of it, to the ford of Little Hunting Creek, at the Gum spring until it comes to a knowl, opposite to an old road which formerly passed through the lower field of muddy hole farm : at which, on the north side of the said road are three red or Spanish oaks marked as a corner, and a stone placed, thence by a line of trees to be marked, rectangular to the back line, or outer boundary of the tract between Thomson Mason & myself,—thence with that line easterly (now double ditching with a post & Rail fence thereon,) to the run of little hunting creek, thence with that run which is the boundary between the lands of the late Humphrey Peake and me, to the tide water of the said creek, thence by that water to Potomac River, thence with the River to the mouth of Dogue creek,—and thence with the said Dogue creek, to the place of beginning at the aforesaid ford ; containing upwards of four thousand acres, be the same more or less—together with the Mansion house, and all other buildings, and improve^m thereon.

"Second. In consideration of the consanguinity between them and my wife, being as nearly related to her as to myself, as on account of the affection I had for, and the obligation I was under to, their father when living, who from his youth had attached himself to my person, and followed my fortunes through the vicissitudes of the late Revolution—afterwards devoting his time to the superintendence of my private concerns for many years, whilst my public employments rendered it impracticable for me to do it myself, thereby affording me essential services, and always performing them in a manner the most filial and respectful : for these reasons, I say, I give and bequeath to George Fayette Washington & Laurence Augustine Washington and their heirs, my estate east of little Hunting creek, lying on the river Potomac : including the farm of 360 acres, leased to Tobias Lear as noticed before—and containing in the whole, by Deeds, two thousand and seventy seven acres —be it more or less, which said Estate it is my will and desire should be equitably & advantageously divided between them, according to quantity, quality and other circumstances when the youngest shall have arrived at the age of twenty one years, by three judicious and disinterested men ;—one to be chosen by each of the brothers, and the third by these two. In the mean time if the termination of my wife's interest therein should have ceased, the profits arising therefrom are to be applied, for their joint uses and benefit :—

"Third.   And whereas it has always been my intention, since my expectation of having issue has ceased, to consider the grandchildren of my wife in the same light as I do my own relations, and to act a friendly part by them ; more especially by the two whom we have reared from their earliest infancy—namely—Eleanor Parke Custis and George Washington Parke Custis. And whereas the former of these hath lately intermarried with Lawrence Lewis, a son of my deceased sister Betty Lewis, by which union the inducement to provide for them both has been increased : Wherefore, I give and bequeath to the said Lawrence Lewis and Eleanor Parke Lewis, his wife, and their heirs, the residue of my Mount Vernon Estate, not already devised to my nephew Bushrod Washington, comprehended within the following description, viz : All the land north of the road leading from the ford of Dogue run to the Gum springs as described in the devise of the other part of the tract, to Bushrod Washington, until it comes to the stone and three red or Spanish oaks on the knowl,—thence with the rectangular line to the back line (between Mr. Mason & me,) thence with that line westerly, along the new double ditch to Dogue run, by the tumbling dam of my mill, thence with the said run to the ford aforementioned : to which I add all the land I possess west of the said Dogue run, and Dogue Cr^k bounded Easterly and Southerly thereby : together with the Mill, Distillery & all other houses and improvements on the premises, making together about two thousand acres, be it more or less.

"Fourth. Actuated by the principle already mentioned, I give and bequeath to George Washington Parke Custis, the Grandson of my wife, and my ward, and to his heirs, the tract I hold on four mile run in the vicinity of Alexandria, containing one thousand Two hundred acres, more or less : and my entire square, number twenty one, in the City of Washington.

"Fifth : All the rest and residue of my Estate, real and personal—not disposed of in manner aforesaid—In whatsoever consisting — wheresoever lying — and whensoever found—a Schedule of which, as far as is recollected, with a reasonable estimate of its value, is hereunto annexed—I desire may be sold by my Executors at such times—in such manner—and on such credits (if an equal, valid, and satisfactory distribution of the specific property cannot be made without,) as, in their judgment shall be most conducive to the interest of the parties concerned : and the monies arising therefrom to be divided into twenty three equal parts, and applied as follows, viz :

To William Augustine Washington, Elizabeth Spots-wood, Jane Thornton and the heirs of Ann Ashton, son and daughters of my deceased brother, Augustine Washington, I give and bequeath four parts ; that is, one part to each of them.—To Fielding Lewis, George Lewis, Robert Lewis, Howell Lewis and Betty Carter, sons and daughter of my deceased sister Betty Lewis, I give and bequeath, five other parts, one to each of them. To George Steptoe Washington, Lawrence Augustine Washington, Harriot

Parks, and the heirs of Thornton Washington, sons and daughter of my deceased brother, Samuel Washington, I give and bequeath other four parts, one part to each of them. To Corbin Washington, and the heirs 'of Jane Washington, son and daughter of my deceased brother John Augustine Washington I give and bequeath two parts : one part to each of them.

To Samuel Washington, Frances Ball and Mildred Hammond, son and daughters of my brother Charles Washington, I give and bequeath three parts : one part to each of them :—And to George Fayette Washington, Charles Augustine Washington and Maria Washington, sons and daughter of my deceased nephew, George Augustine Washington, I give one other part : that is, to each a third of that part. To Elizabeth Parke Law, Martha Parke Peter, and Eleanor Parke Lewis, I give and bequeath three other parts, that is, a part to each of them.

And to my nephews Bushrod Washington and Lawrence Lewis, and to my ward, the Grandson of my wife, I give and bequeath one other part :—that is, a third thereof to each of them.—And if it should so happen, that any of the persons whose names are here enumerated (unknown to me,) should now be deceased, or should die before me, that in either of these cases, the heirs of such deceased person shall, notwithstanding, derive all the benefit of the bequests : in the same manner as if he, or she, was actually living at the time.

And by way of advice, I recommend it to my Executors not to be precipitate in disposing of the landed property (therein directed to be sold,) if from temporary causes the sale thereof should be dull : experience having fully evinced, that the price of land (especially above the Falls of the Rivers and on the western waters,) have been progressively rising, and cannot be long checked in its increasing value. And I particularly recommend it to such of the Legatees (under this clause of my will,) as can make it convenient, to take each a share of my stock in the Potomac Company in preference to the amount of what it might sell for : being thoroughly convinced myself, that no uses to which the money can be applied will be so productive as the Tolls arising from this navigation when in full operation (and this from the nature of things it must be 'ere long,) & more especially if that of the Shenandoah is added thereto.

"The family vault at Mount Vernon requiring repairs, and being improperly situated besides, I desire that a new one of brick, and upon a larger scale, may be built, at the foot of what is commonly called the Vineyard enclosure, on the ground which is marked out.—In which my remains, with those of my deceased relatives (now in the old vault,) and such others of my family as may chuse to be entombed there, may be deposited. And it is my express desire that my corpse may be interred in a private manner, without parade or funeral oration.

" Lastly, I constitute and appoint my dearly beloved wife Martha Washington, my nephews, William Augustine Washington, Bushrod Washington, George Steptoe Washington, Sam¹ Washington & Lawrence Lewis and my ward Geo. Washington Parke Custis, (when he shall have arrived at the age twenty years,) Executrix and Executors, of this will and testament.

" In the construction of which it will readily be perceived that no professional character has been consulted or has had any agency in the draught and that, although it has occupied many of my leisure hours to digest and to through it into its present form, it may, notwithstanding, appear crude & incorrect.—But having endeavored to be plain and explicit, in all the devises—even at the expence of prolixity, perhaps of tautology, I hope, and trust, that no disputes will arise concerning them : but if, contrary to expectation, the case should be otherwise, from the want of legal expression, or the usual technical terms,—or because too much or too little has been said on any of the devises to be consonant with law, my will and direction expressly is, that all disputes (if unhappily any should arise,) shall be decided by three impartial and intelligent men, known for their probity and good understanding : two to be chosen by the disputants, each having the choice of one—and the third by those two.—Which three men thus chosen, shall, unfettered by law, or legal constructions, declare their sense of the testator's intention : and such decision is, to all intents and purposes to be as binding on the parties as if it had been given in the Supreme Court of the United States.

"In witness of all, and of each of the things herein contained I have set my hand and seal this ninth day of July in the year one thousand seven hundred and ninety *—& of the Independence of the United States the twenty fourth.

G Washington   [SEAL.]

* It appears the testator omitted the word "nine."

Schedule of property comprehended in the foregoing will : which is directed to be sold, and some of it, conditionally is sold : with descriptive and explanatory notes relative thereto

IN VIRGINIA.

	Acres.	Price.	Dollars.	
Loudoun County				
Difficult run . . .	300		$6,666	(*a*)
Loudoun & Fauquier				
Ashby's Bent . . .	2,481	$10	24,810 }	(*b*.)
Chattins run . . .	885	$8	7,080 }	
Berkeley				
So Fork of Bullskin .	1,600			
Head of Evan's Mill .	453			
In Wormely's line . .	183			
	2,236	$20	$44,720	(*c*.)
Frederick				
Bought from Mercer .	571	20	11,420	(*d*.)
Hampshire				
On Potmk. river above B.	240	15	3,600	(*e*.)
Gloucester				
On North River . .	400	abt	3,600	(*f*.)
Nansemond,				
Near Suffolk ⅓ of 1119 }	373	$8	2,984	(*g*.)
Acres . . }				
Great Dismal Swamp				
My dividend thereof		abt	20,000	(*h*)
Ohio River				
Round Bottom . .	587			
Little Kenhawa . .	2,314			
	2,901		$124,880	

Schedule—Continued.

			Dol.	Dollars.	
Amount brot. over	.	2,901		$124,880	
16 miles lower down	.	2,448			
Opposite big bent	.	4,395			
		9,744	10	97,440	(*i.*)
Great Kenhawa					
Near the mouth west	.	10,990			
East side above	.	7,276			
Mouth of Cole river	.	2,000			
Opposite thereto	.	2,950			
Burning Spring	.	125			
		23,341		200,000	(*k.*)
Maryland					
Charles County	.	600	6	3,600	(*l.*)
Montgomery do	.	519	12	6,228	(*m.*)
Pennsylvania					
Great Meadows	.	234	6	1,404	(*n.*)
New York					
Mohawk River abt	.	1,000	6	6,000	(*o.*)
North Western Territory					
On little Miami	.	839			
Ditto	.	977			
Ditto	.	1,235			
		3,051	5	15,251	(*p.*)
Kentucky					
Rough Creek	.	3,000			
Ditto adjoing	.	2,000			
		5,000	$2	10,000	(*q.*)
Lots, viz : City of Washington.					
Two near the capitol, sqr. 634					
cost $963, and with Build's.				15,000	(*r*)
Carried over.				479,803	

Schedule—Continued.

	Dollars.
Amt. brought over. . . .	$479,803

Lots. City of Washington.
>   No. 5, 12, 13 & 14, the 3 last, water lots . on the Eastern Branch, in sqr. 667, containing together 34,438 sqr. ft. at 12 cts. . . . . — 4,132 (*s.*)

Alexandria.
>   Corner of Pitt & Prince streets, half an acre—laid out into buildings, 3 or 4 of whi^{ch} are let on ground Rent ' at $30 pr. foot. . . . . . — 4,000 (*t.*)

Winchester.
>   A lot in the town of half an acre, & another in the commons of about 6 acres, supposed. . . . . . — 400 (*u.*)

Bath, or Warm Springs.
>   Two well situated & had buildings to the amount of $150. . . . . — 800 (*v.*)

Stock.
>   United States, 6 P c^{ts.} . . 3,746
>   Do   deferred 1873
>   3 P cts. 2946. . 2500 — 6,246 (*x.*)

Potomack Company.
>   24 shares, cost ea. £100 ster. . . . — 20,666 (*y.*)

James River Company.
>   5 shares, each cost $100. . . . — 500 (*z.*)

Bank of Columbia.
>   170 shares—$40 each. . . 6,800

Bank of Alexandria—besides 20 to   (&.)
>   the free school 5. . . . 1,000

                                     $514,347

Schedule—Continued.

Amt. brought over.　.　.　.　514,347

Stock—living—viz :

    1 Covering horse, 5 Co. Horses, 4 riding
    do—six brood mares—20 working
    horses & mares—2 covering jacks—
    & three young ones—10 she asses,
    42 working mules, 15 younger ones—
    329 head of horned cattle, 640 head of
    sheep, & a large stock of hogs—the
    precise number unknown.

☞ My manager has estimated this live
    stock at $7,000 but I shall set it down
    in order to make said sum at.　　　　15,653

Aggregate Amt.　　.　.　$530,000

NOTES.

(*a.*) This tract for the size of it is valuable : more for its situation—than the quality of its soil, though that is good for farming ; with a considerable portion of gr^d that might, very easily, be improved into meadow. It lies on the Great road from the city of Washington, Alexandria & Georgetown to Leesburgh & Winchester, at Difficult bridge, nineteen miles from Alexandria, less from Washington and Georgetown, and not more than three from Matildaville, at the Great Falls of Potomac. There is a valuable seat on the premises, and the whole is conditionally sold, for the sum annexed in the schedule.

(*b.*) What the selling prices of lands in the vicinity of these two tracts are, I know not ; but compared with those above the ridge, and others below them, the value annexed will appear moderate, a less one would not obtain them from me.

(*c.*) The surrounding land, not superior in soil, situation or properties of any sort, sell currently at from twenty to thirty dollars an acre, the lowest price is affixed to these.

(*d.*) The observations made in the last note applies equally to this tract tract—being in the vicinity of them, and of similar quality, although it lies in another County.

(*e.*) This tract, though small, is extremely valuable: It lies on Potomac River about 12 miles above the town of Bath (or Warm Springs,) and is in the shape of a horse-shoe—the river running almost around it. Two hundred acres of it is rich low grounds : with a great abundance of the largest and finest walnut trees : which, with the produce of the soil, might, (by means of the improved navigation of the Potomac,) be brought to a shipping port with more ease, and at a smaller expence, than that which is transported 30 miles only by land.

(*f.*) This tract of second rate Gloucester low grounds. It has no improvements thereon, but lies on navigable water, abounding in fish and oysters. It was received in payment of a debt (carrying interest), and valued in the year 1789 by an impartial gentleman at £800. N. B. It has lately been sold and there is due thereon, a balance equal to what is annexed the Scedule.

(*g.*) These 373 acres are the third part of undivided purchases made by the deceased Fielding Lewis, Thomas Walker and myself : on full conviction that they would become valuable. The land lies on the road from Suffolk to Norfolk—touches (if I am not mistaken) some part of the navigable water of Nansemond River—borders on and comprehends part of the Rich Dismal Swamp ; is capable of great improvement : and from its situation must become extremely valuable.

(*h.*) This is an undivided interest whch I held in the Great Dismal Swamp Company, containing about 4,000 acres, with my part of the Plantation & the Stock thereon, belonging to the Company in the said swamp.

(*i*) These several tracts of land are of the first quality on the Ohio River, in the parts where they are situated : being almost if not altogether River bottoms. The smallest of these tracts is actually sold at ten dollars an acre, but the consideration therefor, not received—the rest are equally valuable and will sell as high—especially that which lies just below the Little Kenhawa and is opposite to a thick settlement on the west side the River. The four tracts have an aggregate breadth upon the river of sixteen miles and is bounded thereby that distance.

(*k.*) These tracts are situated on the Great Kenhawa river, and the first four are bounded thereby for more than forty miles. It is acknowledged by all who have seen them (and of the tract containing 10990 acres which I have been on myself, I can assert,) that there is no richer or more valuable land in all that Region—they are conditionally sold, for the sum mentioned in the Schedule—that is $200,000. & if the terms of that Sale are not complied with they will command considerably more. The tract of which the 125 acres is a moiety, was taken up by General Andrew Lewis and myself, for & on account of a bituminous spring which it contains, of so inflammable a nature as to burn as freely as spirits, and is as nearly difficult to extinguish.

(*l.*) I am but little acquainted with this land, although I have once been on it.—It was received (many years since.) in discharge of a debt due to me from Daniel Jenifer Adams to the value annexed thereto—& must be worth more. It is very level, lies near the River Potomac.

(*m.*) This tract lies about 30 miles above the City of Washington, not far from Kittoctan. It is good farming land, and by those who are well acquainted with it I am informed that it would sell at twelve or $15 p. acre.

(*n.*) This land is valuable on account of its local situation, & other properties. It affords an exceeding good stand on Braddock's road from Fort Cumberland to Pittsburgh, and besides a fertile soil, possesses a large quantity of natural meadow, fit for the scythe. It is distinguished by the appellation of the Great Meadows, where the first action with the French in the year 1754, was fought.

(*o*) This is the moiety of about 2000 acres, which remains unsold of 6071 acres, on the Mohawk River (Montgomery County) in a patent granted to Daniel Coxe, in the Township of Coxeborough, & Carolaca, as will appear by deed from Marinus Willett & wife to Geo. Clinton (late Governor of New York,) and myself. The latter sales have been at six dollars an acre and what remains unsold will fetch that or more.

(*p*.) The quality of these lands and their situation may be known by the Surveyor's certificates—which are filed along with the patents. They lie in the vicinity of Cincinnati—one tract near the mouth of the little Miami— another seven, and the third ten miles up the same. I have been informed that they will readily command more than they are estimated at.

(*q*.) For the description of these tracts in detail, see General Spotswood's letters filed with the other papers relating to them. Besides the general good quality of the land, there is a valuable Bank of Iron ore thereon—which when the settlement becomes more populous (and settlers are moving that way very fast,) will be found very valuable, as the rough Creek, a branch of Green River affords ample water for Furnices and Forges.

Lots, viz. :

CITY OF WASHINGTON.

(*r*.) The two lots near the capitol, in square 634, cost me $963, only ; but in this price I was favoured, on condition that I should build two brick houses three story high each. Without this reduction the selling prices of those lots would have cost me about $1350. These lots, with the

Buildings thereon, when completed will stand me in
$15000 at least.

(*s.*) Lots No. 5, 12, 13 & 14, on the Eastern branch, are
advantageously situated on the water, & although many
lots much less convenient have sold a great deal higher,
I will rate these at 12 cts. the square foot only.

ALEXANDRIA.

(*t*) For this lot, though unimproved, I have refused $3500.
It has since been laid off into proper sized lots for building
on, three or four of which are let on ground rent, forever—
at three dollars a foot on the street—and this price is asked
for both fronts on Pitt & Princes street.

WINCHESTER.

(*u.*) As neither the lot in the town or common have any
improvements on them, it is not easy to fix a price, but as
both are well situated, it is presumed the price annexed to
them in the schedule is a reasonable value.

BATH.

(*w.*) The lots in Bath (two adjoining) cost me, to the best
of my recollection, between fifty and sixty pounds, 20 years
ago, and the buildings thereon £150 more. Whether property there has increased or decreased in its value, and in
what condition the houses are, I am ignorant—but suppose
they are not valued too high.

(*x.*) These are the sums which are actually funded,—and
though no more in the aggregate than $7,566, stand me in
at least ten thousand pounds Virginia money, being the
amount of bonded and other debts due to me, and discharged during the war, when money had depreciated in
that rate and was so settled by public authority.

(*y.*) The value annexed to these shares is what they
actually cost me and is the price affixed by law, & although

the present settling price is under par ; my advice .to the legatees (for whose benefit they are intended, especially those who can afford to lie out of the money,) is that each should take and hold one : there being a moral certainty of great & increasing profit arising from them in the course of a few years.

(z.) It is supposed that the shares in the James River Company must also be productive : but of this I can give no decided opinion for want of more accurate information.

(&.) These are the nominal prices of the shares in the Banks of Alexandria and Columbia : the selling prices vary according to circumstances. But as the stock usually divide from eight to ten per cent per annum, they must be worth the former at least—so long as the Banks are conceived to be secure, although circumstances may sometimes below it. The value of the live stock depends more upon the quality than quantity of the different species of it, & this again upon the demand and judgment, or fancy of purchasers.

G⁰ WASHINGTON.

Mount Vernon
9th : July 1799.

At a Court held for the County of Fairfax, the 20th, January 1800. This last will and testament of Geo. Washington, deceased, late President of the United States of America, was presented in Court by Geo. Steptoe Washington, Samuel Washington and Lawrence Lewis, three of the Executors therein named, who made oath thereto, and the same being proved by the oath of Charles Little, Charles Simms and Ludwell Lee, to be in the true hand writing of the said Testator, as also the schedule thereto annexed, & the said will being sealed and signed by him, is on motion ordered to be recorded—And the said Executors having given security and performed what the Laws require a

11

certificate is granted them for obtaining a probate thereof
in due form.

Teste :

G. DENEALE, C. Fx.

Examined by
    G. DENEALE.

Virginia, to wit :

I, F. D. Richardson, Clerk of the County Court of Fairfax County, Virginia, do hereby certify, that the foregoing is a full, true and complete copy of the last will & testament of Genl. Go Washington, as the same is now on record among the will records of my said Court. Given under my hand, and the seal of said Court, this 22d. day of October A. D. [SEAL.] 1878, & in the 103rd. year of the Commonwealth of Virginia.

F. D. RICHARDSON, Clerk.

Virginia, to wit :

I, James Sangster, Judge of the County Court of Fairfax County, in the State aforesaid, do certify, that F. D. Richardson, whose genuine signature appears to the foregoing certificate, is Clerk of the said Court and that all his official acts as such are entitled to full faith and credit.

Given under my hand, this 24 day of Oct. 1878.

JAMES SANGSTER, Judge.

Washington,

The Defender of his Country; the Founder of Liberty;
The Friend of Man.
History and Tradition are explored in vain
For a Parallel to his Character.
In the annals of modern Greatness
He stands alone,
And the noblest Names of Antiquity
Lose their Lustre in his Presence.
Born the Benefactor of Mankind,
He united all the Qualities necessary
To an illustrious Career.
Nature made him Great,
He made himself Virtuous.
Called by his Country to the Defense of her Liberties,
He triumphantly vindicated the Rights of Humanity,
And on the Pillars of National Independence
Laid the Foundations of a Great Republic.
Twice invested with Supreme Magistracy
By the Unanimous Voice of a Free People,
He surpassed in the Cabinet
The Glories of the Field.
And, voluntarily resigning the Sceptre and the Sword,
Retired to the Shades of Private Life.
A spectacle so new and so sublime
Was contemplated with the profoundest Admiration;
And the Name of WASHINGTON,
Adding new Lustre to Humanity,
Resounded to the remotest Regions of the Earth.
Magnanimous in Youth,
Glorious through Life,
Great in Death.
His highest Ambition, the Happiness of Mankind,
His noblest Victory the Conquest of himself.
Bequeathing to Posterity the Inheritance of his Fame,
And building his MONUMENT in the Hearts of his Countrymen,
He lived the Ornament of the Eighteenth Century,
He died regretted by a Mourning World.

23 BETTY WASHINGTON, second child of Augustine (by second wife), was born in Stafford county, Virginia, 20 June, 1733.

She married Colonel Fielding Lewis. She was his second wife. A great-grandson now (1876) lives on Hoboken Heights, at Stevens' Castle—Colonel Edward Parke Custis Lewis, 314 Hudson Street, Hoboken. Her children were ·

> **24** FIELDING LEWIS, born in Stafford county, Virginia, about 1755.
>
> **24** BETTY LEWIS, born in Stafford county, Virginia, about 1758.
>
> **24** GEORGE FIELDING LEWIS, born in Stafford county, Virginia, about 1760.
>
> **24** ROBERT LEWIS, born in Stafford county, Virgina, about 1765.
>
> **24** HOWELL LEWIS, born in Stafford county, Virginia, Dec. 12, 1770.
>
> **24** LAURENCE LEWIS, born in Stafford county, Virginia, about 1775.

"Betty Lewis had a number of children, many of whom died young, but five sons and a daughter are yet living."— *General Washington's Letter, May 2, 1752.*

23 MILDRED WASHINGTON, sixth child of Augustine (by second wife), was born 21 June, 1739. Died infant, 28 Oct., 1740.

23 COLONEL SAMUEL WASHINGTON, third child of Augustine (by second wife), was born in Stafford county, Virginia, 16 Nov., 1734.

He was Colonel in the American Army. He died at Harewood, in Berkeley county, Virginia, in 1781. He married first, Jane, daughter of Colonel John Champe. No children. Married second, Mildred, daughter of Colonel John Thornton. He had issue:

b Hall

THE WASHINGTON MONUMENT RICHMOND VA

THOMAS CRAWFORD, SCULPTOR

24 THORNTON WASHINGTON, born in Stafford county, Virginia, about 1760.

24 TRISTAM WASHINGTON, born in Stafford county, Virginia, about 1763.

Married third, Lucy, daughter of Nathaniel Chapman. No children. Married fourth, Anne, daughter of Colonel William Steptoe (widow of Willoughby Allerton). Children by fourth wife :

24 FREDERICK or FERDINAND WASHINGTON, born at Harewood, Berkeley county, Virginia, 1773.

24 GEORGE STEPTOE WASHINGTON, born in Harewood, Berkeley county, Virginia, 1775.

24 LAURENCE AUGUSTINE WASHINGTON, born in Harewood, Berkeley county, Virginia, 1777.

24 HARRIOT PARKS WASHINGTON, born in Harewood, Berkeley county, Virginia, 1780.

His fifth wife was Widow Perrin.

"Samuel Washington, son of Augustine and Mary, was five times married. First, to Jane, daughter of Colonel John Champe. Second, to Mildred, daughter of Colonel John Thornton. Third, to Lucy, daughter of Nathaniel Chapman. Fourth, to Anne, daughter of Colonel William Steptoe, and widow of Willoughby Allerton. Fifth, to Widow Perrin. Samuel by his second wife, Mildred, had issue one son, Thornton, who was twice married, and left three sons. By his fourth wife, Anne, he had three sons, Ferdinand, George Steptoe, and Laurence Augustine, and a daughter, Harriet. Ferdinand was married, but died soon after, leaving no issue. The other two sons and daughter are living (1792), and single. Samuel had children by his other wives, but they all died in their infancy.

"Samuel departed this life, A. D. 1781, at Harewood, in the county of Berkeley, where he was buried."—*General Washington's Letter, May 2, 1792.*

Colonel Samuel Washington built the Harewood House, near Charlestown, Jefferson county, West Virginia, about

A. D. 1752, and lived there until his death in 1781. He often entertained his distinguished brother, General George Washington, beneath his hospitable roof

EXTRACT FROM GENERAL WASHINGTON'S WILL.

" I release, exonerate and discharge the Estate of my deceased brother Samuel Washington, from the payment of the money which is due to me for the land I sold to Philip Pendleton (lying in the County of Berkeley,) who assigned the same to him, the said Samuel : who, by agreement was to pay me therefor : And whereas by some contract (the purport of which was never communicated to me,) between the said Samuel and his son, Thornton Washington, the latter became possessed of the aforesaid land, without any conveyance having passed from me, either to the said Pendleton, the said Samuel, or the said Thornton, and without any consideration having been made, by which neglect neither the legal nor equitable title has been alienated : it rests therefore with me to declare my intentions concerning the premises : and these are to give and bequeath the said land to whomsoever the said Thornton Washington (who is also dead,) devised the same : or to his heirs forever, if he died intestate : Exonerating the estate of the said Thornton, equally with that of the said Samuel from payment of the purchase-money: which, with interest, agreeably to the original contract with the said Pendleton, would amount to more than a thousand pounds. And whereas, two other sons of my said deceased brother Samuel, namely, George Steptoe Washington & Laurence Augustine Washington, were by the decease of those to whose care they were committed, were brought under my protection, and in conseq^e have occasioned advances on my part for their education at College, and other schools, for their board, clothing & other incidental expenses, to the amount of near five thousand dollars, over and above the sum furnished by their Estate, wch sum may be incon-

venient for them, or their father's Estate to refund.—I do
for these reasons acquit them, and the said Estate from the
payment thereof.—My intention being, that all accounts
between them & me and their father's Estate and me, shall
stand balanced."

23 JOHN AUGUSTINE WASHINGTON, fourth child of Augustine
   (by second wife), was born in Stafford county, Virginia,
   13 Jan., 1736.   In 1785 he was chosen one of the Vestry-
   men of Cople Parish, in Westmoreland.   Married Hannah,
   daughter of Col. John Bushrod, of Westmoreland county.
   Had several children who died young, and left two sons
   and two daughters :
      24 JANE WASHINGTON, born in Stafford county, Vir-
         ginia, about 1758.
      24 MILDRED WASHINGTON, born in Stafford county,
         Virginia, about 1760.
      24 BUSHROD WASHINGTON, born in Stafford county,
         Virginia, 5 June, 1762.
      24 CORBIN WASHINGTON, born at Bushfield, West-
         moreland county, Virginia, about 1765.
      24 WILLIAM AUGUSTINE WASHINGTON, born in Stafford
         county, Virginia, about 1767.
   To Hannah, wife of John A. Washington, was left by
General Washington, in his will, a mourning ring of the
value of one hundred dollars.
   " John Augustine Washington died in Feb., 1787, at his
estate on Nomony, in Westmoreland county, and was
there buried."—*General Washington's Letter.*

23 COL. CHARLES WASHINGTON, fifth child of Augustine
   (by second wife), was born in Stafford county, Virginia,
   about 1740.   He was Colonel in the American Army.   He
   married, Mildred, daughter of Colonel Francis Thornton, of Spottswood county, Virginia.   He had issue :

24 GEORGE AUGUSTINE WASHINGTON, born in Stafford
county, Virginia, about 1763.

24 SAMUEL WASHINGTON, born in Stafford county, Virginia, about 1765.

24 FRANCES WASHINGTON, born in Stafford county,
Virginia, about 1772. Married Col. Burgess Ball.

24 MILDRED WASHINGTON, born in Stafford county,
Virginia, about 1777. Married Hammond.

He laid out the town that now bears his name " Charlestown," in Jefferson county, West Virginia. His place of
residence was called " Happy Retreat."

EXTRACTS FROM GENERAL WASHINGTON'S WILL.

Item. " To my brother, Charles Washington, I give and
bequeath the Gold-headed cane, left me by Dr. Franklin,
in his will. I add nothing to it because of the ample provision I have made for his issue."

Item. " To Samuel Washington, Frances Ball and Mildred Hammond, son and daughters of my brother Charles
Washington, I give and bequeath three parts of the residue
of my estate, one part to each of them."

To Mildred, wife of Charles Washington, was left a
mourning ring, of the value of one hundred dollars.

24 WARNER WASHINGTON, first of Warner, first of John,
first of Laurence, first of Col. John, of Bridge's Creek,
Virginia, was born in Gloucester county, Virginia, April
15, 1751. Died in Llewellyn, Clark county, Virginia.

After his father's second marriage he removed with him
to Fairfield, Clark county, Virginia, thence to Clifton,
thence to Audley, thence to Llewellyn, where he died.

Married, first, in Gloucester county, 18 Oct., 1770, to
Mary, daughter of Francis (and Frances Perrin) Whiting,
of Gloucester county, Virginia. She died at Clifton, Virginia, A. D. 1794. " Many sons and daughters."—*George
Washington's Letter*, 2 *May*, 1792. He had issue :

25 WARNER WASHINGTON, born at Clifton, Virginia, Dec. 7, 1771.

25 JOHN WHITING WASHINGTON, born in Kentucky, Oct. 4, 1773.

25 FRANCES WASHINGTON, born at Clifton, Virginia, April 30, 1775.

25 EMILY WASHINGTON, born at Clifton, Virginia, May 8, 1778.

25 SYDNEY WASHINGTON, born at Clifton, Virginia, May 31, 1780. Died young.

25 HENRY WASHINGTON, born at Clifton, Virginia, Mar. 8, 1782.

25 FRANCIS WHITING WASHINGTON, born at Clifton, Virginia, June 18, 1784.

25 BEVERLY WASHINGTON, born at Clifton, Virginia, Aug. 25, 1786.

25 PERRIN WASHINGTON, born at Clifton, Virginia, Feb. 7, 1790.

Married, second, at Elmington, Gloucester county, Virginia, June 13, 1795, to Sarah Warner Rootes, of ———. Children :

25 READE WASHINGTON, born at Audley, Virginia, May 18, 1796.

25 THACHER WASHINGTON, born at Audley, Virginia, Dec. 5, 1797. Died infant.

25 ELIZABETH WARNER WASHINGTON, born at Audley, Virginia, Sept. 28, 1800.

25 FAIRFAX WASHINGTON, born at Audley, Virginia, Mar. 30, 1802.

25 WILLIAM HERBERT WASHINGTON, born at Audley, Virginia, May 30, 1803.

25 ALEXANDER HAMILTON WASHINGTON, born at Audley, Virginia, Mar. 5, 1805.

25 MARY HERBERT WASHINGTON, born at Audley, Virginia, Sept. 25, 1808.

24 MILDRED WASHINGTON, second child of Warner, was born at Fairfield, Virginia, A. D. 1765. Removed to Woodbury, now (1877) Mansfield, Virginia. Died there about 1808. Married at Fairfield, by Rev. Alexander Belmaine, about 1791, to Albion Throckmorton, of Gloucester county, Virginia. He died at Woodbury. Children :

    25 WARNER WASHINGTON THROCKMORTON, born at Woodbury, Virginia, Feb., 1792. Died in Jefferson county, Virginia, in 1855.

    25 HANNAH FAIRFAX THROCKMORTON, born at Woodbury, Virginia, in 1793. Died in Memphis, Tennessee, in 1858.

    25 CATHARINE THROCKMORTON, born at Woodbury, Virginia, in 1796. Died in Nashville, Tennessee.

24 HANNAH FAIRFAX WASHINGTON, third child of Warner, was born at Fairfield, Virginia, in April, 1767. Removed in 1787 to Gloucester county. Returned to Clarke county, about 1811. Died at Berryville, Virginia, Aug. 3, 1828. Married at Fairfield, by Rev. Alexander Belmaine, A. D. 1787, to Peter Beverly, son of Peter Beverly (and Elizabeth Burwell) Whiting, of Elmington, Virginia. He died at Oakley, 1810–11. Children :

    25 BEVERLY WHITING, born in Gloucester county, Virginia, A. D. 1788. Died infant.

    25 WARNER WHITING, born in Gloucester county, Virginia, Dec., 1790.

    25 ANNE BEVERLY WHITING, born in Gloucester county, Virginia, Sept., 1792.

    25 LOUISA WHITING, born in Gloucester county, Virginia, Jan., 1795.

    25 HARRIET THACHER WHITING, born in Gloucester county, Virginia, Sept., 1797.

    25 HANNAH FAIRFAX WHITING, born in Gloucester county, Virginia, Dec., 1799.

    25 PETER BEVERLY WHITING, born in Gloucester county, Virginia, A. D. 1802.

25 MARY BLAIR WHITING, born in Gloucester county, Virginia, A. D. 1804.

25 LOUISA SKAIFE WHITING, born in Gloucester county, Virginia, A. D. 1807.

24 CATHARINE WASHINGTON, fourth child of Warner, was born at Belvoir, Virginia, Apr. 7, 1769. Died at Roseville, Clarke county, Virginia, A. D. 1845. Married at Fairfield, by Rev. Alexander Belmaine, in 1789, to Dr. John Nelson, son of Roger Nelson, of Frederick City, Maryland. He died at Frankfort, Jefferson county, Virginia. Children :

25 PHILIP THOMAS NELSON, born Nov. 6, 1790.
25 LUCINDA   "   "   May 23, 1792.
25 HANNAH FAIRFAX   "   "   Nov. 18, 1793.
25 LOUISA WASHINGTON "   "   A. D. 1796.
25 GEORGE WILLIAM   "   "   A. D. 1798.
25 ELIZABETH CARY   "   "   May, 1800.
25 GERALDINE   "   "   about 1802.
25 ANNE FAIRFAX   "   "   "   1805.

24 ELIZABETH WASHINGTON, fifth child of Warner, was born at Fairfield, Virginia, A. D. 1771. Died there a few months after her marriage. She was married at Fairfield, about 1790, by Rev. Mr. Belmaine, to George Booth, of Gloucester county, Virginia.

24 LOUISA WASHINGTON, sixth child of Warner, was born at Fairfield, Virginia, about 1775. Died at Fairfield, soon after marriage. Married at Fairfield, about 1795, by Rev. Alexander Belmaine, to Thomas Fairfax, eldest son of her uncle, Rev. Bryan (and Miss Cary) Fairfax, of Mount Eagle.

24 FAIRFAX WASHINGTON, seventh child of Warner, was born at Fairfield, about 1778. Removed to Elkton, Kentucky. Died there, in 1860. Married at ———, about

1804, to Sarah Armistead, of Hesse, Gloucester county, Virginia. She died at Elton, Kentucky. Children:

25 WILLIAM ARMISTEAD WASHINGTON, born at Fairfield, Virginia, about 1805.

25 WARNER WASHINGTON, born at Fairfield, Virginia.

25 MARY WASHINGTON, born at Fairfield, Virginia.

25 ANNE OLIVE WASHINGTON, born at Fairfield, Virginia, about 1812.

25 FAIRFAX WASHINGTON, born at Fairfield, Virginia.

25 VIRGINIA WASHINGTON, born at Elton, Kentucky, about 1820. (All living in 1861.)

24 WHITING WASHINGTON, eighth child of Warner, was born at Fairfield, Virginia, about 1780. Removed to Logan county, Kentucky. Died there. Married in Clarke county, Virginia, about 1805, to Rebecca, daughter of Charles Smith, of Berryville, Clarke county, Virginia, widow, living near Elton, Kentucky.

25 CHARLES HENRY WASHINGTON, born at Elmington, Virginia, about 1806.

25 Daughter, in Kentucky, about 1808.

25 Daughter,   "   "   1810.

24 THACHER WASHINGTON, only son of Henry, second of John, first of Laurence, first of Col. John, of Bridge's Creek, Virginia, was born in Gloucester county, Virginia, about 1740.

"He married a daughter of Sir John Peyton, of Gloucester county, and lived on the family estate left to his grandfather, John, at Mahodoe, in Westmoreland county. Had several children."

24 JOHN LEWIS, first child of Catharine Washington (page 123), fifth of John, first of Laurence, first of Col. John, of Bridge's Creek, Virginia, was born at ———, Virginia.

24 'FRANCES LEWIS, second child of Catharine Washington, born at ——, Virginia. Died without issue.

24 ELIZABETH WASHINGTON, first child of Augustine, second of Augustine, second of Laurence, first of Colonel John, was born at Wakefield, Bridge's Creek, Virginia, about 1750. Married General Alexander Spotswood, of Spotsylvania county, Virginia. Children were:

    25 HENRIETTA SPOTSWOOD, born at ——, Virginia, about 1775. Married her cousin, Bushrod Washington, of Mount Zephyr.

    25 PATSY SPOTSWOOD, born at ——, Virginia. Not married.

    25 WILLIAM SPOTSWOOD, born at ——, Virginia.

    25 GEORGE SPOTSWOOD, born at ——, Virginia.

24 JANE WASHINGTON, second child of Augustine, was born at Wakefield, Bridge's Creek, Virginia, about 1752. Married Colonel William Thornton, of Culpepper county, Virginia.

24 ANN WASHINGTON, third child of Augustine, was born at Wakefield, Bridge's Creek, Virginia, about 1755. Married Burdet Ashton, of Westmoreland county, Virginia.

    25 SARAH ASHTON, born at ——, Virginia, about 1775. Married Nickolas Fitzhugh. Left child.

Other children died young.

24 COLONEL WILLIAM AUGUSTINE WASHINGTON, fourth child of Augustine, second of Augustine, second of Laurence, first of Colonel John, fifth of Leonard, first of Laurence, first of Laurence, first of Laurence, first of Thomas, first of Robert, first of John, first of Robert, first of John, first of John, first of John, second of Robert, second of Robert, first of Robert, first of Walter, fourth of Bondo, second of Akaris, first of Bardolf, second of

Torfin the Dane ; was born at Wakefield, Bridge's Creek, Virginia, 25 Nov., 1757. "Removed about 1802 to, and died at, Georgetown, Virginia, 2 or 10 Oct., 1810. Was buried in the Vault at Mount Vernon. He married his cousin Jane, 25 Sept., 1777, daughter of John Augustine Washington, of Bushfield, Westmoreland county, Virginia, by whom he has four children."—*General Washington's Letter*, 2 *May*, 1792. His children were:

   25 AUGUSTINE WASHINGTON, born at Haywood, West-moreland county, Virginia, about 1778. Died, aged 20 years.

   25 CORBIN AYLETT WASHINGTON, born at Haywood, Westmoreland county, Virginia, about 1780. Died young.

   25 HANNAH BUSHROD WASHINGTON, born at Haywood, Westmoreland county, Virginia, about 1782. Died, aged 20 years.

   25 BUSHROD WASHINGTON, born at Haywood, West-moreland county, Virginia, 4 April, 1785.

   25 ANN AYLETTA WASHINGTON, born at Haywood, Westmoreland county, Virginia, about 1787.

   25 GEORGE CORBIN WASHINGTON, born at Haywood, Westmoreland county, Virginia, 20 Aug., 1789.

   25 LAURENCE WASHINGTON, born at Haywood, West-moreland county, Virginia, 26 Feb., 1791 ?

Wife died about 1791. Married second, 10 July, 1792, to Mollie, or Polly, daughter of Richard Henry Lee, of Chantilly, Westmoreland county, Virginia. No children. Married third, at ———, 11 May, 1799, to Sally, sister of Col. John Taylor, of Mount Airy, Richmond county, Virginia. Children by third wife:

   25 SARAH TAYLOR WASHINGTON, born at Haywood, 14 Apr., 1800.

   • 25 WILLIAM AUGUSTINE WASHINGTON, born at Haywood, 30 Aug., 1804.

Other children died young.

" This William Augustine Washington is the same mentioned by General Washington, in his letter to Sir Isaac Heard (*Appendix to Sparks' Life of Washington*, p. 507). The same also named by his will, first after his widow, as one of his Executors, and also as Legatee."

EXTRACTS FROM GENERAL WASHINGTON'S WILL.

Item. " To my nephew, William Augustine Washington and his heirs (if he should conceive them to be objects worth prosecuting), and to his heirs, a lot in the Town of Manchester (opposite to Richmond), No. 265, drawn on my sole account, and also the tenth of one or two hundred acre lots, and two or three half acre lots in the city and vicinity of Richmond, drawn in partnership with nine others, all in the lottery of the deceased William Byrd, are given,—as is also a lot which I purchased of John Hood, conveyed by William Willie and Samuel Gordon, Trustees of the said John Hood, numbered 139, in the town of Edinburgh, in the county of Prince George, State of Virginia."

Item. " To each of my nephews, William Augustine Washington, George Lewis, George Steptoe Washington, Bushrod Washington, and Samuel Washington, I give one of the swords or *cutteaux* of which I may 'die possessed, and they are to *chuse* in the order they are named. These swords are accompanied with an injunction not to unsheath them for the purpose of shedding blood, except it be for self-defence, or in defence of their country and its rights, and in the latter case to keep them unsheathed, and prefer falling with them in their hands to the relinquishment thereof."

NOTE. " These swords have all been presented by the Washington heirs to the people of the United States, through Congress. They are usually to be seen among the valuable Washington relics, in the Patent Office, at Washington City. During the Centennial Exposition they may be seen in the Government building in Fairmount Park."

24 FIELDING LEWIS, first child of Betty Washington, sixth of Augustine, second of Laurence, first of Col. John, of Bridge's Creek, Virginia, was born at ———, about 1755. Children :

    25 CHARLES LEWIS, born at ———, about 1780.

    25 ROBERT LEWIS, born at ———, about 1782.

    25 CATHARINE LEWIS, "   "   " 1785. Married H. C. Dale.

    25 LUCINDA LEWIS, born at ———, about 1787. Married Stetson Foote.

    25 NANCY LEWIS, born at ———, about 1790. Married Thomas Davison.

    25 ELIZABETH LEWIS, born at ———, about 1792. Married Alexander Spotswood.

24 BETTY LEWIS, second child of Betty Washington, second child of Augustine, by second wife, second of Laurence, first of Col. John, of Bridge's Creek, Virginia, and Warton, England ; was born at Fredericksburgh, in Stafford county, Virginia, about 1758. Removed to Culpepper county, thence to Frederick county, and thence to Deerwood, Pittsylvania county, Virginia. Died in April, 1829, at Audley, the seat of Mr. Laurence Lewis, in Clarke county, Virginia. She was married at Fredericksburgh, Virginia, 7 May, 1781, to Charles (of Culpepper county), son of Edward Carter, of Bernheim, Albemarle county, Virginia. Charles Carter removed to Deerwood, Pittsylvania county, Virginia. Died there, 8 May, 1829, aged 64 years.

EXTRACT FROM GENERAL WASHINGTON'S WILL.

Item. "If Charles Carter, who intermarried with my niece, Betty Lewis, is not sufficiently secured in the title to the lots he had of me, in the Town of Fredericksburgh, it is my will and desire that my Executors shall make such conveyances of them, as the law requires to render it perfect." Children of Charles and Betty Lewis Carter :

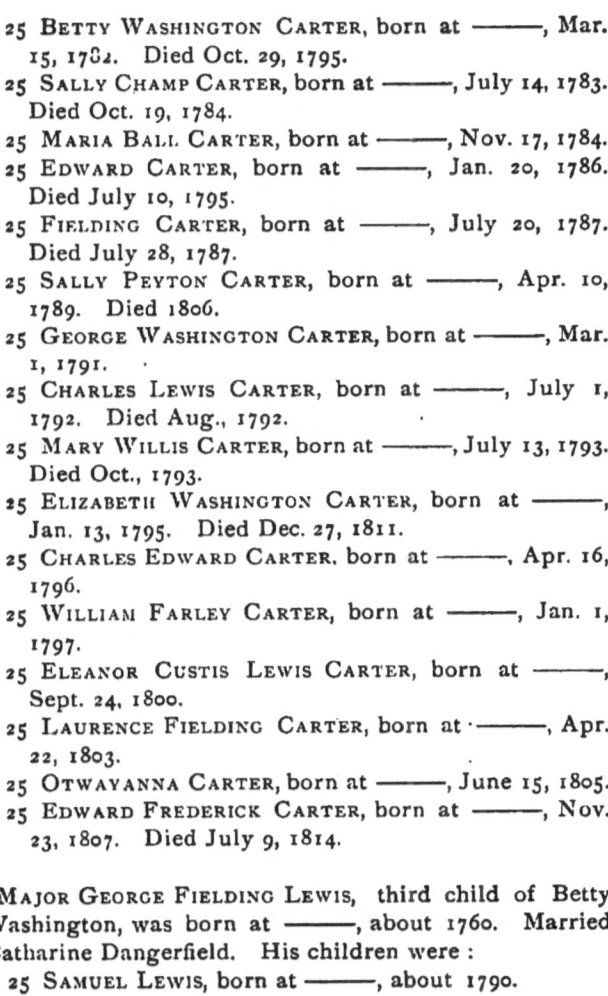

25 BETTY WASHINGTON CARTER, born at ———, Mar. 15, 1782. Died Oct. 29, 1795.

25 SALLY CHAMP CARTER, born at ———, July 14, 1783. Died Oct. 19, 1784.

25 MARIA BALL CARTER, born at ———, Nov. 17, 1784.

25 EDWARD CARTER, born at ———, Jan. 20, 1786. Died July 10, 1795.

25 FIELDING CARTER, born at ———, July 20, 1787. Died July 28, 1787.

25 SALLY PEYTON CARTER, born at ———, Apr. 10, 1789. Died 1806.

25 GEORGE WASHINGTON CARTER, born at ———, Mar. 1, 1791.

25 CHARLES LEWIS CARTER, born at ———, July 1, 1792. Died Aug., 1792.

25 MARY WILLIS CARTER, born at ———, July 13, 1793. Died Oct., 1793.

25 ELIZABETH WASHINGTON CARTER, born at ———, Jan. 13, 1795. Died Dec. 27, 1811.

25 CHARLES EDWARD CARTER, born at ———, Apr. 16, 1796.

25 WILLIAM FARLEY CARTER, born at ———, Jan. 1, 1797.

25 ELEANOR CUSTIS LEWIS CARTER, born at ———, Sept. 24, 1800.

25 LAURENCE FIELDING CARTER, born at ·———, Apr. 22, 1803.

25 OTWAYANNA CARTER, born at ———, June 15, 1805.

25 EDWARD FREDERICK CARTER, born at ———, Nov. 23, 1807. Died July 9, 1814.

24 MAJOR GEORGE FIELDING LEWIS, third child of Betty ⬤Washington, was born at ———, about 1760. Married Catharine Dangerfield. His children were :

25 SAMUEL LEWIS, born at ———, about 1790.

12

25 SAMUEL LEWIS, born at ———, about 1790.
25 DANGERFIELD LEWIS, born at ———, about 1795.
25 POLLY LEWIS,   "   "   "   1800.

EXTRACT FROM GENERAL WASHINGTON'S WILL.

Item. "To each of my nephews, William Augustine Washington, George Lewis, George Steptoe Washington, Bushrod Washington, and Samuel Washington, I give one of the swords or *cutteaux* of which I may die possessed, and they are to *chuse* in the order they are named."

24 LAURENCE LEWIS, sixth child of Betty Washington, second of Augustine, second of Laurence, first of Col. John, of Bridge's Creek, Virginia, was born at Woodlawn, Virginia, about 1775. Married Eleanor Parke Custis, daughter of Mrs. General Washington, Feb. 22, 1799. He had four children.

24 ROBERT LEWIS, fourth child of Betty Washington, was born at Woodlawn, Virginia, about 1765. Married Judith Brown. Had two daughters :
25 JUDY LEWIS, born at ———, about 1805.
25 BETTY BURNETT LEWIS, born at ———, about 1809.

24 HOWELL LEWIS, fifth child of Betty Washington, was born at Woodlawn, Culpepper county, Virginia, Dec. 12, 1770. Removed in 1812 to Kanawha, Mason county, West Virginia, and died there, Dec. 26, 1822. He was married in Richmond, Virginia, Sept. 26, 1795, to Ellen Hackley Pollard (Born Dec. 7, 1776, and died at Marietta, Ohio, 15 Jan., 1859), daughter of Robert Pollard, of Richmond. "She removed, in 1834, to Marietta, Ohio, and died at the house of her daughter, Mrs. Lovell, in 1859."
Howell Lewis was a favorite nephew of General Washington, and inherited from him some 1,300 acres of land,

upon the Kanawha river, in Western Virginia, in Mason county, near the mouth of the Big Buffalo Creek. Of this he took possession, in 1812, with twelve male and six female slaves and their children, under the care of "Old Jack," a trusty old leader among them.

Children of Howell Lewis :

25 BETTY WASHINGTON LEWIS, born at Richmond, Virginia, 14 Oct., 1796. Died at Marietta, Ohio, 2 July, 1866.

25 ROBERT POLLARD LEWIS, born at Richmond, Virginia, 13 Oct., 1798. Died 4 Jan., 1853.

25 GEORGE RICHARD LEWIS, born at Richmond, Virginia, 25 July, 1800. Died 3 Dec., 1843.

25 ELLEN JAEL LEWIS, born at Richmond, Virginia, 28 Jan., 1802. Died 4 Oct., 1850.

25 FRANCES FIELDING LEWIS, born at Richmond, Virginia, 11 Feb., 1805.

25 VIRGINIA LEWIS, born at Richmond, Virginia, 13 Sept., 1806. Died 9 Aug., 1843.

25 HOWELL LEWIS, born at Richmond, Virginia, 10 July, 1808.

25 MARY BALL LEWIS, born at Richmond, Virginia, 2 Jan., 1810. Died 2 Feb., 1810.

25 JOHN EDWARD LEWIS, born at Richmond, Virginia, 5 Nov., 1811. Died ——.

25 LAURENCE LEWIS, born at Kanawha, Virginia, 15 Dec., 1813.

25 HENRY DANGERFIELD LEWIS, born at Kanawha, Virginia, 14 Jan., 1815. Died 1855.

24 THORNTON WASHINGTON, first child of Col. Samuel Washington (by second wife), third of Augustine (by second wife), second of Laurence, first of Col. John, of Bridge's Creek, Virginia ; was born in Stafford county, Virginia, about 1760. He died before 1799, in Jefferson

county, Virginia.   Was named in General Washington's will.

He removed into Jefferson county, Virginia (formerly Berkeley county). Married first, Miss Berry, of Berry Plain on the Rappahannock River. Married second, Miss Washington. Children :

> 25 JOHN THORNTON AUGUSTINE WASHINGTON, born at ———, about 1790.
>
> 25 THOMAS WASHINGTON, born at ———, about 1792. Died young.
>
> 25 SAMUEL WASHINGTON, by second wife, born at ———, about 1795.

Thornton Washington served as an Ensign in the Army, under his uncle General Washington.   He left his home to join the Army before he was 16 years old.

24 TRISTAM WASHINGTON, second child of Colonel Samuel, sixth of Augustine, second of Laurence, first of Colonel John, of Warton, England, and Bridge's Creek, Virginia, fifth of Leonard, first of Laurence, first of Laurence, first of Laurence, first of Thomas, first of Robert, first of John, first of Robert, first of John, first of John, first of John, second of Robert, second of Robert, first of Robert, first of Walter, fourth of Bondo, second of Akaris, first of Bardolf, second of Torfin the Dane ; was born in Stafford county, Virginia, about 1763.

24 FREDERICK (or FERDINAND) WASHINGTON, third child of Colonel Samuel, was born at Harewood, Jefferson county, Virginia, about 1770.   Died without issue.

24 GEORGE STEPTOE WASHINGTON, fourth child of Colonel Samuel, was born in Harewood, Jefferson county, Virginia, about 1773.   Removed about ———, to South Carolina.   Buried in Augusta, Georgia.   Married at Philadelphia, about 1796, to Lucy Payne, daughter of Mr. Payne, of Virginia and Philadelphia.   Children :

25 GEORGE WASHINGTON, born at ———, about 1797. Died infant.

25 SAMUEL WALTER WASHINGTON, born at ———, about 1799.

25 WILLIAM TEMPLE WASHINGTON, born at ———, 16 July, 1800.

25 GEORGE STEPTOE WASHINGTON, born at ———, 15 Oct., 1806.

His widow married Hon. Thomas Todd, of Kentucky, Associate Justice of Supreme Court of United States.

Item. "To each of my nephews William Augustine Washington, George Lewis, George Steptoe Washington, Bushrod Washington, and Samuel Washington, I give one of the swords or *cutteaux* of which I may die possessed, and they are to *chuse* in the order they are named. These swords are accompanied with an injunction, not to unsheath them for the purpose of shedding blood, except it be for self-defence, or in defence of their country and. its rights, and in the latter case to keep them unsheathed, and prefer falling with them in their hands to the relinquishment thereof."

NOTE. "These swords have all been presented by the Washington heirs to the people of the United States, through Congress. They are usually to be seen among the valuable Washington relics, in the Patent Office, at Washington City. During the Centennial Exposition they may be seen in the Government building, in Fairmount Park."

24 LAWRENCE AUGUSTINE WASHINGTON, fifth child of Col. Samuel, sixth of Augustine, was born in Stafford county, Virginia, in 1775. Removed to Wheeling, Virginia, 1815. "He died at Wheeling, Virginia, in Feb., 1824, aged 49. He was a nephew and one of the heirs of General Washington. He married at Winchester, Virginia. A. D. 1798, Mary Dorcas, daughter of James (and Comfort) Wood, of Winchester, Virginia." Children :

25 ROBERT WOOD WASHINGTON, born in Mason county, Virginia, A. D. 1808. Died at Wheeling, 1843.

25 EMMA TELL WASHINGTON, born in Mason county, Virginia, A. D. 1811. Died at Wheeling, 1838.

25 DR. LAURENCE A. WASHINGTON, born in Mason county, Virginia, Dec. 5, 1813, now (1877) at Dennison, Texas.

25 MARY DORCAS WASHINGTON, born in Mason county, Virginia, A. D. 1815. Died in Colorado county, Texas, Nov. 15, 1861.

24 HARRIOT WASHINGTON, sixth child of Col. Samuel, was born in Stafford county, Virginia, about 1780. Removed to Baltimore, A. D. 1796; to Kanawha, Salines, 1818. Died there, Jan. 3, 1822. Married at Richmond, Virginia, 4 July, 1796, to Andrew Parks, of Baltimore, son of John (and Margaret) Parks, of Ireland and Baltimore. Children :

25 ANNE ELIZA PARKS, born at Baltimore, A. D. 1797. Died at Malden, West Virginia, A. D. 1852.

25 LAURENCE AUGUSTINE PARKS, born at Baltimore, A. D. 1801. Died at Kanawha, Salines, A. D. 1822.

25 BUSHROD PARKS, born at Baltimore, A. D. 1806. Died in Louisiana, A. D. 1832.

25 LAURA PARKS, born at Baltimore, 15 Nov., 1809.

25 ANDREW PARKS, born at Baltimore, A. D. 1811. Died at Charleston, West Virginia, A. D. 1863.

25 MARY PARKS, born at Baltimore, A. D. 1813. Died at Clifton, West Virginia.

25 JOHN PARKS, born at Baltimore, A. D. 1816, now (1877) at Kanawha, Salines, West Virginia.

24 JANE WASHINGTON, first child of John Augustine, eighth of Augustine, second of Laurence, first of Colonel John, of Warton, England, and Bridge's Creek, Virginia, fifth of Leonard, of Warton, first of Laurence, first of Laurence, first of Laurence, first of Thomas, first of Robert, first of John, first of Robert, first of John, first of John,

first of John, second of Robert, second of Robert, first of Robert, first of Walter, fourth of Bondo, second of Ak-aris, first of Bardolf, second of Torfin the~Dane~; was born at Bushfield, Westmoreland county, Virginia, about 1758. Removed to Bridge's Creek, Virginia. Died there, A. D. 1791.

She married William, first child of Augustine and Anne Aylett Washington, of Bridge's Creek, Virginia, third child of Augustine, third of Laurence, first of Colonel John, of Bridge's Creek, Virginia. Had 4 children :

    25 BUSHROD WASHINGTON.
    25 GEORGE CORBIN WASHINGTON
    25 WILLIAM WASHINGTON.
    25 JANE WASHINGTON.

These children are given in the line of William Washington.

24 MILDRED WASHINGTON, second child of John Augustine, was born in Bushfield, about 1760. Died at ———, about ———. Married in Selby, Fairfax county, Virginia, about 1780, to Thomas Lee, son of Hon. Richard Henry Lee, of Chantilly, Westmoreland county.

    25 Daughter. Married General Alexander, of ———. Mrs. Alexander died, leaving one son, Sudwell Alexander, of United States Army.

24 HON. BUSHROD WASHINGTON, third child of John Augustine, was born in Westmoreland county, Virginia, 5 June, 1762. He was of Mount Vernon, Virginia, and died in Philadelphia, whilst attending court, 26 Nov., 1829.

He was the favorite nephew of his uncle, George. Removed, first to Richmond, Virginia, thence to Mount Vernon, after General Washington's death.

"Mount Vernon was willed by General Washington to his nephew, Hon. Bushrod Washington."

"He was at an early age admitted to the bar of his native

State, and arrived at such an eminence in his profession, that at the age of 36 he was selected by President Adams as a Justice of the Supreme Court of the United States. He was married at Rippon Lodge, Prince William county, in 1785, to Ann, daughter of Colonel Thomas Blackburn, of Rippon Lodge, Prince William county. No issue. She died of grief at death of her husband, on her way home from Philadelphia, in Nov., 1829."

Bushrod Washington, LL. D. (N. J. Coll., 1803), jurist,' was born in Westmoreland county, Virginia, June 5, 1762, and died in Philadelphia, Nov. 26, 1829. Of William and Mary College, 1778. He was the favorite nephew of the President. Studied law with James Wilson, of Philadelphia, and commenced practice with great success in his native county. He served as a private soldier at York-town ; was a member of the Virginia House of Delegates. in 1787, and the next year was a member of the Convention to ratify the United States Constitution ; afterwards removed to Alexandria and thence to Richmond. Dec. 20, 1798, he was appointed an Associate Justice of the United States Supreme Court. First President of the Colonization Society. Author of Reports in Court of Appeals, Virginia, 1790-6, 2 vols., 8vo, 1798-9 ; Reports of United States Circuit Court, Third Circuit, 1803-27 ; edited by R. Peters, 4 vols., 8vo, 1826-9."

"Judge Bushrod Washington died at Philadelphia, Nov. 26, 1829, aged 67. The first President of the American Colonization Society. The nephew of George Washington, and heir of his books and papers. He was born in 1762, and studied law with James Wilson. At the siege of Yorktown he was a private soldier, under Mercer. In 1797 he was appointed by Mr. Adams, a Judge of the Supreme Court of the United States, an office which he retained till his death. At the first annual meeting of the Colonization Society, he delivered an address which expresses his devout confidence in the blessing of God upon the institution. His widow, the daughter of Mr. Blackburne, died in a few days after him. (His nephew, John Augustine Washington [the son of Corbin Washington], to whom he bequeathed the mansion at Mount Vernon, died June 14, 1832, aged 43.) He was a man of integrity and simplicity of manners, devoted to the performance of his duties, a patriot and a Christian. He published Reports in the Court of Appeals of Virginia, 2 vols., 1798-9."

EXTRACT FROM GENERAL WASHINGTON'S WILL.

Item. "To my nephew, Bushrod Washington, I give and bequeath all the papers in my possession which relate to my civil and military administration of the affairs of this country. I leave to him also such of my private papers as are worth preserving ; and at the decease of my wife, and before, if she is not inclined to retain them, I give and bequeath my library of books and pamphlets of every kind."

EXTRACT FROM GENERAL WASHINGTON'S WILL.

Item. "To each of my nephews, William Augustine Washington, George Lewis, George Steptoe Washington, Bushrod Washington, and Samuel Washington, I give one of the swords or *cutteaux* of which I may die possessed, and they are to *chuse* in the order they are named. These swords are accompanied with an injunction not to unsheath them for the purpose of shedding blood, except it be for self defence, or in defence of their country and its rights, and in the latter case to keep them unsheathed, and prefer falling with them in their hands to the relinquishment thereof."

NOTE. "These swords have all been presented by the Washington heirs to the people of the United States, through Congress. They are usually to be seen among the valuable Washington relics, in the Patent

Office. at Washington City. During the Centennial Exposition they may be seen in the Government building, in Fairmount Park."

24 CORBIN WASHINGTON, fourth child of John Augustine, was born in Bushfield, Westmoreland county, about 1765. He resided at Walnut Farm, Westmoreland county. Died about 1800, at Selby, Fairfax county, Virginia. Married at Chantilly, Westmoreland county, about 1786, to Hannah, daughter of Hon. Richard Henry Lee, of Chantilly, Westmoreland county, Virginia. Four children : His will was dated 19 Oct., 1799.

   25 RICHARD HENRY LEE WASHINGTON, born at Walnut Farm. Westmoreland county, Virginia, A. D. 1787. Died unmarried.

   25 BUSHROD CORBIN WASHINGTON, born at Walnut Farm, Westmoreland county, Virginia, A. D. 1790.

   25 JOHN AUGUSTINE WASHINGTON, born at Walnut Farm, Westmoreland county, Virginia, in Fall of 1792.

   25 MARY LEE WASHINGTON, born at Walnut Farm, Westmoreland county, Virginia, about 1795.

   25 JANE WASHINGTON, born at Walnut Farm, Westmoreland county, Virginia, about 1800.

24 WILLIAM AUGUSTINE WASHINGTON, fifth child of John Augustine, was born in Bushfield, Westmoreland county, Virginia, about 1767.
He was killed whilst at school at ———, in Maryland.

24 COL. GEORGE AUGUSTINE WASHINGTON, first child of Col. Charles, fifth of Augustine, by second wife, second of Laurence, first of Col. John, of Warton, England, and Bridge's Creek, Virginia, fifth of Leonard, of Warton, first of Laurence, first of Laurence, .first of Laurence, first of Thomas, first of Robert, first of John, first of Robert, first of John, first of John, first of John, second of Robert, second of Robert, first of Robert, first of Walter, fourth of Bondo, second of Akaris, first of Bar-

dolf, second of Torfin the Dane, was born in Stafford
county, Virginia, about 1763 Will dated 24 Jan., 1793.
He was Colonel in the American Army.

"He married, Oct. 15, 1785, Frances, daughter of Col.
Burwell Bassett, of New Kent county, Virginia, by whom
he has (1792) had four children, three of whom are living."
—*General Washington's Letter.* Viz. :

    25 GEORGE FAYETTE WASHINGTON, born at ———,
    Apr. 10, 1787. Died infant.

    25 ANNA MARIA WASHINGTON, born at ————, Apr. 3,
    1788.

    25 GEORGE FAYETTE WASHINGTON, born at ———,
    Jan. 17, 1790. Died at Waverly, Sept., 1867.

    25 CHARLES AUGUSTINE WASHINGTON, born at ———,
    Nov. 3, 1791. Died at Cadiz, unmarried.

24 CAPT. SAMUEL WASHINGTON, second child of Col.
Charles, was born in Stafford county, Virginia, about
1767. He was of Fredericksburgh, Virginia; was Captain in the American Army. He removed to Kanawha,
West Virginia. Unmarried in 1792. Married about 1795,
to Dorothea, daughter of ———. Children :

    25 SAMUEL T. WASHINGTON, born about 1796.
    25 AUGUSTINE C.   "   "   1798.
    25 GEORGE F.   "   "   1800.
    25 FRANCES A.   "   "   1805.

24 FRANCES WASHINGTON, third child of Colonel Charles,
was born in Stafford county, Virginia, about 1770.

She married Colonel Burgess Ball, of the American
Army. Had several children :

    25 FAYETTE BALL, born about 1792.
    25 CHARLES   "   "   1795.
    25 MILDRED   "   "   1797.
    25 FRANCES   "   "   1800.
    25 MARTHA   "   "   1805.

Married second, Francis Peyton, of ———.

24 MILDRED WASHINGTON, fourth child of Colonel Charles, was born in Stafford county, Virginia, about 1772. Died without issue.

She married Colonel Thomas Hammond, of the American Army.

25 WARNER WASHINGTON, first child of Warner, first of Warner, first of John, first of Laurence, first of Colonel John, of Warton, England, and Bridge's Creek, Virginia, was born at Clifton, Virginia, 7 Dec., 1771. He died unmarried while attending medical lectures in Philadelphia.

25 JOHN WHITING WASHINGTON, second child of Warner, was born at Clifton, Virginia, 4 Oct., 1773. Removed to Kentucky, where he died. Married Fanny Baylor, of Jefferson county, Virginia. Children :

26 ROBERT WASHINGTON, born about 1800.
26 HENRY   "   "   1802.
26 GWYNN   "   "   1805.
26 TUCKER   "   "   1807.
26 EMILY   "   "   1810.
26 ELIZA   "   "   1812.

25 FRANCES WASHINGTON, third child, was born at Clifton, Gloucester county, Virginia, 30 April, 1775, and died in Clarke county, Virginia, A. D. 1810. She was married in Clarke county, Virginia, to William, son of Edmond (and Elizabeth Taliafiero) Snicker, of Clarke county, Virginia. Died A. D. 1822. Children :

26 MARY SNICKER, born in Clarke county, Virginia, about 1793. Dead.
26 WILLIAM SNICKER, born in Clarke county, Virginia, about 1795. Dead.
26 EMILY SNICKER, born in Clarke county, Virginia, about 1797. Dead.

26 EDWARD SNICKER, born in Clarke county, Virginia, about 1803. Dead.

26 ELIZABETH SNICKER, born in Clarke county, Virginia, 15 Oct., 1806.

26 BEVERLY SNICKER, born in Clarke county, Virginia, about 1808. Dead.

25 EMILY WASHINGTON, fourth child of Warner, was born at Clifton, Virginia, May 8, 1778. Died in Clarke county, Virginia, about 1795.

25 SIDNEY WASHINGTON, fifth child of Warner, was born at Clifton, Virginia, May 31, 1780. Died at ———, about 1800.

25 HENRY WASHINGTON, sixth child of Warner, was born at Clifton, Virginia, Mar. 8, 1782. Removed to Alabama, in 1836, returned to Clarke county, Virginia, in 1841. Died there, in 1852. Married at Berryville, Virginia, by Bishop Meade, May 15, 1815, to Louisa Washington, daughter of P. B. (and Hannah Washington) Whiting, formerly of Elmington, Virginia.

26 WARNER BLAIR WASHINGTON, born at ———.

26 BEVERLY " · " "

26 HENRY SHARPE " " " Not married.

26 HARRIET ANNA " " " Not married.

26 VIRGINIA MEADE " " " Not married.

26 HANNAH " " " Died in childhood.

26 JOHN CARY " " "

25 FRANCIS WHITING WASHINGTON, seventh child of Warner, was born at Clifton, June 18, 1784. Married Miss Hall, of Nashville, Tennessee. Died in Kentucky, leaving children.

25 BEVERLY WASHINGTON, eighth child of Warner, was born at Clifton, Virginia, Aug. 25, 1786. Died unmarried in South America.

25 PERRIN WASHINGTON, ninth child of Warner, was born at Clifton, Virginia, 7 Feb., 1790. Removed to Washington, D. C. Died there, A. D. 1857. Married at the old chapel, in Clarke county, by Bishop Meade, to Hannah Fairfax, daughter of P. B. Whiting (and Hannah Washington).

    26 HANNAH FAIRFAX WASHINGTON, born about 1815. Died unmarried.

    26 WILLIAM DICKINSON   "   "   "   1817. Died unmarried.

    26 LOUISA   "   "   "   1820. Died unmarried.

    27 JOHN HENRY   "   "   "   1822. Married Selina Carter, and lives in Fauquier county, Virginia.

25 READE WASHINGTON, tenth child of Warner, was born at Audley, Virginia, May 18, 1796. Removed to Chambersburgh, Pennsylvania, thence to Pittsburgh, Pennsylvania, where he died. Married at ———, about 1820, to Miss Crawford, of Chambersburgh, Pennsylvania.

    26 WARNER FAIRFAX WASHINGTON, born about 1822. Died infant.

    26 CRAWFORD WASHINGTON, born about 1825. Killed in late war.

    26 AUGUSTUS WASHINGTON, born about 1827.

    26 VIRGINIA   "   "   "   1830.

    26 BUSHROD   "   "   "   1832.

    26 THOMAS   "   "   "   1835.

    26 KATE   "   "   "   1837.

    26 MARY   "   "   "   1840.

    26 LOUISA   "   "   "   1842.

26 HERBERT WASHINGTON, born about 1845.
26 REBECCA   "   "   "   1847.

25 THACHER WASHINGTON, eleventh child of Warner, was born at Audley, Virginia, Dec. 5, 1797. Died infant.

25 ELIZABETH WARNER WASHINGTON, twelfth child of Warner, was born at Audley, Virginia, Sept. 28, 1800. Now (1877) at Berryville, Clarke county, Virginia. Unmarried.

25 FAIRFAX WASHINGTON, thirteenth child of Warner, was born at Audley, Virginia, 30 Mar., 1802. Removed in 183–, to Mississippi. Now (1877) there. Married first, Emily, daughter of Lewis Burwell (and Maria Brown) Whiting. One child :
26 LOUISA WASHINGTON, born about 1825.
Married second, ———. Children :
26 SARAH WASHINGTON, born about 1830.
26 WARNER   "   "   "   1832.
26 MARTHA   "   "   "   1835.
26 JOHN   "   "   "   1837.
26 MARY   ".   "   "   1840.
26 ELIZABETH WARNER WASHINGTON, born about 1842.
26 READE WASHINGTON, born about 1845.

25 WILLIAM HERBERT WASHINGTON, fourteenth child of Warner, was born at Audley, Virginia, 30 May, 1803. Died in Westmoreland county, Virginia. Married at ———, to Lousia, daughter of Lewis Burwell (and Maria Brown) Whiting. No children.

25 ALEXANDER HAMILTON WASHINGTON, fifteenth child of Warner, was born at Audley, Virginia, 5 Mar., 1805. Died in Texas unmarried, in 1876.

25 MARY HERBERT WASHINGTON, sixteenth child of War-

ner, was born at Audley, Virginia, 25 Sept., 1808. Died in
Texas, in 187–. Married Dr. Beasley. Children :
> 26 HERBERT BEASLEY, born in Texas, about 1830.
> 26 HAMILTON   "   "   "   "   1832.
> 26 SARAH   "   "   "   "   1835.
> 26 LUCY   "   "   "   "   1837.
> 26 JOHN   "   "   "   "   1840.

25 WARNER WASHINGTON THROCKMORTON, first child of
Mildred Washington, second of Warner, first of Warner,
first of John, first of Laurence, first of Colonel John, of
Warton, England, and Bridge's Creek, Virginia ; was
born at Woodbury, Virginia, in Feb., 1792. and died in
Jefferson county, West Virginia, in 1855.

25 HANNAH FAIRFAX THROCKMORTON, second child of Mildred Washington, was born at Woodbury, Virginia, A. D
1793. Died at Memphis, Tennessee, in 1858.

25 CATHARINE THROCKMORTON, third child of Mildred
Washington, was born at Woodbury. Virginia, A. D.
1796. Died at Nashville, Tennessee.

25 BEVERLY WHITING, first child of Hannah Fairfax Washington, third of Warner, first of Warner; first of John,
first of Laurence, first of Col. John, of Warton, England, and Bridge's Creek, Virginia, was born in Gloucester county, Virginia, A. D. 1788.   Died infant.

25 WARNER WASHINGTON WHITING, second child of Hannah Fairfax Washington, was born at Gloucester county,
Virginia, in Dec., 1790. Died in Sumter county, Alabama, A. D. 1840.

25 ANN BEVERLY WHITING, third child of Hannah Fairfax
Washington, was born in Gloucester county, Virginia,
in Sept., 1792. Died in Richmond, A. D. 1870.

25 LOUISA WASHINGTON WHITING, fourth child of Hannah Fairfax Washington, was born in Jan., 1795. Now (1877) at Berryville.

25 HARRIET THACHER WHITING, fifth child of Hannah Fairfax Washington, was born in Gloucester county, Virginia, in Sept., 1797. Died in Richmond, Virginia, 1873.

25 HANNAH FAIRFAX WHITING, sixth child of Hannah Fairfax Washington, was born in Gloucester county, Virginia, in Dec., 1799. Now (1877) in Fauquier county, Virginia.

25 PETER BEVERLY WHITING, seventh child of Hannah Fairfax Washington, was born in Gloucester county, Virginia, A. D. 1802. Died in Sumter county, Alabama.

25 MARY BLAIR WHITING, eighth child of Hannah Fairfax Washington, was born in Gloucester county, Virginia, A. D. 1804. Died at Richmond, Virginia, 1828.

25 LOUISA SKAIFE WHITING, ninth child of Hannah Fairfax Washington, was born in Gloucester county, Virginia, A. D. 1807. Died in Richmond, Virginia.

25 PHILIP THOMAS NELSON, first child of Catharine Washington, fourth of Warner, first of Warner, first of John, first of Laurence, first of Col. John, of Warton, England, and Bridge's Creek, Virginia, was born at Rossville, Clarke county, Virginia, Nov. 6, 1790. Died in Alexandria, Virginia, about 1810.

25 LUCINDA N. NELSON, second child of Catharine Washington, was born at Rossville, Clarke county, Virginia, May 23, 1792. Died in Clarke county.

13

25 HANNAH FAIRFAX NELSON, third child of Catharine Washington, was born at Rossville, Clarke county, Virginia, Nov. 18, 1793. Died at Beverly, Jefferson county, West Virginia.

25 LOUISA WASHINGTON NELSON, fourth child of Catharine Washington, was born at Rossville, Clarke county, Virginia, A. D. 1796. Died in Clarke county, in Feb., 1858.

25 GEORGE WILLIAM NELSON, fifth child of Catharine Washington, was born at Rossville, Clarke county, Virginia, A. D. 1798. Died in Clarke county, Virginia.

25 ELIZABETH CARY NELSON, sixth child of Catharine Washington, was born at Rossville, Clarke county, Virginia, in May, 1800. Died at Winchester, Virginia, in Feb., 1876.

25 GERALDINE NELSON, seventh child of Catharine Washington, was born at Rossville, Clarke county, Virginia, A. D. 1802. Died there, in 1828.

25 ANN FAIRFAX NELSON, eighth child of Catharine Washington, was born at Rossville, Clarke county, Virginia, about 1805. Died in childhood.

25 WILLIAM ARMISTEAD WASHINGTON, first child of Fairfax Washington, seventh of Warner, first of John, first of Laurence, first of John, of Warton, England, and Bridge's Creek, Virginia, was born at Fairfield, Virginia, about 1805. Was living, 1861.

25 WARNER WASHINGTON, second child of Fairfax Washton, was born at Fairfield, Virginia, about 1807. Living, 1861.

25 MARY WASHINGTON, third child of Fairfax Washington, was born at Fairfield, Virginia, about 1810. Living, 1861.

25 ANN OLIVE WASHINGTON, fourth child of Fairfax Washington, was born at Fairfield, Virginia, about 1812. Living, 1861.

25 FAIRFAX WASHINGTON, fifth child of Fairfax Washington, was born at Fairfield, Virginia, about 1815. Living, 1861.

25 VIRGINIA WASHINGTON, sixth child of Fairfax Washington, was born at Elkton, Kentucky, about 1818. Living, 1861.

25 CHARLES HENRY WASHINGTON, first child of Whiting Washington, eighth of Warner, first of John, first of Laurence, first of Col. John, of Warton, England, and Bridge's Creek, Virginia, was born at Elmington, Virginia, about 1805.

25 Daughter of Whiting Washington, was born at Elmington, Virginia, about 1807.

25 Daughter of Whiting Washington, was born at Elmington, Virginia, about 1810.

25 AUGUSTINE WASHINGTON, first child of William Augustine Washington, fourth of Augustine, second of Augustine, second of Laurence, first of Col. John, of Warton, England, and Bridge's Creek, Virginia, was born at Haywood, Westmoreland county, Virginia, about 1778. Died, aged 20 years.

25 CORBIN AYLETT WASHINGTON, second child of William

Augustine Washington, was born at Haywood, Westmoreland county, Virginia, about 1780. Died young.

25 HANNAH BUSHROD WASHINGTON, third child of William Augustine Washington, was born at Haywood, Westmoreland county, Virginia, about 1782. Died, aged 21 years.

25 BUSHROD WASHINGTON, fourth child of William Augustine Washington, fourth of Augustine, second of Augustine, second of Laurence, first of Col. John, and of Jane Washington, first of John Augustine, seventh of Augustine, second of Laurence, first of Col. John, of Bridge's Creek, Virginia, was born at Haywood, Virginia, Apr. 4, 1785. Settled at Mount Zephyr, Virginia. Married his cousin, Henrietta, daughter of General Alexander Spotswood, of Spotsylvania county, Virginia. Children :

26 SPOTSWOOD AUGUSTINE WASHINGTON.
26 ANNE   "
26 JANE MILDRED   "   Died unmarried.
26 GEORGE   "
26 JOHN   "
26 MARY   "
26 CORBIN   "
26 FRANCES or FANNY   "   Married Finch.
    Widow. Now (1877) at Morrisania.

Bushrod Washington died at Mount Zephyr, in 1830, and was interred in vault at Mount Vernon.

25 ANN AYLETTE WASHINGTON, fifth child of William Augustine Washington, was born at Haywood, Westmoreland county, Virginia, about 1787. Died, and was buried at Mount Vernon. Married William Robinson, of Westmoreland. No children.

25 GEORGE CORBIN WASHINGTON, sixth child of William Augustine, third of Augustine, second of Augustine, second of Laurence, first of Colonel John, of Bridge's Creek, Virginia; was born at Harewood, Virginia, 20 Aug., 1789. Removed about ——, to Georgetown, D. C. Died there, 17 July, 1854.

Married at Dunbarton, near Georgetown, in 1807, to Eliza Ridgeley Beall, daughter of Thomas (and Ann Orme) Beall, of Dunbarton, near Georgetown, D. C. She died at Georgetown, 1 July, 1820. Eight children. All died young except:

> **26** LEWIS WILLIAM WASHINGTON, born at Georgetown, 30 Nov., 1812.
>
> **26** ELEANOR WASHINGTON (by second wife, Ann Peter, daughter of Colonel John Peter). Died, aged 20, unmarried.
>
> **26** GEORGE CORBIN WASHINGTON, born at Georgetown, about ——. Died July, 1854, at Georgetown, D. C., and was buried at Oak Hill, near there.

25 LAURENCE WASHINGTON, seventh child of William Augustine, was born at Haywood, Virginia. 26 Feb., 1791, and died 15 Mar., 1875.

25 SARAH TAYLOE, eighth child of William Augustine Washington, was born at Haywood, Virginia, 14 Apr., 1800, and died in ——, Mar. 15, 1875. Married at Haywood, Virginia, by Rev. W. Wilmer, of Alexandria, 20 Oct., 1819, to Lawrence Washington, third child of Henry Washington, of Westmoreland county, Virginia. Eight sons and three daughters:

> **26** HENRY AUGUSTINE WASHINGTON, born at Haywood, Virginia, 24 Aug., 1820.
>
> **26** JOHN TAYLOE WASHINGTON, born at Blenheim, Virginia, 20 Dec., 1822.
>
> **26** GEORGE WASHINGTON, born at Cedar Hill, Virginia, 24 July, 1825.

26 RICHARD BUSHROD WASHINGTON, born at Blenheim, Virginia, 21 June, 1827.

26 MARY WEST WASHINGTON, born at Blenheim, Virginia, 13 Oct., 1828.

26 SARAH ASHTON WASHINGTON, born at Campbelltown, Virginia, 17 Aug., 1831. .

26 WILLIAM AUGUSTINE WASHINGTON, born at Blenheim, Virginia, 5 Mar., 1833.

26 LAURENCE WASHINGTON, born at Campbelltown, Virginia, 1 May, 1836.

26 ELIZABETH WASHINGTON, born at Blenheim, Virginia, 23 Nov, 1838.

26 ROBERT J. WASHINGTON, born at Campbelltown, Virginia, 16 Sept., 1841.

26 LLOYD WASHINGTON, born at Blenheim, Virginia, 2 Nov., 1846.

Mr. Laurence Washington, now (1877) at Blenheim, on Bridge's Creek, Westmoreland county, Virginia.

25 WILLIAM AUGUSTINE WASHINGTON, ninth child of William Augustine Washington, was born at Haywood, Virginia, 30 Aug., 1804. Died there, 26 Jan., 1830. Married at ———, about ———, to Julia E. Bayard, of Princeton, New Jersey. Three children :

26 JULIA AUGUSTA WASHINGTON, born at ———. Now (1877) Mrs. Dabney C. Wirt, at Oak Grove, Virginia, son of William Wirt.

Two children died infants.

25 JUDY LEWIS, first child of Robert Lewis, fourth of Betty Washington, sixth of Augustine, second of Laurence, first of John, of Warton, England, and Bridge's Creek, Virginia, was born at Fredericksburgh, Virginia, about 1800. Died young.

25 LEWIS, second child of Robert Lewis, was born at Fredericksburgh, Virginia, about 1803.

25 LEWIS, third child of Robert Lewis, was born at Fredericksburgh, Virginia, about 1805.

25 JUDY LEWIS, fourth child of Robert Lewis, was born at Fredericksburgh, Virginia, about 1807.

25 BETTY BURNETT LEWIS, fifth child of Robert Lewis, was born at Fredericksburgh, about 1809. Removed about 1828, to Etham, New Kent county, Virginia, and to Hanover county, about 1847. Now (1877) there. Married at Fredericksburgh, by Rev. E. C. McGuire, in Aug., 1827, to George Washington Bassett, son of John (and Betty Carter Browne Burwell) Bassett. Children :

    26 BETTY BURWELL BASSETT, born at Etham, New Kent county, Virginia, about 1828.

    26 GEORGE WASHINGTON BASSETT, born at Etham, New Kent county, Virginia, about 1832.

    26 ANNA VIRGINIA BASSETT, born at Etham, New Kent county, Virginia, about 1835.

    26 ELLA MORE BASSETT, born at Etham, New Kent county, Virginia, Sept. 7, 1837.

    26 JUDITH FRANCES CARTER BASSETT, born at Etham, New Kent county, Virginia, about 1840.

    26 MARY BURNETT BASSETT, born at Etham, New Kent county, Virginia, about 1842.

    26 ANNETTE LEWIS BASSETT, born at Etham, New Kent county, Virginia, about 1845.

    26 ROBERT BASSETT, born at Etham, New Kent county, Virginia, about ——.

    26 WILLIAM AUGUSTINE BASSETT, born at Etham, New Kent county, Virginia, about ——.

25 BETTY WASHINGTON CARTER, first child of Mrs. Betty Lewis Carter, first of Mrs. Betty Washington Lewis, second of Augustine Washington, by second wife, second of Laurence, first of Colonel John, of Warton, England, and

Bridge's Creek, Virginia; was born at ——. Virginia, 15 Mar., 1782, and died there, 29 Oct., 1795.

25 SALLY CHAMP CARTER, second child of Mrs. Betty Lewis Carter, was born at ——, 14 July, 1783, and died, 19 Oct., 1784.

25 MARIA BALL CARTER, third child of Mrs. Betty Lewis Carter, was born at ——, 17 Nov., 1784, and died at ——, 29 Jan., 1823. Married at ——, A. D. 1801, to George Tucker, of Richmond, Virginia. Children :

    26 DANIEL GEORGE TUCKER, born at ——, 20 Nov., 1802.

    26 ELEANOR ROSALIE TUCKER, born at ——, 8 May, 1804. Died, Oct., 1818.

    26 MARIA FARLEY TUCKER, born at ——, 6 Nov., 1805.

    26 ELIZA LEWIS CARTER TUCKER, born at ——, 9 Dec., 1808.

    26 MARY LELIA TUCKER, born at ——, 5 Aug., 1810. Died, July, 1816.

25 EDWARD CARTER, fourth child of Mrs. Betty Lewis Carter, was born at ——. 20 Jan., 1786, and died, 10 July, 1795.

25 FIELDING CARTER, fifth child of Mrs. Betty Lewis Carter, was born at ———, 20 July, 1787, and died, 28 July, 1817.

25 SALLY PEYTON CARTER, sixth child of Mrs. Betty Lewis Carter, was born at ——, Apr. 10, 1789, and died, A. D. 1806.

25 GEORGE WASHINGTON CARTER, seventh child of Mrs. Betty Lewis Carter, was born at ——, Mar. 1, 1791, and removed about ——, to Mississippi. Married at Fredericksburgh, Virginia, to Mary, daughter of ——, Wormley, of ——. Left four daughters.

25 CHARLES LEWIS CARTER, eighth child of Mrs. Betty Lewis Carter, was born at ———, July 1, 1792, and died in Aug., 1792.

25 MARY WILLIS CARTER, ninth child of Mrs. Betty Lewis Carter, was born at ———, July .13, 1793, and died in Oct., 1793.

25 ELIZABETH WASHINGTON CARTER, tenth child of Mrs. Betty Lewis Carter, was born at ———, Jan. 13, 1795, and died, Dec. 27, 1811.

25 CHARLES EDWARD CARTER, eleventh child of Mrs. Betty Lewis Carter, was born at ———, Apr. 16, 1796.

25 WILLIAM FARLEY CARTER, twelfth child of Mrs. Betty Lewis Carter, was born at ———, Jan. 1, 1797, and removed about ———, to Kentucky. Left three children.

25 ELEANOR CUSTIS LEWIS CARTER, thirteenth child of Mrs. Betty Lewis Carter, was born at ———, Sept. 24, 1800. Married in 1823, Henry Brown. Two children. Married, second, in 1835, to Dr. Patterson, of Lynchburgh, Virginia, and died in 1845, leaving four children.

25 LAWRENCE FIELDING CARTER, fourteenth child of Mrs. Betty Lewis Carter, was born at ———, Apr. 22, 1803. Stationed at Fort Smith, in Arkansas. Married and died there, leaving two sons.

25 OTWAYANNA CARTER, fifteenth child of Mrs. Betty Lewis Carter, was born at ———, June 15, 1805. Married Dr. W. Owens, of Lynchburgh, Virginia, and died without issue.

25 EDWARD FREDERICK CARTER, sixteenth child of Mrs.

Betty Lewis Carter, was born at ———, Nov. 23, 1807, and died, July 9, 1814.

25 BETTY WASHINGTON LEWIS, first child of Howell Lewis, fourth of Betty Washington, second of Augustine, by second wife, second of Laurence, first of Colonel John, of Warton, England, and Bridge's Creek, Virginia ; was born at Richmond, Virginia, 14 Oct., 1796. Removed to Marietta, Ohio. Died there, 2 July, 1866. Married at ———, 19 Feb., 1818, to Colonel Joseph Lovell, of Charlestown, West Virginia. He died there, 25 Nov., 1835, whose father was of England. Children :

    26 ALFRED LOVELL, born at Charlestown, West Virginia, Kanawha C. H., 27 Dec., 1818. Dead.

    26 RICHARD CHANNING MOORE LOVELL, born at Charlestown, West Virginia, Kanawha C. H., 3 Mar., 1822.

    26 HOWELL LEWIS LOVELL, born at Charlestown, West Virginia, Kanawha C. H., 9 July, 1824. *

    26 JOSEPH LOVELL, born at Georgetown, West Virginia, Kanawha C. H., 31 Mar., 1827. Died, 22 Mar., 1865.

    26 BETTY LOVELL, born at Georgetown, West Virginia, Kanawha C. H., about 1829.

    26 FAYETTE AUGUSTINE LOVELL, born at Georgetown, West Virginia, Kanawha C. H., about 1830.

25 ROBERT POLLARD LEWIS, second child of Howell Lewis, was born at Richmond, Virginia, 13 Oct., 1798. Died at ———, unmarried, 4 Jan., 1853.

25 GEORGE RICHARD LEWIS, third child of Howell Lewis, was born at Richmond, Virginia, 25 July, 1800. He died at Osceola, Missouri, 3 Dec., 1843.

He was married at Morgansfield, Kentucky, in 1833, to Widow Eliza McLean, daughter of William Bayless, of Culpepper county, Virginia. Children :

    26 ELLEN ELIZA LEWIS, born at ———, 18 July, 1834.

26 JEANNETTE LEWIS, born at ———, 2 July, 1837. Died, Dec., 1843.

26 HAROLD LEWIS, born at ———, 14 Aug., 1839. Died 1863.

26 GEORGE LEWIS, born at ———, 14 Sept., 1842.

25 ELLEN JAEL LEWIS, fourth child of Howell Lewis, was born at Richmond, Virginia, 28 Jan., 1802. Removed in Dec., 1812, to Charlestown, West Virginia. To Marietta, Ohio, in Feb., 1834. Returned to Charlestown, Nov., 1843. Died there, 4 Oct., 1850.

Married first, at Charlestown, 21 Jan., 1819, by Rev. Henry Ruffner, to Robert McAmey Steele, of Charlestown, West Virginia, son of Richard (and Martha McAmey) Steele, of Lexington, Kentucky. Children:

26 WILLIAM STEELE, born at Charlestown, West Virginia, 12 Dec., 1819. Died at Windsor, Missouri, 7 Oct., 1872.

26 MARTHA ELLEN STEELE, born at Charlestown, West Virginia, 5 July, 1821.

26 HOWELL LEWIS STEELE, born at Charlestown, West Virginia, 31 Dec., 1822. Died at Ophir, California, 26 Dec., 1850.

26 ROBERT McAMEY STEELE, born at Charlestown, West Virginia, 28 Dec., 1824. Died at Charlestown, West Virginia, 16 July, 1844.

26 BETTY WASHINGTON STEELE, born at Charlestown, West Virginia, 10 Dec., 1826.

Her husband died at Charlestown, West Virginia, 28 Feb., 1827. She was married second, at Marietta, Ohio, by Rev. Edward Winthrop, 28 Nov., 1843, to Dr. Spicer Patrick, of Charlestown, West Virginia. No children. He now (1876) resides at Charlestown, West Virginia.

25 FRANCES FIELDING LEWIS, fifth child of Howell Lewis, was born at Richmond, Virginia, 11 Feb., 1805. Now

(1877) there. Married there, by Rev. Dr. John D. Blair,
27 June, 1822, to Humphrey Brooke Gwathmey, son of
Temple (and Ann) Gwathmey, of Richmond. He died
at Richmond, 22 Oct., 1852. Children :

26 WILLIAM GASTON GWATHMEY, born at Savannah,
Georgia, 2 April, 1823. Died, 5 Aug., 1852.

26 ELLEN JAEL GWATHMEY, born at Richmond, Virginia, 26 Sept., 1824. Died at Rockbridge Baths,
Virginia, 5 Oct., 1870.

26 HUMPHREY BROOKE GWATHMEY, born at Richmond.
Virginia, 5 June, 1826. Died, 5 Nov., 1826.

26 MATILDA CUMING GWATHMEY, born at New York,
6 Jan., 1828.

26 VIRGINIA GWATHMEY, born at New York, 31 Dec.,
1830.

26 THEODORE FRANCIS GWATHMEY, born at Norfolk,
Virginia, 21 May, 1832.

26 TEMPLE GWATHMEY, born at Norfolk, Virginia, A.
D. 1834. Died, 12 Nov., 1840.

26 FANNY BROOKE GWATHMEY, born at Norfolk, Virginia, 8 Sept., 1835.

26 CAROLINE HETH GWATHMEY, born at Mobile, Alabama, A. D. 1837. Died at Richmond, Virginia, 9
May, 1842.

26 MARY ANN GWATHMEY, born at Richmond, Virginia, A. D. 1841. Died, 9 May, 1849.

26 EMILY CARTER GWATHMEY, born at Richmond, Virginia, A. D. 1843. Died, 26 Mar., 1849.

26 ROBERT WASHINGTON GWATHMEY, born at Richmond, Virginia, 22 June, 1846.

25 VIRGINIA LEWIS, sixth child of Howell Lewis, was born
at Richmond, Virginia, 13 Sept., 1806. Removed to
Buffalo, West Virginia. Died, 9 Aug., 1843, at Moren's
Bottom, Mason county, West Virginia. Married at Buffalo, in Mason county, West Virginia, 6 Jan., 1825, to

Robert Ammon Hereford (died at Warrensburgh, Missouri, Oct., 1860), son of Robert Hereford, of Mason county, Virginia. Children :

26 ROBERT HEREFORD, born at Buffalo, Mason county, West Virginia, 17 July, 1827.

26 BROOK GWATHMEY HEREFORD, born at Buffalo, Mason county, West Virginia, 16 Dec., 1829.

26 MARY BRENAUGH HEREFORD, born at Buffalo, Mason county, West Virginia, 25 Jan., 1832. Died, 23 Mar., 1836.

26 FRANCES ELIZA HEREFORD, born at Buffalo, Mason county, West Virginia, 4 June, 1834.

26 KATHERINE ELLEN HEREFORD, born at Buffalo, Mason county, West Virginia, about 1836.

26 LAWRENCE LEWIS HEREFORD, born at Buffalo, Mason county, West Virginia, about 1838

26 BETTY STRIBLING HEREFORD, born at Buffalo, Mason county, West Virginia, about 1840.

25 HOWELL LEWIS, seventh child of Howell Lewis, was born at Richmond, Virginia, 10 July, 1808. Removed to Calhoun or Lewis, Missouri, in Nov., 1836, now (1877) Lewis, Henry county, Missouri. Married in Mason county, Virginia, 14 Jan., 1831, to Emily G., daughter of William (and Grace) Burch. She died near Calhoun, Missouri, 13 May, 1866. Children :

26 GEORGE LEWIS, born in Mason county, Virginia, 27 Oct., 1831.

29 MARY ELLEN LEWIS, born at Mason county, Virginia, 28 Jan., 1834. Died at Salem, Illinois.

26 AUGUSTUS D. LEWIS, born at Mason county, Virginia, 8 Nov., 1836. Died near Calhoun, 10 Feb., 1853.

26 FIELDING LEWIS, born at Calhoun, Missouri, 9 Mar., 1839. Died 21 Mar., 1863.

26 COLUMBIA LEWIS, born at Calhoun, Missouri, 24
Sept., 1842.

26 VIRGINIA LEWIS, born at Calhoun, Missouri, 11
Mar., 1845.

26 BETTIE F. LEWIS, born at Calhoun, Missouri, 28
Sept., 1848.

26 WILLIAM HOWELL LEWIS, born at Calhoun, Missouri, 26 Jan., 1850.

26 GASTON G. LEWIS, born at Calhoun, Missouri, 28
Jan., 1853.

26 EMMA A. LEWIS, born at Calhoun, Missouri, 28
Sept., 1855.

25 MARY BALL LEWIS, eighth child of Howell Lewis, was
born at Richmond, Virginia, 2 Jan., 1810. Died 2 Feb.,
1810.

25 JOHN EDWARD LEWIS, ninth child of Howell Lewis, was
born at Richmond, Virginia, 5 'Nov., 1811. Died ——.
Widow, Mary M. Lewis, resides (1877) Osceola, Missouri.

25 DR. LAWRENCE LEWIS, tenth child of Howell Lewis, was
born in Mason county, Virginia, 15 Dec., 1813. Removed
in 1839, to Osceola, Missouri. Now (1877) there. He was
married, first, in Benton county, Missouri, 14 Feb., 1843,
to Mary, daughter of Robert (and Diademia) Ferguson.
She died in Benton county, Missouri, 26 Dec., 1845. Her
children were:

26 MARTHA ELLEN LEWIS, born in Osceola, Missouri,
8 Feb., 1844.

Martha Ellen Lewis, married, 26 Aug., 1869, Henry
Waite Douglass. Children:

27 RALPH DOUGLASS, born 29 Oct., 1870. Died
31 July, 1872.

27 LAWRENCE LEWIS DOUGLASS, born 24 Jan.,
1873. Died 30 July, 1874.

27 NELLIE DOUGLASS, born 7 Nov., 1874.

Married, second, at Lewisburg, Virginia, by Dr. Mc-Elhenney, 4 Mar., 1853, to Mary Emma, daughter of Johnson (and Elizabeth) Reynolds.

Children of Dr. Lawrence Lewis, by second wife :

26 LAWRENCE LEWIS, born at Osceola, Missouri, 15 Dec., 1853. Died 30 Mar., 1858.

26 BETTIE BLAIN LEWIS, born at Osceola, Missouri, 17 Sept., 1855.

26 HOWELL REYNOLDS LEWIS, born at Osceola, Missouri, 27 Jan., 1857. Died 31 Oct., 1858.

26 EDWIN LILLEY LEWIS, born at Osceola, Missouri, 1 Apr., 1859.

26 SAMUEL REYNOLDS LEWIS, born at Osceola, Missouri, 31 Oct., 1860.

26 EMMA JOHNSON LEWIS, born at Osceola, Missouri, 5 Mar., 1862.

26 LAWRENCE HENRY LEWIS, born at Osceola, Missouri, 13 May, 1864.

26 KATE HENDRY LEWIS, born at Osceola, Missouri, 25 Nov., 1866.

26 LELIA VERNON LEWIS, born at Osceola, Missouri, 2 Dec., 1868.

26 MARIA HAMNER LEWIS, born at Osceola, Missouri, 26 Aug., 1871.

25 HENRY DANGERFIELD LEWIS, eleventh child of Howell Lewis, was born at Richmond, Virginia, 14 Jan., 1815. Died, 1855.

25 SAMUEL LEWIS, first child of Major George Fielding Lewis, second of Mrs. Betty Washington Lewis, sixth of Augustine, second of Laurence, first of Colonel John, of Warton, England, and Bridge's Creek, Virginia ; was born at ———, about 1790. Married Atway Miller. Children :

26 GEORGE WASHINGTON LEWIS, born at ———, about 1815. Married his cousin, daughter of Dangerfield Lewis.

26 HENRY HOWELL LEWIS, born at ———, about 1818. Married Rebecca, daughter of Colonel John Taylor, of Mount Airy, Virginia.

26 CATHARINE LEWIS, born at ———, about 1820. Married her cousin, Fielding, son of Dangerfield Lewis.

25 DANGERFIELD LEWIS, second child of Major George Fielding Lewis, was born at ———, about 1795. Married Miss Pratt.

26 FIELDING LEWIS, born at ———, about ———. Married his cousin, Catharine, daughter of Samuel Lewis.

26 Daughter, born at ———, about ———. Married her cousin George, son of Samuel Lewis.

25 POLLY LEWIS, third child of Major George Fielding Lewis, was born at ———, about 1800.

25 JOHN THORNTON AUGUSTINE WASHINGTON, first child of Thornton, first of Col. Samuel, by second wife, third of Augustine, by second wife, second of Laurence, first of Col. John, of Warton, England, and Bridge's Creek, Virginia, was born in Berkeley county, Virginia (now Jefferson county, West Virginia), 20 May, 1783. Died 9 Oct., 1841, at Cedar Lawn. He was married at Shepherdstown, West Virginia, 2 Sept., 1810, to Elizabeth Conrad, daughter of Major Daniel Bedinger, of Shepherdstown, West Virginia. She died about 1835. Major Bedinger was an officer in the Revolutionary War. His second wife was Sarah, daughter of Hon. Robert Rutherford, M. C. Married about 1836. She was born 27 Sept., 1793. Died 21 Oct., 1837, at Cedar Lawn, West Virginia. Children by first wife:

26 LAWRENCE BERRY WASHINGTON, born at Cedar

Lawn, Jefferson county, West Virginia, 26 Nov., 1811. Died — Sept., 1856.

26 DANIEL BEDINGER WASHINGTON, born at Cedar Lawn, Jefferson county, West Virginia, 8 Feb., 1814.

26 VIRGINIA THORNTON WASHINGTON, born at Cedar Lawn, Jefferson county, West Virginia, 2 Mar., 1816.

26 SALLY ELEANOR WASHINGTON, born at Cedar Lawn, Jefferson county, West Virginia, 7 Apr., 1818.

26 BENJAMIN F. WASHINGTON, born at Cedar Lawn, Jefferson county, West Virginia, 7 Apr., 1820.

26 GEORGIANA AUGUSTA WASHINGTON, born at Cedar Lawn, Jefferson county, West Virginia, 3 Mar., 1822.

26 MARY ELIZABETH WASHINGTON, born at Cedar Lawn, Jefferson county, West Virginia, 4 Mar., 1824.

26 JOHN THORNTON AUGUSTINE WASHINGTON, born at Cedar Lawn, Jefferson county, West Virginia, 22 Jan., 1826.

26 MILDRED BERRY WASHINGTON, born at Cedar Lawn, Jefferson county, West Virginia, 3 Sept., 1827. Died 12 Sept., 1827.

26 MILDRED BERRY WASHINGTON, born at Cedar Lawn, Jefferson county, West Virginia, 8 Mar., 1829. Died.

26 GEORGE WASHINGTON, born at Cedar Lawn, Jefferson county, West Virginia, 9 Dec., 1830.

26 SUSAN ELLSWORTH WASHINGTON, born at Cedar Lawn, Jefferson county, West Virginia, 1 Apr., 1833.

26 HENRIETTA GRAY WASHINGTON, born at Cedar Lawn, Jefferson county, West Virginia, 30 Sept., 1835. Died 18 Dec., 1838.

25 GEORGE WASHINGTON, first child of George Steptoe Washington, fourth of Colonel Samuel Washington, sixth of Augustine, second of Laurence, first of Colonel John, of Warton, England, and Bridge's Creek, Virginia, fifth of Leonard, first of Laurence, first of Laurence, first

14

of Laurence, first of Thomas, first of Robert, first of John, first of Robert, first of John, first of John, first of John, second of Robert, second of Robert, first of Robert, first of Walter, fourth of Bondo, second of Akaris, first of Bardolf, second of Torfin the Dane ; was born at Harewood, Jefferson county, Virginia, about 1797. Died infant.

25 Dr. Samuel Walter Washington, second child of George Steptoe Washington, was born at Harewood, Jefferson county, Virginia, about 1799. Died there in 1831. Married at Philadelphia, about 1822, to Louisa, daughter of Thomas G. Clemsen, of Philadelphia. Mrs. Louisa Washington. Widow now (1876) at Claymont, Delaware. Children :

   26 Lucy Elizabeth Washington, born at Harewood, Virginia, 4 July, 1824.
   26 George La Fayette Washington, born at Harewood, Virginia, 12 Jan., 1825.
   26 Christine Maria Washington, born at Harewood, Virginia, 17 Dec., 1827.
   26 Annie Steptoe Clemson Washington, born at Harewood, Virginia, in Sept., 1831.

25 William Temple Washington, third child of George Steptoe Washington, was born at Harewood, Jefferson county, West Virginia, 16 July, 1800. Removed to Megwillie, April, 1856, a portion of the Harewood estate. Thence to Falmouth, Stafford county, Virginia, about 1857. Now (1876) there. Married by Rev. Mr. Chapman, in Lexington, Kentucky, A. D. 1821, to Margaret, daughter of General Thomas Fletcher, of Bath county, Kentucky. She died in Falmouth, 9 Jan., 1865. Children :

   26 Lucy Washington, born in Lexington, Kentucky, 8 Oct., 1822. Died, 12 Oct., 1822.

26 MILLICENT WASHINGTON, born in Bath county, Kentucky, 4 Aug., 1824.

26 WILLIAM WASHINGTON, born in Lexington, Kentucky, 7 Jan., 1827.

26 THOMAS WASHINGTON, born in Maysville, Virginia, 17 Mar., 1829. Died in Missouri, 12 April, 1849.

26 JANE WASHINGTON, born in Maysville, Virginia, 27 June, 1834.

26 EUGENIA WASHINGTON, born in Maysville, Virginia, 24 June, 1840.

26 FERDINAND STEPTOE WASHINGTON, born in Maysville, Virginia, 22 Jan., 1843.

25 GEORGE STEPTOE WASHINGTON, fourth child of George Steptoe Washington, was born at Harewood, now Jefferson county, West Virginia, 15 Oct., 1806. Removed to Belvidere, a portion of the Harewood estate. Died there, 1 Oct., 1831. Married at Frankfort, Kentucky, about 1827, to Augusta Hawkins, of Frankfort, Kentucky. No children. The wife is now (1876) Mrs. Tarleton, and resides in Louisiana.

25 ROBERT WOOD WASHINGTON, first child of Laurence Augustine Washington, fifth of Samuel, seventh of Augustine, second of Laurence, first of Col. John, of Warton, England, and Bridge's Creek, Virginia, was born at Winchester, Frederick county, Virginia, A. D. 1808. Died at Wheeling, Virginia, A. D. 1843.

25 EMMA TELL WASHINGTON, second child of Laurence Augustine Washington, was born at Winchester, Frederick county, Virginia, A. D. 1811. Died at Wheeling, Virginia, A. D. 1838.

25 DR. LAWRENCE AUGUSTINE WASHINGTON, third child of Laurence Augustine Washington, was born in Winchester,

Frederick county, Virginia, 5 Dec., 1813. Removed to Texas, A. D. 1850. To Colorado, and then, A. D. 1872, to Dennison City, Texas. Now (1877) there. Married in Kanawha county, Virginia, by Rev. Mr. Martin, 29 Nov., 1839, to Martha Dickinson, daughter of John (and Julia) Shrewsbury, of Charlestown, Kanawha county, Virginia. Children :

26 LAWRENCE AUGUSTINE WASHINGTON, born in Frederick county, Virginia, 21 Mar., 1841. Died at Dennison City, Texas, 20 Aug., 1852.

26 WALTER GOOD WASHINGTON, born in Frederick county, Virginia, 21 Feb., 1843.

26 JOHN SHREWSBURY WASHINGTON, born in Frederick county, Virginia, 27 Apr., 1845.

26 JAMES TURNER WASHINGTON, born in Frederick county, Virginia, 3 Mar., 1847.

26 EMMA TELL WASHINGTON, born in Frederick county, Virginia, 27 Sept., 1849.

26 JULIA WOOD WASHINGTON, born in Texas, 29 May, 1850.

26 CECIL WOOD WASHINGTON, born in Colorado, 1 June, 1858.

25 MARY DORCAS WASHINGTON, fourth child of Laurence Augustine Washington, was born at Winchester, Frederick county, Virginia, A. D. 1815. Died in Colorado, 15 Nov., 1861.

25 ELIZA PARKS, first child of Harriet Parks, sixth of Col. Samuel Washington, seventh of Augustine, second of Laurence, first of Col. John, of Warton, England, and Bridge's Creek, Virginia, was born at Baltimore, Maryland, A. D. 1797. Died at Malden, West Virginia, 1852.

25 LAWRENCE AUGUSTINE PARKS, second child of Harriet

Parks, was born at Baltimore, Maryland, A. D. 1801.
Died at Kanawha Salines, West Virginia, 1822.

25 BUSHROD PARKS, third child of Harriet Parks, was born
at Baltimore, Maryland, A. D. 1806.   Died in Louisiana,
A. D. 1832.

25 LAURA PARKS, fourth child of Harriet Parks, was born
at Baltimore, Maryland, 15 Nov., 1809. Removed to
Kanawha Salines, A. D. 1818. To Charlestown, West
Virginia, 1864. Now (1877) there. Married, 1828, at Kanawha Salines, by Rev. N. W. Calhoun, to Samuel, son of
John (and Martha Dickinson) Shrewsbury, of Kanawha
county, West Virginia.   He died at Charlestown, 24
Mar., 1865.   Children :
  26 MARTHA DICKINSON SHREWSBURY, born at Shrews-
     bury, Kanawha county, West Virginia, 3 Feb., 1828.
  26 LAURENCE WASHINGTON SHREWSBURY, born at
     Shrewsbury, Kanawha county, West Virginia, 11
     Oct., 1831.
  26 ALBERT SHREWSBURY, born at Shrewsbury, Kanawha
     county, West Virginia, A. D. 1833.   Died.
  26 ANDREW PARKS SHREWSBURY, born at Shrewsbury,
     Kanawha county, West Virginia, 6 July, 1836.
  26 HARRIET WASHINGTON SHREWSBURY, born at Shrews-
     bury, Kanawha county, West Virginia, 15 May,
     1840. Died 1 Jan., 1876.
  26 CORNELIA SHREWSBURY, born at Shrewsbury, Kan-
     awha county, West Virginia, 4 Apr., 1842.
  26 LAURA SHREWSBURY, born at Shrewsbury, Kanawha
     county, West Virginia, 16 Apr., 1844.
  26 SAMUEL SHREWSBURY, born at Shrewsbury, Kan-
     awha county, West Virginia, 27 Nov., 1847.
  26 HENRY SHREWSBURY, born at Shrewsbury, Kanawha
     county, West Virginia, 12 Oct., 1853.

25 Major Andrew Parks, fifth child of Harriet Parks, was born at Baltimore, Maryland, 1811. Removed to Charlestown, Kanawha Salines, 1818. Died at Charlestown, West Virginia, 27 June, 1863. Married at Charlestown, by Dr. James Brown, A. D. 1842, to Margaret, daughter of John (and Margaret) Creed, of Lancaster, Ohio. She died at Charlestown, West Virginia, 9 June, 1866. Children :

26 Creed Parks, born at Charlestown, West Virginia, about 1843.

26 Bushrod Washington Parks, born at Charlestown, West Virginia, about 1845.

26 Harriot Parks, born at Charlestown, West Virginia, 27 Oct., 1848. Married Theodore Talmadge, of Columbus, Ohio.

26 Andrew Parks, born at Charlestown, West Virginia, 27 Oct., 1852.

25 Mary Parks, sixth child of Harriet Parks, was born at Baltimore, Maryland, about 1813. Died at Clifton, West Virginia. Married at ———, about ———, to Milton Hansford, of ———.

25 Dr. John Parks, seventh child of Harriet Parks, was born at Baltimore, Maryland, A. D. 1816. Removed A. D. 1818, and now (1877) at Kanawha Salines, Kanawha county, West Virginia. Married at Kanawha Salines, Dec., 1845, by Rev. Stuart Robinson, Lucy M., daughter of Robert N. (and Maria C.) Anderson, of Kanawha Salines. Children :

26 Albert Washington Parks, born at Kanawha Salines, 14 May, 1853.

26 Laura Shelton Parks, born at Kanawha Salines, 27 Oct., 1855. Died, Oct., 1862.

26 Anna Wall Parks, born at Kanawha Salines, 21 Aug., 1859.

25 RICHARD HENRY LEE WASHINGTON, first child of Corbin, fourth of John Augustine, seventh of Augustine, second of Laurence, first of Col. John, of Warton, England, and Bridge's Creek, Virginia, was born at Walnut Farm, Westmoreland county, Virginia, A. D. 1787. Removed to Selby, Fairfax county, and died at Prospect Hill, Jefferson county, Virginia, about 1819. Not married.

25 BUSHROD CORBIN WASHINGTON, second child of Corbin, was born at Walnut Farm, Westmoreland county, Virginia, Fall of 1790. Removed to Claymont, Jefferson county, West Virginia, and died there, 28 July, 1851. Married, first, in Prince William county, Virginia, about 1810, to Anna Maria (died at Duffield, Virginia, 24 Nov., 1850), second daughter of Major Richard Scott Blackburn, of United States Army. Two children :

> **26** HANNAH LEE WASHINGTON, born at Rippon Lodge, Prince William county, Virginia, 19 May, 1811. Married William P. Alexander. Now (1877) a widow, at Duffield, Jefferson county, Virginia. Had three children.

> **26** THOMAS BLACKBURN WASHINGTON, born at Rippon Lodge, Prince William county, Virginia, about 1813.

Wife died in 1833. Married, second, in 1835, at Leesburg, Loudon county, Virginia, in 1835, to Maria Powell, daughter of Matthew Harrison, of Loudon county, Virginia. No issue.

25 JOHN AUGUSTINE WASHINGTON, third child of Corbin, was born at Walnut Farm, Westmoreland county, Virginia, about 1792. He removed to, and died at Mount Vernon, Virginia, in June, 1832. He was married at ————, A. D. 1814, to Jane Charlotte, daughter of Major Richard Scott Blackburn, of United States Army. Children :

26 George Washington, born at Blakeley, West Virginia, about 1815. Died young.

26 Ann Maria Washington, born at Blakeley, West Virginia, A. D. 1817. Died, 29 Mar., 1850.

26 John Augustine Washington, born at Blakeley, West Virginia, 3 May, 1821.

26 Richard Blackburn Washington, born at Blakeley, West Virginia, 12 Nov., 1822.

26 Daughter. Died young.

Widow died at Blakeley, Jefferson county, West Virginia, in Aug., 1856.

25 Mary Lee Washington, fourth child of Corbin, was born at Walnut Farm, Westmoreland county, Virginia, about 1797. Removed about ——, to Alexandria, Virginia, and died at Blakeley, Jefferson county, West Virginia, A. D. 1827. Married at Mount Vernon about 1819, to Noblet Herbert, of Alexandria, Virginia. He died there. Children :

26 Bushrod Washington Herbert, born at Alexandria, Virginia, about 1820. Now (1877) living at Prospect Hill, near Charlestown, West Virginia. Not married.

26 Robert Herbert, born at Alexandria, Virginia, about 1822. Died.

26 Noblet Herbert, born at Alexandria, Virginia, about 1825. Died.

25 Jane Washington, fifth child of Corbin, was born at Walnut Farm, Westmoreland county, Virginia, about 1800.

25 Anna Maria Washington, second child (first child, George Frederick, died infant), of Col. George Augustine, first of Col. Charles, fifth of Augustine, by second wife, second of Laurence, first of Col. John of Warton,

England, and Bridge's Creek, Virginia, was born at ———, 3 Apr., 1788. Married at ———, about 1810, Captain Reuben Thornton. Children :

    26 CHURCHILL JONES THORNTON, born at ———, about 1812.

    26 CHARLES AUGUSTINE THORNTON, born at ———, about 1815.

Their descendants are in the South.

25 GEORGE FAYETTE WASHINGTON, third child of Col. George Augustine, was born at ———, 17 Jan., 1790. Died at Waverly, Virginia, in Sept., 1867.' Married at Charlestown, West Virginia, 18 Nov., 1813, to Maria, daughter of Mathew (and Massey) Traner, of Charlestown. She died at Waverly, about 1860. Children :

    26 MATHEW BARWELL BASSETT WASHINGTON, born at Charlestown, West Virginia, 15 Aug., 1810. Died at Waverly, Virginia, 1 Aug., 1868.

    26 ———. Died young.

    26 CHARLES AUGUSTINE WASHINGTON, born at Charlestown, West Virginia, 9 Aug., 1814. Died at Georgetown, D. C., A. D. 1861.

    26 FRANCIS MASSEY WASHINGTON, born at Charlestown, West Virginia, 21 Jan., 1816.

    26 GEORGE FAYETTE WASHINGTON, born at Charlestown, West Virginia, 21 Feb., 1823. Died at Waverly, Virginia, about 1853.

" George Fayette Washington spent part of his life at Mount Vernon. Was educated at Williamsburgh, Virginia. Lived a while at Wellington, below Alexandria. Removed to Frederick county, thence to Waverly, six miles from Winchester."

25 CHARLES AUGUSTINE WASHINGTON, fourth child of Col. George Augustine, was born at ———, about 1795.

" He fell into bad health, and his brother George Fayette

went abroad with him, hoping that a sea voyage would be beneficial, but their hopes were vain, as Charles died at Cadiz," A. D. ——.

25 FAYETTE BALL, first child of Frances Washington, third of Col. Charles, fifth of Augustine, by second wife, second of Laurence, first of Col. John, of Warton, England, and Bridge's Creek, Virginia, was born at ——, about 1790. He died about 1835. Married, about 1811, Mary Maria, daughter of George Thompson Mason, of Fairfax county, Virginia. One son :

> 26 GEORGE WASHINGTON BALL, born at ——, about 1812. Married Miss Randolph, daughter of Col. Randolph, of Fauquier county, and resides (1877) in Loudon county, Virginia.

25 CHARLES BALL, second child of Frances Washington, was born at ——, about 1792. Lived in Loudon county, Virginia. Married Miss Potter. Had issue.

25 MILDRED BALL, third child of Frances Washington, was born at ——, about 1795. Married William Thorner. Had issue.

25 FRANCES BALL, fourth child of Frances Washington, was born at ——, about 1797.

25 MARTHA BALL, fifth child of Frances Washington, was born at ——, about 1800. Married John C. Gibson.

26 LEWIS WILLIAM WASHINGTON, first child of George Corbin Washington, sixth of William Augustine, third of Augustine, second of Augustine, second of Laurence, first of Col. John, of Warton, England, and Bridge's Creek, Virginia, was born at Georgetown, D. C., 30 Nov., 1812. Removed to Jefferson county, West Virginia. Died there, 1 Oct., 1871. Married at Baltimore,

Maryland, by Rev. Dr. Wyatt, 17 Nov., 1836, to Mary
Ann, daughter of James (and Mary Ann Crockett) Barroll, of Baltimore, Maryland. Children :

   27 GEORGE CORBIN WASHINGTON, born at Baltimore,
     Maryland, Mar., 1837. Died 30 Sept., 1843.

   27 JAMES BARROLL WASHINGTON, born at Baltimore,
     Maryland, 26 Aug., 1839.

   27 MARY ANN WASHINGTON, born at Baltimore, Mary-
     land, 1 June, 1839.

   27 ELIZA RIDGELEY WASHINGTON, born in Jefferson
     county, West Virginia, 16 Nov., 1844.

Children by second wife :

   27 BETTY LEWIS WASHINGTON, born in Jefferson
     county, West Virginia, 26 Aug., 1861. Died 25 July,
     1862.

   27 WILLIAM DE HERTBURN WASHINGTON, born in Jeffer-
     son county, West Virginia, 29 Jan., 1863.

Wife died in Jefferson county, West Virginia, 16 Nov.,
1844. Married, second, at Clover Lea, Hanover county,
Virginia, by Rev. G. S. Carraway, 6 Nov., 1860, to Ella
Bassett, daughter of George Washington (and Betty Burnett) Bassett, of Clover Lea. Two children above. Mrs.
Ella Bassett Washington, now (1876) resides at Charlestown, West Virginia.

26 ELEANOR WASHINGTON, second child of George Corbin
   Washington, was born at Georgetown, D. C., about 1814,
   and died about 1834, aged 20 years. Unmarried.

26 GEORGE CORBIN WASHINGTON, third child of George
   Corbin Washington, was born at Georgetown, D. C.,
   about 1816. Died at Georgetown, D. C., in July, 1854.
   Was buried at Oak Hill, near there.

26 MARY SNICKERS, first child of Fanny Washington, third
   child of Warner, first of Warner, first of Warner, first of
   John, first of Laurence, first of Col. John, of Warton

England, and Bridge's Creek, Virginia, was born at Claymont, in Clarke county, Virginia, about 1795. **Dead.**

26 WILLIAM SNICKERS, second child of Fanny Washington, was born at Claymont, in Clarke county, Virginia, about 1798. Unmarried. Dead.

26 EMILY SNICKERS, third child of Fanny Washington, was born at Claymont, in Clarke county, Virginia, about 1800. Unmarried. Dead.

26 EDWARD SNICKERS, fourth child of Fanny Washington, was born at Claymont, in Clarke county, Virginia, about 1804. Unmarried. Dead.

26 ELIZABETH SNICKERS, fifth child of Fanny Washington, was born at Claymont, in Clarke county, Virginia, 15 Oct., 1806. Removed to Baltimore, Maryland, 1835. Now (1877) there. Married at Martinsburgh, West Virginia, by Rev. Mr. Johnson, 17 Feb., 1835, to Charles H. H. Browne, of Westmoreland county, Virginia, son of William (and Sarah Hammond) Browne, of Westmoreland, Virginia. Seven children :

    27 HENRY BROWNE, born at Baltimore, Maryland, 23 Apr., 1836. Died 13 Feb., 1839.

    27 WILLIAM BROWNE, born at Baltimore, Maryland, 10 July, 1838. Died 5 May, 1866.

    27 CHARLES BROWNE, born at Baltimore, Maryland, 10 Nov., 1839. Died 1 Jan., 1860.

    27 FREDERICK BROWNE, born at Baltimore, Maryland, 15 Nov., 1841.

    27 FRANK BROWNE, born at Baltimore, Maryland, 21 Dec., 1843.

    27 ALBERT BROWNE, born at Baltimore, Maryland, 30 Nov., 1845.

    27 FANNY BROWNE, born at Baltimore, Maryland, 7 Feb., 1849.

26 BEVERLY SNICKERS, sixth child of Fanny Washington, was born at Claymont, Clarke county, Virginia, about 1808. Died unmarried.

26 HENRY AUGUSTINE WASHINGTON, first child of Sarah Tayloe Washington, eighth of William Augustine, third of Augustine, second of Augustine, second of Laurence, first of Col. John, of Warton, England, and Bridge's Creek, Virginia, was born at Haywood, Virginia, 24 Aug., 1820. Died at Washington, D. C., 28 Feb., 1858. He was educated at Princeton, New Jersey. Removed to Williamsburgh, Virginia. Was Professor of William and Mary's College. Married at Williamsburgh, by Rev. Mr. Wilmer, 8 July, 1852, to Cynthia B., daughter of Hon. Nathaniel Beverly (and Lucy Ann) Tucker, of Williamsburgh. Professor of Moral Philosophy and Political Economy, of William and Mary's College. Children :

    27 LUCY B. WASHINGTON, born at Williamsburgh, Virginia, 22 July, 1854. Died 30 July, 1854.

    27 SARAH TAYLOE WASHINGTON, born at Williamsburgh, Virginia, 26 Dec., 1856. Died 1 Oct., 1862.

26 JOHN TAYLOE WASHINGTON, second child of Sarah Tayloe Washington, was born at Blenheim, Westmoreland county, Virginia, 20 Dec., 1822. Died at Albion, King George's county, Virginia, 18 May, 1854. Married at Washington, D. C., 10 June, 1850, to Mary D., daughter of George D. (and Roberta) Ashton, of King George's county, Virginia. Children :

    27 SARAH TAYLOE WASHINGTON, born at Albion, King George's county, Virginia, 4 May, 1851. Died 5 Apr., 1857.

    27 JOHN WASHINGTON, born at Albion, King George's county, Virginia, 9 Aug., 1852.

    27 MARY ASHTON WASHINGTON, born at Albion, King George's county, Virginia, 12 June, 1858.

27　RICHARD HENRY WASHINGTON, born at Albion, King
George's county, Virginia, 22 Mar., 1863.

26　GEORGE WASHINGTON, third child of Sarah Tayloe
Washington, was born at Cedar Hill, Virginia, 24 July,
1825. Removed to Alexandria, Virginia. Now (1877)
there. Married at Warrenton, Virginia, 1 Dec., 1852, to
Sallie, daughter of J. W. Massie, of Alexandria, Virginia. Children :
　　27　ORLANDO FAIRFAX WASHINGTON, born at Alex-
　　andria, Virginia, 18 Nov., 1853. Died Oct., 1857.
　　27　HENRY AUGUSTINE WASHINGTON, born at Alex-
　　andria, Virginia, 29 Sept., 1856.
　　27　EFFIE WASHINGTON, born at Alexandria, Virginia,
　　17 Dec., 1358. Died 24 Dec., 1858.
　　27　GEORGE WASHINGTON, born at Warrenton, Virginia,
　　28 May, 1861.
　　27　CLARENCE EDGAR WASHINGTON, born at Alexandria,
　　Virginia, 23 June, 1868.
　　27　MARY STUART WASHINGTON, born at Alexandria,
　　Virginia, 19 July, 1871.
　　27　LAURENCE R. WASHINGTON, born at Alexandria,
　　Virginia, 14 Sept., 1873.

26　RICHARD BUSHROD WASHINGTON, fourth child of Sarah
Tayloe Washington, was born at Blenheim, Virginia, 21
June, 1827. Removed to Hastings, Minnesota. Died at
Hagerstown, Maryland, 6 July, 1863. Married at Hast-
ings, Minnesota, 28 June, 1859, to Ellen, daughter of ——
Center, of Hastings, Minnesota, Children :
　　27　LAURENCE GIBSON WASHINGTON, born at Hastings,
　　Minnesota, 2 June, 1860.
　　27　MARY WHALEY WASHINGTON, born at Hastings,
　　Minnesota, 5 Aug., 1862.

26　MARY WEST WASHINGTON, fifth child of Sarah T. Washington, was born at Blenheim, Virginia, 13 Oct., 1828. Now (1877) there, or at Haywood, or Campbelltown. Married at Blenheim, Virginia, by Rev. William Chesley, 19 Dec., 1856, to Dr. Walker, son of William Fetner Washington, of Clifton, Caroline county, Virginia. Children :

27 LAURENCE AUGUSTINE WASHINGTON, born at Clifton, Virginia, 9 Nov., 1857.

27 WALKER WASHINGTON, born at Clifton, Virginia, 23 Oct., 1860.

27 RICHARD WASHINGTON, born at Campbelltown, Virginia, 1 Nov., 1862.

27 ANNA WASHINGTON, born at Clifton, Virginia, 25 Dec., 1865. Died 4 Feb., 1867.

27 BESSIE WASHINGTON, born at Clifton, Virginia, 7 June, 1869. Died 8 Aug., 1870.

26 SARAH ASHTON WASHINGTON, sixth child of Sarah Tayloe Washington, was born at Campbelltown, Westmoreland county, Virginia, 17 Aug., 1831, and died there, 2 Jan., 1832.

26 WILLIAM AUGUSTINE WASHINGTON, seventh child of Sarah Tayloe Washington, was born at Blenheim, Virginia, 5 Mar., 1833. Removed about 1859 to Florence, South Carolina. To Merced City, California, 1870. Now (1877) there. Married at Florence, South Carolina, 19 Sept., 1860, to Sallie A., daughter of —— James, of Florence, South Carolina. Children :

27 Infant, born at Florence, South Carolina, about 1861. Died infant.

27 JULIA J. WASHINGTON, born at Florence, South Carolina, 11 July, 1862.

27 MARY E. WASHINGTON, born at Florence, South Carolina, 13 Oct., 1866. Died 18 Apr., 1871.

27 EDITH H. WASHINGTON, born at Campbelltown, Virginia, 30 Sept., 1868. Died 30 July, 1869.

27 WILLIAM AUGUSTINE WASHINGTON, born at Baltimore, Maryland, 13 Oct., 1870.

27 EMMA ETHEL WASHINGTON, born at Merced City, California, 5 Sept., 1875.

26 LAURENCE WASHINGTON, eighth child of Sarah Tayloe Washington, was born at Campbelltown, Virginia, 1 May, 1836. Not married.

26 ELIZABETH WASHINGTON, ninth child of Sarah Tayloe Washington, was born at Blenheim, Virginia, 23 Nov., 1838. Removed to Wakefield, Virginia. Now (1877) there. Married at Campbelltown, Virginia, by Rev. William Chesley, 22 Oct., 1856, to John E. Wilson, son of John T. Wilson, of Anne Arundel county, Maryland. Children :

27 SUSAN WILSON, born at Campbelltown, Virginia, 9 Sept., 1857.

27 HENRIETTA WILSON, born at West Wakefield, Virginia, 26 Mar., 1859.

27 JOHN F. WILSON, born at Campbelltown, Virginia, 19 Aug., 1860.

27 WILLIAM WILSON, born at West Wakefield, Virginia, 8 Feb., 1862.

27 LAWRENCE W. WILSON, born at West Wakefield, Virginia, 28 May, 1866.

27 SARAH TAYLOE WILSON, born at West Wakefield, Virginia, 5 Nov., 1867. Died 26 Aug., 1868.

27 GEORGE WILSON, born at West Wakefield, Virginia, 27 Jan., 1874. Died 8 Sept., 1875.

26 ROBERT JAMES WASHINGTON, tenth child of Sarah Tayloe Washington, was born at Campbelltown, Virginia, 16 Sept., 1841. Now (1877) there. Married at Wirtland, Virginia, 30 Oct., 1867, to Bessie Payne, daughter of Dr. William Wirt, of Wirtland, Virginia. Children :

27 SELINA PAYNE WASHINGTON, born at Wirtland, Virginia, 16 Apr., 1870.

27 ROBERT WIRT WASHINGTON, born at Wirtland, Virginia, 25 Feb., 1872.

27 HENRY TAYLOE WASHINGTON, born at Campbelltown, Virginia, 27 Dec., 1874.

27 WILLIAM DABNEY WASHINGTON, born at Campbelltown, Virginia, 14 Jan., 1876.

27 FANNIE WIRT WASHINGTON, born at Campbelltown, Virginia, 28 Feb., 1877.

26 LLOYD WASHINGTON, eleventh child of Sarah Tayloe Washington, was born at Blenheim, 2 Nov., 1846. Removed in Dec., 1866, to Chicago, Illinois. Now (1877) there. Not married.

26 DANIEL GEORGE TUCKER, first child of Maria Ball Tucker, third of Mrs. Betty Lewis Carter, first of Mrs. Betty Washington Lewis, second of Augustine Washington, by second wife, second of Laurence, first of Col. John, of Warton, England, and Bridge's Creek, Virginia, was born at ———, 20 Nov., 1802.

26 ELEANOR ROSALIE TUCKER, second child of Maria Ball Tucker, was born at ———, 8 May, 1804. Died Oct., 1818.

26 MARIA FARLEY TUCKER, third child of Maria Ball Tucker, was born at ———, 6 Nov., 1805. Married ——— Rives, of ———.

26 ELIZA LEWIS TUCKER, fourth child of Maria Ball Tucker, was born at ———, 9 Dec., 1808.

26 MARY LELIA TUCKER, fifth child of Maria Ball Tucker, was born at ———, 5 Aug., 1810. Died 28 July, 1817.

26 ELLEN ELIZA LEWIS, first child of George Richard Lewis,

15

third child of Howell Lewis, fourth of Mrs. Betty Washington Lewis, second of Augustine, by second wife, second of Laurence, first of John, of Warton, England, and Bridge's Creek, Virginia, was born at Morgansfield, Kentucky, 18 July, 1834. Removed about ——, to Marietta, Ohio. Now (1876) there. Married at Baltimore, Maryland, 9 Oct., 1856, to Anselm Tupper Nye, son of Anselm Tupper Nye, of Baltimore. Children :

27 GEORGE LEWIS NYE, born at ——, 27 July, 1857.
27 HAROLD BAYLESS NYE, born at ——, 3 Feb., 1859.
27 ANSELM TUPPER   "   "   "   27 Sept., 1860.
29 ELLEN LEWIS   "   "   "   22 Nov., 1863.

26 JEANNETTE LEWIS, second child of George Richard Lewis, was born at Morgansfield, Kentucky, 2 July, 1837. Died — Dec., 1843.

26 HAROLD LEWIS, third child of George Richard Lewis, was born at Morgansfield, Kentucky, 14 Aug., 1839. Died at ——, 1863.

26 GEORGE LEWIS, fourth child of George Richard Lewis, was born at Morgansfield, Kentucky, 14 Sept., 1842.

26 ALFRED LOVELL, first child of Betty Washington Lewis, first of Howell Lewis, fourth of Betty Lewis, second of Augustine Washington, by second wife, second of Laurence, first of Col. John, of Warton, England, and Bridge's Creek, Virginia, was born at Charlestown, West Virginia, 27 Dec., 1818. He died at Marietta, Ohio, 6 Sept., 1842. Not married.

26 RICHARD CHANNING MOORE LOVELL, second child of Betty Washington Lewis, was born at Charlestown, West Virginia, 3 Mar., 1822. Removed about ——, to Covington, Kentucky. Married at Charlestown, West Virginia, about

——, to Sallie, daughter of —— Patrick, of Charlestown, West Virginia.

26 HOWELL LEWIS LOVELL, third child of Betty Washington Lewis, was born at Charlestown, West Virginia, 9 July, 1824. Removed about —, to Covington, Kentucky. Now (1877) there.

26 JOSEPH LOVELL, fourth child of Betty Washington Lewis, was born at Charlestown, West Virginia, 31 Mar., 1827. Removed about ——, to Nashville, Tennessee. To Marietta, Ohio, where he died, 22 Mar., 1865. Married at Marietta, Ohio, 15 Nov., 1852, to Sarah Sophia, daughter of Anselm Tupper (and Rebecca Dodge Cram) Nye, of Marietta, Ohio. Widow, now (1877) at Marietta, Ohio. One child:

    27 BETTY WASHINGTON LOVELL, born at Marietta, Ohio, 13 Oct., 1853. Married 12 Jan., 1876, to Francis Fox Oldham.

26 BETTY LOVELL, fifth child of Betty Washington Lewis, was born at Charlestown, West Virginia, about 1829. Married Charles Carter.

26 FAYETTE AUGUSTINE LOVELL, sixth child of Betty Washington Lewis, was born at Charlestown, West Virginia, about 1832, and died there. Widow, Mrs. Sally S. Lovell, now (1877) there.

26 WILLIAM STEELE, Lawyer, first child of Ellen Jael Steele, second of Howell Lewis, fourth of Betty Lewis, second of Augustine Washington, by second wife, second of Laurence, first of Col. John, of Warton, England, and Bridge's Creek, Virginia, was born at Charlestown, West Virginia, 12 Dec., 1819. He settled, first, at Calhoun, Missouri, a lawyer. Removed to Windsor, Missouri, where he died, 7 Oct., 1872. He was married at ———, to Fanny, daughter of —— Delany, of ———. Children :

27 ROBERT FLEMING STEELE, born at ———, 23 Sept., 1846.

27 FANNY MARIA STEELE, born at ———, 2 Nov., 1848. Died 19 Mar., 1873.

27 JOSEPH PERKINS STEELE, born at ———, 3 Dec., 1850.

27 LOUISE STEELE, born at ———, 28 Mar., 1853. Died 9 Nov., 1872.

27 WILLIAM STEELE, born at ———, 24 Apr., 1855.

27 ELLEN JAEL STEELE, born at ———, 14 Dec., 1857. Died young.

27 BETTY CALDWELL STEELE, born at ———, 1 Mar., 1860. Died 28 Oct., 1873.

27 LOVELL STEELE, born at ———, 1865. Died 2 Apr., 1870.

26 MARTHA ELLEN STEELE, second child of Ellen Jael Steele, was born at Charlestown, West Virginia, 5 July, 1821. Removed in Fall of 1834, to Marietta, Ohio. To Cleveland, Ohio, in April, 1852. Now (1876) there. Married at Marietta, Ohio, 25 Oct., 1841, by Rev. Dr. Thomas Weeks, to Joseph Perkins, son of General Simon Perkins, of Warren, Ohio. Her children :

27 OLIVE PERKINS, born at Marietta, Ohio, 1 Aug., 1842. Died at Cleveland, Ohio, 26 May, 1853.

27 CHARLES PERKINS, born at Marietta, Ohio, 10 Feb., 1844. Died at Cleveland, Ohio, 18 Aug., 1864.

27 ELLEN STEELE PERKINS, born at Marietta, Ohio, 11 Dec., 1846. Married Robert L. Chamberlain, and died 4 July, 1876.

27 DOUGLAS PERKINS, born at Cleveland, Ohio, 28 Apr., 1854. Married Emma Keller.

27 Joseph Perkins, born at Cleveland, Ohio, 20 Nov., 1858.

27 Lawrence Lewis Perkins, born at Cleveland, Ohio, 6 Mar., 1862.

26 Howell Lewis Steele, third child of Ellen Jael Steele, was born at Charlestown, West Virginia, 31 Dec., 1822. He died at Ophir, California, 26 Dec., 1850.

26 Robert McAmey Steele, fourth child of Ellen Jael Steele, was born at Charlestown, West Virginia, 28 Dec., 1824. Died there, 16 July, 1844.

26 Betty Washington Steele, fifth child of Ellen Jael Steele, was born at Charlestown, West Virginia, 10 Dec., 1826. Removed to Marietta, Ohio, in Fall of 1834. To Akron, Ohio, in 1849. Now (1876) there. Married at Charlestown, West Virginia, by Rev. Mr. Nash, 1 May, 1849, to David Leicester King (born 25 Dec , 1825), of Akron, Ohio, son of Hon. Leicester (and Julia Ann Huntington) King, of Warren, Ohio. Children :

27 Ellen Lewis King, born at Akron, Ohio, 13 June, 1850. Married David R. Paige, Jr., of Akron, Ohio, 19 Jan., 1870.

27 Betty Steele King, born at Cleveland, Ohio, 22 Dec., 1851. Married John Gilbert Raymond, of Akron, Ohio, 10 Dec., 1873.

27 Howell Steele King, born at Cleveland, Ohio, 3 May, 1853.

27 Susan Huntington King, born at Cleveland, Ohio, 16 Jan., 1855.

27 Martha Perkins King, born at Cleveland, Ohio, 6 Apr., 1863.

26 William Gaston Gwathmey, first child of Frances Fielding Lewis, fifth of Howell Lewis, fourth of Betty

Washington, second of Augustine, by second wife, second of Laurence, first of Col. John, of Warton, England, and Bridge's Creek, Virginia, was born at Savannah, Georgia, 2 Apr, 1823. Removed to New York, about 1830, to Mobile, Alabama, in 1836, to Richmond, Virginia, in 1840. Died there, 5 Aug., 1852. Married in Carolina county, Virginia, Oct., 1846, by Rev. Dr. Friend, to Anna Henry Moore, daughter of —— Moore, of ——. Widow living, 1878. Children:

    27 ELIZABETH TAYLOR GWATHMEY, born at Richmond, Virginia, about 1847.

    27 FANNY FIELDING GWATHMEY, born at Richmond, Virginia, about 1850.

    27 BROOKE GWATHMEY, born at Richmond, Virginia, about 1852. Died.

26 ELLEN JAEL GWATHMEY, second child of Frances Fielding Lewis, was born at Richmond, Virginia, 26 Sept., 1824, and died at Rockbridge Baths, Virginia, 5 Oct., 1870. Married in North Carolina, 26 May, 1844, to James Kerr Caskie, son of John (and Martha Norvell) Caskie, of Richmond, Virginia. He died in Sept., 1868. Children:

    27 MARTHA NORVELL CASKIE, born at Richmond, Virginia, about 1845.

26 HUMPHREY BROOKE GWATHMEY, third child of Frances Fielding Lewis, was born at ——, 5 June, 1826, and died, 5 Nov., 1826.

26 MATILDA CUMMING GWATHMEY, fourth child of Frances Fielding Lewis, was born in New York, 6 Jan., 1828. Removed to Norfolk, Virginia, in 1832. Mobile, Alabama, in 1837. To Richmond, Virginia, 1840, to Nashville, Tennessee, in 1868. Now (1878) there. Married at Philadelphia, 12 May, 1852, by Rev. William S. Plumer,

D.D., to Thomas Verner Moore, son of John (and Rachel) Moore, of Newville, Pennsylvania. He died at Nashville, Tennessee, 5 Aug., 1871. Children:

  27 FANNY BROOKE MOORE, born at Richmond, Virginia, 15 Apr., 1853.

  27 THOMAS VERNER MOORE, born at Richmond, Virginia, 24 Nov., 1856.

26 VIRGINIA GWATHMEY, fifth child of Frances Fielding Lewis, was born at New York, 31 Dec., 1830. Removed to Norfolk, Virginia, in 1831. To Mobile, Alabama, in 1836, to Richmond, Virginia, in 1840, to Wilmington, North Carolina, in 1853. Now (1878) there. Married at Richmond, Virginia, 27 Dec., 1853, by Rev. Adam Empie, to Adam, son of Rev. Adam (and Ann Eliza Wright) Empie, of Richmond, Virginia. Husband died at Wilmington, North Carolina, 10 July, 1877. Children:

  27 SWIFT MILLER EMPIE, born at Wilmington, North Carolina, about 1854.

  27 BROOKE GWATHMEY EMPIE, born at Wilmington, North Carolina, about 1856.

  27 ANN ELIZA EMPIE, born at Wilmington, North Carolina, about 1858.

  27 FANNY LEWIS EMPIE, born at Wilmington, North Carolina, about 1860.

  27 VIRGINIA EMPIE, born at Wilmington, North Carolina, about 1862. Died.

  27 ELLEN CASKIE EMPIE, born at Wilmington, North Carolina, about 1865.

  27 ADAM EMPIE, born at Wilmington, North Carolina, about 1867. Died young.

  27 THEODORE FRANCIS EMPIE, born at Wilmington, North Carolina, about 1870.

  27 ADAM EMPIE, born at Wilmington, North Carolina, about 1872.

26 THEODORE FRANCIS GWATHMEY, sixth child of Frances Fielding Lewis, was born at Norfolk, Virginia, 21 May, 1832. Removed to Mobile, Alabama, in 1836. To Richmond, Virginia, in 1840, to New Orleans, in 1848. Now (1878) there. Unmarried.

26 TEMPLE GWATHMEY, seventh child of Frances Fielding Lewis, was born at Norfolk, Virginia, A. D. 1834. Died at ——, 12 Nov., 1840.

26 FANNY BROOKE GWATHMEY, eighth child of Frances Fielding Lewis, was born at Norfolk, Virginia, 8 Sept., 1835. Removed to Mobile, in 1836. To Richmond, Virginia, in 1840, to Baltimore, Maryland, in 1853. Now (1878) there. Married at Richmond, Virginia, 8 Dec., 1853, by Rev. T. V. Moore, to Andrew, son of George (and Elizabeth) Reed, of Scotland (who removed to Norfolk, Virginia, in 1801). Children :

    27 IMOGEN REED, born at Baltimore, Maryland, 2 Oct., 1854.

    27 BROOKE GWATHMEY REED, born at Baltimore, Maryland, 23 Apr., 1856. Died 19 Jan., 1875.

    27 FANNY FIELDING REED, born at Baltimore, Maryland, 2 June, 1857. Died 8 Aug., 1858.

    27 HARRY FIELDING REED, born at Baltimore, Maryland, 18 May, 1859.

    27 ELLEN REED, born at Baltimore, Maryland, 5 June, 1860.

    27 ANDREW MELVILLE REED, born at Baltimore, Maryland, 16 Aug., 1861.

    27 FANNY LEWIS REED, born at Baltimore, Maryland, 6 Sept., 1862.

26 CAROLINE HETH GWATHMEY, ninth child of Frances Fielding Lewis, was born at Mobile, Alabama, about 1837, and died at Richmond, Virginia, 9 May, 1842.

26 MARY ANN GWATHMEY, tenth child of Frances Fielding Lewis, was born at Richmond, Virginia, A. D. 1841. Died at Richmond, Virginia, 9 May, 1849.

26 EMILY CARTER GWATHMEY, eleventh child of Frances Fielding Lewis, was born at Richmond, Virginia, A. D. 1843, and died there, 26 Mar., 1849.

26 ROBERT WASHINGTON GWATHMEY, twelfth child of Frances Fielding Lewis, was born at Richmond, Virginia, 22 June, 1846. Removed to Baltimore, Maryland, in 1865. Now (1878) there.

26 ROBERT HEREFORD, first child of Virginia Lewis, sixth of Howell Lewis, fourth of Betty Washington, second of Augustine, by second wife, second of Laurence, first of Col. John, of Warton, England, and Bridge's Creek, Virginia, was born at Buffalo, Mason county, West Virginia, 17 July, 1827. Now (1877) at Fort Bridger, Wyoming Territory.

26 REV. BROOKE GWATHMEY HEREFORD, second child of Virginia Lewis, was born at Buffalo, Mason county, West Virginia, 16 Dec., 1829. Removed in 1864, to Gallia county, Ohio, and in 1869, to Greasy Ridge, Lawrence county, Ohio, now (1877) there. Married at Buffalo, Mason county, West Virginia, by Rev. Charles Carroll, 30 Oct., 1851, to Meriam (born in Mason county, West Virginia, in 1832), daughter of Esom (and Elizabeth) Hannan, of Mason county, West Virginia. She died at ———, Gallia county, Ohio, 6 Apr., 1869. Children :

  27 VIRGINIA FRANCES HEREFORD, born at Buffalo, Mason county, West Virginia, 9 Nov., 1852. Married 11 Apr., 1872, William Massie. Two children :

    28 BROOKE HERSCHEL MASSIE, born 22 Feb., 1873.

    28 JOSEPH OSCAR MASSIE, born 3 Nov., 1874.

27 ELLEN LEWIS HEREFORD, born at Buffalo, Mason county, West Virginia, 3 Dec., 1854. Married Daniel S. Vermillion, 30 Sept., 1874. One child:

    28 JENNY FLORENCE VERMILLION, born 8 June, 1875.

27 ROBERT ESOM HEREFORD, born in Henry county, Missouri, 8 June, 1857.

27 NANCY EMMA HEREFORD, born in Buffalo, Mason county, West Virginia, 1 Dec., 1861.

27 WILLIAM CARTER HEREFORD, born in Gallia county, Ohio, 28 Oct., 1864.

27 MARY EVELYN HEREFORD, born in Gallia county, Ohio, 25 Jan., 1869.

He was married, second, by Rev. John Houck, in Lawrence county, Ohio, 16 Oct., 1869, to Mrs. Elizabeth Jane Lewis (born 18 Feb., 1833), daughter of Isaac (and Catharine) Miller, of Lawrence county, Ohio.

26 MARY BRENAUGH HEREFORD, third child of Virginia Lewis, was born at Buffalo, Mason county, West Virginia, 25 Jan., 1832. Died 23 Mar., 1836.

26 FRANCES ELIZA HEREFORD, fourth child of Virginia Lewis, was born at Buffalo, Mason county, West Virginia, 4 June, 1834. Removed to Marietta, Ohio. Now (1876) there. Married at Cleveland, Ohio, 14 Dec., 1853, to John, son of Joseph E. Hall, of Marietta, Ohio. Children:

    27 ALFRED LOVELL HALL, born at Cleveland, Ohio, 7 Sept., 1854.

    27 RHODA VIRGINIA HALL, born at Cleveland, Ohio, 25 Oct., 1855.

    27 BERTHA COTTON HALL, born at Cleveland, Ohio, 26 Jan., 1857.

    27 ELLEN LEWIS HALL, born at Cleveland, Ohio, 29 Oct., 1860.

27 GERTRUDE BUTLER HALL, born at Cleveland, Ohio, 28 Oct., 1867.

27 JOHN CHARLES HALL, born at Cleveland, 'Ohio, 13 Feb., 1869.

26 KATHERINE ELLEN HEREFORD, fifth child of Virginia Lewis, was born at Buffalo, West Virginia, about 1836. Removed in July, 1853, to Clinton, Henry county, Missouri. Now (1877) at Clinton. Married in Henry county, Missouri, by Rev. Dr. Browning, 10 July, 1853, to William H., son of C. H. (and Anna) Schroeder, of St.' Louis. Children: **o**

27 WILLIAM H. SCHROEDER, born at Clinton, Missouri, 17 July, 1855.

27 MATTIE A. SCHROEDER, born at Clinton, Missouri, 18 June, 1857.

27 ROBERT LEE SCHROEDER, born at Clinton, Missouri, 23 June, 1859.

27 JOSEPH SCHROEDER, born at St. Louis, Missouri, 21 Aug., 1862.

27 BETTIE G. SCHROEDER, born at Jerseyville, Illinois, 18 Sept., 1865.

26 LAURENCE LEWIS HEREFORD, sixth child of Virginia Lewis, was born at Buffalo, Mason county, West Virginia, about 1838. Now (1877) at Sherman, Texas. He was married at Jerseyville, Illinois, by Rev. W. H. Reed, 16 Apr., 1871, to Nellie, daughter of J. B. Schroeder, of Jerseyville, Illinois. One child:

27 INEZ FEWELL HEREFORD, born at Jerseyville, Illinois, 31 Jan., 1872.

26 BETTY STRIBLING HEREFORD, seventh child of Virginia Lewis, was born at Buffalo, Mason county, West Virginia, about 1840.

26 GEORGE LEWIS, first child of Howell Lewis, seventh of Howell Lewis, fourth of Mrs. Betty Lewis, sixth of Augustine Washington, second of Laurence, first of Col. John, of Warton, England, and Bridge's Creek, Virginia, was born at ——, Mason county, Virginia, 27 Oct., 1831. Removed in 1852, to California, thence to White Spring, Nye county, Nevada. Now (1877) there. Married in ——, Nevada, in 1874, to ——. Child born in 1876.

26 MARY ELLEN LEWIS, second child of Howell Lewis, was born in ——, Mason county, Virginia, 28 June, 1834. She died in Salem, Illinois. Married in Calhoun, Henry county, Missouri, 25 Oct., 1855, by Rev. William Hoag, to Robert H. Hogan. One child :

    27 ALICE HOGAN, born in Calhoun, Missouri, A. D. 1856.

26 AUGUSTUS D. LEWIS, third child of Howell Lewis, was born in ——, Mason county, Virginia, 8 Nov., 1836. Died in Henry county, Missouri, 10 Feb., 1853.

26 FIELDING LEWIS, fourth child of Howell Lewis, was born at Calhoun, Missouri, 9 Mar., 1839. Removed to Grayson county, Texas. Died 21 Mar., 1863. Married near Calhoun, Missouri, 10 Jan., 1861, by Rev. William Garrett, to Mary S. Rains. One child :

    27 LAWRENCE H. LEWIS, born near Calhoun, Missouri, 11 Jan., 1862.

26 COLUMBIA LEWIS, fifth child of Howell Lewis, was born at Calhoun, Missouri, 24 Sept., 1842. Removed to Lewis, Henry county, Missouri. Now (1877) there. Married at ——, by Rev. L. C. Marvin, D.D., 14 Jan., 1866, to Lawrence W., son of John (and Mary) Good, formerly of West Virginia. Children :

27 IDA GOOD, born at Lewis, Missouri, about 1867.

27 ARCHIE L. GOOD, born at Lewis, Missouri, about 1870.

27 HARRY C. GOOD, born at Lewis, Missouri, about 1872.

27 LAWRENCE B. GOOD, born at Lewis, Missouri, about 1875.

26 VIRGINIA LEWIS, sixth child of Howell Lewis, was born at Calhoun, Missouri, 11 Mar., 1845. Removed 26 Sept., 1867, to Choctaw Nation, Indian Territory. Now (1877) at Stringtown, Indian Territory. Married near Calhoun, Missouri, by Rev. Mr. Dolby, 10 June, 1867, to C. H. Gatewood, son of James M. (and Ann A.) Gatewood, of Sherman, Texas. Children :

27 JAMES HOWELL GATEWOOD, born at Boggy Depot, Indian Territory, 1 June, 1868.

27 EMMA ANN GATEWOOD, born at Stringtown, Indian Territory, 12 Jan., 1873.

27 MARY FRANKLIN GATEWOOD, born at Stringtown, Indian Territory, 5 June, 1875.

26 BETTY F. LEWIS, seventh child of Howell Lewis, was born at Calhoun, Missouri, 28 Sept., 1848. Now (1877) resides near Calhoun. Married at Lewis, Missouri, by Rev. J. Warder, 26 Jan., 1871, to Milton D., son of Mark (and Eliza) Finks, of Calhoun, Missouri. Children :

27 LELAND FINKS, born near Calhoun, Missouri, in Jan., 1872.

27 EMMA MAY, born near Calhoun, Missouri, in June, 1875.

26 WILLIAM HOWELL LEWIS, eighth child of Howell Lewis, was born at Calhoun, Missouri, 26 Jan., 1850. Removed to Lewis, Missouri. Now (1877) there. Married at Lewis, by Rev. William Lawler, 26 Feb., 1874, to Nettie,

daughter of George (and Mary) Dean, of ———. One child :

27 EMMA LEWIS, born at Lewis, Missouri, 28 Feb., 1875.

26 GASTON G. LEWIS, ninth child of Howell Lewis, was born at Calhoun, Missouri, 28 Jan., 1853. Removed Oct., 1875, to White River, Nye county, Nevada. Now (1877) there. Unmarried.

26 EMMA A. LEWIS, tenth child of Howell Lewis, was born at Calhoun, Missouri, 28 Sept., 1855. Removed to Lewis, Missouri. Now (1877) there. Married at Lewis, by Rev. Mr. Hudson, 9 Mar., 1876, to Monroe, son of James (and Martha) Wiley, of Calhoun, Missouri. No children.

26 LAURENCE BERRY WASHINGTON, first child of John Thornton Augustine Washington, first child of Thornton Washington, first of Col. Samuel, by second wife, second of Augustine, by second wife, second of Laurence, first of Col. John, of Warton, England, and Bridge's Creek, Virginia, was born at Cedar Lawn, Jefferson county, West Virginia, 26 Nov., 1811. Never married. "He was a lawyer by profession, served as a Lieutenant in a Virginia regiment in the Mexican War. Went to California, in 1849, thence to Missouri, in 185–. To Virginia, in 185–, to Missouri, in 1856, where he died on a steamboat, on Mississippi River, 21 Sept., 1856. Was an author and poet of no mean ability."

26 DANIEL BEDENGER WASHINGTON, second child of John Thornton Augustine Washington, was born at Cedar Lawn, Jefferson county, West Virginia, 8 Feb., 1814. "Was a farmer by profession, though sometimes editor and writer for political newspapers. Removed to Putnam county, West Virginia, in 1846. To Johnson county,

Missouri, in 1856. Served in Confederate Army during the Civil War. Now (1877) near Index, Cass county, Missouri. Married at Harper's Ferry, Virginia, 24 Oct., 1843, to Lucy (she was daughter of Samuel Washington, half brother of John T. A. Washington), A. Wharton, widow of Dr. John J. Wharton, of Newport; Kentucky. Had five children, two sons and three daughters, all alive except the eldest, a son," Children :

27 SAMUEL THORNTON WASHINGTON, born at Cedar Lawn, West Virginia, 22 Dec., 1844. Died 15 Nov., 1850.

27 KATE TOWNSEND WASHINGTON, born in Putnam county, West Virginia, 11 Sept., 1846.

27 ELIZABETH BEDENGER WASHINGTON, born in Putnam county, West Virginia, 3 Sept., 1848.

27 THORNTON AUGUSTINE WASHINGTON, born in Putnam county, West Virginia, 23 Apr., 1854.

27 MARIAN WALLACE WASHINGTON, born in Putnam county, West Virginia, 17 June, 1856.

26 VIRGINIA THORNTON WASHINGTON, third child of John Thornton Augustine Washington, was born at Cedar Lawn, Jefferson county, West Virginia, 22 May, 1816. Died unmarried, 13 Nov., 1838, in Jefferson county, West Virginia.

26 SALLY ELEANOR WASHINGTON, fourth child of John Thornton Augustine Washington, was born at Cedar Lawn, Jefferson county, West Virginia, 7 Apr., 1818. Removed to Johnson county Missouri, in 1856–7, thence to Cass county, Missouri, in 1857, where she died unmarried, 21 Jan., 1858.

26 BENJAMIN FRANKLIN WASHINGTON, fifth child of John Thornton Augustine Washington, was born at Cedar Lawn, Charlestown, Jefferson county, West Virginia,

7 Apr., 1820. Removed to San Francisco, California, A. D. 1849. Died there 22 Jan., 1872. Married 22 Oct., 1845, at Charlestown, West Virginia, to Georgianna Hite Ransom, daughter of James L. Ransom, of Charlestown, Jefferson county, West Virginia. She died in Dec., 1860, at San Francisco, California. Children :

> 27 JOHN THORNTON WASHINGTON, born at Charlestown, West Virginia, 26 July, 1846.
>
> 27 FRANKLIN BEDENGER WASHINGTON, born at Charlestown, West Virginia, 23 June, 1848.
>
> 27 FANNIE MADISON WASHINGTON, born at San Francisco, California, Aug., 1853. Married 18 Apr., 1876, to Lieutenant D. Delhanty.
>
> 27 LILLIAN WASHINGTON, born at San Francisco, California, A. D. 1855. Died 1856, at Charlestown, West Virginia.
>
> 27 BERTHA JAMES WASHINGTON, born at San Francisco, California, 3 Mar., 1858.

" Lawyer and Editor by profession. He emigrated to California in 1849. Was elected Recorder and Police Judge of Sacramento City, in 1850, and took an active part in suppression of 'the squatter riots.' Became part owner and Editor-in-Chief of the *Democratic State Journal*, in 1852. Also edited and partly owned the *Times and Transcript*, of San Francisco, in 1853 to 1855. In 1857 was appointed Collector of the Port of San Francisco, by President Buchanan, served four years. Retired to farm in Tehama county, California, during the War. In June, 1865, became first Editor of the *Examiner*, which he controlled until the day of his death."

26 GEORGIANNA AUGUSTA WASHINGTON, sixth child of John Thornton Augustine Washington, was born at Cedar Lawn, Charlestown, Jefferson county, West Virginia, 13 Mar., 1822. Removed to West Poultney, Vermont, thence to Washington, D. C., thence to Johnson

county, Missouri, in 1857, thence to Little Rock, Arkansas, in 1866, where she now (1877) resides. Married at Cedar Lawn, West Virginia, 20 Nov., 1851, by Rev. Dudley A. Tyng, to John Wheeler, son of Samuel Mansfield (and Eliza) Smith, of Washington, Connecticut. Children :

27 EDWIN CURRAN SMITH, born at West Poultney, Vermont, 3 Feb., 1853.

27 VIRGINIA EMELINE SMITH, born at East Poultney, Vermont, 25 Dec., 1855.

27 MARY WASHINGTON SMITH, born at Washington, D. C., 25 Nov., 1857.

27 ELIZA MANSFIELD SMITH, born at Rose Hill, Missouri, 1 Feb., 1859.

27 WHEELER EATON SMITH, born at Rose Hill, Missouri, 23 Oct., 1862.

26 MARY ELIZABETH WASHINGTON, seventh child of John Thornton Augustine Washington, was born at Cedar Lawn, near Charlestown, West Virginia, 24 May, 1824. Removed to Johnson county, Missouri, in 1857. Now (1877) resides in Index, Cass county, Missouri. Married in Johnson county, Missouri, 21 Sept., 1858, to Squire Asbury, a grand-nephew of President Zachary Taylor. Had three children. One son and two daughters. Two daughters died. Children :

27 CHARLES HORACE ASBURY, born in Johnson county, Missouri, 17 Nov., 1859.

27 BESSIE ASBURY, born in Johnson county, Missouri, Sept., 1861. Died 21 June, 1863.

27 MIDA HOPE ASBURY, born in Johnson county, Missouri, 19 Feb., 1864. Died.

26 COL. JOHN THORNTON AUGUSTINE WASHINGTON, Civil Engineer by profession, eighth child of John Thornton Augustine Washington, was born at Cedar Lawn, Charlestown, Jefferson county, West Virginia, 22 Jan., 1826. Was in United States Army. Now (1877) at Galveston,

16

Texas. Entered West Point, 1845. Graduated June, 1849. Entered Army as Brevet-Lieutenant, Sixth United States Infantry, 1849. Second Lieutenant, Fifth Infantry. First Lieutenant, First Infantry, and Aid-de-Camp to Major-General D. E. Twiggs, when the War commenced. Resigned 8 Apr., 1861. Served in the Confederate Army through the War. Was at one time General Lee's Chief-of-Staff. Now Civil Engineer. Married 8 Mar., 1860, at San Antonio, Texas, by Rev. R. F. Bunting, to Olive Ann, daughter of Enoch (and Olive Ann) Jones, of San Antonio, Texas. Children :

27 FLORA MARY WASHINGTON, born at Indianola, Texas, 1 May, 1861.

27 GEORGE THORNTON WASHINGTON, born at San Antonio, Texas, 13 Apr., 1863.

27 LEE HOWARD WASHINGTON (girl), born at San Antonio, Texas, 15 Apr., 1865.

27 SARAH WASHINGTON, born at San Antonio, Texas, 12 Apr., 1867.

27 LAWRENCE BERRY WASHINGTON, born at San Antonio, Texas, 12 July, 1869.

27 OLIVE ANN WASHINGTON, born at Galveston, Texas, 17 Sept., 1875.

He was Instructor of Tactics at West Point, when Jefferson Davis was Secretary of War.

26 MILDRED BERRY WASHINGTON, ninth child of John Thornton Augustine Washington, was born at Cedar Lawn, Charlestown, West Virginia, 3 Sept., 1827. Died 12 Sept., 1827.

26 MILDRED BERRY WASHINGTON, tenth child of John Thornton Augustine Washington, was born at Cedar Lawn, Charlestown, West Virginia, 8 Mar., 1829. Removed 1854, to Lewis county, Kentucky. Removed to Johnson county, Missouri, in 1853, to Conway county,

Arkansas, in 1866. Died 7 Nov., 1871, near Lewisburg, Conway county, Arkansas. Married at Cedar Lawn, West Virginia, 8 Feb., 1854, by Rev. Mr. Ambler, to Solomon Singleton Bedinger (dead), of Lewis county, Kentucky. Five children. Three sons and two daughters. One son dead. Children :

27 HENRIETTA GRAY BEDINGER, born in Lewis county, Kentucky, 17 Nov., 1854.

27 LAVINIA BEDINGER, born in Lewis county, Kentucky, 29 May, 1857.

27 HENRY CLAY BEDINGER, born in Lewis county, Kentucky, 13 Sept., 1859.

27 ARTHUR SINGLETON BEDINGER, born in Lewis county, Kentucky, 7 Mar., 1862. Died 9 Nov., 1869.

27 SOLOMON BERRY BEDINGER, born in Conway county, Arkansas, 7 Nov., 1871.

26 HON. GEORGE WASHINGTON, Attorney-at-Law, and Judge of the County Court of Johnson county, Missouri, eleventh child of John Thornton Augustine Washington, first child of Thornton, first of Col. Samuel, by second wife, second of Augustine, by second wife, second of Laurence, first of Col. John, was born at or near Charlestown, in Jefferson county, West Virginia, 9 Dec., 1830. Removed in Mar., 1856, to Johnson county, Missouri. To San Francisco, California, in June, 1857. Returned to Johnson county, Missouri, in Aug., 1861. Was engaged in the War until 1866. Now (1876) at Centre View, Johnson county, Missouri. Married at Otterville, Cooper county, Missouri, by Rev. J. B. Logan, 11 Apr., 1871, to Mary Virginia, daughter of William Rowland (and Mahala) Dempsey, of Otterville, Missouri. She was born in Cooper county, Missouri, 23 May, 1844. Children :

27 ROBERT WASHINGTON, born at Centre View, Missouri, 17 Mar., 1872. Dead.

27 Mary Virginia Washington, born at Centre View, Missouri, 14 June, 1873.

27 Vernon de Hertburn Washington, born at Centre View, Missouri, 27 July, 1876.

" He was Cashier of Customs, under his brother B. F. Washington, during his administration as Collector of the Port of San Francisco, in 1857 to 1861. He edited the *Daily and Weekly National,* during the years 1858–9, in conjunction with George P. Johnston. Obtained license to practice law in Supreme Court of California, in Spring of 1861. Resigned position as Cashier of Customs when the Civil War commenced. Reached Missouri in Summer of 1861, and entered State service on Confederate side. Was in the service of the Confederate States ; wounded and captured whilst on Price's raid into Missouri, near Fort Scott, 25 Oct., 1864. Sent to Johnson's Island and remained there until surrender .of Richmond. Transferred to Cairo, then to New Orleans, and finally exchanged at mouth of Red River, 4 May, 1865. Returned to St. Louis, in Summer of 1865, and to Johnson county, in Spring of 1866."

26 Susan Ellsworth Washington, twelfth child of John Thornton Augustine Washington, was born at Cedar Lawn, Jefferson county, West Virginia, 1 Apr., 1833. Removed to Clarke county, Kentucky, about 1855. Moved to Johnson county, Missouri, in 1856, to Rose Hill, Index, Cass county, Missouri, 1857. Now (1877) there. Married at ———, 22 May, 1857, to Henry Clay, son of ——— Bedinger, of Lewis county, Kentucky. Eight children. Three boys, five girls ; one girl dead. Children :

27 George Washington-Bedinger, born at Rose Hill, Index, Cass county, Missouri, 28 Feb., 1858.

27 Lillian Thornton Bedinger, born at Rose Hill, Index, Cass county, Missouri, 27 Dec., 1859.

27 EMMA BIRD BEDINGER, born at Rose Hill, Index, Cass county, Missouri, 23 Feb., 1862.

27 SUSAN AUGUSTA BEDINGER, born at Rose Hill, Index, Cass county, Missouri, 14 June, 1867.

27 HENRY CLAY BEDINGER, born at Rose Hill, Index, Cass county, Missouri, 18 Sept., 1869.

27 SOLOMON SINGLETON BEDINGER, born at Rose Hill, Index, Cass county, Missouri, 3 Oct., 1871.

26 HENRIETTA GRAY WASHINGTON, thirteenth child of John Thornton Augustine Washington, was born at Cedar Lawn, Jefferson county, West Virginia, 30 Sept., 1835. Died 18 Dec., 1838.

26 LUCY ELIZABETH WASHINGTON, first child of Dr. Samuel Walter Washington, second of George Steptoe Washington, fourth of Col. Samuel, sixth of Augustine, second of Lawrence, first of Col. John, of Warton, England, and Bridge's Creek, Virginia, was born at Harewood, Jefferson county, Virginia, about 1823. Now (1876) resides at Locust Hill, near Charlestown, Jefferson county, West Virginia. Married at Baltimore, Maryland, 4 Mar., 1840, by Rev. Dr. Henshaw, to John Bainbridge Packett, of Charlestown, West Virginia, son of Lieutenant John (and Fanny Hammond) Packett, of United States Navy, and of Charlestown, West Virginia. Her husband died at Locust Hill, West Virginia, 18 Nov., 1872. Children :

27 LOUISE CLEMSON PACKETT, born at Locust Hill, West Virginia, 4 Mar., 1848.

27 FANNIE HAMMOND PACKETT, born at Locust Hill, West Virginia, 6 May, 1850.

27 ELIZABETH BARTON PACKETT, born at Locust Hill, West Virginia, 2 Sept., 1852.

27 WILLIAM BAINBRIDGE PACKETT, born at Locust Hill, West Virginia, 14 Feb., 1854.

27 GEORGE WASHINGTON PACKETT, born at Locust Hill, West Virginia, 13 Aug., 1855.

27 CHRISTINE WASHINGTON PACKETT, born at Locust Hill, West Virginia, Feb., 1858. Died infant.

27 LUCY MADISON PACKETT, born at Locust Hill, West Virginia, 22 Feb., 1860.

27 WALTER HAREWOOD PACKETT, born at Locust Hill, West Virginia, 2 Nov., 1863.

26 GEORGE LA FAYETTE WASHINGTON, second child of Dr. Samuel Walter Washington, was born at Harewood, Jefferson county, Virginia, 12 Jan., 1825. Removed to Claymont, Delaware, 1865. Died at Lehigh Valley, Pennsylvania, 7 Feb., 1872. Married at Claymont, Delaware, 29 Apr., 1859, to Anna Bull Clemson, daughter of Rev. John B. Clemson, of Claymont. Widow, now (1876) at Claymont, Delaware. Children :

27 MARGARETTA WASHINGTON, born at Harewood, Virginia, 11 June, 1860.

27 LOUISA CLEMSON WASHINGTON, born at Harewood, Virginia, 29 Apr., 1862. Died June, 1865.

27 JOHN CLEMSON WASHINGTON, born at Harewood, Virginia, 5 Jan., 1865.

27 MARTHA WASHINGTON, born at Claymont, Delaware, 29 Aug., 1867.

27 ANNIE HAREWOOD WASHINGTON, born at Claymont, Delaware, 26 Nov., 1869.

27 ELIZABETH FISHER WASHINGTON, born at Lehigh Valley, 20 Dec., 1871.

26 CHRISTINE MARIA WASHINGTON, third child of Dr. Samuel Walter Washington, was born at Harewood, Jefferson county, West Virginia, 16 Dec., 1826. Now (1876) there. Married at Philadelphia, by Rev. John B. Clemson, 20 Nov., 1844, to Richard Blackburn Washington,

son of John Augustine (and Jane Blackburn) Washington, of ———. Children :

27 ELIZABETH CLEMSON WASHINGTON, born at Harewood, Virginia, 21 Aug., 1845.

27 JOHN AUGUSTINE WASHINGTON, born at Harewood,
Virginia, 27 May, 1847.

27 ANNA M. T. BLACKBURN WASHINGTON, born at
Harewood, Virginia, 1 Nov., 1849.

27 LOUISA CLEMSON WASHINGTON, born at Harewood,
Virginia, 17 Nov., 1851.

27 SAMUEL WALTER WASHINGTON, born at Harewood, Virginia, 1 Nov., 1853.

27 RICHARD BLACKBURN WASHINGTON, born at Harewood, Virginia, 21 Mar., 1856.

27 CHRISTINE MARIA WASHINGTON, born at Harewood,
Virginia, 13 June, 1858.

27 GEORGE STEPTOE WASHINGTON, born at Harewood,
Virginia, 7 June, 1860.

27 WILLIAM DE HERTBURN WASHINGTON, born at Harewood, Virginia, 14 Feb., 1864.

26 ANNIE STEPTOE CLEMSON WASHINGTON, fourth child of
Dr. Samuel Walter Washington, was born at Harewood,
West Virginia, 8 Sept., 1831. Removed to Missouri in
1858, and returned in 1865, to Charlestown, West Virginia, where she now (1876) resides. Married in St.
Mark's Church, at Philadelphia, by Rev. John B. Clemson, 17 Oct., 1854, to Thomas Augustus Brown, of
Charlestown, West Virginia, son of William (and Elizabeth Forrest) Brown. Children :

27 FORREST WASHINGTON BROWN, born at Harewood,
West Virginia, 15 Oct., 1855.

27 MARY HARRISON BROWN, born in Randolph county,
Missouri, 11 Feb., 1859.

27 LOUISA CLEMSON BROWN, born in Randolph county,
Missouri, 8 July, 1861.

27 ANNIE AUGUSTA BROWN, born in Missouri, 10 Aug.,
1863.   Died 14 Nov., 1863.

27 ANNA FLORIDE BROWN, born at Sulgrave, near
Charlestown, West Virginia, in Aug., 1872.

26 MISS R—— B—— WASHINGTON, fifth child of Dr. Samuel Walter Washington, was born at Harewood, Jefferson
county, West Virginia, about 1835.   Now (1877) at
Charlestown, Jefferson county, West Virginia.

26 LUCY WASHINGTON, first child of William Temple Washington, third of George Steptoe, fourth of Col. Samuel,
sixth of Augustine, second of Laurence, first of Col.
John, of Warton, England, and Bridge's Creek, Virginia,
was born at Lexington, Kentucky, 8 Oct., 1822.   Died 12
Oct., 1822.

26 MILLISSENT WASHINGTON, second child of William Temple Washington, was born in Bath county, Virginia, 4
Aug., 1824.   Removed to Frederick City, Maryland, in
1853.   Now (1877) there.   Married at Megwille, Jefferson
county, Virginia, 10 Dec., 1840, by Rev. Alexander Jones,
to Robert Grier, son of Robert G. (and Maria) McPherson.   Children :
  27 MARIA MCPHERSON, born in Jefferson county, Virginia, 11 Feb., 1842.   Married to Dr. Robert F.
  Wier, 37 West Thirty-third street, New York.   One
  daughter :
    28 ALICE WASHINGTON WIER.
  27 ROBERT GRIER MCPHERSON, born in Jefferson
  county, Virginia, 6 Feb., 1844.   Died 4 Sept., 1847.
  27 WILLIAM WASHINGTON MCPHERSON, born in Jefferson county, Virginia, 10 June, 1846.   Resides (1877)
  at Stillwater, Minnesota.
  27 CATHARINE DAVIS MCPHERSON, born in Jefferson
  county, Virginia, 17 Oct., 1850.
  27 MILLISSENT WASHINGTON MCPHERSON, born in Jef-

ferson county, Virginia, 17 Oct., 1850. Died 5 Sept., 1852.

27 FRANK McPHERSON, born in Jefferson county, Virginia, 5 Nov., 1852. Died 9 Sept., 1853.

27 MARGARET WASHINGTON McPHERSON, born at Frederick City, Maryland, 26 Sept., 1855.

27 ROBERT GRIER McPHERSON, born at Frederick City, Maryland, 16 Feb., 1858.

26 WILLIAM TEMPLE WASHINGTON, third child of William Temple Washington, was born at Lexington, Kentucky, 7 Jan., 1827. Removed to Indiana, in 1851. Now (1877) in Missouri. Married in 1846, in Kentucky, Lydia, daughter of —— Herndon, of ———. No children. Wife died in Indiana, in 1850.

26 THOMAS WASHINGTON, fourth child of William Temple Washington, was born at Megwille, Virginia, 17. Mar., 1829. Died in or on the way to Missouri, 12 Apr., 1849.

26 JANE CHARLOTTE WASHINGTON, fifth child of William Temple Washington, was born at Megwille, Virginia, 29 June, 1834. Removed April, 1855, to Falmouth, Stafford county, Virginia. Now (1876) there. Married at Falmouth, Virginia, 1 Mar., 1866, by Rev. Magruder Maury, to Thomas G. Moncure, son of Hon. R. C. L. Moncure, Chief Justice of Virginia, Stafford county. Children :

27 TEMPLE WASHINGTON MONCURE, born in Stafford county, Virginia, 14 Dec., 1868.

27 R. C. L. MONCURE, born in Stafford county, Virginia, 16 Dec., 1869. Died 5 July, 1870.

27 EUGENIA WASHINGTON MONCURE, born in Stafford county, Virginia, 22 May, 1872.

27 HULL MONCURE, born in Stafford county, Virginia, 11 Dec., 1873.

26 EUGENIE WASHINGTON, sixth child of William Temple

Washington, was born at Megwille, Virginia, 24 June, 1840. Removed to Falmouth, Virginia, A. D. 1856, to Washington, D. C., A. D. 1866. Now (1877) there.

26 FERDINAND STEPTOE WASHINGTON, seventh child of William Temple Washington, was born at Megwille, Virginia, 22 Jan., 1843. Removed to Falmouth, Virginia, A. D. 1856. To Arkansas, 1869. Now (1877) in Arkansas.

26 LAURENCE AUGUSTINE WASHINGTON, first child of Dr. Laurence Augustine Washington, third of Laurence Augustine, fifth of Col. Samuel, seventh of Augustine, second of Laurence, first of Col. John, of Warton, England, and Bridge's Creek, Virginia, was born in Kanawha county, West Virginia, 21 Mar., 1846. Removed to Colorado county, Texas, and died there, 20 Aug., 1852.

26 WALTER GOOD WASHINGTON, second child of Dr. Laurence Augustine Washington, was born in Mason county, West Virginia, 21 Feb., 1843. Removed in 1874 to Denison, Texas. Now (1877) there. Unmarried.

26 JOHN SHREWSBURY WASHINGTON, third child of Dr. Laurence Augustine Washington, was born in Mason county, West Virginia, 27 Apr., 1845. Removed, 1874, to Denison, Texas. Now (1877) there. Unmarried.

26 JAMES TURNER WASHINGTON, fourth child of Dr. Laurence Augustine Washington, was born in Mason county, West Virginia, 3 Mar., 1847. Removed in 1875 to Comanche county, Texas. Now (1877) there. Married at Brownwood, Brown county, Texas, in 1875, to Josephine Burras. One child:

27 MARTHA WASHINGTON, born in Comanche county Texas, Nov., 1876.

26 EMMA TELL WASHINGTON, fifth child of Dr. Laurence Augustine Washington, was born in Mason county, West

Virginia, 27 Sept., 1849. Removed to Eagle Lake, Colorado county, Texas ; to Junction City, Kansas, in Sept., 1868 ; to Denison, Texas, in Apr.. 1873. Now (1877) there. Married 14 Sept., 1865, at Eagle Lake, Texas, by Rev. Mr. Foote, to George Lee Patrick, son of George Washington (and Margaret) Patrick, of Visalia, California. Children :

    27 GEORGE WASHINGTON PATRICK, born at Eagle Lake, Texas, 16 Aug., 1866.

    27 LAURENCE AUGUSTINE PATRICK, born at Eagle Lake, Texas, 4 Oct., 1868. Died at Junction City, Kansas, 4 Feb., 1869.

    27 MARGARET PATRICK, born at Junction City, Kansas, 10 Feb., 1870. Died 13 July, 1870.

    27 MARTHA WOOD PATRICK, born at Junction City, Kansas, 1 Oct., 1871.

    27 ISABELLA LUCY PATRICK, born at Denison, Texas, 12 Feb., 1874.

    17 CHARLES FOX PATRICK, born at Denison, Texas, 30 May, 1876.

26 JULIA WOOD WASHINGTON, sixth child of Dr. Laurence Augustine Washington, was born at Columbus, Colorado county, Texas, 29 May, 1850. Removed in June, 1873, to St. Louis, Missouri, thence to Galveston, Texas. Now (1877) there. Married at Columbus, Texas, by Rev. Mr. Trader, 19 June, 1873, to Sidney Thurston, son of Henry Whiting (and Susan Elizabeth) Fontaine, of Houston, Texas. Children :

    27 ANNIE WASHINGTON FONTAINE, born at St. Louis, Missouri, 23 Mar., 1874. Died at Denison, Texas, 3 June, 1875.

    27 SHIRLEY WASHINGTON FONTAINE, born at Denison, Texas, 1 Jan., 1876.

26 CECIL WOOD WASHINGTON, seventh child of Dr. Laurence Augustine Washington, was born in Colorado county, Texas, 1 Jan., 1858. Removed to Denison, Texas, in 1874. Now (1877) there. Unmarried.

26 MARTHA DICKINSON SHREWSBURY, first child of Laura Shrewsbury, fourth of Harriet Parks, sixth of Col. Samuel Washington, seventh of Augustine, second of Laurence, first of Col. John, of Warton, England, and Bridge's Creek, Virginia, was born at Shrewsbury, Virginia, 3 Feb., 1828. Died at Charlestown, West Virginia, 24 Mar., 1875. Married at Shrewsbury, 4 Feb., 1847, by Rev. Mr. Ward, to Major Nicholas Fitzhugh, of Charlestown, West Virginia, son of Henry (and Henrietta) Fitzhugh, of Ravenswood, Jackson county, North Virginia. Children :

　　27 LAURA FITZHUGH, born at Charlestown, West Virginia, 27 Nov., 1848. Married A. A. Preston, of Richmond, Virginia.
　　27 HENRY FITZHUGH, born at Charlestown, West Virginia, 28 Dec., 1853.
　　27 MATTIE FITZHUGH, born at Charlestown, West Virginia, 27 July, 1856.
　　27 NICHOLAS FITSHUGH, born at Charlestown, West Virginia, 30 Jan., 1858.
　　27 LAURENCE SHREWSBURY FITZHUGH, born at Charlestown, West Virginia, 15 Sept., 1860.

26 LAURENCE WASHINGTON SHREWSBURY, second child of Laura Shrewsbury, was born at Shrewsbury, Virginia, 11 Oct., 1831. Removed in 1850 to Klamath county, California.

26 ALBERT SHREWSBURY, third child of Laura Shrewsbury, was born at Shrewsbury, Virginia, about 1833. Died infant.

26 Andrew Parks Shrewsbury, fourth child of Laura Shrewsbury, was born at Shrewsbury, Virginia, 6 July, 1846. Removed 1864, to ———, Nevada.

26 Harriet Washington Shrewsbury, fifth child of Laura Shrewsbury, was born at Shrewsbury, Virginia, 15 May, 1840. Died 1 Jan., 1876. She removed in 1864, to Charlestown, West Virginia, where she died.

26 Cornelia Shrewsbury, sixth child of Laura Shrewsbury, was born at Shrewsbury, Virginia, 4 Apr., 1842. Removed in 1864, to Charlestown, West Virginia, and thence to San Francisco, California, in 1872. Now (1877) there. Married at Charlestown, West Virginia, 9 Oct., 1872, by Rev. Mr. Callaway, to Enoch South Gany, of Pittsburgh, Pennsylvania, and San Francisco. Children :

27 Herbert Gany, born at San Francisco, California, 14 Aug., 1872.
27 Laura Mattie Gany. Died infant.

26 Laura Shrewsbury, seventh child of Laura Shrewsbury, was born at Shrewsbury, Virginia, 16 Apr., 1844. Removed in 1864, to Charlestown, West Virginia. Now (1877) there.

26 Samuel Shrewsbury, eighth child of Laura Shrewsbury, was born at Shrewsbury, Virginia, 27 Nov., 1847. Removed 1864, to Charlestown, West Virginia ; thence to Independence, Missouri. Now (1877) there.

26 Henry Shrewsbury, ninth child of Laura Shrewsbury, was born at Shrewsbury, Virginia, 12 Oct., 1853. Removed 1864, to Charlestown, West Virginia. Now (1877) there.

26 Creed Parks, first child of Major Andrew Parks, fifth

of Mrs. Harriet Parks, sixth of Col. Samuel Washington, third of Augustine, by second wife, second of Laurence, first of Col. John, of Warton, England, and Bridge's Creek, Virginia, was born at Charlestown, West Virginia, A. D. 1842. Died at ———, 27 July, 1864.

26 BUSHROD PARKS, second child of Major Andrew Parks, was born at Charlestown, West Virginia, A. D. 1845. Removed about ———. Now (1877) at Neosho, Newton county, Missouri. Married at ———.

26 HARRIOT PARKS, third child of Major Andrew Parks, was born at Charlestown, West Virginia, 27 Oct., 1848. Removed to Lancaster, Ohio. Thence to Columbus, Ohio. Now (1877) there. Married at Lancaster, Ohio, 27 June, 1867, to Theodore W. Tallmadge, Attorney-at-Law, of Columbus, Ohio. Children :
> 27 FLORA TALLMADGE, born at Columbus, Ohio, 1 Oct., 1868.
> 27 ANDREW TALLMADGE, born at Columbus, Ohio, 16 Jan., 1870.

26 ANDREW PARKS, fourth child of Major Andrew Parks, was born at Charlestown, West Virginia, 27 Oct., 1852. Now (1877) there.

26 GEORGE WASHINGTON, first of John Augustine, second of Corbin, fourth of John Augustine, seventh of Augustine, second of Laurence, first of Col. John, of Warton, England, and Bridge's Creek, Virginia, was born at Blakeley, West Virginia, about 1815. Died young.

26 ANNE MARIA WASHINGTON, second child of John Augustine, was born at Blakeley, West Virginia, 5 Nov., 1817. Removed in May, 1834, from Mount Vernon to Howard, near Alexandria, and to Vine Hill, A. D. 1835, thence to Walnut Farm, Virginia, about 1840. Died at

Blakeley, 29 Mar., 1850.   Married at Mount Vernon, by
Rev. Dr. E. R. Leppett, 15 May, 1834, to Dr. William
Fontaine Alexander, son of Charles (and Mary Bowles
Armisted) Alexander, of Mount Ida, near Alexandria,
Virginia.   He died at Walnut Farm, West Virginia, in
Jan., 1862.   Children :

27 JEAN CHARLOTTE ALEXANDER; born at Alexandria,
28 Jan., 1835.   Married Dr. J. A. Straith.   Lives at
Staunton, Virginia.

27 WILSON CARY SELDEN ALEXANDER, born at Vine
Hill, 8 Feb., 1836.   Died 1859.

27 LOUISA FONTAINE ALEXANDER, born at Blakeley,
13 Nov., 1837.   Died April 24, 1839.

27 JOHN AUGUSTINE ALEXANDER, born at Blakeley, 24
Oct., 1839.   Died Aug. 11, 1854.

27 MARY FONTAINE ALEXANDER, born at Walnut
Farm, 12 Mar., 1845.   Married —— Ransom.   Now
(1877) at Staunton, Virginia.

27 CHARLES ARMISTED ALEXANDER, born at Walnut
Farm, 12 May, 1843.   Died in March, 1864.

27 ANN BURNETT ALEXANDER, born at Walnut Farm,
9 July, 1848.   Died in July, 1864.

26 JOHN AUGUSTINE WASHINGTON, third child of John
Augustine, was born at Blakeley, 3 May, 1820.   He was
killed at Cheat Mountain, West Virginia, 13 Sept., 1861.
He was married at Exeter, Loudon county, Virginia, in
Feb., 1842, to Eleanor Love, daughter of Wilson Cary
Selden, of Exeter, Loudon county, Virginia.   Chil-
dren :

27 LOUISA FONTAINE WASHINGTON, born at Mount
Vernon, Virginia, 19 Feb., 1844.

27 JANE CHARLOTTE WASHINGTON, born at Mount
Vernon, Virginia, 26 May, 1846.

27 ELIZA SELDEN WASHINGTON, born at Mount Vernon, Virginia, 17 July, 1848.

27 ANNE MARIA WASHINGTON, born at Mount Vernon, Virginia, 17 Nov., 1851.

27 LAWRENCE WASHINGTON, born at Mount Vernon, Virginia, 14 Jan., 1854. *died Feby 9·1920- Wash D.C.*

27 ELEANOR LOVE WASHINGTON, born at Mount Vernon, Virginia, 14 Mar., 1856.

27 GEORGE WASHINGTON, born at Mount Vernon, Virginia, 22 July, 1858.

26 RICHARD BLACKBURN WASHINGTON, fourth child of John Augustine, was born at Blakeley, West Virginia, 12 Nov., 1822. Removed about ——, to Harewood, Jefferson county, West Virginia. Now (1877) there. . Married at Philadelphia, by Rev. John B. Clemson, 20 Nov., 1844, to Christine Maria, daughter of Dr. Samuel Walter Washington, of Harewood, Virginia. Children :

27 ELIZABETH CLEMSON WASHINGTON, born at Harewood, Virginia, 21 Aug., 1845.

27 JOHN AUGUSTINE WASHINGTON, born at Harewood, Virginia, 27 May, 1847.

27 ANNA M. F. BLACKBURN WASHINGTON, born at Harewood, Virginia, 1 Nov., 1849.

27 LOUISA CLEMSON WASHINGTON, born at Harewood, Virginia, 17 Nov., 1851.

27 SAMUEL WALTER WASHINGTON, born at Harewood, Virginia, 1 Nov., 1853.

27 RICHARD BLACKBURN WASHINGTON, born at Harewood, Virginia, 21 Mar., 1856.

27 CHRISTINE MARIA WASHINGTON, born at Harewood, Virginia, 13 June, 1858.

27 GEORGE STEPTOE WASHINGTON, born at Harewood, Virginia, 7 June, 1860.

27 WILLIAM DE HERTBURN WASHINGTON, born at Harewood, Virginia, 14 Feb., 1864.

26 SPOTSWOOD AUGUSTINE WASHINGTON, first child of

Bushrod, fourth of William Augustine, first of Augustine, second of Laurence, first of Colonel John, of Warton, England, and Bridge's Creek, Virginia ; was born at Mount Zephyr, Virginia, about 1810. Removed to Illinois. Has children.

26 ANN WASHINGTON, second child of Bushrod, was born at Mount Zephyr, Virginia, about 1812. Died at ———. Married at ———, about ——, to Rev. W. P. C. Johnson. "Several children. One married Dr. Magruder, of Montgomery county, Maryland."

26 JANE MILDRED WASHINGTON, third child of Bushrod, was born at Mount Zephyr, Virginia, about 1814. Died unmarried.

26 GEORGE WASHINGTON, fourth child of Bushrod, was born at Mount Zephyr, Virginia, about 1816. Married, and died without issue.

26 JOHN WASHINGTON, fifth child of Bushrod, was born at Mount Zephyr, Virginia, about 1818. Died unmarried.

26 MARY WASHINGTON, sixth child of Bushrod, was born at Mount Zephyr, Virginia, about 1820.

26 CORBIN WASHINGTON, seventh child of Bushrod, was born at Mount Zephyr, Virginia, about 1822.

26 FRANCES (or FANNY) WASHINGTON, eighth child of Bushrod, was born at Mount Zephyr, Virginia, about 1825. Married Finch. Now (1877) a widow, living at Morrisania, Westchester county, New York.

26 CHURCHILL THORNTON, first child of Ann Maria Washington, second of Col. George Augustine, first of Col. Charles, fifth of Augustine, by second wife, second of

17

Laurence, first of Col. John, of Warton, England, and Bridge's Creek, Virginia, was born at ———, about 1812.

26 CHARLES THORNTON, second child of Ann Maria Washington, was born at ———, about 1815.

26 CHARLES AUGUSTINE WASHINGTON, first child of George Fayette, third of Col. George Augustine, first of Col. Charles, fifth of Augustine, by second wife, second of Laurence, first of Col. John, of Warton, England, and Bridge's Creek, Virginia, was born at Charlestown, West Virginia, 9 Aug., 1814. Lived at Wellington, below Alexandria. Sold his place and returned to Waverly. He died at Georgetown, West Virginia, in 1861. Not married.

26 FRANCIS MASSEY WASHINGTON, third child of George Fayette (second child died young), was born at Charlestown, West Virginia, 21 Jan., 1816.

26 GEORGE FAYETTE WASHINGTON, fourth child of George Fayette, was born at Charlestown, West Virginia, 21 Feb., 1823. Resided for some time at Greenwood, Virginia, and died at Waverly, Virginia, about 1853. Not married.

26 MATHEW BARWELL BASSETT WASHINGTON, fifth child of George Fayette, was born at Charlestown, West Virginia, 15 Aug., 1830. Removed to Winchester in Nov., 1863; to Waverly, in May, 1865. Died there, 1 Aug., 1868. Married at the University of Virginia, 20 Mar., 1862, by Rev. William Hoge, to Nannie Bird Dandridge, daughter of Thomas Ely (and Ann Spottswood Dandridge) Buckannan, of Waverly. She now (1877) resides, a widow, at Waverly, near Stephenson's Depot, Frederick county, Virginia. One child :

27 NANNIE BIRD WASHINGTON, born at Winchester, Virginia, 17 Mar., 1864.

26 HANNAH LEE WASHINGTON, first child of Bushrod Corbin Washington, third of Corbin, fourth of John Augustine, seventh of Augustine, second of Laurence, first of Col. John, of Warton, England, and Bridge's Creek, Virginia, was born at Rippon Lodge, Prince William county, Virginia, 19 May, 1811. Removed 9 Feb., 1869, to Duffield, Virginia. Now (1877) there. Married at ———, about 1830, William P. Alexander, of ———. Husband died at .Alexandria, Virginia, A. D. 1862. . Children :

   27 DR. WILLIAM F. ALEXANDER, of Duffield Depot, Jefferson county, Virginia, born about 1832.

   •27 JENNIE ALEXANDER, of Duffield Depot, Jefferson county, Virginia, born about 1835.

   27 RICHARD A. ALEXANDER, of Charlestown, Jefferson county, West Virginia, born about 1837.

   27 THOMAS ALEXANDER, of Charlestown, Jefferson county, West Virginia, born about 1840. Dead.

   27 HERBERT ALEXANDER, of Charlestown, Jefferson county, West Virginia, born about 1845. Dead.

26 THOMAS BLACKBURN WASHINGTON, second child of Bushrod Corbin Washington, was born at Rippon Lodge, Prince William county, Virginia, about 1813. He died in Aug., 1854, leaving five children. Married Rebecca, daughter of William Cunningham, of Richlands, Frederick county, Maryland. Five children :

   27 BUSHROD CORBIN WASHINGTON, born about 1842.

   27 THOMAS BLACKBURN WASHINGTON, born about 1845.

   27 ANNA WASHINGTON, born about 1850.

   27

   27   .

His widow married Rev. Mr. Lyle, and is living in China.

27 EDWIN CURRAN SMITH, first child of Georgiana Augusta Washington, sixth of John Thornton Augustine, first of Thornton Washington, first of Colonel Samuel, by second wife, second of Augustine, by second wife, second of Laurence, first of Colonel John, of Warton, England, &c.; was born at West Poultney, Vermont, 3 Feb., 1853. Removed to Little Rock, Arkansas. Now (1877) at Deadwood, Dakotah Territory. Married at ———, 3 Jan., 1875, to Elizabeth Turrell, of ———. One child :

    28 EDWIN CURRAN SMITH, born at ———, 23 Oct., 1875.

27 VIRGINIA EMELINE SMITH, second child of Georgiana Augusta Washington, was born at East Poultney, Vermont, 25 Dec., 1815. Removed to Little Rock, Arkansas. Now (1877) there.

27 MARY WASHINGTON SMITH, third child of Georgiana Augusta Washington, was born at Washington, D. C., 25 Nov., 1857. Removed to Little Rock, Arkansas. Now (1877) there.

27 ELIZA MANSFIELD SMITH, fourth child of Georgiana Augusta Washington, was born at Rose Hill, Missouri, 1 Feb., 1859. Removed to Little Rock, Arkansas. Now (1877) there.

27 WHEELER EATON SMITH, fifth child of Georgiana Augusta Washington, was born at Rose Hill, Missouri, 23 Oct., 1862. Removed to Little Rock, Arkansas. Now (1877) there.

27 GEORGE CORBIN WASHINGTON, first child of Lewis William, first of George Corbin Washington, sixth of William Augustine, third of Augustine, second of Augustine, second of Laurence, first of Colonel John, of Warton, England, &c.; was born at Baltimore, Maryland, Mar., 1837. Died there, 30 Sept., 1843.

27 JAMES BARROLL WASHINGTON, second child of Lewis William, was born at Baltimore, Maryland, 26 Aug., 1839. Removed in 1873 to Pittsburgh, Virginia. Now (1876) there. Secretary and Auditor of Baltimore & Ohio Railroad Company. Married at Montgomery, Alabama, by Rev. J. M. Mitchell, to Mrs. Jane Britney Lanier Cabell, daughter of William L. (and Virginia Armisted) Lanier, of Selma, Alabama. His children were :

28 WILLIAM LANIER WASHINGTON, born at Montgomery, Alabama, 30 Mar., 1865.

28 BENJAMIN CABELL WASHINGTON, born near Baltimore, Maryland, 16 Nov., 1866.

28 LEWIS WILLIAM WASHINGTON, born at Baltimore, Maryland, 20 Nov., 1869.

28 MARY WASHINGTON, born at Baltimore, 4 Oct., 1871. Died 22 Aug., 1872.

27 MARY ANN WASHINGTON, third child of Lewis William, was born at Baltimore, Maryland, 1 June, 1841. Now (1876) there. Married in Grace Church, at Baltimore, Maryland, 17 Nov., 1864, by R. A. A. Curtis, to Henry Irvine Keyser, son of Samuel Keyser, of Baltimore, Maryland. Children :

28 HENRY BARROLL KEYSER, born at Baltimore, Maryland, 9 Sept., 1865.

28 SAMUEL IRVINE KEYSER, born at Baltimore, Maryland, 30 June, 1869. Died 4 Mar., 1874.

28 LEWIS WASHINGTON KEYSER, born at Baltimore, Maryland, 21 Nov., 1870. Died 5 June, 1871.

28 IRVINE KEYSER, born at Baltimore, Maryland, 30 Apr., 1872.

28 MARY WASHINGTON KEYSER, born at Baltimore, Maryland, 20 Nov., 1874.

27 ELIZA RIDGELEY WASHINGTON, fourth child of Lewis William Washington, was born at ———, Jefferson

.county, West Virginia, 16 Nov., 1844. Removed to Baltimore, in 1844. Now (1876) there. Married there, 25 Apr., 1865, by Rev. Dr. M. Mahan, to Elias Glenn Perine, son of David M. (and Mary) Perine, of Baltimore, Maryland. Children :

28 MARY PERINE, born at Baltimore, Maryland, 30 May, 1866.

28 WILLIAM B. PERINE, born at Baltimore, Maryland, 28 Nov., 1867.

28 DAVID M. PERINE, born at Baltimore, Maryland, 13 Feb., 1869.

28 WASHINGTON PERINE, born at Baltimore, Maryland, 14 Oct., 1870.

28 GLENN PERINE, born at Baltimore, Maryland, 5 Sept., 1871.

28 EVELYN PERINE, born at Baltimore, Maryland, 10 Mar., 1873.

28 GEORGE CORBIN PERINE, born at Baltimore, Maryland, 3 June, 1874.

28 MILDRED WASHINGTON PERINE, born at Baltimore, Maryland, 30 Sept., 1875.

27 BETTY LEWIS WASHINGTON, fifth child of Lewis William Washington, was born at Baltimore, Maryland, 26 Aug., 1861. Died 25 July, 1862.

27 WILLIAM DE HERTBURN WASHINGTON, sixth child of Lewis William Washington, was born at Baltimore, Maryland, 29 June, 1863.

27 ELLEN LEWIS KING, first child of Mrs. Betty Washington King, fifth of Mrs. Ella Jael Steele, fourth of Howell Lewis, fourth of Mrs. Betty Washington Lewis, sixth of Augustine Washington, second of Laurence, first of Col. John, of Warton, England, and Bridge's Creek, Virginia, was born at Akron, Ohio, 13 June, 1850. Now

(1877) there.   Married at Akron, 19 Jan., 1870, to David
Raymond Paige, son of Judge David R. (and Nancy)
Paige, of Painesville, Ohio.   Children :
> 28 CHARLES CUTLER PAIGE, born at Akron, Ohio, 25
> Nov., 1870.
> 28 DAVID KING PAIGE, born at Akron, Ohio, 20 May,
> 1872.

27 BETTY STEELE KING, second child of Mrs. Betty Washington King, was born at Cleveland, Ohio, 22 Dec., 1851.
Removed to Akron, Ohio.   Now (1877) there.   Married
at Cleveland, Ohio, 10 Dec., 1873, to John Gilbert Raymond, of Akron, Ohio.

27 HOWELL KING, third child of Mrs. Betty Washington
King, was born at Cleveland, Ohio, 3 May, 1853.

27 SUSAN HUNTINGTON KING, fourth child of Mrs. Betty
Washington, was born at Cleveland, Ohio, 16 Jan., 1855.

27 MARTHA PERKINS KING, fifth child of Mrs. Betty Washington King, was born at Cleveland, Ohio, 6 Apr., 1863.

27 JOHN THORNTON WASHINGTON, first child of Benjamin
Franklin Washington, fifth of John Thornton Augustine
Washington, first of Thornton, first of Colonel Samuel,
by second wife, third of Augustine, by second wife, second of Laurence, first of Colonel John, of Warton, England, &c.; was born at Charlestown, West Virginia, 26
July, 1846.   Removed to Sacramento, 1852, to San Francisco, California, A. D., 1854.   Now (1877) there.   Not
married.

27 FRANK B. WASHINGTON, second child of Benjamin
Franklin Washington, was born at Charlestown, West
Virginia, 20 June, 1848.   Removed to San Francisco,
California, in Sept., 1852.   Now (1877) there, unmarried.

27 Fanny Madeline Washington, third child of Benjamin Franklin Washington, was born at San Francisco, California, Aug., 1853. Now (1877) there. Married at San Francisco, California, in Apr., 1875, to D. Delhanty.

27 Lilian Washington, fourth child of Benjamin Franklin Washington, was born at San Francisco, California, A. D. 1855. Died 1856.

27 Bertha James Washington, fifth child of Benjamin Franklin Washington, was born at San Francisco, California, in March, 1858. Now (1877) there.

27 Jane Charlotte Alexander, first child of Anne Maria Washington, second of John Augustine, second of Corbin, fourth of John Augustine, seventh of Augustine, second of Laurence, first of Colonel John, of Warton, England, &c.; was born at Alexandria, Virginia, in Feb., 1834. Married Dr. J. A. Straith. Lives (1877) at Staunton, Virginia.

27 Wilson Cary S. Alexander, second child of Anne Maria Washington, was born at Alexandria, Virginia, about 1836. Died before marriage.

27 Louisa Fontaine Alexander, third child of Anne Maria Washington, was born at Alexandria, Virginia, about 1838. Died.

27 John Augustine Alexander, fourth child of Anne Maria Washington, was born at Alexandria, Virginia, about 1840. Died.

27 Mary Fontaine Alexander, fifth child of Anne Maria Washington, was born in Jefferson county, Virginia, 12 Mar., 1845. Removed in April, 1871, to Staunton, Augusta county, Virginia. Now (1877) there. Married at

Charlestown, Jefferson county, Virginia, by Rev. Wm. H. Meade, of Zion Episcopal Church, 12 April, 1871, to Thos. Davis Ransom, son of James M. (and Eleanor Baldwin) Ransom, of Charlestown, West Virginia.

    28 CHARLOTTE ALEXANDRA RANSOM, born at Staunton, Virginia, 12 Apr., 1872.

    28 JOHN BALDWIN RANSOM, born at Staunton, Virginia, 4 Jan., 1874.

    28 MARIA WASHINGTON RANSOM, born at Staunton, Virginia, 29 Sept., 1875.

27 CHARLES ARMISTED ALEXANDER, sixth child of Anne Maria Washington, was born at Alexandria, Virginia, about 1847. Died young.

27 ANN BURNETT ALEXANDER, seventh child of Anne Maria Washington, was born at Alexandria, Virginia, about 1849. Died young.

27 LOUISA FONTAINE WASHINGTON, first child of John Augustine Washington, third of John Augustine, second of Corbin, fourth of John Augustine, seventh of Augustine, second of Laurence, first of Col. John, of Warton, England, and Bridge's Creek, Virginia, was born at Mount Vernon, Virginia, 19 Feb., 1844. Removed about ——, to Blakeley, West Virginia. Now (1876) there. Married at ———, about ——, to Col. R. P. Chew, son of —— Chew, of ———.

27 JANE CHARLOTTE WASHINGTON, second child of John Augustine Washington, was born at Mount Vernon, Virginia, 26 May, 1846. Removed about ——, to Rock Hall, Jefferson county, West Virginia. Now (1876) there. Married at ———, about ——, to Nathaniel H. Willis, son of —— Willis, of ———.

27 ELIZA SELDEN WASHINGTON, third child of John Augustine Washington, was born at Blakeley, Jefferson county, West Virginia, 17 July, 1848. Removed in 1860, to Waveland, Fauquier county, Virginia, and in 1861, to Jefferson county, West Virginia; thence to. Warsaw, Virginia. Now (1877) there. Not married.

27 ANN MARIA WASHINGTON, fourth child of John Augustine Washington, was born at Mount Vernon, Virginia, 17 Nov., 1851. Removed 1860, to Fauquier county; to Jefferson county, in 1861, and in 1873, to Warsaw, Richmond county, Virginia. Now (1876) there. Married by Rev. Mr. Leavell, at Charlestown, West Virginia, 22 July, 1873, to Rev. Beverly Dandridge Tucker, son of Beverly (and Jane Ellis) Tucker, of Richmond, Virginia. Children :

    28 HENRY ST. GEORGE TUCKER, born at Warsaw, Virginia, 16 July, 1874.

    28 EMILY SELDEN TUCKER, born at Warsaw, Virginia, 1 Nov., 1875.

27 LAURENCE WASHINGTON, fifth child of John Augustine Washington, was born at Mount Vernon, Virginia, 14 Jan., 1854. Removed about ——, to Waveland, near Salem, Fauquier county, Virginia. Now (1876) there. Married at Charlestown, West Virginia, 14 June, 1876, to Fanny, daughter of Thomas Lackland, of Charlestown, West Virginia. *died Feb 9. 1920 · Washington D.C.*
left 12 children

27 ELEANOR LOVE WASHINGTON, sixth child of John Augustine Washington, was born at Mount Vernon, Virginia, 14 Mar., 1856. Removed 1860, to Fauquier county, Virginia; to Jefferson county, West Virginia, in 1861. Now (1877) resides in Jefferson county, West Virginia. Not married.

27 GEORGE WASHINGTON, seventh child of John Augustine Washington, was born at Mount Vernon, Virginia, 22 July, 1858. Removed to Fauquier county, Virginia, in 1860. Now (1877) in Jefferson county, West Virginia. Unmarried.

24 LAURENCE LEWIS (see page 178) had four children :

    25 ELEANOR PARKE LEWIS, born in Fairfax county, Virginia, 1 Dec., 1799. She married Colonel Butler, of Louisiana.

    25 ANGELA LEWIS, born in Fairfax county, Virginia, about 1801. She married C. M. Conrad, of New Orleans.

    25 LORENZO LEWIS, born in Fairfax county, Virginia, in Nov., 1803.

    25 AGNES LEWIS, died at the age of 16 years.

" Laurence Lewis was a favorite nephew of General Washington, and one of his Executors. He married one of his adopted daughters, Nellie Custis."

25 LORENZO LEWIS (above), removed to Audley, Clarke county, Virginia, about 1840, and died there, in Aug., 1847. He was married in Philadelphia in 1826, to Esther Marion, daughter of John Redman Coxe, of Philadelphia. His children were :

    26 GEORGE WASHINGTON LEWIS, born in Philadelphia, 12 Feb., 1829.

    26 JOHN REDMAN COX LEWIS, } twins, born at Audley,
    26 LAURENCE FIELDING LEWIS, } Clarke county, Virginia, 13 April, 1834. Laurence died in January, 1857.

    26 EDWARD PARKE CUSTIS LEWIS, born at Audley, Clarke county, Virginia, 7 Feb., 1837.

    26 CHARLES CONRAD LEWIS, born at Audley, Clarke county, Virginia, in Oct., 1840, and died in Mar. 1859.

26 H. L. DAINGERFIELD LEWIS, born at Audley, Clarke county, Virginia, 25 April, 1843.

Mrs. Lorenzo Lewis, now (1878) resides at Audley, Virginia.

26 EDWARD PARKE CUSTIS LEWIS (above), removed in 1869 to, and now (1878) resides at Hoboken, New Jersey. He is a member of the New Jersey Assembly. He was married, first, in Clarke county Virginia, to Lucy Belmain Ware, daughter of Colonel Josiah William Ware, of Clarke county, Virginia, by whom he had five children:

27 ELEANOR ANGELA LEWIS, died at Fredericksburgh, Virginia, in Feb., 1860.

27 LAURENCE FIELDING LEWIS, died at Audley, Clarke county, Virginia.

27 JOHN GLOPELL WARE LEWIS, died at Audley, Clarke county, Virginia.

27 EDWARD PARKE CUSTIS LEWIS, died at Audley, Clarke county, Virginia.

27 LUCY WARE LEWIS, born at Audley, Clarke county, Virginia, A. D. 1866.

His wife died at Audley, Clarke county, Virginia, in August, 1866. He was married, secondly, at Baltimore, Maryland, by Rev. ——, 1 June, 1869, to Mary Picton, daughter of Edwin Augustus Stevens, of Hoboken, New Jersey. Has four children by his second wife, viz. :

27 EDWIN AUGUSTUS STEVENS LEWIS, born at Hoboken, New Jersey, A. D. 1870.

27 ESTHER MARIA LEWIS, born at Hoboken, New Jersey, A. D. 1872.

27 JULIA STEVENS LEWIS, born at Hoboken, New Jersey, A. D. 1874.

27 ELEANOR PARKE CUSTIS LEWIS, born at Hoboken, New Jersey, A. D. 1876.

APPENDIX.

G ENEALOGY may be considered the mathematics of the human race, and serves to *identify* the individual, or family, of whom a history has 'been preserved.

The preceding pages have consisted mainly of the *Genealogy* of the Washington Family, and designed to settle all controverted points on the subject. The following pages will contain scraps of history in regard to members found in the *line of descent from Odin*, of sufficient importance to interest the general reader.

It will be observed, that the succession is complete and unbroken in thirty-two generations, from Odin, the Founder of Scandinavia, B. C. 70, down to Earl Thorfin, one of the " Lords of the Isles," Founder of the Washington Family, in England, circa A. D. 1000 ; from whom the line of descent is also complete and unbroken, in twenty-three generations, down to the first President of the United States, embracing a period of about eighteen centuries.

For about nine hundred years prior to Thorfin, there are no controversies, but in the tenth and eleventh centuries there is considerable confusion among the Genealogists, owing to their anxiety to *identify* a number of individuals as *belonging to our* Washington Family, on account of a *similarity* of cognomen. They took advantage of the

fact that in those (and all preceding) centuries there were
no surnames ; and hence, many bearing the names of de
Wass, d'Oulston, de Weston, de Walston, de Wessington,
de Walsingham, de Weiston, de Weisington, &c., ad infini-
tum, all derived from the names of the places or locality
where they resided (as proved by the prefix "de," before their
names, signifying of), and *changed* in cases of removal, or
the names of the new places added, instances of which are
frequently met with in Genealogical history.   These
names have been merged into the Genealogy as *Washingtons,* to *prove* that the *family* was of *Saxon origin.*   Others
have endeavored to *prove,* from a similarity of names, that
the ancestors of the Washingtons in England were descended from the Dukes of Brittany, in France, and the
Earls of Richmondshire, in England.   By carefully following *our* line of descent, it will be seen that all these ambi-
tious Genealogists had no other basis for their assertions
than analogy, supposition and inference.

The simple, brief, and efficient manner of preserving the
identity and derivation of individuals, pursued in the Ancient Cartularies of the Monks in the Monasteries and
Abbeys (pages 6, 8, 9, 10, 11, 12 and 13), has been the means
of tracing *accurately* the line of succession.   Thus Alet *fil*
(son of) Bodin, Henry fil Bardolf, Akary fil Bardolf, Hervey *fitz* (son of) Akaris (page 5), and Robert fil Akary de
Ashton (page 9), *i.e.,* Robert, the son of Akary, or Akaris,
of the Manor of Ashton, at Kirkby, in Ravenswarth, Yorkshire.

Having settled the *Genealogy* of the Washington Family
on a firm, authentic and rational foundation, we may proceed to give some of the historical narrations.

"Biography is the record of persons : History, of events.
In their more perfect form the two studies are seen to
blend together, rather than encroach upon each other.
History relieving the dryness of Genealogy by the attrac-
tive narration of events, and Biography, by its minute de-

scription of persons, imparts a deeper, and, as it were, a more dramatic interest to History.

3 FRYER, surnamed YNGVE, after his father, Yngve, or Niord (page vii.), the son of Odin, succeeded to the Government of *Sweden* on the death of his father, B. C. 20. He reigned thirty years, and died A. D. 10. His son was :

    4 FIOLNER, who became Governor in Sweden, A. D. 10.

FRYER removed his capitol from Sigtuna to Upsala, where he is said to have built a palace, and a magnificent temple, which he surrounded with a chain of gold, and endowed with considerable wealth in lands and other revenues. He adopted the surname of YNGVE, and hence the sacred race of the YNGLINGS derived their historical appellation.

4 FIOLNER (who died A. D. 41) was the son of Freyer (who died A. D. 10), the son of Yngve or Niord (page vii.), King of Sweden, who reigned at Upsala, and died B. C. 20, second son of Odin (page v.). He reigned in Sweden four years, not as King, but as *Drotter*, or Lord of Sweden. He lost his life in a remarkable manner, A. D. 14, and was succeeded by his son Visbur. "He was drowned in a large vat of mead, into which he had stumbled while under the dominion of liquor. His three immediate successors perished by violent means ; the fourth, Donald, was slain by the advice of his councillors, under the superstitious idea that a severe famine which afflicted the country could only be removed by sprinkling the altars of the offended deities at Upsala, with blood of their King. War was the principal occupation of their reign, and numerous bloody battles were fought in repressing the incessant piracies of the neigh-

boring nations. Yet several of them were distinguished for their encouragement of civilization and social improvement."

Fiölner had three sons, viz.:

   5 VISBUR, who succeeded his father, A. D. 10.

   5 DONALD, who succeeded his brother, A. D. 98.

   5 DOMAR, who succeeded his brother, A. D. 130.

The successor of Fiolner was his son

5 VISBUR, who reigned in Sweden eighty-four years, and died, A. D. 98, when he was succeeded by his brother:

5 DONALD, who reigned in Sweden thirty-two years, and died, A. D. 130, when he was succeeded by his brother:

5 DOMAR, who reigned in Sweden thirty-two years, and died, A. D. 162, when he was succeeded by his nephew.

6 DYGGVE, the son of Visbur (obit A. D. 98), the son of Fiolner (obit A. D. 14), the son of Fryer (obit A. D. 10), the son of Yngve or Niord (obit B. C. 20), the son of Odin (page v.), succeeded to his uncle Domar, as King of Sweden at Upsala, A. D. 162, and reigned thirty years. His wife was sister of Dan Mykillati (page viii.). His son was:

   7 DAG SPAKER.

DYGGVE is alleged to have been the first that assumed the regal title, his predecessors being merely called " Drottar," or " Lord," and their queens Drottingar.

The son of Dyggve was named:

7 DAG SPAKER, who succeeded to the government of Sweden at the death of his father, A. D. 190. He reigned thirty years, and died, A. D. 220. His son was:

   8 AGNE.

8 AGNE, the son of Dyggve (above) succeeded to the throne of Sweden, at the death of his father at Upsala, A. D. 220, and reigned forty years. He died, A. D. 260. He had two sons, Alrek and Eric. He was succeeded by his sons:

9 ALREK, } in the government of Sweden.
9 ERIC, }

" At the death of AGNE, A. D. 260, the Kingdom, which had hitherto remained entire, was shared between his two sons, Alrek and Eric—an unwise policy, which had the effect of dividing the prerogatives as well as the dominions of the crown among a multitude of provincial chiefs, who assumed an independent authority."

9 ALREK, the first son of Agne, succeeded to the government of Sweden at the death of his father, A. D. 260, and reigned twenty years. He joined with him his brother

9 ERIC, in the Kingdom. At the death of Alrek, A. D. 280, his son Yngve (named after his ancestor Yngve or Niord, the son of Odin), succeeded him in the Kingdom.

Alrek had two sons :
   10 YNGVE, who succeeded him, and,
   10 ALF.

10 YNGVE II., first son of Alrek, succeeded to the government of Sweden, at the death of his father, A. D. 280, and reigned twenty years. He died, A. D. 300, and was succeeded by his son,

11 HUJLECK, who reigned but two years. He died A. D. 302. Hujleck had two sons :
   12 JORNSIDER.
   12 ERIK.

12 JORNSIDER, first son of Hujlek, succeeded to the government of Sweden, at the death of his father, A. D. 302, and reigned 10 years. " He was deposed, A. D. 312, when the prerogatives as well as the dominions of the Crown became divided among a multitude of provincial Chiefs, who assumed an independent authority."

This state of anarchy continued for above a century,

18

when the old Dynasty was restored in the person of a descendant (probably grandson) of Jornsider, named,

13 AUN HINN GAMLE, who had a peaceful reign and died A. D. 448. He was succeeded by his son,

14 EGIL TUNNEDOLGI, who reigned eight years. He died A. D. 456, and was succeeded by his son,

15 OTTAR VENDILKRAKA, who reigned four years. He died A. D. 460, when he was succeeded by his son.

16 ADILS, son of Ottar Vendilkraka, succeeded to the throne of Sweden, at the death of his father, A. D. 460. His wife was named Yrsa. His son and successor was named :

17 EYSTEIN, who became King of Sweden, A. D. 505.

"ADILS was involved in a protracted quarrel with the Norwegians, which was at length terminated in his favor by a pitched battle on the Lake Wener, the two armies being drawn up on its frozen surface."

ADILS reigned forty-five years, and died A. D. 505, and was succeeded by his son, .

17 EYSTEIN, who reigned twenty-six years, and died A. D. 531, when he was succeeded by his son,

18 YNGVAR, who reigned fourteen years, and died A. D. 545, when he was succeeded by his son,

19 ONUND BRAUT, who became King of Sweden, as successor of his father, YNGVAR, A. D. 545, reigned twenty years, and died A. D. 565.

ONUND received the name of BRAUT (the road-maker), from his exertions in draining marshes, extending cultivation, and opening up channels of intercourse to every province in the kingdom.

The hereditary occupant of the throne at Upsala continued to enjoy a pre-eminence in dignity and power, until the fatal reign of INGIALD ILLRADA, son of Frode VII. (page x.), when the hallowed sceptre was transferred from the line of the YNGLINGS to that of the SKIOLDUNGS in the earlier part of the seventh century (A. D. 630).

Onund having died without issue, the throne of Sweden became the hereditary right of Denmark, and reverted to the Skioldungs in the person of Frode VII. (page x.), whose younger son Ingiald proceeded to Upsala to take possession of the Kingdom, A. D. 565.

Ingiald Illrada, son of Frode VII., or Olaf (page x.), became King of Sweden, at Upsala, at the death of Onund Braut, A. D. 565. He reigned 65 years, and lost his life, A. D. 630.

"That Prince, when young, is said to have been of gentle disposition, but. being vanquished in some juvenile contest, such as the sons of the nobility were then accustomed to display at their annual festivals, the Saga relates that in order to alter his temper he was fed with wolves' hearts. Judging from his future actions, this regimen appears to have had the desired effect.

"His long reign, from its commencement to its close, was a series of cruel and lawless atrocities. It was the ancient custom at the Royal inauguration (which always took place at the funeral of the deceased Prince), for the next heir to seat himself on the lowest step of the vacant throne, in the midst of the grandees, until presented with a huge ox horn filled with wine. After taking the usual oaths he drank off the liquor, mounted the chair of State, and was proclaimed amidst the shouts of the people. This initiatory rite INGIALD accompanied with the additional ceremony of swearing, before draining the mystic cup, that he would either double the extent of his Kingdom, or perish in the attempt. The fulfillment of his vow led to those acts of treachery and murder which procured him the name of

ILLRADA (the deceitful), and ultimately occasioned his own destruction.

" Fire and sword were employed to exterminate the chiefs and nobles, many of whom were consumed in the flames of the palace, where they had been hospitably entertained by their perfidious sovereign. Twelve princes in Sweden fell victims to the rapacity of the tyrant, who seized their possessions, and added them to the dominions of the crown. But a just retribution awaited the perpetration of his crimes. His daughter Asa had been given in marriage to GUDROD, the Gothic King of Seania ; at her instigation, he assassinated his brother, Halfdan III., of Denmark, A. D. 580 (page x.), and was afterwards himself cut off in a plot, by the artifices of his own wife. Having sacrificed her husband she fled to the court of Upsala, where she became an accomplice in the death of her father. IVAR VIDFADME (page xi.), son of HALFDAN III., had invaded Sweden, A. D. 630, with a powerful host, to avenge the murder of his *kindred.* His ravages filled the guilty INGIALD with terror and despair. As the victorious foe approached, he was entertaining his courtiers at a grand banquet ; when, finding it impossible to resist or make his escape, he resolved, with the aid and advice of his daughter, to terminate his life by setting fire to the hall.

"OLAF, his son, unable to repel the invaders, was driven into exile. Passing to the westward of the Wener Lake, he settled, with the few companions, that still adhered to his standard, in the province of Wermeland ; there he hewed down the immense forests, hence his name of TRAETELIA (the tree-cutter), and laid the basis of a new kingdom, where, in short time, the star of the Ynglings rose again with more than its ancient splendor in the person of HARALD HAAR-FAGER, founder of the Norwegian Monarchy."

BARONS OF BRIQUEBEC.

. Robert Turstain (see Introduction, page xvi.), the first

Baron, had two sons : Anselec, ancestor of the Barons of Bec, and Aunsfred the Dane. The latter had two sons : Turstain Goz (ancestor of the house of Averanches, Earls of Chester, in England), and William. The latter was Baron of Bec, and ancestor of the Barons of Bec-Crespin. His son, or grandson, Gilbert Crepon, Baron of Bec, and Castellan de Tillierers, aided in founding the Abbey of Bec. He had sons, William and Gilbert. William the 2nd of Bec, 1054, came to England in 1066. He had 1st William (see family of Mitford), and Milo De Wallingford, 1086, who left a son William.

From the ancestor, Harold Blatrand, Duke Rollo, afterward Bertrand, this family derive their origin.

BARDOLF.

1 WILLIAM BARDOLF, probable grandson of Bardolf fil Thorfin (page 4), was Sheriff of the counties of Norfolk and Suffolk, in 16 Henry II. (1169), and from that time to 21 Henry II. (1174) inclusive. He had two sons :

   2 THOMAS BARDOLF, below.

   2 HUGH BARDOLF, of whom hereafter.

2 THOMAS BARDOLF, in 18 Henry II. (1171), upon levying the Scutage of such Barons as did not then attend the King into Ireland, nor send soldiers, or money for that service, paid £cxxv. for the Scutage of those Knights' Fees, which formerly did belong to Raphe Hanselyn, a Baron in Nottinghamshire, whose daughter and heir, called Rose, he had taken to wife.

This Thomas Bardolf obtained from William, brother to King Henry II., the Lordship of Bradewell (in Essex), to hold to himself and his heirs, by the service of one Knight's Fee ; three parts of which Lordship he gave in marriage to his three daughters. The first married to Robert de St. Remegio ; the second to William Bacun ;

the third to Baldwin de Thone.   Thomas Bardolf had two sons :

>   3 DOUN BARDOLF, below.
>   3 WILLIAM BARDOLF, of whom hereafter.

To Thomas Bardolf, succeeded his son and heir, by her the said Rose.

3 DOUN BARDOLF, who married Beatrix, daughter and heir to William de Warren, of Wirmegay, in Norfolk (whereby the Barons of Wirmegay came to this family of Bardolf). He died in 11 John (1210).   Which Beatrix then surviving, had the Lordship of Kiskynton assigned for her Dower ; and gave three thousand and one hundred Marks to the King, for livery of her father's lands belonging to her husband ; as also that she might not be compelled to marry again.

This Doun and Beatrix left issue :

4 WILLIAM BARDOLF, who, in 17 John (1215), had Livery of all his lands, and in 26 Henry III. (1241), amongst other of the great men of that time, attended the king in person, in that expedition which he then made into France ; and obtained such favor for his services there done, that of all the debts he owed unto the Exchequer, as well those which were due from William de Warren, his grandfather, as those from Beatrix, his mother, fifty Marks per annum was accepted, until they should be fully paid.

In 27 Henry III. (1242), he had Livery of the Honour of Wirmegay, which, during his minority, had been in the hands of Hubert de Burgh, sometime Earl of Kent.   And in 28 Henry III. (1243), obtained the King's charter for a market at Wirmegay, on the Monday every week ; as also a Fair every year at his Lordship of Stowe, upon the day and morrow after the Feast of the Holy Trinity.

In 29 Henry III. (1244), upon collection of the Aid then

levied for marriage of the King's eldest daughter, he paid
xiv£ vs. for the Knight's Fees he then held, which were
xiv and a fourth part, and in 38 Henry III. (1253), upon
collection of the Aid for making the King's eldest son
Knight, accounted xxviii£ xs. for the same Knight's Fees,
but by reason he was then going to the King, he had
respite for part of that sum.

In which year also he obtained a Charter for Free-warren
throughout all the lordships and lands whereof he was
then possessed, viz. : Wirmegay, Westbrigg, Lotenhill,
Watlington, Thorpe, Festome, Sechie l'Estowe, Wynebodes-
ham, Dunham, Welbes, Kungetone, another Sechie, West-
weniz, Herdwike, Biddeltone, Halgane, Wyneberg, Inkes-
ham, Westfeld, Batestal, Thurston, Lerabeston, and
Keymestone in Norfolk ; Kyskinton, Digeby, Levesing-
ham, Blokesham, Amewik, Latelmund, Blanchewill, West-
burg, Dedinton, Stebinton, and Thorpe in Lincolnshire ;
Shelcford in Nottinghamshire ; Okebror and Eleton in
Derbyshire ; "Plumpthon, Winpelesfield, Lindeskeld, Had-
leg, Standen, Poleston, Ardingeley, Pipesteye, Bercamp,
and Flefang, in Sussex.

In 41 Henry III. (1256), he attended the King in his expedition into Wales. And in 42 Henry III. (1257), was
made Governor of Nottingham Castle. So also in 47
Henry III. (1262). After which, viz., in 48 Henry III. (1263),
in that great Insurrection of the Barons, adhering to the
King, he was taken prisoner with him in that fatal battle
of Lewes, and died in 4 Edward I. (1277), as it seems, for
then his son and heir :

5 WILLIAM BARDOLF, doing homage, had Livery of all his
lands, lying in the counties of Leicester, Lincoln, Nottingham, Norfolk and Sussex ; the King accepting of his
Relief (which was cl£), by l£ per annum.

Which William being personally in that expedition into
Wales, 10 Edward I. (1283), had scutage of all his tenants

that held of him by Military Service, and about two years following obtained the King's Charter for a Market at his Mannor of Halluton, in Leicestershire, to be kept upon the Tuesday every Week ; with two Fairs every year ; the one upon the Eve, Day and Morrow, after the Feast of the Nativity of St. John Baptist, and two days following ; the other on the Eve, Day and Morrow, after the Feast of Simon and Jude, and two days after. And likewise, a Fair at Tilney, in Norfolk, upon the Eve, Day and Morrow, and two days next following the Feast of St. Laurence. And moreover, a Fair, yearly, at Cauntele, in the same County, upon the Eve, Day and Morrow, after the Feast of St. Margaret the Virgin.

By Julian, the daughter and Heir of Hugh de Gurnay (whom he took to wife), he left issue a son, called,

6 HUGH BARDOLF, born A. D. 1256, who in June, 22 Edward I. (1295), having Summons (with other of the Great Men) to attend the King with his Advice, touching the weighty Affairs of the Realm, accompanied him soon after into Gascoigne.

Upon the death of which Julian (his Mother), in 23 Edward I. (1296), being xl years of age, and in Gascoigne, he had Livery of all the Lands of her Inheritance, by the King's Special Favour, in regard he was then in his Service ; when he had the hard fate to be taken Prisoner by the King of France at his Siege of Rifunce.

In 25 Edward I. (1298), he continued still in the King's Service in Gascoigne. And in the 28 Edward I. (1301), was in that Expedition then made into Scotland. So also, in 29 Edward I. (1302).

In 32 Edward I. (1305), he went again into Scotland, the King himself, with his Army, being there, but departed this Life the same year (1305), the Lands whereof he then died seized being these, viz. : the Mannor of Birling, in Sussex, parcel of the Barony of Gourney ; Westburgh, in the County of Lancaster, with the Hamlets of Dodington. Stubton, Stocking, and Thorpe, as a Member of his Barony. of Shelford ; Kyskinton, in Lincolnshire, with the Hamlets of Digby. Lebestingham, Rokingham, and Brauncewell, Members also of the same Barony ; the Mannor of Wyrmegay, in Norfolk (being the Head of another Barony), with Certain Lands in Surget, Fincham, Stowe and Quinebergh. And in the right of Isabell, his Wife, the Mannor of Bures, in Suffolk ; Perting and Plumpton, in Sussex ; with Certain Lands in Emsworth, in Southampton.

Which Isabell, by the consent of her son Thomas, had the Mannor of Bercamp, in Sussex ; Kyskinton, with the Hamlets of Digby, and Lestingham, and certain Lands in Fillingham, in Lincolnshire ; as also in Kungitone and Scrimpesbagh, in Norfolk, assigned for her Dowry. And the same year obtained a Grant from the King, of the Mannors of Watton, in Hertfordshire ; Addington in Survey ; and Emesworth in Southampton, for Life, with Remainder to her younger son William, and the Heirs of his Body ; and for default of such issue, to her Right Heirs.

Hugh Bardolf had issue by Isabell, his wife, two sons, viz. :

7 THOMAS BARDOLF, born 10 Edward I. (1283), and

7 WILLIAM BARDOLF, born 13 Edward I. (1286).

This Thomas Bardolf was made Knight of the Bathe, in 34 Edward I. (1306), together with Edward, Prince of Wales, and many others, at the Feast of Pentecost ; and had allowance of Robes out of the King's Wardrobe, for that ceremony, as for a Baneret. After which, viz., the same year, he Marched with the Prince into Scotland.

In 8 Edward II. (1315), he had (with divers other Great Men) Summons to come to New Castle upon Tine, at the Feast of the Assumption of the Blessed Virgin, well provided with Horse and Arms, thence to march against the Scots. His death happened in 3 Edward III. (1329). He

was buried in the Priory of Shelford, Nottinghamshire.
His son was :

8 JOHN BARDOLF, born A. D. 1307. He was xvii years of
age at the death of his father, 3 Edward III. (1329).

Which John making proof of his age in 9 Edward III.
(1335), and doing Homage, had Livery of his Lands. In
which year he Marched into Scotland, in the King's Service.
And in 10 Edward III. (1336), wedded Elizabeth, Daughter
and Heir of Sir Roger Damory (by that great Woman,
Elizabeth de Burgh, his Wife), by whom at length he had
a fair Inheritance, viz. : the Mannors of Craneburne,
Larent, Gundebill, Pymperne, and Wyke ; with the Bur-
roughs of Warham, and Maymouth in Dorsetshire.

In 14 Edward III. (1340), he was in the King's Service in
the parts of Almaine. And in 16 Edward III. (1342), in
Brittany. Moreover in 18 Edward III. (1344), he was retained to serve the King with twelve Men at Arms, and
twenty Archers on Horseback, in his Irish Wars.

In 19 Edward III. (1345), he received Command to pre-
pare himself with Horse and Arms, to go again in his Service into Britanny, being then a Baneret. And in 26
Edward III. (1352), upon that apprehension of danger,
which there was, of an Invasion by the French, was joyned
in Commission with Robert de Ufford, Earl of Suffolk,
and Robert, Lord Morlee, for defence of the Norfolk
Coasts. Also in 37 Edward III. (1363), he was again beyond the Sea in the King's Service.

His death happened 3 Aug., 45 Edward III. (1371), at
which time he was seized of the Mannors of Clopton, in
Suffolk ; Cauth, Strumpesham, Rugeton, Fincham, Stowe,
Wermegay and Quinnebergh, in Norfolk ; Dons, Watton,
and Stone, in Hertfordshire ; Westburgh, with its Members,
viz. : Dodington, Coling, and Stubton, in Lancashire ;
Kyskinton, with its Members, Scil-Digby, Ammyke, Bor-
ham and Branswell ; Cathorpe, with its Members, viz. :

Trestone, Normenton, Sudbroke, Hambeck and Willoughby
juxta Ancaster in Lincolnshire. Stoke-Bardolf, parcel of
the Barony of Shelford, and xxix Knight's Fees, belonging to the Count of Shelford, in Nottinghamshire ; the
Mannor of Hallughton, in Leicestershire ; Okebrok, in
Derbyshire, parcel of the Barony of Shelford ; Addington,
in Surrey ; with Bereling and Bercamp, in Sussex.

To whom succeeded :

9 WILLIAM BARDOLF, his Son and Heir, born (A. D. 1357),
then, 45 Edward III. (1371), xiv years of age, whose
Wardship and Marriage was granted by Queen Philippa
(wife to King Edward the Third), in 40 Edward III.
(1366), under Sir Michaell Poynings, Knight ; to the intent that he should marry Agnes, daughter of the said
Michaell. Which William, upon proof of his age, and
doing his Homage, in 45 Edward III. (1371), had Livery
of his Lands, and the next year following was in that
Expedition then made into France.

In the same year he was retained to serve the King in
his Irish Wars, with two Knights, xxvii Esquires (all Men
at Arms), and thirty Archers.

In 47 Edward III. (1373), he was again retained to serve
the King for one whole year, in his French Wars, under
the Conduct of John of Gaunt, Duke of Lancaster, with xl
Men at Arms, xl Archers, all on Horseback.

This William made his Testament, 12 Sept., Anno 1384
(9 R. 2), being then at Cathorpe, in Lincolnshire ; by which
he bequeathed his Body to be buried in the Quire of the
Fryers-Carmelites at Lewne, in Norfolk, and to his Heir-
male, whomsoever it should be, a part of the very Cross
of our Saviour, set in Gold. And departed this Life the
same year (1384), leaving Agnes his widow, who had for
her Dowrie, the Lordships Wyrmegeye, Stowe, Fyncham,
Cantile, and Strumpethagh, then assigned to her.

10 THOMAS, his Son and Heir, born 1367, being then xvii years of age.

Which Thomas, in 13 R. 2 (1388), having made proof of his age, and doing his Homage, had Livery of his Inheritance, and within two years after obtained License to travel beyond the Seas with xii Servants, their Horses, and all necessary Accommodations.

In 18 R. II. (1393), he was beyond Sea in the King's Service. And in 20 R. II. (1395), had the like License. Moreover, in 21 R. II. (1396), he was sent by the King, together with the Lord Scales, upon some special Service into France : and in 22 R. II. (1397) was in Ireland.

In 1 H. IV. (1399), as Cousin and Heir to Sir Roger Damory, by Agnes his Mother, he obtained a Confirmation to himself and his Heirs, of that Grant which King Edward the Third, in 13th (1339) of his Reign (in consideration of special Services), made to the same Sir Roger and his Heirs, of the Mannors of Sandball, in Yorkshire, Halghton, in Oxfordshire, and Faukeshall, in Surrey.

Which Lady Agnes, being afterwards the wife of Sir Roger Mortimer, and surviving him, in 4 H. IV. (1402), had License to go on Pilgrimage to Rome and Colein, attended with xii Servants, their Horses, and all Accoutrements fit for such a Journey. Soon after which, she declared her will, whereby she bequeathed her Body to be buried in the Priory Church of the Holy Trinity, without Algate, in the Suburbs of London, making Henry, Earl of Northumberland, with her Son,

11 THOMAS, LORD BARDOLF, Supervisors thereof, and departed this life on Tuesday next after the Feast of St. Barnabas the Apostle, the same Year (1402), her Son Thomas, born 1372, been then xxx years of age.

This Thomas, in 6 H. IV. (1404), taking part with Henry, Earl of Northumberland ; Thomas, Earl Marshal and Notingham, and Richard Scrope, Archbishop of Yorke, in that Insurrection then by them made (for which the Archbishop and Earl Marshal were beheaded, at Yorke), was, together with the Earl of Northumberland, pursued by the King, with a powerful Army; whereupon he fled, with that Earl, first into Scotland and afterwards into Wales. But about three years after, returning into England, and so to Threske, in Yorkshire, they made Proclamation for Liberty to all that would put themselves in Arms and joyn with them, insomuch as many flocked in to their Assistance. But the Sheriff of Yorkshire having raised the Power of the County, met with them about Haselwood, and in a sharp Skirmish, slew the Earl, and wounded this Thomas so much, that he soon died of those Hurts, in 1407, leaving Anne and Joane, his Daughters and Heirs, the one then xix, the other xviii years of age.

After which, being attainted in Parliament, Anno 7 H. IV. (1406), his Honor, of Wyrmegay, with divers other fair Mannors in Norfolk, were given by the King to Thomas Beaufort (his Brother), other great Lordships to Sir George Dunbar, Knight, and the Mannors of Shelford and Stoke-Bardolf, in Nottinghamshire, with Hallughton, in Leicestershire, to the Queen.

But the next year following (1407) Sir William Clifford, Knight, in right of Anne, his wife, and William Phelip, in right of Joane, his wife, daughters to the said Thomas, humbly representing to the King, That Henry the Second long since King of England (his Royal Progenitor), having by his Letters Patents given to Thomas Bardolf, Ancestor to this Thomas, and to the Heirs of his Body, by Rose, the Daughter of Raphe Hanselyne, the Lordships of Shelford and Stoke-Bardolfe, in Nottinghamshire, and likewise the Mannor of Halughton, in Leicestershire, as the whole Inheritance of Raphe Hanselyn, her Grandfather: and that the said Thomas Bardolf, their Father, lately attainted, being the Lineal Heir to the before specified Thomas Bardolfe and Rose, the Inheritance of those

Lordships did of right belong unto them the said Anne and Joane · The King thereupon, having a conscientious regard to this their Right and Title, granted to the said Sir William Clifford and Anne, his wife, and to William Phelip, and Joane, his wife, the Reversion of those Lordship, as also of the Mannor of Birlyng, in Sussex, after the death of his Royal Consort the Queen, to hold and enjoy to them and the Heirs of their Bodies.

Which William Phelip, and Joane, his wife, in 9 II. V. (1421), had the Livery of their Purparty of certain lands in Suffolk, of the Inheritance of Avicia, late wife of the same Thomas Bardolf attainted, and Mother to her, the said Joane, Daughter to Raphe Lord Cromwell, of Tatshall, and died in 9 H. V. (1421).

It seems that though this Thomas Lord Bardolf did die of his wounds (as hath been already observed), yet his Body was Quartered, and the Quarters disposed of, to be set upon the Gates of these several Cities and Town, viz.: London, Yorke, Denne, and Shrewsbury, and his Head upon one of the Gates of Lincolne; for it appeareth, That afterwards, upon the Petition of Avicia, his widow, the King was pleased to give her leave to take them down and bury them.

Whether Anne, the eldest Daughter of this Thomas, had any Issue by Sir William Clifford, her Husband, appeareth not, but certain it is, that she buried him, and was afterwards the wife of Sir Reginald Cobham.

Of this Family, there was also

2 HUGH BARDULF (a younger Son to the first WILLIAM BARDOLF [page 13]), who in 22 H. II. (1175) was amerced at five Marks, for trespassing in the King's Forests, and was Sheriff of Cornwall, in 31 H. II. (1184).

In 33 H. II. (1186), the King being in Normandy, he was constituted one of his Lieutenants here in England, for conservation of the Peace in his absence.

This Hugh continued Sheriff of Cornwall, in 33 H. II. (1186), and executed the same Office for Wiltshire, for half that year, and likewise in 34 H. II. (1187).

So also for the Counties of Somerset and Dorset, in 1 R. I. (1189). In which year he had the Custody of the Lands of Fulke Paynel, by reason that he fled, and paid not his fine to the King for the Honor of Baenton. And the same year, upon the going of that King into the Holy Land, was constituted (with William Briwere), an Associate to the Bishops of Durham and Ely, during his absence, for administering Justice to every man, according to the Laws and Customs of the Realm. Moreover, in Anno 1190 (2 R. 1), he was at Messana, in Sicilie, with King Richard, and one of those, who, on the behalf of that King, undertook that the Articles of Peace and Friendship, which were there agreed on, betwixt King Richard and Tancred, King of Sicilie, should be firmly kept.

Upon his return, he was also one of that number whom the Pope had then Excommunicated, as Enemies to the Church, but chiefly for adhering to John, Earl of Moreton (the King's Brother) and those who with him opposed William de Longchamp, Bishop of Ely, then Chancellor of England, in his oppressive way of Governing (the King being absent), but was particularly excepted by that Bishop, upon denouncing the Sentenex, in regard he was not personally with those that ejected and laid hold on the same Bishop, upon condition he would, upon demand, resign unto William de Stutevill, the Castle of Scardeburgh, and all other in Yorkshire and Westmerland, which he then had in Custody. Moreover, in 2 R. I. (1190), he executed the Office for Sheriff, for Warwick and Leicestershires, for the one half of that year. So also for the whole year in 3 R. I. (1191). And in 4 and 5 R. I. (1192–3), for Yorkshire, being in such high esteem with King Richard, that in the third year of his Reign, when he was in the Holy Land, and suspected his Chancellor in England, to whom he had chiefly committed the Charge of Governing in his absence, he wrote his Letter to this Hugh Bardulf, and three others, requiring them, in case the Chancellor did not do as he ought, that they should take upon them the rule in all things. From which time, it evident, from divers Fines levied before him that he was one of the King's Justices for some years, as also a Justice Itinerant.

In those great contests which were betwixt the Bishop of Ely (Governor of the Kingdom in King Richard's absence), and John, Earl of Moreton (the King's brother), when Windsore Castle (which was the Earl of Moreton's), had Siege laid to it by all the Nobility of England, this Hugh, being then the King's Justice, and Sheriff of Yorkshire, joyn'd with the Archbishop of Yorke, and William de Stuteville, who having raised a great Power, fortified Doncaster, but would not take part with that Archbishop in the Siege of Tickhill Castle, belonging to the Earl of Moreton, in regard to his special obligations unto him.

In 6 R. I. (1194) he was Sheriff of Northumberland, Westmerland and Yorkshire. Howbeit, upon the return of King Richard from his Restraint in Almaine, he took the Sheriffalty of Yorkshire and Westmerland, and likewise the Custody of the Castles of Yorke and Scarborough. Nevertheless, the next year following he was again Sheriff of Northumberland, Westmerland, Lancashire, Yorkshire, Warwick, and Leicestershires, and sent with Earl, Roger Bigot, William de Warren, and others, to hear and determine that great Controversie betwixt the Archbishop of Yorke and Canons of that Church. Moreover, he was then constituted one of the Justices Itinerant throughout all the Counties of England. And upon the death of Hugh, Bishop of Durham, had the Custody of the Castles of Durham and Norham.

This Hugh had the Inheritance of the Honor of Baenton given to him by King Henry the Second (upon the forfeit-

ure of Fulke Painel), and in 8 R. I. (1196), passed it back
to the King, in exchange for the Mannor of Hou.

In that year he continued Sheriff of Westmerland, and
again executed the same Office for that County, in 10 R. I.
(1198), and 1 John (1199). So likewise for Notingham and
Derbyshires, Devon and Cornwall, for the one half of that
year.

In 9 R. I. (1197), he was again Constituted one of the Justices Itinerant for the Counties of Lincoln, Nottingham,
Derby, Yorke, Northumberland, Westmerland, Cumberland, and Lancaster. And in 3, 4, and 5 John (1202-3-4),
executed the Sheriffalty for Notingham and Derbyshires.

But in 5 John (1204), he died without Issue ; unto whom
succeeded his brother.

2 ROBERT, as his Heir, who then (1204) gave 1000£ for the
Livery of his Lands. And for his widow, William de
Braose gave 1000£ to the King, that he might have her
to be wife for one of his Sons, to whom she accordingly
was married.

This Robert had the Lordship and Hundred of Hou, in
Kent, which after his death were given to Hubert de Burgh,
Justice of England ; And died without Issue, in 9 H. III.
(1224). Whereupon his Lands were shared amongst his
Nephews and Heirs, viz. : Jordan Foliot, Isolda Grey,
Raphe Paynel, Hugh Poinz, and Maud Bardolf.

Hugh and Robert Bardolf, had nieces as follows, viz. :

3 A niece, who married Jordan Foliot.

"Henry Foliot, with Lecia de Muntenei his wife, Daughter and Coheir to Jordan Briset, Founder of the Nunnery
at Clerkenwell, in the Suburbs of London, confirmed the·
Grant of those Lands whereon that Religious house was
built. To him succeeded Jordan, his Son and Heir ; who
in 9 Henry III. (1224), with Isolda de Grey, and Raphe

19

Paynell, performed his Homage for the Lands of Robert Bardolf their Uncle, whereunto they were some of the Coheirs.—*Dugdale's Baronage*, v. 1, p. 679.

3 "Isolda, who married Henry de Grey, of Codnovre, unto whom King Richard I. in the sixth year of his reign (1194), gave the manor of Turrock, in Essex, which King John Confirmed ; and by his Publick Charter vouchsafed to him a Special privilege, viz. : to hunt the Hare and Fox in any Lands belonging to the Crown, excepting the King's own Demesn-Parks.

Which Henry, in 1 Henry III. (1216), had also a Grant of the Mannor of Grimston, in Nottinghamshire (part of the possessions of Robert Bardolf), for his Support in the King's Service. And having afterwards married Isolda, Niece and Co-heir to the Same Robert, in 9 Henry III. (1224), shared in the Inheritance in all his Lands. By which Isolda he had issue Six Sons, viz. :

    4 Richard de Grey, whose principal Seat was at Codnobre, in Derbyshire.

    4 John de Grey, of Wilton, Sometime Justice of Chester, and Progenitor to the Lords Graye, of Wilton and Ruthin.

    4 William de Grey, of Landford, in Nottinghamshire, and Sandiacre, in Derbyshire.

    4 Robert de Grey, of Rotherfield.

    4 Walter de Grey, Archbishop of Yorke.

    4 Henry de Grey.

For account of these six sons, and their descendants, see *Dugdale's Baronage*, pages 709, 722.

3 William Bardolf (son to the first Thomas), which William first married the Daughter of Almarick le Dispenser, and afterwards, Elizabeth, the Daughter of William

Fitz William, with whom he had all the Thenage which the said William Fitz William held in Hapedale and Rokedale. But this William lived not long, for in 7 John (1205), John Bec (a great Baron in Lincolnshire) gave 100£ and four Palfreys for License to marry his widow ; Yet he did not marry her, for it appears, that in the year following, she (viz. Elizabeth) gave to the King 100£ Fine and two Palfreys, that she might not be compelled to marry, and that in 13 John (1212), Ivo Tailboys, on her behalf, gave xcvi£ ivs. vd. and two Palfreys to the King upon the same account.—*Dugdale's Baronage,* pages 681–684.

Whittaker, in his *History of Richmondshire,* has no pedigree of the Washington family, and only a brief reference to the name, as having a territorial origin. He says, "Prior to the Conquest a family residing on the river Wass, in Yorkshire, seated at Wharleton and Wassington, the names of the territory and river adjoining." This is made significant by the same author in an illusion to Wassington juxta Ravensworth (page 1), and he confirms it still further in another statement. " In the tower of the church in the parish of Wharleton are the *arms* of the *Washington* family—an old family of considerable note in this Parish ; from whence it may be inferred that one of them built the tower " (see also *Burton's History of York,* 148, 149).

Wharleton was in the Parish of Alan, county of York. The *name* of Wassington is *anterior* to the Conquest. "The village of Wassengton is mentioned in a Saxon charter by King Edward, in 973, of Thorneby Abbey." (*Collectanea Typographica,* vol. 4, p. 55.) The *records* of this Abbey refer to the manor of Washbourn and Wharton, hence the name of Wassengtone.

It is certain that within this diocese was the manor of

Washbourn, valued at the dissolution of the monasteries, temp. Henry VIII. (1509-1547), at £11 3s. 11d., and Wharton also went as an endowment of the church.

The Northumberland family mingled in stirring scenes. This was a border county, and a theatre of perpetual strife. Here a castle was erected and a parish founded. It was not, properly speaking, a county, at that period—only a territory north of the river Humber.

William De Bradwell (son of Alet [page 5], son of Bodin, the Monk), born about 1135, was contemporary with Robert Wharlton, or de Wyssington, and Walter de Wharlton, or de Wyssington, in the county of York, who held land north of the Humber, in the same county, afterwards called Richmondshire. They were called "De Wharlton." William de Wharlton held 11 bovates of land in Wharlton, in Wastyale and Newsam, for capital service. (*Testa de Neville*, p. 406.) Newsam was owned by Bodin. (See *Whittaker*, p. 124.)

William, Count of Boulogne, brother to Henry II., gave this land to Walter, uncle of William Wharlton, in the time of Stephen, 1135-1154.

We find among the benefactors of St. Mary's, York. Askettle de Ferneaux (or fern waters), Odo, the Chamberlain, Ackeris (page 5), Hervey fil Akaris (page 7), Ribald and Stephen, Earl of Richmond. Radulphus (doubtless of Reyne Hall), is called a son of Ribald. Odo Dapiser left heirs, and of his descent was Brian *Aquarius*, or waters. Brian had a son Conan.

ORIGIN, CAUSE AND ACCOUNT OF THE YORK AND LANCASTER TROUBLES IN ENGLAND.

"The York and Lancaster troubles had their *origin* at the Conquest, and their *cause* in the antagonism of two nations, Norman and Saxon, and the two issues were sufficient to impel the most disastrous action. Great battles, where hosts were slain, were fought out to the exhaustion of both parties. Change of owners of the territories, to an almost unbounded extent, both in England and in France, was the result. The *Welch* became the staunch allies of Henry II., 1154, though only through stipulations, that varied the fortunes of many families, and alienated their estates. Richmondshire was taken from the county of York, and the title of "the Earls of Richmond" was given to the younger sons of the Dukes of Brittany. Many of the descendants of the governing Saxon families before the Conquest, ceased to exist altogether, though, by virtue of alliances with remaining heiresses, the names of many of the old race survived,* and the names of their *Manors* (the new incumbents *taking territorial names*), mingled with the descendants of the original owners ; and this led to great confusion among the cognomens of the families, and has greatly increased the difficulty of tracing genealogies.

" It has become customary to adduce or assign the origin of the York and Lancaster troubles to the two powerful leagues that were formed in the reign of Henry IV. (1399–1413), elder son of John of Gaunt, Duke of Lancaster, and Earl of Richmondshire. From the time of the Conquest there were two nationalities, Saxon and Norman, struggling for existence. This embraced, however, something more than a governing ascendency. On the part of the original inhabitants, it comprehended the possession of their Laws, Manners, and Language, as well as political institutions. While there was any existence of these accepted as the nucleus of a league, a people could not be entirely subjugated. This diversity of principles bore sway until the beginning of the 'Wars of the Roses,' in the reign of Henry VI. (1429–1464), and England was swept by the diverse currents as by a tempest, and the contest en-

---

* As was the case with Thorfin and his sons Bodin and Bardolf (see pages 1 to 4).

dured for the ensuing thirty years. It ceased at length, after immolating at the shrines of the conflicting factions, four score at least of the princes of the blood Royal, with almost the entire body of the ancient nobility of England. Not one of the kings succeeded to the Throne, in regular constitutional order. If some Nero of those days had made his horse a Consul, it would have expressed something of the dominion exercised. To appear in arms in favor of some new chief, whose right had never been recognized before, was the customary alternative.

"The words 'York' and 'Lancaster' revive in the mind not a mere picture of war; on the contrary, a large territory constituting a Kingdom, and embracing a field of wide political action, and a pristine grandeur of achievement. York county seemed a land of destiny, echoing on every side with the solution of fearful problems. What was the assured advantage accruing from so many changes? What were the promptings of so many sad events? Why should one portion of a people become so vividly alive to a need of defence from another portion? It could only have been a strong faith, that in the issues involved, was a remedy for all social wrongs, bad laws, and abuses. The test of law was a final solution of the political problem.

"The Kings of England, from the fall of the Plantagenets, accompanied their efforts of rule with peculiar characteristics. The people could not do anything *for* them, nor *with* them, nor *without* them. Their Regal services were necessary, but not valuable; they would not employ the aid of others to give them higher importance, always opposing this duty whenever the influence was to be superseded by subsidiary eminence. They brooked no control by others, and would exercise none exceptionably themselves.

"These painful conditions brought together precarious contrasts, and very unhappy attendants of force. Cruel disasters to families, the best in the realm, struggling to make prominent position respectable, and official moral duty, sapped away the vital elements of exalted life. The great Councillors of the nation were warned of those fatal issues, attendant upon rectitude of conduct. The first Tudor dishonored and dismissed the Councillor Sir Thomas More, whom his successor sent to the block. This corresponded with the act that destroyed the young Earl of Warwick, the last of the Plantagenets. Henry VII. acted up to the dictates of the popular will in superseding Richard III., though the constitution and laws were violated. After the death of Gloucester, the Princess Elizabeth was the real heir to the throne, but she was set aside by a compulsory marriage with Henry. Her rights were invaded and the woman's inheritance ignored. It is manifest that the leading families—Saxon, Norman and Ancient British—were compacted into close alliances at the period. Such arrangements were made as best secured the objects aimed at,—*i. e.*, the tranquillity of the country and a harmony of conflicting interests."

It is evident that one branch of the Washington family was originally allied to the York faction, and the other to the Lancastrian interest.

We attach no credence to reports of the Cavalier sentiments of the Washington Family. That they showed any excessive zeal for the monarchy under the Stuarts, may be doubted. The want of love for power without principle was hereditary in the family of the Spencers, with which family they were allied ; and this was shown in the letters of Lord Spencer to General Washington, recommending Steuben to the command of the American Army. The Washington and Fairfax relationship, moreover, conspicuously confirms kindred political sentiments. Saxon opposition to the Norman rule in England took the form of liberalism, and throughout all the civil commotions this element prevailed, until a *Saxon* dynasty was re-established under George I. Earl Farrars, who married Elizabeth Washington, was a Shirley, and the Shirleys of the Peak, Derby-

shire, intermarried with the Vernons, of Haddon Hall.
" Mount Vernon " formularizes these antecedents, and it
accounts for Admiral Vernon's kindness to Lawrence
Washington, while the latter was in the service of his
country, under the Admiral's command, at the siege of
Carthagena.

From the time of the " Wars of the Roses " until their removal to America,—a period of about five centuries,—these
antecedents of the Washingtons bore sway. They had
weight also in our colonial acts and regulations. They
formed the Confederative system. They united the colonies
and gave national independence to the Government. They
illustrate the idea that men may die, but principles must
survive. Washington was not a lawyer nor politician.
He was simply the arm of strength, which supported legislative enactments — the embodiment in force of those
thoughts in council, which had strength enough for success, if they did not solve for all time the problems of
Government.

In the reign of Edward III. (1327 to 1377), we find the
De Wessingtons mingling in chivalrous scenes in Durham.
The name of Sir Stephen De Wessyngton is on a list of
Knights (noble chevaliers) who were to tilt at a tourna-
ment at Dunstable in 1334. He bore for his device a
golden rose on an azure field. (*Collectanea Typographica et
Genealogica*, table IV. page 395.)

He was soon called to exercise his arms on a sterner
field. In 1346, Edwardaw, his son (the Black Prince being
absent with the armies in France), King David of Scotland, invaded Northumberland with a powerful army.
Queen Philippa, who had remained in England as Regent,
immediately took the field, calling the northern prelates
and nobles to join her standard. They all hastened to
obey. Among the prelates was Hatfield, the Bishop of
Durham. The sacred banner of St. Cuthbert was again
displayed, and the chivalry of the palatinate assisted at the

famous battle of Nevil's cross, near Durham, in which the Scottish army was defeated and King David taken prisoner.

Queen Philippa hastened with a victorious train to cross the sea at Dover, and join King Edward in his camp before Calais. The prelate of Durham accompanied her. His military train consisted of three Baronets, forty-eight Knights, one hundred and sixty-four esquires, and eighty Archers, on horseback. (*Collin's Ecclesiastical History*, Book VI., Century XIV.) They all arrived to witness the surrender of Calais in 1346, on which occasion Queen Philippa distinguished herself by her noble interference in saving the lives of its patriot citizens.

Such were the warlike and stately scenes in which the de Wessyngtons were called to mingle by their feudal duties as Knights of the palatinate. A few years after the last event (1350), Sir William de Washington (page 36), at that time lord of the manor of Wessyngton, had license to settle it and the village upon himself, his wife, and " his own right heirs." He died in 1367, and his son and heir, William (page 41), succeeded to the estate.

1400. But though the name of " de Wessyngton " no longer figured on the chivalrous roll of the palatinate, it continued for a time to flourish in the cloisters. In the year 1416, John de Wessyngton, probable brother of William Washington (page 43), was elected prior of the Benedictine Convent attached to the Cathedral. The monks of this convent had been licensed by Pope George VII. to perform the solemn duties of the Cathedral in place of secular clergy, and William the Conqueror had ordained that the priors of Durham should enjoy all the liberties, dignities, and honors of the Abbots, should hold their lands and churches in their own hands and free disposition, and have the Abbot's seat on the left side of the choir—thus taking the rank of every one except the Bishop (*Dugdale, Monasticon Anglicanum*, T. I. page 231, London edition, 1846).

In the course of three centuries and upwards, which had

since elapsed, these honors and privileges had been subject to repeated dispute and encroachment, and the prior had nearly been elbowed out of the Abbot's chair by the Archdeacon. John de Wessyngton was not a man to submit tamely to such infringements of his rights. He forthwith set himself up as the champion of his priory, and in a learned tract, *De Juribus et Possessionibus Ecclesiæ Dunelin*, established the validity of the long-controverted claims, and fixed himself firmly in the Abbot's chair. His success in this controversy gained him much renown among his brethren of the cowl, and in 1426 he presided at the general chapter of the order of St. Benedict, held at Northampton.

The stout prior of Durham had other disputes with the bishop and the secular clergy, touching his ecclesiastical functions, in which he was equally victorious, and several tracts remain in manuscript in the dean and chapter's library ; weapons hung up in the church armory as memorials of his polemical battles.

Finally, after fighting divers good fights for the honor of his priory, and filling the Abbot's chair for thirty years, he died, to use an ancient phrase, "in all the odor of sanctity," in 1446, and was buried like a soldier on his battlefield, at the door of the north aisle of his church, near to the altar of St. Benedict. On his tombstone was an inscription in brass (now unfortunately obliterated), which may have set forth the valiant deeds of this "Washington of the Cloisters."

By this time the primitive stock of the de Wessyngtons had separated into divers branches, holding estates in the various parts of England, some distinguishing themselves in the learned professions, others receiving Knighthood for public services. Their names are to be found honorably recorded in County histories, or engraved on Monuments in time-worn churches and cathedrals, those garnering places of English worthies.

By degrees the Seignorial sign of "*de*" disappeared before

the family surname, which also varied from Wessyngton to Wassington, Wasshington, and finally to Washington (*Hutchinson's Durham*, vol. 2, *passim*). A parish in the county of Durham bears the name as last written, and in this probably the Ancient manor of Wessyngton was situated. There is another parish of the name in the county of Sussex (Bardolf, *Dugdale*, 681).

Robert Washington (page 65) and his wife Elizabeth (page 66), spent their last days at Brington, Northamptonshire, both dying in 1622, justifying the words found on their epitaph : " After they lived lovingly together many years in this parish."

MEMORIALS IN THE CHURCH AT BRINGTON, WHERE THE WASHINGTONS WERE BURIED.

The tombstone in the nave marks the last resting place of Robert and Elizabeth Washington, who both died in 1622. The inscription is on a brass plate let into the stone :

" Here lies interred yᵉ bodies of Elizabeth Washington, Widdowe, who changed this life for immortalitie yᵉ 19th of March, 1622.

"As also yᵉ body of Robert Washington, gent., her late husband, sonne of Robert Washington of Sulgrave, in yᵉ County of Northampton, who depted this life yᵉ 10th of March, 1622, after they lived lovingly together many yeares in this parish."

" Below the inscription there is a brass shield let into the stone, which has still greater interest. It represents the Washington Family Escutcheon : 'Argent, two bars gules ; in chief, three mullets of the second,' as it is described in Heraldric phraseology ; or, in simpler language : 'On a shield of silver (or white), two red bars ; and in chief (the upper third of the shield), three stars, also red.'

" In this shield, therefore, we have the origin of the National Flag of America, and the stars and stripes were indeed copied from General Washington's signet ring."

1622. Mr. Robert Washington (page 65), was buried March yᵉ 11th.

1622. Mrs. Elizabeth Washington (page 66), widow, was buried March yᵉ 20th.

MEMORIAL IN BRINGTON CHURCH, NORTHAMPTONSHIRE.

" A tombstone in the chancel covers the remains of Laurence Washington (page 78), who died in 1616." The inscription reads as follows :

" HERE LIETH THE BODI OF LAURENCE
WASHINGTON SONNE AND HEIRE OF
ROBERT WASHINGTON OF SOOLGRAVE
IN THE COUNTIE OF NORTHAMTON
ESQUIER WHO MARRIED MARGARET
THE ELDEST DAUGHTER OF WILLIAM
BUTLER OF TEES IN THE COUNTIE
OF SUSSEXE ESQUIER WHO HAD ISSU
BY HER 8 SONNS AND 9 DAUGHTERS
WHICH LAURENCE DECEASED THE 13
OF DECEMBER A DNI 1616
Those that by chance or choyce
of this hast sight
Know life to death resignes
as day to night ;
But as the sunns retorne
Revives the day
So Christ shall us
Though turnde to dust & clay."

" Above the inscription is chiselled in stone, the Arms of the Washington and Butler Families."

"The Parish register records that a child of Laurence Washington (page 79), named Gregory (page 92), was baptized and buried in Brington, 16 Jan., 1607." It also contains the following :

" 1616. Mr. Laurence Washington was buried the 15th day of December."

HERE LIES INTERRED Yᵉ BODIES OF ELIZAB. WASHINGTON WIDDOWE WHO CHANGED THIS LIFE FOR IMORTALLITIE Yᵉ 19ᵗʰ OF MARCH 1622. AS ALSO Yᵉ BODY OF ROBERT— WASHINGTON GENT. HER LATE HVSBAND SECOND SONNE OF ROBERT WASHINGTON OF SOLGRAVE IN Yᵉ COUNTY OF NORTH: Esqᵢ WHO DEPTED THIS LIFE Yᵉ 10ᵗʰ OF MARCH 1622 AFTER THEY LIVED LOVINGLY TOGETHER

WASHINGTON MEMORIALS NEAR NORTHAMPTON.

1 and 4. Inscription and Shield of one of Washington's Ancestors in Brington Church, Northamptonshire, the Shield showing the supposed Original of the "Stars and Stripes."—A. House at Little Brington formerly occupied by Washington's Ancestors.—8. Brington Church, containing the Graves of Lawrence Washington and Robert Washington, Direct Ancestors of President Washington.

" 1620. Mr. Philip Custis and Miss Amy Washington (page 90), were married August 8."

WASHINGTON MEMORIALS IN NORTHAMPTONSHIRE.

" Of all the places of interest visited by the Royal Arch-æological Institute on the occasion of a visitation to North-ampton, in 1877, few could have presented more points of attraction than the tombs and other memorials of the WASHINGTON Family, still to be seen at Brington, (about six miles from Northampton).

" In the year 1532, and again in 1545, there was a Lau-rence Washington, Mayor of Northampton (page 52). He was the son of John Washington, of Warton, Lancashire, and a member of Grey's Inn. Afterward, however, he relin-quished the profession of the law and settled in North-ampton, where he rose to great influence. His wife was sister of Sir Thomas Kitson, a merchant and Alderman of London, whose daughter had been espoused by Sir John Spencer, of Althrop. In 1538 he obtained a grant of the manor and lands of Sulgrave, Northamptonshire, together with other estates, which until then had belonged to the monastery of St. Andrews, at Northampton. Retiring to Sulgrave, he died there in 1584, at a ripe old age. Two generations of Washingtons only retained possession of Sulgrave—Robert (page 65) and Laurence (page 68), sons of the grantee, being obliged to sell it and retire to Bring-ton, where he would be under the protection of his kins-men, the Spencers. The house in Little Brington is still shown where he is supposed to have lived. Over the door is the inscription : ' The Lord giveth, the Lord taketh away : Blessed be the name of the Lord.—*Constructa*, 1606.'

" The parish register of Little Brington, Northampton-shire, among other Washington records, contains the bap-tism and burial of a son of (page 92) Lawrence Washington, son of Robert (page 65), in 1606-7. The latter died in 1616, and his remains lie buried in the chancel of the parish church. One of our illustrations represents the shield bearing his arms, impaled with those of his wife, Margaret, engraven on his tombstone. Near to him, but in the nave, is the grave of his brother Robert (page 65). It also bears a shield on brass, showing the same blazon (argent, two brass gules, in chief three mullets of the second). This shield, of which we also give a sketch, exhibits, even more plainly than the other, the characteristics which have caused the device to be regarded as the origin of the American flag—namely, the five-pointed stars and the alternate red and white stripes. Robert Washington died without issue. Laurence, however, had a large family. The first son was Sir William Washington, of Packington, Lieccestershire (page 87), who wedded Agnes or Anne, a half-sister of George Villiars, Duke of Buckingham, through whose influence the fortunes of the family seem to have revived. The second son was Sir John (see page 88). Repeated mention is made of him in the household books of Althrop, where he and several of his brothers were frequent guests. He was married to Mary, daughter of Philip Custis, of Islip, Northamptonshire, by whom he had three sons. A mural tablet to her memory still exists in the Islip church.

"The Washingtons did not stay at Brington many years. The depression of their fortunes was but temporary. They recovered wealth and position by a singular marriage. Sir William Washington (see page 87) married a half-sister of George Villiers, afterward Duke of Buckingham, an alliance which at that time was not beyond the pretensions of the Washingtons. They appear in consequence soon to have risen again to affluence and prosperity.

"Colonel Edward Apsley, of the Parliamentary Army, son of Sir Edward, had a sister Alice, who married Sir John Butler, son and heir of Sir Oliver Butler, of Teston,

Kent. His widow married secondly, George Fenwick, of Brinkburn, county Northumberland, a colonel in the army of Oliver Cromwell. They had two daughters.

"Lady Alice Butler is called on the tombstones in Connecticut, wife of George Fenwick. Colonel Fenwick returned to England, and married Kate, daughter of Sir Arthur Haselrig. She survived her husband and married, thirdly, Philip Babbington, member of Parliament for Berwick. The last family becomes associated with Washington. On the 36th of Henry VIII., 1544, there was granted to Thomas Babbington, to be held in Capite in Wigwall; the Manor of *Wassington* in Crick Derbey, late the property of Darley Abbey, and tithes of hay and corn in Wassington. Thomas Babbington, second son of Sir John, by heiress of Ward, was Chief Justice of the King's Bench, 1423. He had four sons—Anthony and three others. The great grandson of Anthony was beheaded in 1586. There was something pathetic in the plea of George Babbington, for the manor of Washington and the other property after this execution. 'Lord D'Arcy, my uncle, promised to re-acquire the estates and protect the heirs.' His lordship's mutilated form filled a bloody grave, and the intended beneficence was thwarted. He married a sister of Sir Thomas Kitson, and another sister married, about 1499, John Washington (page 47). Cresacre More, great grandson of Sir Thomas More, Lord Chancellor (connection of Richard Washington [page 75], of Ardwick le Street), married a daughter of Sir Thomas Gage, of Furles, Sussex. Colonel Henry Gage married a granddaughter of Sir Peter Warren, and the sister of James De Lancey, of New York, was Sir Peter's wife. D'Arcy Washington (page 83), mentioned in Thorsby's *History of Leeds*, derived his name from this source, *i. e.*, D'Arcy.

Mary Woombwell, county of York, wife of William Woombwell. Her mother was Jane, daughter of Mathew Wentworth, of Monk Bretton. William Woombwell's daughter married, about 1630, Richard Washington, of Ardwick le Street (page 84).

We shall see that there was a cord that bound the existence of these families together in Kent. After James I. confiscated the manor of Bretton, the Woombwells, Washingtons, and Wentworths appear, as per Will of Hovendon, previously quoted, and there can be little doubt, that John Wentworth, Rector of Snargate, Kent, 1770, was a descendant of Philip.

Thorsby, in his *History of Leeds*, presented to his readers, a pedigree of the Washingtons of Ardwick le Street. In that work it is asserted that D'Arcy Washington (page 83) married Anne, daughter of Mathew Wentworth, of Bretton, 9 James I. (1611).

"Will of John Hovendon, in the Prerogative Court of Canterbury, dated 26th December, 1629, proved 17th March, by Thomas Radcliff. He locates himself in University College, Oxford, England, and mentions, ' My sister, Mary Hovenden £100, now in hands of my father-in-law, Thomas Radcliff, sole executor. My friends, Thos. Bancroft, Master, University College, and *Richard Washington*, overseers.' He gives rings to Richard Washington (page 84), Mr. Philip Wentworth, and others."

"Thomas Hovenden, of Canterbury and Cranbrook. Will witnessed by Robert Washington " (page 90).

John Washington (page 88) is first entered in the Althorp household books, as Mr. Washington, and is so styled in January, 1622–3, but in the following March, and afterwards, he is called "Sir John Washington." There is a memorial of this Sir John, at Islip, Northamptonshire. In the church there is the following epitaph : "Here lieth the body of Dame Mary ; wife unto Sir John Washington, daughter of Philip Curtis, Gent., who had issue by her sayd husbande, three sonns, Mordaunt, John and Phillipe, deceased, the 1 of Janu. 1624." It will be recollected that in the Brington Register there is the record of the marriage of a Philip Curtis with Amy Washington (page 90), the latter being a sister of Sir John (page 88), so that both brother and sister were married into the same family. Sir John's connection with the Islip epitaph is shown by the fact that he was frequently accompanied to Althorp by Mordaunt Washington (page 98).

When the Civil War broke out, the Washingtons took the side of the King, and fought for him with all that bravery of devotion which appears to have been a characteristic of the males of the family. The name of Sir Henry Washington (page 97) is well known to those who are acquainted with the history of the Civil War ; how he led the storming party at Bristol and defended the city of Worcester against the parliamentary forces, in 1646.

We have it on the contemporary authority of Lloyd, that this Colonel Washington was so well known for his bravery that he became a proverb in the army.

Lord Astley, who had succeeded Colonel Sandys as Governor of Worcester, being taken prisoner and confined at Warwick, Sir Henry Washington was made Governor and Colonel in his absence. In the Herald's College it appears that the last entry of this gentleman's family was made there in 1618, at which time the name of Henry Washington, son and heir of Sir William Washington, of Packington, in the county of Leicester, occurs. His mother was half-sister to the famous George Villiers, Duke of Buckingham, which accounts for his great attachment to the King.

In the appendix to the second volume of Nash's *History of Worcestershire*, there is a highly interesting narrative of the siege of Worcester, drawn from the diary of a gentleman who was in the city during the siege. The conduct of Governor Washington appears throughout to the greatest advantage. His spirit and firmness are displayed in his first letter to General Fairfax, who demanded a surrender

20

on the 16th May, 1646, eleven days after the King had escaped in disguise from Oxford.

"It is acknowledged by your books, and by report out of your own quarters, that the King is in some of your armies. That granted, it may be easy for you to procure His Majesty's commands for the disposal of this garrison. Till then I shall make good the trust reposed in me. As for conditions, if I shall be necessitated, I shall make the best I can. The worst I know and fear not, if I had, the profession of a soldier had not been begun, nor so long continued, by your Excellency's humble servant,

"HENRY WASHINGTON, Colonel."

The King's fortunes were now desperate, but the siege was maintained, even against all hope, for nearly three months, when honorable conditions were granted.

Colonel Henry Washington is mentioned by Clarendon as having distinguished himself at the taking of Bristol, in 1643, three years before the siege of Worcester.

Though the division led on by Grandison was beaten (he himself being hurt); and the other by Colonel Bellasis had no better fortune; yet Colonel Washington, with a less party, was soon victorious.

Joseph Washington (page 100), an eminent lawyer of Gray's Inn, London, Thorsby says, "Is to be remembered among the authors." He wrote the first volume of "Modern Reports;" "Observations upon the Ecclesiastical Jurisdiction of the Statutes to 1687;" a translation of part of "Lucian's Dialogues," and other tracts.

Toland says that he was the translator of Milton's *Defensis pro populo Anglicana*, in reply to Salamasius. (*Life of Milton*, p. 84.) The translator's name is not prefixed to the first edition; but the publisher states, in a advertisement "that the person who took the pains to translate it did it partly to gratify one or two of his friends, without any design of making it public, and is since deceased."

This edition was printed in 1693, and it is probable that Joseph Washington died not long before. The translation is that usually printed with Milton's prose writings. The interest he took in this performance indicates the tenor of his political sentiments, as well as the fact, mentioned by Hunter, that he was an intimate friend of the celebrated Lord Somers.

He was buried in the Bencher's Vault, of the Inner Temple. He was of the Ardwick le Street family, and son of Robert Washington (page 96), a wealthy merchant, who lived and died at Anstrope Hall, near Leeds, Yorkshire.

"Col. William Augustine Washington, a distinguished cavalry officer of the Revolution, was born in Stafford county, Virginia, 28 Feb., 1752, and died at Charleston, South Carolina, 6 March, 1810. Designed for the Church by his father, Bailey Washington, probably descended from Laurence (page 101), brother of Col. John Washington, of Bridge's Creek, Virginia. His attainments as a scholar were respectable. A captain under Mercer, in the Virginia line. He distinguished himself at Long Island, also at Trenton, New Jersey (where he was severely wounded), and at Princeton. He was Major and Lieutenant-Colonel of Baylor's dragoons, and present at its surprise by Gen. Grey, at Tappan, in 1778. He was active in command of a light corps in the vicinity of Charleston, South Carolina, in 1779–80, and was worsted at Monk's Corner and at Lancan's Ferry ; attached to the division of Gen. Morgan, he carried by stratagem the fort at Rugely's Mill, capturing a large force ; and for his valor at the Cowpens, where he commanded the cavalry, and contributed much to the victory. He had a personal encounter with Col. Tarleton, both being wounded, received from Congress a silver medal and sword. He was active in Greene's celebrated retreat ; was conspicuous at Guilford ; behaved gallantly at Hobkirk's Hill and also at Eutaw Springs, where he was taken prisoner, remaining till the close of the war. He then married and settled at Sandy Hill, near Charleston, South Carolina, the family seat of his wife, Jane Elliott, where he was a member of the Legislature, but declined being a candidate for Governor as he could not make a speech. Upon Washington's appointment as commander of the army by President Adams in 1798, he selected Col. Washington as one of his staff, with the rank of Brigadier-General. Tall, strong, and active in person, he was taciturn and modest in deportment, and exceedingly hospitable, generous and benevolent. His son William died at Charleston, South Carolina, in March, 1830, aged 45."

There were a number of Washingtons in Virginia, who were unknown to General Washington as blood relatives. He makes mention of some two or three in his will, viz. : " To the acquaintances and friends of my juvenile years, Laurence Washington and Robert Washington, of Chotank," &c. " To my friends Eleanor Stuart, Hannah Washington, of Fairfield, and Elizabeth Washington, of Hayfield," &c. (page 145).

They were, doubtless, descendants of Laurence Washington, of Bridge's Creek—the brother who emigrated with John in 1659.

Edward Washington, born about 1745, who lived and died in Truro Parish, county of Fairfax, whose will is given below, dated June 30, 1791, cotemporary with General George Washington, was probably a great-grandson of the above Laurence (page 101), and grandson of his son John Washington (page 111). He had a sister named Sarah Washington, named in the will of his son, who was living Apr. 8, 1813, on the east side of Polrick Run, Fairfax county.

WILL OF EDWARD WASHINGTON, OF TRURO PARISH, FAIRFAX COUNTY, VIRGINIA.

In the name of God, Amen ! I, Edward Washington, of Truro Parish, and county of Fairfax, being of weak body,

but of sound sence and memory, thanks to God, do make and ordain this to be my last will and testament. Imp^s I give and bequeath to my son Edward Washington, all my Estate, real and personal, forever, and after his decease to be disposed of as he shall think proper.

Lastly. I nominate, constitute and appoint, my son Edward Washington, to be my whole and sole Executor of this my last will and testament, ratifying and confirming this, and disannulling all former and other will and testaments.

In testimony whereof, I have hereunto set my hand and affixed my seal, this 30 day of June, one thousand seven hundred and ninety-one.

EDWARD WASHINGTON.   [SEAL.]

Signed, sealed and delivered, in the presence of
JOSHUA COFFER.
JAMES HEREFORD.
JOSEPH REED.

P. S.—It is my desire that there be no appraisement of my Estate.

At a Court continued and held for the County of Fairfax, 18th of September, 1792. This will was presented in Court, and proved by the oaths of James Hereford and Joseph Reed, and ordered to be recorded.

Teste :
P. WAGONER, Clerk.

A true Copy.   Teste :
F. W. RICHARDSON, Deputy Clerk,
21 Nov., 1878.

There were probably only three children of above Edward Washington. His son was named Edward, born about 1770, who lived also in Fairfax county, Virginia ; a daughter who married Mr. Sanford ; and another, who married Mr. Manly. The son's will was dated, 8 April, 1813, and he probably died soon afterward. He was a widower at date of will, as no wife is mentioned therein. His children were as named :

> MARGARET SANFORD WASHINGTON, born in Fairfax county, Virginia, about 1795.
>
> JOHN WASHINGTON, born in Fairfax county, Virginia, about 1797.
>
> MARY ANN WASHINGTON, born in Fairfax county, Virginia, about 1800.
>
> ELIZABETH CATHARINE WASHINGTON, born in Fairfax county, Virginia, about 1802.
>
> EDWARD SANFORD WASHINGTON, born in Fairfax county, Virginia, about 1805.
>
> GEORGE WILLIAM WASHINGTON, born in Fairfax county, Virginia, about 1807.
>
> JOSEPH HOUGH WASHINGTON, born in Fairfax county, Virginia, about 1810.

He had a niece, Peggy Sanford, whose father was probably Edward Sanford, one of the Executors of his will, and brother-in-law, from whom one of his sons was named.

He had a nephew, John .H. Manly. His aunt was Sarah Washington, to whom he gave the land whereon she then resided, "lying on the east side of Polrick Run, Fairfax county, Virginia, and his own household furniture and stock, &c., on farm."

As Margaret, the eldest child, was unmarried in 1813, she was probably born about 1795, and the other children at corresponding dates, all young.

WILL OF EDWARD WASHINGTON, OF FAIRFAX COUNTY, VIRGINIA, DATED 8 APRIL, 1813.

"In the name of God, Amen! I, Edward Washington, of the county of Fairfax, and State of Virginia, being sick and weak of body, but of sound mind and disposing memory, do make this my last will and testament hereby revoking all former wills by me hertofore made.

Item. It is my will and desire that my body be decently buried at the discretion of my executors hereinafter named, and that all my just debts, due either by bond, note or open account be by them paid without any regard to the act of limitation.

Item. I give and bequeath unto my daughter, Margaret Sanford Washington, the following slaves with their future increase, To wit: Belinda, Tom Nokes, Joshua, Jemima (wife of Dennis Seales), Harriet, daughter of said Jemima and Henson (son of Fanny), also a bay filly rising two years old.

Item. I give and bequeath unto my son, John Washington, the following slaves with their future increase, to wit: Old Lett, Dennis, Corner, Doctor, Susanna, Winny, and Ann, as also one half of the tract of land whereon I now live (including the mansion house, barn, stables, &c.), to be equally divided agreeable to quantity and quality.

Item. I give and bequeath unto my daughter, Mary Ann Washington, the following slaves, with their future increase, to wit: Jane, John (son of old Winny), Charles Seales, Fanny, Flora, Caroline, Solomon, and Jemima, daughter of Fanny.

Item. I give and bequeath unto my daughter, Elizabeth Catherine Washington, the following slaves, with their future increase, to wit: Daniel, Frank, Ned, Sarah, Harriot, daughter of Fanny, Cato Seales, and John, son of Sarah.

Item. I give and bequeath unto my son, Edward Sanford Washington, the following slaves, with their future increase, to wit: James Straight, Old Harry, Sandy, Kitty, Seales, Linny, Dennis Seals, and Nathaniel, also one half of the tract of land whereon I now live to be divided as before directed.

Item. I give and bequeath unto my son, George William Washington, the following slaves, with their future increase, to wit: Jesse, Duke, Reuben, Ella, Letty Seals,

Jemima Seals, and Alfred ; also two lotts of land in the county of Prince William, and State of Virginia, designated in the general Plotts by Lotts Nos. 1 and 2, containing 400 acres, be the same more or less, which said lotts was purchased by me of Wm. H. Dorsey.

Item. I give and bequeath unto my son Joseph Hough Washington, the following slaves with their future increase, to wit, Malbourne, Isaac, David, Sinah and her child, Rosetta, Rose, Thomas, Person, Julius and Milly, also two lotts of land purchased by me of Wm. H. Dorsey, in the County of Prince William, and State of Virginia, lying near Baconrace meeting-house, and adjoining the lands of Hezekiah Fairfax, Designated in the General Plott by lotts No. 15 and 16, containing 271 acres, be the same more or less.

Item. It is my further will and desire, that if any of my children herein named should die before they arive at full age or without lawful issue, that in such case, whatever they may die seized of, shall be equally divided between my Surviving children or their heirs.

Item. It is my will and desire that my niece Peggy Sanford, or her heirs, keep and peaceably enjoy the negro girl Lett, with her present and future increase, which girl I gave her heretofore, and which she has been possessed of for several years.

Item. I give and bequeath unto my nephew John H. Manley all my wearing apparel of every description.

Item. It is further my will and desire, that the land whereon my aunt, Sarah Washington, now lives, lying on the east side of Polrick run, in the County of Fairfax and State of Virginia, and adjoining the lands of Doddridge Pitt Chichester, and the land generally known by the name of the Ravensworth tract, for which there is a suit now pending in the Superior Court of the County of Fairfax, be sold when recovered, also my household and kitchen furniture, my stock of horses, a bay filly excepted, cattle, hogs, and sheep, Plantation and Farming utensils, and the crop, and it is also my will and desire that my Exors. do as soon as convenient, collect all monies that is now due, and that will become due on the first day of January, one thousand eight hundred and fourteen, which monies, with the amount of the sales, is to be applied to the discharge of my just debts. Reserving in the hands of my Executors after such debts are discharged, a sufficiency for the support of my children, and other necessary Purposes during this present year; and then the balance (if any) to be equally divided and laid out in Bank Stock, or otherwise as may be deemed most advisable for the benefit of my three daughters, namely : Margarett Sandford Washington, Mary Ann Washington, and Elizabeth Catharine Washington, and it is further my will and desire that each and every one of my children may have their smith's work done gratis by the Black Smiths belonging to my estate, herein devised, as long as they may be convenient or wish it.

And lastly, it is my will and sincere desire that my much esteemed friends, Edward Sanford, Doddridge Pitt Chichester and Reasin Offitt, do act and I do hereby appoint them my whole and Sole Executors to this my last will and testament. In witness whereof, I have hereunto set my hand and affixed my seal, this 8th day of April, one thousand eight hundred and thirteen.

EDW^D WASHINGTON. [SEAL.]

Signed, sealed, and acknowledged in the presence of Sinah Ellen Lee, Ann Talbott, Reazin Haislip, Mary Offitt.

N. B.—I do hereby authorize my Executors to proceed at their discretion to getting Timber, Tan bark, &c., off of any lands herein devised for the express purpose of discharging my just debts, and that it shall be a joint expence between all of my children.

EDW^D WASHINGTON.

Witness: ANN TALBOTT, SINAH ELLEN LEE.

At a Court held for Fairfax county, the 21st day of June, 1813.

This last will and testament of Edward Washington, dec., was presented in court by Edward Sandford, one of the Executors therein named, who made oath thereto, and the same being proved by the oaths of Ann Talbott and Sinah Ellen Lee, is admitted to record, and the said Exor, having performed what the law requires, a certificate is granted him for obtaining a probat thereof in due form.

Teste: WM. MOSS, Clerk.

A true copy. Teste:

F. W. RICHARDSON, Deputy Clerk.

1878, Nov. 21.

Laurence Washington, of Belmont, Fairfax county, Virginia, probably a near relative of the first Edward, above (page 308), and great-grandson of the first Laurence. Also probably the Laurence Washington, legatee of a "gold-headed cane," in General Washington's will (page 145), died at Belmont, Fairfax county, Virginia, probably about the beginning of the year 1800, as his will is dated Nov. 15, 1799, one month previous to the death of General Washington (14 Dec., 1799).

WILL OF LAURENCE WASHINGTON, OF BELMONT, FAIRFAX COUNTY, VIRGINIA, DATED 15 NOV., 1799.

In the name of God, Amen. I, Laurence Washington, of Belmont, in the County of Fairfax, and State of Virginia, being of sound mind and memory, do make this my last will and testiment in manner and form following. Imprimis. I give to my niece Ann Thompson, wife of Wm. Thompson, of Colchester, the tract of land whereon I live, called Belmont, and containing about a 1000 acres, to hold the same during her natural life, without impeachment of waste, and after her death I give the same to her son, Robert Townshend Thompson, and his heirs, but in case he should die before he arrives at the age of 18 years, then, and in that case I give the said tract of land (after the death of his mother), to his two sisters, Elizabeth Lund Thompson and Catharine Foote Thompson, and their heirs, to be equally divided between them.

Item. I give to the said Ann Thompson all the slaves and furniture I bought of her husband, the said Wm. Thompson and described in the conveyance from him to me, to hold the same as her absolute property.

Item. I give the said Ann Thompson the following slaves, Joe, Aaron, Isaac, Bob, Will, Winkey, Ned, Peter, Harry, Sukey, and Alice, to hold the same until the 25th day of Dec., in the year one thousand eight hundred and one, after which period it is my will and desire that the said slaves and each of them shall be liberated and remain free from Bondage for the remainder of their lives.

Item. I give to the said Ann Thompson the following young slaves, Davy, Hanson, Paris, Anna, Berkley, Titus, James, Jenny, John and Jeffrey, to hold the same until they arrive at the age of 25 years, respectively, after which time it is my will and desire that the last mentioned slaves, and each of them respectively, shall be liberated and remain free from bondage during the remainder of their lives : And I direct my Executor at the time of proving my will, to exhibit a list of their present ages, and have the same recorded, in order to enable them hereafter to prove the time of their liberation.

Item. I give to the said Ann Thompson after payment of my just debts all the residue of my Estate not hereinbefore mentioned, to hold the same as her absolute property.

Item. It is my will and express intention that none of the property above given to the said Ann Thompson, shall be subject to the disposal of her husband Wm. Thompson or to the payment of his debts present or future, but be held by her in her own right as fully to all intents and purposes as if she were a feme sole, it being intended by me as a certain support for her and her children.

Item. I nominate and appoint my nephew Haywood Foote Sole Executor of this my this my last will and testament revoking all others by me heretofore made. In witness whereof, I have hereunto set my hand and seal the 15th day of Nov., Anno Domini 1799.

L. WASHINGTON. [SEAL.]

Signed, Sealed, published and declared by the testator as and for his last will and testament, in presence of us, who, at his request and in his presence subscribed our names as witnesses thereto Lee Massey, Eliz. Washington, Robt. Washington, Alexander Wade.

At a Court held for Fairfax county, the 16th day of December, 1799.

The last will and testament of Laurence Washington dec., was presented in court by Haywood Foote, the Executor therein named, who made oath thereto, and the same being proved by the oaths of Lee Massey, Elizabeth Washington and Alexander Wade, witnesses thereto, is ordered to be recorded.

And the said Executor having performed what the law requires, a certificate is granted him for obtaining a probate thereof in due form.

Teste :	G. DENEALE, C. C.
A true Copy.	Teste :
	F. W. RICHARDSON,
	D. C.
	21 Nov., 1878.

In the name of God amen. I Laurence Washington, of Truro Parish in Fairfax County & Colony of Virginia, gent. Knowing the uncertainty of this transitory life, and being in sound & disposing mind and memory do make this my last will & testament, hereby revoking & disannulling all other wills and testaments by me at any time heretofore made. Imprimis. My will and desire is that a proper vault for interment may be made on my home plantation, wherein my remains together with my three children may be decently placed & to serve for my wife & such other of the family as may desire it. Item. My will & desire is that my funeral charges and respective debts be first paid & discharged out of such of my personal Estate as my Executors hereafter to be named shall think best and most advisable to be disposed of for that purpose. Item. My will & desire is that my loving wife, have the use, benefits and profits of all my lands on Little Hunting & Dog's Creeks in the Parish of Truro & County of Fairfax, with all the houses & edifices thereon during her natural life likewise the use, labour and profit arising from the one half of all my negroes, as my said wife & Executors may agree in dividing them. Negro Moll & her issue to be included in my wife's part of the said negroes. I also desire that my said wife may have the use of the lands surveyed on the south fork of Bull Skin in the County of Frederick during her natural life. But in case of my daughter Sarah dying without issue before her said mother, then I give & devise my said Bull Skin tract to my said wife to her & her heirs forever. Item. It is my will & desire that all my household goods & furniture with the liquors be appraised & valued by three persons, to be chosen by my wife & Executors, & that my wife have the liberty to choose any part of the said household goods & furniture to the amount of a full moiety, of the whole sum which they shall be appraised to, which part I give and bequeath to her and her heirs forever, the other moiety to be sold and the money arising applied towards the payment of my debts. Item. What I have herein devised and left to my wife I intend to be in lieu & instead of her right of dower, provided my wife according to her promise sells her several tracts of land near Salisbury plains, & applies the said money to the discharge of my debts due at the time of my death, but in case of her refusal then my will is that all my household furniture be sold & the whole amount applied towards the discharge of my debts.

Item. I give and bequeath to my daughter Sarah, & the heirs of her body lawfully begotten forever after my just debts are discharged all my real & personal Estate in Virginia & the Province of Maryland, not otherwise disposed of. But in case it should please God my said daughter should die without issue, it is then my will & desire that my Estate, both real & personal, be disposed of in the following manner. First. I give and bequeath unto my loving brother Augustine Washington & his heirs forever, all my stock, interest & Estate in the Principio, Accokeek, Kingsbury, Laconshire & No. East Iron works, in Virginia & Maryland reserving one third of the profits of the said works to be paid my wife as hereafter mentioned & two tracts of land lying & being in Frederick County which I purchased of Col. Cresap & Gerrard Pondegrass.

Second. I give & bequeath unto my loving brother George Washington & his heirs forever after the decease of my wife, all my lands in Fairfax Co. with the improvements thereon, & further it is my Will and desire that during the natural life of my wife that my said brother Geo. shall have the use of an equal share & proportion of all the. lands hereafter given & devised unto my brothers Samuel, John & Charles.

Third, I give and bequeath all those several tracts of land which I am possessed of & claim in the County of Frederick (except the tract on the S° fork of Bull Skin bequeathed to my wife & the two tracts purchased of Col. Cresap & Gerrard Pondegrass, devised unto my brother Augustine), unto my brothers Samuel, John & Charles reserving as above an equal proportion for my brother Geo. provided they Saml. John or Chas. pay or cause to be paid unto my & their sister Betty Lewis, the sum of one hundred and fifty pounds.

Fourth. My will also is that upon the death of any or all of my said brothers Geo. Saml. John & Chas. dying without lawful issue such lands as was given them or any of them in case of my said daughter's demise as aforesaid to become the property & right of my brother Augustine & his heirs.

Fifth. My further will & desire is that after the demise of my said wife the negro woman Moll & her increase be given unto my said brother Augustine, his heirs, Admors &c., & likewise give him an equal proportion with his other brothers of the other part of the negroes & personal Estate upon their paying my said wife one hundred pounds Sterling, my intent and meaning is that the said one hundred pounds sterling be paid by my said brothers to my said wife immediately, or soon after it may please God to remove by death my said daughter. Item. I further give and bequeath unto my loving wife during her natural life one full third part of the profits from the share I hold in all the Several Iron works, both in the Colony of Virginia and Maryland to be paid unto my said wife from time to time by my Executors, immediately upon notice given them by the partners residing in England of the annual amount of the profits to be paid either

in Bills or cash at the current exchange as she shall choose.
Item.   I give unto my brother, John Washington, fifty
pounds in lieu of the land taken from him by a suit at
law, by Capt. Maxmn. Robinson, after my debts are paid.
Item.   My will and desire is that my two tracts of land
one joining my wife's tract near Salisbury plain, the other
on a branch of Goose creek being 303 acres, my two lots
in the Town of Alexandria, with the edifices thereon, and
my share and interest in the Ohio Company all be sold by
my Executors and the money applied towards discharging my debts.   Also my arrears of half pay which Col.
Wilson the agent or Mr. Stuart his kinsman and clerk
be addressed for and money applied to the same use.
Item.   Whereas the purchasing negroes and land may
greatly tend to the advantage of my daughter, I therefore
fully empower my Executors to lay out the profits of my
Estate or any part thereof in lands and negroes at their discretion, *i. e.* I mean such part of my Estate as I have devised to my daughter Sarah which said several purchases
in case of her decease without issue shall be deemed and
accounted personal estate and be accordingly equally
divided among my brothers as above provided.   Item.   I
also desire that my just suit of complaint at law pending against Gersham Keys, of Frederick County for
breach of trust be effectually prosecuted by my Executors.
Item.   It is furthermore my will and desire that all my
Estate be kept together till the debts are discharged.
Item.   I give to my wife, my mother-in-law, and each of
my Executors a mourning ring.

Lastly.   I constitute and appoint the Honble Wm.
Fairfax and Geo. Fairfax Esqs., my said brothers Augustine and Geo. Washington, and my Esteemed friends Mr.
Nathl. Chapman and Major John Carlyle, Executors of
this my last will and testament, whereof I have hereunto
set my hand & seal this 20th day of June, one thousand

seven hundred & fifty two, in the 26th year of his majesty King George the second's reign.

LAWRENCE WASHINGTON. [SEAL.]

Signed, Sealed & delivered in the presence of us, Wm. Waite, Jno. North, Andrew W. Warren, Joseph Gound.

At a Court held for Fairfax County, Sep. 26, 1752. This last will & testament of Laurence Washington Gent. deceased, was presented in Court by the Honb^le Wm. Fairfax & Geo. William Fairfax Esqs., John Carlyle & Geo. Washington Gents. four of the Executors therein named, who made oath thereto according to law & being proved by the oaths of Wm. Waite, Jno. North, & Andrew Warren three of the witnesses is admitted to record & the said Executors performing what is usual in such cases, certificate is granted them for obtaining a probate in due form.

Teste :   JOHN GRAHAM, Clerk.

A true Copy.   Teste :

F. W. RICHARDSON,
Deputy Clerk,
1878, Nov. 21st.

WILL OF BUSHROD WASHINGTON (PAGE 183), OF MOUNT VERNON, VIRGINIA, DATED 19 JULY, 1828.

In the name of God Amen. I Bushrod Washington, of Mount Vernon, do make this my last will and testament hereby revoking all former wills by me made.

Imprimis. I give to my dear & most excellent wife, and her heirs the following negroes, viz. Ann, Luisa, & the children she now has, or may hereafter have, Sam, Jessy, Clark & Silvia his wife and Lucy their daughter, with all the future increase of the females, and also Jenny who I purchased from Mr. Turner.

Second. I give to my said wife during her life, the

21

whole of my Mt. Vernon land, except such parts thereof as will be hereafter given in trust for my nephew, Bushrod Washington, & also all the rest of my negroes of which I may die possessed or entitled to.

Third. I give to my said wife during her life the interest which may accrue after my death upon the debts now due or which may hereafter become due to me, as well as the dividends & interest which may accrue and to be declared upon my bank and road stock, upon my share in the Dismal Swamp Land Company, and all other stocks to which I may be entitled at the time of my death. I also give to her during her *her* life the whole of my household and kitchen furniture liquors, so much thereof as she may require for the use of her Family, riding carriages, horses, mules, cattle, sheep, hogs, plantation utensils, *waggons*, & carts, crops on hand & provisions laid in for the use of my family at the time of my death, or fattening at that time for such use. The use only of the above articles is intended to be given to my said wife during her life. Fourth. It is my will that as soon & as fast as the debts to me are collected, their amount, including whatever I may be entitled to receive from the estate of my deceased uncle General George Washington, in my own right or as assignee of Major Geo. Lewis, & on account of my commissions as Executor, and all rents due to me at the time of my death may be invested by my Executors in publick or other safe stocks, the interest whereof which may accrue during the life of my wife I give to her.

Fifth. I give to my said wife all the *all the furniture furniture* of her chamber, also the organ and pianos, books of musick & her Library of books kept by herself separate from mine, her Jewels and paraphernalia of every kind. And whereas there are certain prints hanging in some of the rooms which I have given and now confirm to my said wife, but which I cannot now describe, it is my will that she shall have such of them as she may by some writing under her hand, attested by one witness at least, and delivered during her life to one of my Executors, destinctly point out and describe unless my wife should dispose of the organ by will or by some other act during her life, I give the same to the person to whom I shall hereafter devise the mansion house as it would hardly suit any other room than that in which it now stands. Sixth. After the death of my said wife, I give to my nephew John A. Washington and to his heirs all that part of my Mount Vernon Land included within the following boundaries, to wit: Beginning at the Gum Spring on or near the line between Mr. Peake & myself and running thence the straight road along where the post and rail fence, ran to the gate leading in to the house, & pursuing the road passing the said Gate leading to the old Ferry house occupied lately by James Dorsey till it comes to the corner of the fence on the road leading to the Union farm barn, & thence along the fence and road leading to said barn to the first wattle fence made by Ja : Dorsey, (at which point it is my intention to put down a post.) and then along said wattle fence, rectangular or nearly so, to the last line to the creek, and so with the meanders of said creek, the river and hunting creek, including the fisheries and marshes to the beginning. I also give to my said nephew John, after the death of my said wife, all the green house and hot house plants and tools or instruments belonging to the gardens. I also give to my said nephew after the death of my said wife all the furniture belonging, & which at the time of my death may belong to, and be in the mansion house, Kitchen & other houses (not before given to my wife,) in which bequest to avoid disputes, I mean to include not only the standing furniture, but all the silver and plated ware, cut & other glass, pictures, prints, Table & bed furniture, & in short everything used and generally considered as furniture. All the Liquors of every kind remaining in the house at the death of my wife unused by her, I give to be equally divided between my nephews, Bushrod Washington, of Mt Zephire, Geo. C. Washington, John A. Washington, & Bushrod C. Washington. Seventh. After the death of my wife I give to my dear niece Mary Lee Herbert, & to her heirs, all that part of my Mount Vernon Tract of land. Beginning at the Knowl opposite to the old road, which formerly passed through the lower field of Muddy hole farm, at which on the north side of said road, are or were three red or Spanish oaks, marked as a corner, (which spot is mentioned in the Will of General Washington,) thence rectangular by a line of trees to the back line or outer boundary of the tract between General Thompson Mason, (now in possession of his son,) and myself, thence with that line easterly along the double ditch to the run of .Little Hunting creek, thence with that run to the gum spring, thence along the most northerly of the two roads being that leading to Major Lewis' mill, to the beginning.

Eighth. I give to my nephew George C. Washington, and his heirs, on my death all the land from the Gum spring aforesaid lying between the road leading to Mt Vernon until it comes to the lower end or corner of the field, (Nº 3.) in the plot made by Genl. Washington, amongst my Mount Vernon Land papers by James Nugent's quarter, that was, & the road leading from the said Gum spring to Major Lewis' mill 'till it comes to the inner and upper corner of my new ground 216 acre field & thence with the inner fence of the said new ground field, dividing the same from the Mt. Zephyr land to the lower end or corner of the said inner fence near the spring, thence easterly along the lower fence of Bushrod Washington Jr's new ground as it now runs and crosses the swamp 'till it comes to the edge of the woods on the easterly side of the swamp to an old road, & thence with said old road & along the edge of the woods to the lower fence of the said Bushrod Washington's Jr. meadow, below his house, and thence easterly following the fence as it now runs to the road at James Nugent's where there is a gate which said lines enclose the whole of the cleared land now in possession of the said Bushrod Washington, Jr. Also a small part of the swamp on the east side of the ditch to the edge of the woods, and also a small angle of wood land lying between the aforesaid two roads in which stood the school house. I also give to the said Geo. C. Washington in fee one half of the aforesaid new ground field being that half which lies to the northward of the red line run from the corner of the fence before mentioned, near the spring before mentioned called A in S^m Summers' plat & survey of the said new ground field to B, which half in the said plat is marked N°. 2, as by reference to said plat and survey, dated July, 1813, amongst the Mount Vernon Land papers will more fully appear. I also give to the said Geo. C. Washington & his heirs, one equal half part of the wood land adjoining the afs^d clear land to be laid off by a line running from the road leading from the Gum spring to the porter's lodges, northwesterly to the old road by the swamp & edge of the woods before mentioned in this clause, the said division to be according to the quantity : The other half of the wood land here intended extending to the road leading from the porter's lodge to the union farm gate being contiguous to that part of the Estate will be disposed of by a future clause of this will to the person to whom that part of the land will be devised. If any disagreements should arise respecting the lines of division mentioned in this Will, it is my desire that the parties concerned should submit the same to arbitration, and I declare that all the lands mentioned in this clause and devised to the said Geo. C. Washington, are given in trust to permit my nephew Bushrod Washington, Jr. his Brother, to receive the rents, issues and profits thereof *thereof* during his life and after his death then in trust for the children of the said Bushrod Washington, living at his death & their heirs equally to be divided.

Ninth. All the rest and residue of my Mt. Vernon estate not before disposed of, I give, after the death of my wife to be equally divided between my nephews George C. Washington & Bushrod C. Washington and their heirs. Tenth. I give my Ohio tract of land immediately on my death as follows, one equal fifth part to my nephew Geo. C. Washington, and his heirs, one other fifth part to my niece Mary L. Herbert and her heirs, one other fifth part to the said Geo. Washington, and his heirs to the same uses and under the same limitations as are mentioned in the 8th clause aforesaid, in respect to the part of the Mt. Vernon Land devised to him in trust, and the other two fifths I give to my nephews Jno. A. Washington & Bushrod C. Washington and their heirs equally to be divided : Should the said Geo. C. Washington, think it most to the advantage of the said Bushrod Washington Jr. to sell the part of the Ohio land hereby devised to him, in trust, he may do the same at public or private sale, on such terms as he may think best, the proceeds to be invested in some productive fund & the interest or dividends to be paid to the said Bushrod Washington Jr. during his life and after his death to be equally divided between the children of the said Bushrod Washington Jr. who shall be living at his death, their heirs and assigns.

Eleventh. I desire that all my law books in Philadelphia and a few others left with Mr. Berkham in Trenton may be removed to Mt. Vernon and together with those now there may remain in the study under the care of Jno. A. Washington, until Bushrod Washington Herbert son of my niece aforesaid arrives to the age of 21 & in case he should be educated & prepared to practice law I give all the said books to him ; But if at the above period he should not be destined to the bar or in case of his death before the said age, I desire the said books may be sold and the proceeds to sink into the residuum of my Estate. Wheaton's Reports belong to the United States and are to be delivered to the person authorized to receive them. Twelfth. After the death of my wife, I give all the rest and residue of my Estate real and personal in possession or expectancy and not by this will otherwise disposed of as follows; viz: one fifth part to my nephew Geo. C. Washington & his heirs, one other fifth. part to John A. Washington, my nephew and his heirs, one other fifth part to his brother Bushrod C. Washington and his heirs, another fifth part to my niece Mary L. Herbert, & her heirs, & the remaining fifth part to the said Geo. C. Washington & his heirs in trust for the same uses & under the same limitations as are mentioned in the eighth clause of this will in respect to the part of the Mt. Vernon land devised to him in trust for Bushrod Washington Jr. & his children. It is further my will that my nephew John A. Washington may be at liberty after my wife's death to take the Gardner Phil at his appraised value to be paid my Executors.

Thirteenth : All the papers and letter books devised to me by my uncle Genl. Washington, as well as the books in my study, other than law books, I give to my nephew, Geo. C. Washington, the books in the cases in the dining room, I give to my nephew John A. Washington.

Fourteenth. The sword left to me by Genl. Washington, I give to the aforesaid Geo. C. Washington under the same injunctions that it was bestowed to me. My gold watch I give to my friend Robt. Adams, of Philadelphia, knowing that he will appreciate the gift not for the intrinsic value of the article but because it was worn by the father of our country and afterwards by his friend : After the death of the said Robt. Adams I give the said watch to his son Bushrod. I give Cooke's Edition of Hogarth with the key, to my nephew John, and Alexander's victories to my nephew Bush : C. Washington. I also give to my said nephew John, the two Globes & the busts of Genl. Washington & Neckar. The bust of Paul Jones I give to Mr. Mumford for his musuem. My double barrel gun I give to my nephew Bushrod Washington Jr. and the pistols which belonged to, & were used by Genl. Washington, to Geo. C. Washington. Watts' Views I give to my highly valued friend Mr. Justice Story.

· Fifteenth. The debts due to me from the Estates of my deceased friends. Major Richard Blackburn & Thomas Blackburn, I hereby forgive and release.

Sixteenth: I give to West Ford the tract of land on Hunting creek adjoining Mr. Geo. Mason and that occupied by Dr. Peake, which I purchased from Nollet Herbert deceased, which was conveyed to him by Francis Adams, to him the said West Ford, & his heirs. Whatever appears by my Ledger to be due to said West Ford is to be paid to him, & it is my request that he will continue in his present situation & employment during the life of my wife provided she wishes him to do so on the terms he is now living with me.

Seventeenth : Whereas, as Trustee for the creditors of my nephew Bushrod Washington Jr. I have made advances greatly beyond the value of the property conveyed to me, besides being a considerable creditor of my said nephew, & entitled to come in as such under the deed of trust, & whereas the unsold trust property, that is to say the following negroes, Nat, Sue, Isaac, Joshua, Tetia & her 7 children, James, William, Nancy, John, Henry, Betsy & Judy. Also Eliza, & her two children Warren & Geo. Also Nanny, who have this day been valued by Laurence Lewis and Saml. Collard at the price of $2205, fall very short of the amount due to me from the said trust estate and for which the said property is answerable, I do hereby give the said negroes and the future increase of the females to my aforesaid nephew George C. Washington & his heirs upon the same trusts and under the same limitations as are mentioned in the 8th clause of this will in respect to the part of the Mt. Vernon land devised to him in trust. I also give & release to my said nephew Bushrod Washington, Jr., all

& every sum and sums of money due by him to me, and which yet remain unsatisfied.

Lastly. I nominate and appoint my nephews John A. Washington & Bushrod C. Washington my Executors, who are to give no security for the discharge of their duties. In witness whereof, I have hereto set my hand and affixed my seal, having written the whole of this will with my own hand this 10th day of July 1826.

BUSH : WASHINGTON. [SEAL.]

Memorandum. All the erasures & interlineations in this will have been made with my own hand. B. W.

This is a codicil to my will written and dated this 10th day of July 1826.

Whereas Chief Justice Marshall & myself contemplate publishing some volumes of letters from Genl. Washington, all or the most of which are already copied & also publishing a second edition of the life of Washington, it is my will that whatever sum of money may accrue from these sources be invested by my Executor in some productive fund, the interest or dividends whereof are to be paid to my wife during her life and after her death to be divided and to vest in the persons to whom the residue of my Estate is given to and for the same uses and under the same limitations. Item. I give to our niece Jane C. Washington, wife of my nephew John A. Washington, & to her heirs a negro boy called Lewis son of Ozman & Aggy.

Item. And whereas it may so happen that my wife may die without making any disposition of the property, I have devised to her in fee simple, I give to her niece Jane C. Washington, in that event, and that only the organ and piano forte, together with all the musick, also all the books in the chamber book cases and chamber closet, also the chamber furniture and the prints mentioned in my will. All the rest of the property so devised to my wife, I give, in the said event, to be equally divided between such of the nieces of my said wife as may be living at the time of her death. The property which I have purchased from the Executors of Nob : Herbert dec ; and from the Administrators of Richard H. L. Washington decd, & which I have conveyed to my niece, Mary L. Herbert, for whom I bought the whole, and have given her possession, I hereby confirm and ratify.

In witness whereof, I have hereunto set my hand and affixed my seal this 10th, day of July 1826, the whole of this codicil being written with my own hand & all erasures & interlineations in the will and codicil being made by myself before they were signed and sealed.

BUSH : WASHINGTON. [SEAL.]

This is a second codicil to my will. Imprimis, my beloved niece Mary L. Herbert having died since the making of my former will, I hereby give and bequeath all the property real and personal in possession or expectancy devised to her to be equally divided between her two sons Bushrod W. Herbert and Noblet Herbert and their heirs, & in the case of the death of either without child or children his part to go to the survivor, & in case of the death of both without child or children, the whole then remaining I give to be divided amongst my four nephews & their heirs, the part of my nephew Bushrod under the same trust & to the same trustee as are mentioned in the 8th Clause of my will : All the personal property except negroes, now in possession of my said nephew Bushrod Washington on hire I give to him. Item. If Bushrod W. Herbert should not practice law, I give my law library to such of the sons of my nephew John A. Washington as may practice it, & if more than one should, then to the eldest, and if neither should, then the same is to be sold and the proceeds disposed of as directed by the eleventh clause of my will. Item. Having subscribed for 50 shares, in the Chesapeake & Ohio Canal which I trust may be paid for without a sale of other property, I hereby appropriate for that purpose, whatever ready money I may have in any bank or banks at my death, & whatever salary may be due to me at that time, & I further empower my Executor to apply to the same purpose so much of the income of my Estate, or monies he may collect, as may remain after amply supplying the wants of my dear wife, to whom I hereby give during her life the dividends which may arise on said canal stock. But if these funds should be insufficient to comply with the calls of the company, my said Executors may sell as much of my bank stock as may be sufficient. In witness whereof I have hereunto set my hand & affix my seal the 9th day of January 1828, the whole of this codicil being written with my own hand & all erasures and interlineations being made by myself before signing and sealing this codicil.

BUSH: WASHINGTON. [SEAL.]

This is a third codicil to my will.

Whereas the line between Major Lewis & myself from the tree red or Spanish oaks marked as a corner and a stone placed, thence by a line of trees to be marked rectangular to the back line or outer boundary of the tract between Thompson Mason & Genl. Washington, as described in the clause of Genl. Washington's will which devises a part of the Mount Vernon estate to me, has never been run by the major and myself and there subsists a difficulty of opinion between us to the construction of the said will in relation to that line which my frequent and long absences from home have hitherto prevented us from adjusting, it is my will that my nephews, the Executors & Trustees of my deceased niece Mary L. Herbert, (in case it should not be in my power to settle this matter with Major Lewis, during my life,) do as soon as possible Settle and adjust with him this controverted line & in order that it may be done in the most amicable manner, I do hereby empower my said nephews John A. and Bushrod C. Washington or either of them or the survivor of them to submit any disputed point relative to that subject to arbitration hereby declaring any award or awards to be made in the premises to be final and binding on the persons who may be entitled to that part of the land devised by the preceeding codicil to the sons of my niece Mary L. Herbert in like manner as it would were the submission made by me during my life.

Item. I give the interest which after my death may become due on Geo. Atkinson's bond until George W. Washington son of Bushrod Washington of Mt. Zephyr shall arrive at the age of 18 (and which my Executor is to collect as it becomes due), to be divided as follows : viz. : one third to Ann Eliza, one third to Jane Mildred, daughters of the said Bushrod Washington Jr. of Mt. Zephyr, & the other third to the before mentioned Geo. W. son of the said Bushrod Washington Jr. towards his education & fitting him for the navy, & after he has arrived at the age of 18, then I give the whole of the said debt principal & interest with all the Securities for the same to be equally divided between the said Ann Eliza and Jane Mildred Washington & their assigns. The above bequest is intended to be made to my Executors in strict trust for the uses above mentioned & the principal to be paid to my nieces on their respective marriages and not before.

Item. It is my wish that my Executor may add to the above bequest to the said Geo. W. as much out of the income of my Estate as will complete his Education till his arrival at the age aforesaid, if in his Judgment the same can be spared after paying up my subscription to the Chesapeake & Ohio canal company, & any other debts and providing for the comfortable and abundant support of my dear wife. All benefit under this clause in favor of the said Geo. W. to cease after he arrives at the af^{sd} age, ex-

cept a moderate outfit which is to be given him in case he
should be received as a midshipman in our Navy. In witness whereof I have hereunto set my hand & affixed my seal
this 19th day of July 1828, the whole of this Codicil being
written with my own hand, & all erasures & interlineations
being made by myself before signing & sealing the same.

BUSH: WASHINGTON.

At a Court held for Fairfax county, the 21st. day of December 1829.

This last will & testament of the Honorable Bushrod
Washington, of Mt. Vernon, deceased, together with three
Codicils thereto annexed was presented in court by Jno.
A. Washington, one of the Executors therein named & the
same being proved to be wholly in the handwriting of the
said Bushrod Washington by the oaths of Geo. Mason,
Geo. Millan, Dennis Johnson, & Wm. Moss, is admitted to
record. And the said John A. Washington having in open
court executed bond in the penalty of $100,000 conditioned
as the law directs, & taken the oath prescribed by law, a
certificate is granted him for obtaining a probate thereof in
due form.

Teste: WM. MOSS, C. C.

A true copy. Teste :

F. W. RICHARDSON,

Deputy Clerk.

21 Nov., 1878.

WILL OF CORBIN WASHINGTON (PAGE 186), OF FAIRFAX CO.,
VA., DATED 19 OCT., 1799.

In the name of God amen. I Corbin Washington, of
Fairfax County in the State of Virginia, being sick & weak
in body, but of sound mind & disposing memory, & calling
to mind the uncertainty of human life & being anxious to
dispose of my worldly property in the most judicious manner, I am capable of for the comfort, ease & advantage of

my family after I am gone, do hereby, revoking all other or former wills or Testaments by me heretofore made & make and declare this as my only proper last will & testament, in manner & form following to wit, First, it is my will & desire that all my just debts be paid & discharged as soon as possible by my Executrix hereinafter mentioned.

Secondly. I do give and bequeath unto my most dear wife and friend Hannah Washington, all my Estate of every kind and description whatsoever, both real & personal in possession, remainder & revertion, and every species of Estate or property that I have any right to dispose of by will to have & to hold unto her during her widowhood, & I do hereby authorize and fully empower my said wife Hannah, (provided she should not marry) to divide my said Estate among my children and grand children in any manner she may think proper.

Thirdly. If the profits of the Estate should prove insufficient for the plentiful and comfortable support of my said dear wife, & the education of my children, It is my will & desire that she may let & dispose of any of the negroes or other personal property to raise money for that purpose.

Fourthly. As it is not uncommon for negroes to become disobedient to their mistresses after the death of their masters, to prevent any inconvenience on this head I do hereby give my said dear wife full power & authority to sell and dispose of any of them so offending in her opinion & vest the moneys arising therefrom in other negroes, or such other property as she may consider most beneficial to herself & children.

Fourthly. It is my will & desire that my Executrix be not compelled to give security on qualifying to my will & that she may not be put to the trouble of having the Estate appraised.

Lastly. I do hereby constitute and appoint my most

justly beloved wife & very faithful & sincere friend, Hannah Washington, sole Executrix of this my last will & testament & Sole Guardian to all my children. In witness whereof, I have hereunto set my hand & affixed my seal, this 19th day of Oct. 1799.

CORBIN WASHINGTON. [SEAL.]

At a Court held for Fairfax County, the 21st. day of April 1800. This last will & testament of Corbin Washington deceased, was presented in Court by Thos. Lee Senr. & the same being proved by the oaths of Edmund I. Lee, Thos. Lee, Senr. & Nicholas Fitzhugh, to be wholly writ by the said Testator, & Signed by him, is on motion ordered to be recorded.   Teste :

G. DENEALE, C. C.

A Copy.   Teste :

F. W. RICHARDSON,
Deputy Clerk,
21 Nov., 1878.

WILL OF COL. GEORGE AUGUSTINE WASHINGTON (PAGE 186), OF FAIRFAX CO., VA., DATED 24 JAN., 1793.

In the name of God, Amen. I George Augustine Washington of the county of Fairfax being of my usual soundness of mind & of sufficient recollection do make & constitute this my last will & testament for a disposition of my property after my death as follows, to wit : To my wife Frances Washington whilst she shall remain a widow & whilst my children are under lawfull age or unmarried I give all my Estate real and personal to maintain herself & support and educate my children as she shall think proper out of the annual Interest &.profits thereof, subject however to the discharge of my debts & the legacies & bequests in the manner as they are hereinafter made. Whenever my said wife shall choose it, whilst she shall remain sole &

before any of my children shall arive to lawfull age or
marry, it is my will that she may take to her seperate use
all the Slaves which I received with her from her father &
their increase, and the Lott & house in the town of Alexandria, purchased by me of a Wm. Hunter, to hold the same
to her & her heirs, and then divide the parts of my Estate
allotted to my children, among them as hereafter devised &
directed. And if my said wife shall not choose to make
such seperation whilst she shall remain Sole & before any
of my Children shall arrive to lawful age or marry, then
when either of those events shall take place or when she
shall marry herself, I give to her and her heirs the said
slaves & their increase & the said Lott & house in Alexandria. I give to my said wife my chariot horses, my riding
chair & harness & all furniture of the household kind that
I may leave not particularly disposed of herein to other
persons or uses. I give to my said wife one fourth part of
my plantation, stocks of horses, cattle, sheep & hogs whenever a division or seperation of my Estate is made. To my
son George Fayette, & his heirs, I give that part of my tract
of land in Berkley county included in the following description to wit, Begining at the corner thereof on the south
side of Chaˢ Town & running along the Road leading therefrom to Harper's Ferry as far as the said tract is bounded
by the said road & along the Known boundary line from
where it leaves the said road to where it reaches Hite's
great road, thence along Hite's road to where it intersects
with the new cut road leading to the line dividing Eph-
raim Worthington's land from my said tract, & so along the
said new cut road & line to the begining at the Charles
Town corner," which part of my said tract so described &
bounded contains about 510 acres be it more or less. I
give to my said son Geo. Fayette & his heirs 1000 acres of
land situate in the District set apart for the officers & soldiers of the Virginia line, on the Ohio river, which I hold
by a patent from the State of Virginia, dated the 29th. day

of July 1789. I also give to my said son Geo. Fayette, my Gold watch. To my son Charles Augustine & his heirs I give all the remaining part of my said tract of land in Berkley county not given as above to my son Geo. Fayette. I also give to my said son Chas. Augustine 1000 acres of land which I claim as an officer of the Virginia line, it being that part of my said claim which is not yet surveyed & patented & all my Estate & right therein. To my daughter Maria I give a tract of 666 ⅔ acres which I hold by a Patent from the State of Virginia, dated the 3rd. day of Feby, 1787 & is situated in the District set apart for the officers and soldiers of the Virginia Continental line. I give to my said daughter my Lott in the town of Alexandria purchased of Laurison & adjoining the Clerk's office, together with four Lotts in the Town of Fredericksburg purchased of John Lewis. I also give to my said daughter two negro men named Gabriel & Frederick & two debts due to me by Bond, one from Alexander Spotswood & the other from Robert Brooke of Fredericksburg. I give to each of my said children one fourth part of my Plantation, stocks of horses, cattle, Cattle, sheep & hogs plantation utensils, to be delivered to them respectively whenever a division of my Estate shall take place as herein before directed or when my said wife shall marry. I give to my sisters Frances Ball & Mildred Washington each the sum of fifty pounds to be paid out of Estate for the year 1792, if the said profits shall amount to the sum of four hundred pounds, & if the said profits for the year 1792 shall not amount to that sum, then I will that only twenty five pounds to each of my said sisters to be. paid thereout, & the remaining twenty five pounds each, to be paid to them out of the profits of my Estate for the year 1793. To Mr. John Packett, as a friendly testimonial of my sence of his faithful services to me I give the sum of fifty pounds to be paid to him out of the profits of my Estate for the year 1793, if such profits shall amount to the sum of three hun-

22

dred pounds, & if such profits shall not amount to that sum,
I will that twenty five pounds of the said fifty be paid to
him out of the said profits of the year 1793, & the balance
out of the profits of my Estate for the year 1794. I desire
ten pounds yearly to be paid out of my Estate to my negro
man Charles whom I give to my said wife during her
widowhood & when my said wife shall marry or at her
death (if she shall not marry again,) I hereby liberate my
said man Charles, & charge the said property which I have
herein given to my sons (from the time a division of my
Estate shall be made,) with the payment of the said ten
pounds : that is to say, the respective portion of each son
with the several sum of five pounds annually to be paid to
the said man Chas. during his life. I also give to my said
man Chas. my cassemor blue coat, striped great coat & all
my shirts not herein particularly and other wise disposed
of—I give to my brother Samuel Washington my brown
coat, buff vest & breeches, my best blue coat, striped scar-
let vest & green breeches & half a dozen new ruffled shirts :
I give to my brother in law Col. Ball my double milled
drab great coat. I give to my young friend Geo. W. P.
Custis my silver hilted sword. I desire my Executors to
present to my dear father & mother & to my aunt Martha
Washington each a ring of five Guineas value to be in
wrought with some of my hair in token of my affectionate
remembrance of them : To my dear uncle & friend the
President of the United States, I return the golden headed
cane which I received from him, I request him to accept of
my gray riding horse & new saddle and bridle as the last
Testimonial of my most grateful & affectionate regard for
him. If my debt from John Lewis cannot be recovered
within 6 months after my decease & no other money can be
conveniently spared from my Estate, I desire my Executors
to apply as much of the debts collected from Robt. Brooke
or Alexander Spotswood as will be sufficient to the discharge of a debt which I owe to John Hopkins of Rich-

mond & that the same may be replaced to my daughter Maria's portion out of the said debt from John Lewis when recovered.

Finally, I commit the execution of this my will to my said uncle George Washington, and my most affectionate & beloved wife Frances Washington on whom I rely therefor, with the most perfect satisfaction & I hereby nominate and appoint my said uncle & wife Executors of this my last will & testament, desiring that my estate may not be appraised or inventoried & that no security be required of my said Executors at their qualification.

In witness of all which I have hereunto set my hand & affixed my seal this the 24th. day of January in the year of Christ 1793.

GEO. A. WASHINGTON. [SEAL.]

Signed, Sealed & published as his last will by the above named G. A. Washington, in presence of us, who in his presence have hereunto subscribed our names as witnesses thereof. J᷎ DANDRIDGE, BENJ. BASSETT, C. P. LYONS, M. W. DANDRIDGE.

At a Court held for the County of Fairfax, 15 July 1793. This will was presented in court by Frances Washington Executrix therein named, who made oath thereto, & the same being proved by the oath of John Dandridge, *Burrell* Bassett & M. W. Dandridge ; is ordered to be recorded, & the said Frances Washington, having performed what the laws require, a certificate is granted her for obtaining a probate thereof in due form.

Teste :   P. WAGONER, Clk.

A true copy.   Teste :

F. W. RICHARDSON,

Deputy Clerk.

21st Nov., 1878.

WILL OF JOHN AUGUSTINE WASHINGTON (PAGE 215), OF JEF-
FERSON CO., VA., DATED JULY 8, 1830.

In the name of God amen. I John A. Washington, of
Jefferson county, in the State of Virginia, being in perfect
health of body & of sound and disposing mind, memory
and understanding, considering the certainty of death &
the uncertainty of the time thereof & being desirous to settle my worldly affairs & therefore be the better prepared to
leave this world, when it shall please God to call me hence,
do therefore make this my last will and testament, in manner and form following, that is to say. First. It is my will
& desire that all my just debts and funeral charges be paid
& discharged as soon as possible, by my Executrix hereinafter mentioned.

Secondly. I give & bequeath unto my most dear wife &
friend Jane C. Washington, all my negroes and other real
& personal Estate of every kind & description whatsoever,
that I now have or may hereafter have any right to dispose
of by will or otherwise in possession, to hold during her
widowhood. Thirdly. I do hereby fully empower my dear
wife Jane C. Washington, to divide my said Estate among
my children in any way she may think proper.

Fourthly. As it frequently happens that negroes becomes extremely disobedient to their mistress after the
death of their masters, I do hereby give my said dear wife
full power & authority should any act so unfaithfully to
her orders, to sell and dispose of any of them so offending
in her opinion, & vest the money arising therefrom, in other
negroes, property or public stock, which at the death of my
dear wife Jane C. Washington is to be divided between my
children as she may direct.

Fifthly. It is my will & desire that my Executrix shall
not be compelled to give security upon qualifying to my
will, and that she may not be put to the trouble of having

the Estate appraised, also I do hereby appoint her sole Guardian to all my children, without giving security for the same.

Lastly. I do hereby constitute & appoint my most dear & affectionate wife Jane C. Washington my sole Executrix to this my last will & testament, revoking & annulling all former wills by me heretofore made, ratifying and confirming this & none other to be my last will & testament. In testimony whereof I have hereunto set my hand & affixed my seal in my own hand writing this 6th. day of August 1822. The erasures in lines 7 & 8 on page second I did myself before I set my hand and affixed my seal.

JOHN A. WASHINGTON. [SEAL.]

Codicil—Whereas, I John A. Washington, in the County of Jefferson, & State of Virginia, have made & duly executed my last will & testament in writing, bearing date as above, which said last will & testament, & every clause, bequest and devise therein contained, I do hereby ratify and confirm & being desirous to alter some parts thereof, provided my dear wife Jane C. Washington should die without making her last will devising my estate as she may think proper between my children, in that case only do therefore hereby make this my codicil, which I will & direct shall be taken & held as my will & testament in manner & following that is to say, I hereby give & devise all my negroes & other real & personal Estate of every kind & description whatsoever that I now have or may hereafter have any right to dispose of by will or otherwise, in possession, reversion or remainder, to my sons and to their heirs forever in equal proportions to be allotted to each of them as soon as they arrive at the age of 21 years, except what I shall hereafter devise. I do hereby declair that should either of my sons die without lawful issue the property so descending shall go to the surviving brother or brothers. Item. I give & bequeath to my dear daughter

Anne Mariah J. B. Washington ten thousand 'dollars current money of the United States to bear interest from the death of my wife Jane C. Washington, to be raised in the most convenient manner to the Estate as speedily as possible after her deceased a negro man and woman not to exceed 25 years of age, also a good riding horse, saddle & bridle, to be paid to her when she arrives at the age of 21 years or marries. In testimony whereof I have hereunto set my hand & affixed my seal, in my own hand writing, this 10th day of Sept. 1822, the erasure in lines 7 & 8 on page second I did myself before I set my hand & affixed my seal.

                    JOHN A. WASHINGTON. [SEAL.]

Codicil 2nd. Whereas my late uncle Bushrod Washington did by will give to me Mount Vernon house and a certain parcel of land attached thereto, I do hereby authorize my Executrix or administrator should they deem it advisable for my children's interest to sell to the Government of the United States only if they should be dispose to purchase Mount Vernon & as much of the land as they may want, the proceeds to be laid out in public stock for the benefit of my children. If the Congress of the United States will take Mt. Vernon & part of the land my Executrix or Administrator may sell the balance to any person or persons, also all undivided property received from the said Bushrod Washington & the amount laid out in public stock for the benefit of my children. In testimony whereof, I have hereunto set my hand & affixed my seal, in my own hand writing this Eight day of July in the year of our Lord one thousand eight hundred & thirty.

                    JOHN A. WASHINGTON. [SEAL.]

State of Virginia, ⎫
County of Jefferson. ⎰ *Sct.:*

In the county court. July Term 1832.
At a court held for the said county on the 16th. day of

July 1832. The last will & testament of Jno. A. Washington dec. is this day proved in open courts by the oaths of Bushrod C. Washington and Edmund I. Lee Junr. to be altogether in the hand writing of the said testator, & ordered to be recorded, & on the same day on motion of Mrs. Jane C. Washington, the Executrix named in the said will, who made oath according to law, & entered into and acknowledged a bond without security, in the penalty of $50,000 with condition according to law, the said testator having directed that no security should be required of her, certificate is granted her for obtaining letters testamentary in due form.

Teste :   SAMUEL J. CRANE, Clerk.

And afterwards, to wit: At a Court held for the said County on the 16th day of July 1849. It appearing to the satisfaction of the Court, that in making the entry of the proof of the last will & testament of John A. Washington, deceased, at July Term 1832, of this court, it was proved that both wills & codicils were in the handwriting of the Testator, & that the record inadvertantly mentions that the will had been proved omitting the codicils, on motion leave is given to examine the same witnesses again, which being done & it being proved by the said witnesses Bushrod C. Washington & Edmund I. Lee, that the said will & codicils are all in the hand writing of the said Jno. A. Washington, the said testator, the same is ordered to be entered of record, which is accordingly hereby done.

Teste :
T. A. MOORE, Clerk.

And at a Court held for the said county on the 12th day of Oct. 1857. On motion of Richard B. Washington who made oath according to law & with Robt. W. Baylor his security, entered into & acknowledged a Bond in the penalty of $5000 with condition according to law, certificate is granted him for obtaining letters of administration de bonis non,[1] with the will annexed of Jno. A. Washington deceased in due form (the Executrix who heretofore qualified having departed this life.) Teste: T. A. MOORE.

True copies.　Teste: T. A. MOORE,
Clerk.

State of Virginia, .} *Sct.*
County of Jefferson. }

I Thos. A. Moore, Clerk of the County Court of said County certify that the foregoing are true copies of the last will & testament of Jno. A. Washington dec. & codicils thereto, & also of the orders of the said court relative to the same. Given under my hand & the seal of said court, the 7th day of Dec. 1859.

[SEAL.]   THOS. A. MOORE, Clerk.

At a County Court held for the County of Fairfax, on the 16th day of January 1860. An authenticated copy of the last will and testament of John A. Washington, late of Jefferson county, deceased, was this day presented to the Court by John A. Washington of Mt. Vernon, & on his motion it is ordered to be recorded.

Teste: ALFRED MOSS,
Clerk.

A true Copy.   Teste:
F. W. RICHARDSON,
Deputy Clerk,
1878, Nov. 21.

INDEX.

[345]

INDEX.

Havard, Prince of the Orkneys, xx
Harald I., King of Norway, xx
Halfdan the Swart, xx
Hringo, Prince of Hringa, xx
Hrolf or Rollo, First Duke of Normandy, xxi
Haquin, King of Norway, xx, xxi
Hemingur, Prince of Norway, xxi
Holmfrida, of Sweden, xxi
Hastings, xxi
Humboldt, xxviii
Henry fil Bardolf, 4, 5
Hervey fitz Akaris, 5, 6, 7, 8, 9, 12
Herasculfus fil Akery, 6, 9, 10, 11
Hugo fil Walter, 5, 12, 15
Henry fil Akaris, 7
Henry fil Henry, 7, 12
Henry de Ravensworth, 8, 16, 19, 24, 27, 29, 32
Hugh de Ravensworth, 8, 13, 19, 20, 21, 27
Henry fil Hervey, 9, 12, 13
Huestachio Karlyle, 10
Henry fil Ranulf, 10, 20
Henry fil William, 13
Henry de Washington, 16, 17, 20, 23, 24, 27, 29, 34
Hugh fil Ranulph, 17
Henry Fitz Randolph, 20
Hugh de Washington, 20, 28, 34
Hugh de Kerneford, 25
Hugh de Lastington, 28
Henry Fitz Hugh, 32, 33
Henry Lord Percy, 33
Sir Henry Vavasor, 33
Hugh Fitz Hugh, 33
Hugh de Ask, 34
Henry Washington, 47, 49, 51, 60, 63, 74, 82, 83, 87, 97, 114, 123, 169, 188, 197, 305, 306
Henry Dore, 100
Henry Sandy, Jr., 104, 105

Hannah Washington, 122, 145, 167, 186, 189, 196, 308, 334, 335
Hannah Whiting, 123
Henry Clinton, 135
Humphrey Peake, 147
Howell Lewis, 149, 164, 178, 179, 205
Harriot Parks, 150, 182, 214
Harriot P. Washington, 165
Hannah F. Throckmorton, 170, 192
Harriet T. Whiting, 170, 193
Hannah F. Whiting, 170, 193
Hannah F. Nelson, 171, 194
Henrietta Spotswood, 173
Hannah B. Washington, 174, 196
H. C. Dale, 176
Henry D. Lewis, 179, 207
Henry S. Washington, 189
Harriet A. Washington, 189
Hannah F. Washington, 190
Herbert Washington, 191
Herbert Beasley, 192
Hamilton Beasley, 192
Henrietta Washington, 196
Henry Aug. Washington, 197, 221, 222
Howell L. Lovell, 202
Harold Lewis, 203, 226
Howell L. Steele, 203, 227, 229
Rev. Henry Ruffner, 203
Humphrey B. Gwathmey, 204, 230
Henry W. Douglass, 206
Howell R. Lewis, 207
Henry H. Lewis, 208
Henrietta G. Washington, 209, 245
Harriet W. Shrewsbury, 213, 253
Henry Shrewsbury, 213, 253
Hannah L. Alexander, 215, 259
Henry Browne, 220
Henrietta Wilson, 224
Henry T. Washington, 225
Harold B. Nye, 226
Howell S. King, 229, 263

THE END.